—THREE VIEWS—
ON THE
MILLENNIUM
AND
BEYOND

BOOKS IN THE COUNTERPOINTS SERIES

►COUNTERPOINTS◄

—THREE VIEWS—
ON THE
MILLENNIUM
AND
BEYOND

Premillennialism
Craig A. Blaising

Postmillennialism
Kenneth L. Gentry Jr.

Amillennialism
Robert B. Strimple

Darrell L. Bock
General Editor

ZondervanPublishingHouse
Grand Rapids, Michigan

A Division of HarperCollinsPublishers

Three Views on the Millennium and Beyond
Copyright © 1999 by Darrell Bock, Craig Blaising, Ken Gentry Jr., Robert Strimple

Requests for information should be addressed to:

ZondervanPublishingHouse
Grand Rapids, Michigan 49530

Library of Congress Cataloging-in-Publication Data

Blaising, Craig A.
    Three views on the millennium and beyond / Craig A. Blaising, Kenneth
  L. Gentry, Robert B. Strimple; Darrell L. Bock, general editor.
       p. cm.
    Includes bibliographical references and index.
    ISBN: 0–310–20143-8 (softcover)
    1. Millennialism—Comparative studies. I. Gentry, Kenneth L. II. Strimple,
  Robert B., 1935- III. Bock, Darrell L. IV. Title.
  BT891 .B55 1999
  236'.9—ddc21   98–37483
                                                      CIP

Printed in the United States of America

---

00 01 02 03 04/ ❖ DC / 10 9 8 7 6 5 4 3

CONTENTS

EDITOR'S PREFACE

It is my pleasure to welcome the reader to what I believe is an unprecedented study of the issue of eschatology as it addresses our future. I know of no other recent work where proponents of the three major millennial schools are brought together for an interactive presentation of their views in an irenic environment.

Eschatology is *the study of the last things*. For some that means "future things" only, but all of these authors note that we already live in an era of initial fulfillment of promises concerning the Messiah Jesus. We are in a world where eschatology is now at work.

This book picks up the eschatological discussion by treating the question of the Millennium and beyond. This question concerns whether or not there is a future intermediate earthly kingdom of a literal thousand years over which Christ will rule before the new heavens and new earth are established. It is also called chiliasm. Those who argue that Christ comes again before such a kingdom are called *premillennialists*. Those who argue that the present church age represents that intermediate kingdom come in two types. *Postmillennialists* see the church as moving toward the complete fulfillment of kingdom promise, which gradually moves to victory until Christ appears. *Amillennialists* argue that there is no future literal Millennium, but when Christ returns we are ushered immediately into a new heaven and new earth. Nevertheless, postmillennialists are not the same as amillennialists. Postmillennialists see the church as marching gradually but most certainly to victory in the present age, while amillennialists see the church as delivered from the pressures and persecutions of a fallen world when Jesus returns.

All of these views have various subcategories, as our contributors will note, but their basic responsibility is to trace the hermeneutical, theological, and exegetical rationale for their millennial view. Each has also been asked to provide a brief history of his view.

Since the focal point of this book is the issue of the Millennium and beyond, certain questions often given prominence in books on end-time eschatology are not prominent here. Issues like the Rapture and Tribulation receive attention only as they relate to the discussion of the Millennium. Other works in Zondervan's Counterpoints series, such as those on the Rapture and the book of Revelation, treat such questions in more detail.

I promise you, as a student of Scripture, a fascinating read. The discussion shows how and why evangelical Christians differ on questions about the future. The essays also indicate how each millennial view impacts how one sees the task and destiny of God's people in God's plan, both present and future. The side-by-side presentation of views allows you to assess the case for each option.

Each contributor presents an essay surveying the rationale for his particular view. The premillennial essay is a little longer than the other two because of its treatment of history. To redress the balance the responses of the other two views were allowed to be a little longer so that these contributors could comment on both the history and the textual discussion. Each essay is followed by short responses to raise questions and issues the main essay raised. It is here that the reader will see the differences in readings and views articulated most directly. As becomes clear, key issues include the reading of texts like Revelation 20 and Romans 11, the role of the destruction of the temple in early Christian thinking, the relationship of Old Testament texts to those in the New Testament, and how the book of Revelation should be read both with respect to its message and in terms of the canon.

I conclude the book with an essay summarizing the issues involved in thinking about the Millennium and beyond. I will not try to resolve the debate within my concluding essay, but will articulate the hermeneutical, theological, and exegetical issues at the center of the discussion of this topic and the disagreements that arise from it. Each view must face these issues as it attempts to determine what Scripture teaches about this topic. You deserve to know that I am a premillennialist, but I have attempted to write the final essay as a reflective student of the topic, trying to help other students of the Bible navigate their way through the complex terrain of the debates surrounding futuristic eschatology.

My thanks goes to our three contributors for faithfully carrying out their assignments. I have enjoyed working through the essays and considering the case for each view in this side-by-side format. I have learned much about each view and why some hold to each position. I hope you will have the same experience, as well as receive the resources "to search the Scriptures" to see which of these views best reflects God's Word.

DARRELL L. BOCK
FEBRUARY 28, 1998

Chapter One

POSTMILLENNIALISM

Kenneth L. Gentry Jr.

POSTMILLENNIALISM

Kenneth L. Gentry Jr.

Eschatology is easily, often, and much abused. Nevertheless, it is foundationally important to a distinctly biblical worldview. Though we are creatures constrained by time (Job 14:1–6) and space (Acts 17:26), God has set eternity in our hearts (Eccl. 3:11). Consequently, we have an innate interest in the future— which necessarily affects our conduct in the present.

Given these realities, how could the inscripturated disclosure of the future not be important and practical for God's people? Does not 2 Timothy 3:16–17 teach us that "all Scripture is God-breathed" (hence important) and profitable in preparing us for "every good work" (hence practical)? Eschatology's considerable task is to explore the whole revelation of the inerrant Word of God in order to discern the divinely ordained, prophetically revealed flow of world history from creation to consummation with a view to issuing "a call to action and obedience in the present."[1]

In this chapter I will present the biblical foundations for and basic contours of that system of eschatology known as *postmillennialism*. I will begin by defining its basic idea: *Postmillennialism expects the proclaiming of the Spirit-blessed gospel of Jesus Christ to win the vast majority of human beings to salvation in the present age. Increasing gospel success will gradually produce a time in history prior to Christ's return in which faith, righteousness, peace, and prosperity*

---

[1]Stanley J. Grenz, *The Millennial Maze: Sorting Out Evangelical Options* (Downers Grove, Ill.: InterVarsity, 1992), 202.

will prevail in the affairs of people and of nations. After an extensive era of such conditions the Lord will return visibly, bodily, and in great glory, ending history with the general resurrection and the great judgment of all humankind.[2] Hence, our system is *post*millennial in that the Lord's glorious return occurs *after* an era of "millennial" conditions. Thus, the postmillennialist confidently proclaims in a unique way that history is "His story."

HISTORICAL DEVELOPMENT OF POSTMILLENNIALISM

Despite the frequent appearance of prophetic statements in the early church fathers, an intriguing phenomenon presents itself to us: *No ancient creed affirms a millennial view.* Though subsidiary to the Scripture, creeds play an important role in defining Christian orthodoxy by protecting the church from the corruption of belief within and against the assaults of unbelief from without.

Ancient Postmillennialism

The early creedal formulations of Christianity provide only the most rudimentary elements of eschatology. For instance, the Apostles' Creed simply affirms: "He ascended into heaven; and sitteth on the right hand of God the Father Almighty; from thence he shall come to judge the quick and the dead," and "I believe ... the resurrection of the body, and the life everlasting." The eschatology of the Nicene Creed makes only slight advances, asserting that he "ascended into heaven, and sitteth on the right hand of the Father; and he shall come again, with glory, to judge the quick and the dead; whose kingdom shall have no end."

Both amillennialism and postmillennialism fit comfortably within these and other ancient creedal affirmations. Premillennialism's fit is a bit more awkward, however, because of its requiring two separate resurrections and two distinct judgments rather than general ones involving all people simultaneously. Consequently, as classic dispensationalist Robert P. Lightner

---

[2]For a more detailed definition, see my *He Shall Have Dominion: A Postmillennial Eschatology*, 2d. ed. (Tyler, Tex.: Institute for Christian Economics, 1997), ch. 4.

admits: "None of the major creeds of the church include pre-millennialism in their statements."[3] Not one of the millennial views, though, is expressly affirmed by any early creed as the orthodox position. This is not surprising in that, as Erickson explains, "all three millennial positions have been held virtually throughout church history."[4]

This noted, we should expect to find a *gradual* development of the millennial schemes, rather than a fully functioning system in early Christian history. For example, Walvoord confesses when defending dispensationalism: "It must be conceded that the advanced and detailed theology of pretribulationism is not found in the Fathers, but neither is any other detailed and 'established' exposition of premillennialism. *The development of most important doctrines took centuries.*"[5] And although premillennialism finds slightly earlier development (especially in Irenaeus, A.D. 130–202[6]), theologian Donald G. Bloesch notes: "Postmillennialism was already anticipated in the church father Eusebius of Caesarea" (A.D. 260–340).[7] Schaff traces it back even farther, observing that Origen (A.D. 185–254) "expected that Christianity, by continual growth, would gain the dominion over the world."[8]

---

[3]Robert P. Lightner, *The Last Days Handbook: A Comprehensive Guide to Understanding the Different Views of Prophecy* (Nashville: Thomas Nelson, 1990), 158.

[4]Millard J. Erickson, *Christian Theology*, 3 vols. (Grand Rapids: Baker, 1985), 3:1207.

[5]John F. Walvoord, *The Rapture Question* (Grand Rapids: Zondervan, 1957), 52 (emphasis mine).

[6]Brian E. Daley provides extensive research and argumentation suggesting that the early presence of apocalyptic interest in general and of premillennialism in particular was born within a persecution setting that confidently anticipated the imminent end of history. Because of various historical factors at work and the range of images and ideas among the Christian writers, Daley wonders: "At the end of this survey of Patristic eschatological thought, one might justly wonder if it is proper at all to speak in the singular of 'the hope of the early Church'" (Daley, *The Hope of the Early Church: A Handbook of Patristic Eschatology* [Cambridge: Cambridge Univ. Press, 1991], 216).

[7]Donald G. Bloesch, *Essentials of Evangelical Theology: Vol. 2: Life, Ministry, and Hope* (San Francisco: Harper and Row, 1979), 192. In speaking of Old Testament prophecies, Eusebius writes: "The whole world [will] partake of the virtues of wisdom and sound discretion, through the almost universal prevalence of those principles of conduct which the Saviour would promulgate, over the minds of men; whereby the worship of God should be confirmed, and the rites of superstition established" (*Constantine*, 16).

[8]Philip Schaff, *History of the Christian Church*, 5th ed. (Grand Rapids: Eerdmans, rep. n.d. [1910]), 2:591, cf. 122. For more information see: D. H. Kromminga, *The*

Two other prominent church fathers whose historical confidence appears to express a nascent postmillennialism are Athanasius (A.D. 296–372) and Augustine (A.D. 354–430).[9] As Zoba notes, Augustine taught that history "would be marked by the ever-increasing influence of the church in overturning evil in the world before the Lord's return."[10] This would eventually issue forth in a "future rest of the saints on earth" (Augustine, *Sermon* 259:2) "when the Church will be purged of all the wicked elements now mixed among its members and Christ will rule peacefully in its midst."[11] This early incipient postmillennialism contains the most basic element of the later developed system: a confident hope in gospel victory in history prior to Christ's return.

Reformation Postmillennialism

Later, as Bloesch notes, "postmillennialism experienced an upsurge in the middle ages," as illustrated in the writings of Joachim of Fiore (1145–1202) and others.[12] But a more fully developed postmillennialism enjoys its greatest growth and influence in the seventeenth through nineteenth centuries, especially under Puritan and Reformed influence in England and America. Rodney Peterson writes that "this perspective had undergone changes, particularly since Thomas Brightman (1562–1607)." Brightman is one of the fathers of Presbyterianism in England.[13] His postmillennial views are set forth in detail in his

---

Millennium in the Church: Studies in the History of Christian Chiliasm (Grand Rapids: Eerdmans, 1945). Origen expected that "every form of worship will be destroyed except the religion of Christ, which will alone prevail. And indeed it will one day triumph, as its principles take possession of the minds of men more and more every day" (Origen, *Against Celsus*, 8:68).

[9]For documentation see Gentry, *He Shall Have Dominion*, ch. 4. For Augustine, see Erickson, *Christian Theology*, 3:1206–7. For Athanasius, see David Chilton, *Paradise Restored: An Eschatology of Dominion* (Fort Worth: Dominion, 1985), ch. 1.

[10]Wendy Murray Zoba, "Future Tense," *Christianity Today* (Oct. 2, 1995), 20. Cf. John O'Meara, "Introduction," in Augustine, *City of God*, trans. Henry Bettensen (New York: Penguin, 1984), viii.

[11]Brian E. Daley, *The Hope of the Early Church*, 133.

[12]Bloesch, *Essentials of Evangelical Theology*, 2:192. See fuller discussion in Kromminga, *The Millennium in the Church*, 129–36, 159ff.

[13]Rodney Peterson, "The Debate Throughout Church History," in John S. Feinberg, ed., *Continuity and Discontinuity: Perspectives on the Relationship Between the Old and New Testaments* (Westchester, Ill.: Crossway, 1988), 32.

book *A Revelation of the Revelation*, which was published posthumously in 1609 and quickly established itself as one of the most widely translated works of the day. In fact, some church historians consider this work the "most important and influential English revision of the Reformed, Augustinian concept of the millennium."[14] Thus, Brightman stands as the modern systematizer (not creator) of postmillennialism.

Bloesch lists subsequent "guiding lights" from "the heyday of postmillennialism": Samuel Rutherford (1600–1661), John Owen (1616–1683), Philipp Spener (1635–1705), Daniel Whitby (1638–1726), Isaac Watts (1674–1748), the Wesley brothers (1700s), and Jonathan Edwards (1703–1758).[15] To this list we could add John Calvin (1509–1564) as an incipient postmillennialist.[16] In his "Prefatory Address" to King Francis I of France, Calvin writes:

> Our doctrine must tower unvanquished above all the glory and above all the might of the world, for it is not of us, but of the living God and his Christ whom the Father has appointed King to "rule from sea to sea, and from the rivers even to the ends of the earth...." And he is so to rule as to smite the whole earth with its iron and brazen strength, with its gold and silver brilliance, shattering it with the rod of his mouth as an earthen vessel, just as the prophets have prophesied concerning the magnificence of his reign.[17]

Calvin is a forerunner to the flowering of the postmillennialism of the Reformers Martin Bucer (1491–1551) and Theodore Beza (1519–1605). Following in their train but with greater clarity still are the Puritans William Perkins (1558–1602), William

---

[14]Peter Toon, ed., *Puritans, the Millennium and the Future of Israel* (Cambridge: James Clarke, 1970), 26. See also Bryan W. Ball, *A Great Expectation: Eschatological Thought in English Protestantism to 1660* (Leiden: E. J. Brill, 1975).

[15]Bloesch, *Essentials of Evangelical Theology*, 2:193.

[16]For documentation see Greg L. Bahnsen, "The Prima Facie Acceptability of Postmillennialism," *Journal of Christian Reconstruction* (Winter, 1976): 69–76. See also John Calvin, *The Institutes of the Christian Religion*, ed. John T. McNeil (Philadelphia: Westminster, 1960), 2:904, n. 76; J. A. De Jong, *As the Waters Cover the Sea: Millennial Expectations in the Rise of Anglo-American Missions 1640–1810* (Kampen: J. H. Kok, 1970), 8ff; Iain Murray, *The Puritan Hope: Revival and the Interpretation of Prophecy* (Edinburgh: Banner of Truth, 1971), 89–90.

[17]John Calvin, *Institutes of the Christian Religion*, 1:12.

Gouge (1575–1653), Richard Sibbes (1577–1635), John Cotton (1584–1652), Thomas Goodwin (1600–1679), George Gillespie (1613–1649), John Owen (1616–1683), Elnathan Parr (d. 1632), Thomas Brooks (1608–1680), John Howe (d. 1678), James Renwick (d. 1688), Matthew Henry (1662–1714), and others.

The Puritan form of postmillennialism generally holds not only to a future glory for the church, but that the millennial era proper will not begin until the conversion of the Jews and will flower rather quickly thereafter, prevailing over the earth for a literal thousand years. A purified church and a righteous state governed by God's law arises under this intensified effusion of the Spirit. This culminates eventually in the eschatological complex of events surrounding the glorious Second Advent. Many of the Puritans also held that the Jews would return to their land during this time.[18]

Modern Postmillennialism

Generic postmillennialists[19] of the nineteenth and twentieth centuries generally did not hold that the Jewish people would return to their land as a fulfillment of prophecy—though Iain Murray and Erroll Hulse are notable contemporary exceptions. They also believed that the Millennium spans *all* of the new covenant phase of church history, developing incrementally from the time of Christ until his Second Advent.

Prominent generic postmillennial writers include: Jonathan Edwards (1703–1758), William Carey (1761–1834), Robert Haldane (1764–1842), Archibald Alexander (1772–1851), Charles Hodge (1797–1878), Albert Barnes (1798–1870), David Brown (1803–1897), Patrick Fairbairn (1805–1874), Richard C. Trench (1807–1886), J. A. Alexander (1809–1860), J. H. Thornwell (1812–1862), Robert L. Dabney (1820–1898), William G. T. Shedd (1820–1894), A. A. Hodge (1823–1886), Augustus H. Strong (1836–1921), H. C. G. Moule (1841–1920), B. B. Warfield (1851–1921), O. T. Allis (1880–1973), J. Gresham Machen (1881–1937),

---

[18]See Murray, *The Puritan Hope.* For an extensive bibliography of original sources, see De Jong, *As the Waters Cover the Sea,* 232–42.

[19]I call them "generic postmillennialists" to set them over against the postmillennialism of the Puritans, which, in addition to an interest in conversions, holy living, and missions, has a strong involvement in civil governmental matters.

John Murray (1898–1975), Loraine Boettner (1903–1989), and J. Marcellus Kik (1903–1965). Contemporary defenders include Norman Shepherd, John Jefferson Davis, Erroll Hulse, Iain Murray, Donald Macleod, Douglas Kelly, John R. deWitt, J. Ligon Duncan, Henry Morris III, and Willard Ramsey.

A development within the postmillennial tradition since the 1960s is known as Christian Reconstructionism, involving "theonomic" ethics ("theonomy" = "God's law"). Theonomic postmillennialism (a feature of Christian Reconstructionism) combines the inter-advental gradualism of the modern generic variety with the socio-political interests of the older Puritan form. The theonomic postmillennialist sees the *gradual* return to biblical norms of civil justice as a *consequence* of widespread gospel success through preaching, evangelism, missions, and Christian education. The judicial-political outlook of Reconstructionism includes the application of those justice-defining directives contained in the Old Testament legislation, when properly interpreted, adapted to new covenant conditions, and relevantly applied.[20]

Despite widespread misunderstanding of the Reconstructionist interest in socio-political matters, evangelical theologian Ronald H. Nash notes: "It does not take a postmillennialist to see that their account of the central role that evangelism and Christian obedience to the Word of God must play in the transformation of society is miles removed from the repeated distortions" common among certain opponents.[21] As Mark Noll expresses it:

---

[20]For a thorough and academic presentation and defense of theonomic ethics, see Greg L. Bahnsen, *Theonomy in Christian Ethics*, 2d ed. (Phillipsburg, N.J.: Presbyterian and Reformed, 1984). For more popular introductions, see Bahnsen, *By This Standard: The Authority of God's Law Today* (Tyler, Tex.: Institute for Christian Economics, 1985); Kenneth L. Gentry Jr., *God's Law in the Modern World: The Continuing Relevance of Old Testament Law*, 2d ed. (Tyler, Tex.: Institute for Christian Economics, 1997); and William O. Einwechter, *Ethics and God's Law: An Introduction* (Mill Hill, Penn.: Preston/Speed, 1995). For a dialogue on the matter, see Wayne G. Strickland, ed., *The Law, the Gospel, and the Modern Christian: Five Views* (Grand Rapids: Zondervan, 1993) and Gary Scott Smith, *God and Politics: Four Views on the Reformation of Civil Government* (Phillipsburg, N.J.: Presbyterian and Reformed, 1989).

[21]Ronald H. Nash, *Great Divides: Understanding the Controversies That Come Between Christians* (Colorado Springs, Colo.: NavPress, 1993), 164–65. See also Bruce Barron, *Heaven on Earth? The Social and Political Agendas of Dominion Theology* (Grand Rapids: Zondervan, 1992), and Bob and Gretchen Passantino, *Witch Hunt* (Nashville: Thomas Nelson, 1990), 164–98.

"Theonomy sounds a good deal like populist libertarianism, yet by insisting on carefully formulated theological foundations for political action, it too pushes toward a more self-conscious political reflection than is customary in the evangelical tradition."[22]

Reconstructionists hold strongly to a separation of church and state.[23] Consequently, they reject the sometimes overly close church-state relationship advocated by many of the English and New England Puritans. Nevertheless, they do admire the Puritans' deep interest in and work for the application of the whole Word of God to all matters of life, including civil jurisprudence. One Puritan example who serves as a clear forerunner to the Reconstructionist outlook is the prominent Scottish divine George Gillespie, who is known as "one of the brightest stars" of the Westminster Assembly.[24] Gillespie argues: "The Christian Magistrate is bound to observe the judicial laws of Moses, as well as the Jewish Magistrate was." He also notes that Christ's words in Matthew 5:17–19 (a favorite text of Reconstructionists) "are comprehensive of the judicial law, it being a part of the law of Moses."[25] In that many opponents of Reconstructionism rec-

---

[22]Mark A. Noll, *The Scandal of the Evangelical Mind* (Grand Rapids: Eerdmans, 1994), 225.

[23]See Greg L. Bahnsen, *Theonomy in Christian Ethics*, ch. 20; *No Other Standard: Theonomy and Its Critics* (Tyler, Tex.: Institute for Christian Economics, 1991), ch. 8; Gentry, *God's Law in the Modern World*.

[24]Philip Schaff, *The Creeds of Christendom; Vol. 1: The History of Creeds*, 6th ed. (New York: Harper and Row, 1931; reprint, Grand Rapids: Baker, 1990), 746. That the Westminster Standards endorse the theonomic outlook is not only evident in its proof texts (see especially those on the Second Commandment in the Larger Catechism), but also in the writings of its framers. For an important and helpful compendium, see Martin A. Foulner, *Theonomy and the Westminster Confession* (Edinburgh: Marpet, 1997). See also Kenneth L. Gentry Jr., "Theonomy and Confession: A Review and Report," *Chalcedon Report* 388 (November, 1997): 12–16.

[25]George Gillespie, "Wholesome Severity Reconciled with Christian Liberty," reprinted in vol. 4 of Christopher Coldwell, ed., *Anthology of Presbyterian and Reformed Literature* (Dallas, Tex.: Naphtali, 1991), 182. His postmillennialism couples with a strong theonomic-like interest in civil jurisprudence in his "Sermon Preached Before the Honourable House of Commons at Their Late Solemn Fast, Wednesday, March 27, 1644," reprinted in George Gillespie, *The Works of George Gillespie*, 2 vols, (Edmonton, Alta.: Still Waters Revival Books, rep. 1991), vol. 2. The New England Puritans follow the same pattern: "The Old Testament texts were copied directly into the New England law books" (George M. Marsden, "America's 'Christian' Origins: Puritan New England as a Case Study," in W. Stanford Reid, ed., *John Calvin: His Influence in the Western World* [Grand Rapids: Zondervan, 1982], 247).

ognize the similarity between it and Puritanism in this regard,[26] Reconstructionism is also known as "neo-Puritanism."

Another feature of theonomic postmillennialism (though not essential to it) is its preterist approach to a number of the great judgment passages of the New Testament. The preterist (Latin: "gone by") approach to certain prophecies holds that the Great Tribulation (Matt. 24:21) occurred in the generation living when Christ spoke (Matt. 24:34); the book of Revelation expects its events to transpire "soon" (Rev. 1:1; 22:7, 12), because in John's day "the time is near" (Rev. 1:3; 22:10); and the Antichrist was a first-century phenomenon (1 John 2:18, 22; 4:3; 2 John 7).[27]

Preterism places the prophecies of intense evil and foreboding gloom in the first century, focusing on the events surrounding the forty-two-month long Neronic persecution (A.D. 64–68, cf. Rev. 13:5), the forty-two-month long Jewish war with Rome (A.D. 67–70, cf. Rev. 11:1–2), and the destruction of the temple (A.D. 70, cf. Matt. 23:36–24:34). The preterist viewpoint is not unique to theonomic postmillennialism; it has been held, for instance, by the ancient church father Eusebius, seventeenth-century Puritan Talmudic scholar John Lightfoot, nineteenth-century Methodist theologian and hermeneutics authority Milton S. Terry, and modern Reformed writers J. Marcellus Kik

---

[26]Meredith G. Kline, "Comments on an Old/New Error," *Westminster Theological Journal* 41:1 (1978): 172–74; Michael D. Gabbert, "An Historical Overview of Christian Reconstructionism," *Criswell Theological Review* 6:2 (1993): 281–301; Sinclair B. Ferguson, "An Assembly of Theonomists? The Teaching of the Westminster Divines on the Law of God," in William S. Barker and W. Robert Godfrey, eds, *Theonomy: A Reformed Critique* (Grand Rapids: Zondervan, 1990), 326–34.

[27]Kenneth L. Gentry Jr., *The Beast of Revelation*, 2d ed. (Tyler, Tex.: Institute for Christian Economics, 1995); C. Marvin Pate, ed., *Four Views on the Book of Revelation* (Grand Rapids: Zondervan, 1998); Gary DeMar, *Last Days Madness: Obsession of the Modern Church*, 3d ed. (Atlanta: American Vision, 1997); David Chilton, *The Great Tribulation* (Fort Worth: Dominion, 1987); Chilton, *The Days of Vengeance: An Exposition of the Book of Revelation* (Tyler, Tex.: Institute for Christian Economics, 1987). For the preterist understanding of Daniel's Seventy Weeks (Dan. 9), the Great Tribulation (Matt. 24), the man of sin (2 Thess. 2), and the Babylonian harlot (Rev. 17), see Kenneth L. Gentry Jr., *Perilous Times: A Study in Eschatological Evil* (Bethesda, Md.: Christian Universities Press, 1998). Even some dispensationalists are influenced by preterism: C. Marvin Pate and Calvin B. Haines Jr., *Doomsday Delusions: What's Wrong With Predictions About the End of the World* (Downers Grove, Ill.: InterVarsity, 1995). David L. Turner, "Structure and Sequence of Matthew 24:1–41: Interaction With Evangelical Treatments," *Grace Theological Journal* 10:1 (Spring, 1989): 3–28.

and Jay E. Adams.[28] Nevertheless, this view is greatly emphasized by the theonomic strain of postmillennialism.

Published advocates of theonomic postmillennialism in-
clude: Greg L. Bahnsen (1948–1995), Gary North, Rousas J. Rush-
doony, Kenneth L. Gentry Jr., David Chilton, Gary DeMar,
George Grant, Francis Nigel Lee, Steve Schlissel, Douglas Jones,
Reuben Alvarado, Curtis Crenshaw, Grover E. Gunn, Douglas
Wilson, Stephen C. Perks, Jack Van Deventer, Stephen J. Hayhow,
Andrew Sandlin, Colin Wright, and Joseph C. Morecraft III.

THEOLOGICAL FOUNDATIONS
OF POSTMILLENNIALISM

Postmillennialism expects the vast majority of the world's
population to convert to Christ as a consequence of the Spirit-
blessed proclamation of the gospel. In light of present world conditions, however, many Christians are surprised at the resilience
of the postmillennial hope. Before actually providing positive
exegetical evidence for the postmillennial position, I will briefly
show that though the hope of gospel victory sounds strange to
the modern evangelical, the basic theology of Scripture is congenial to it. Indeed, these factors suggest the prima facie plausibility of postmillennialism.

God's Creational Purpose

In Genesis 1 we find the record of God's creation of the universe in the space of six days.[29] As a result of God's purposeful

---

[28]Eusebius, *Ecclesiastical History*, 3:5–9; John Lightfoot, *Commentary on the New Testament From the Talmud and Hebraica: Matthew–1 Corinthians* (Peabody, Mass.: Hendrickson, rep. 1989 [1674]); Milton S. Terry, *Biblical Apocalyptics: A Study of the Most Notable Revelations of God and of Christ* (Grand Rapids: Baker, rep. 1988 [1898]), chs. 18–19; J. Marcellus Kik, *The Eschatology of Victory* (Phillipsburg, N.J.: Presbyterian and Reformed, 1971); Jay E. Adams, *The Time Is at Hand* (Nutley, N.J.: Presbyterian and Reformed, 1966).

[29]Kenneth L. Gentry Jr., "Reformed Theology and Six Day Creationism," *Christianity & Society* 5 (October, 1995): 25–30. See also Robert L. Dabney, *Lectures in Systematic Theology* (Grand Rapids: Zondervan, rep. 1972 [1878]), 254–63; Louis Berkhof, *Systematic Theology* (Grand Rapids: Eerdmans, 1941), 152–58; Douglas F. Kelly, *Creation and Change* (Ross-shire, Great Britain: Mentor, 1997); Kenneth L. Gentry Jr., et al. "The Biblical Doctrine of Creation," set of six audio tapes from Covenant Media Foundation.

creative power, all was originally "very good" (Gen. 1:31). Of course, we expect this in that God created the world for his own glory: "For from him and through him and to him are all things. To him be the glory forever! Amen" (Rom. 11:36). "All things were created by him and for him" (Col. 1:16b). Frequently, Scripture reaffirms God's love of his created order and his ownership claim over all things: "The earth is the LORD's, and everything in it, the world, and all who live in it."[30] The postmillennialist holds that God's love for his creation prompts his concern to bring it back to its original purpose of bringing positive glory to him. *Thus, the postmillennialist's hope-filled expectation is rooted in creational reality.*

God's Sovereign Power

Our evangelistic task in God's world should be emboldened by the certainty that God "works out everything in conformity with the purpose of his will" (Eph. 1:11). We confidently believe that God controls history by means of his decree, whereby he determines "the end from the beginning" (Isa. 46:10). Consequently, postmillennialists assert that God's Word, as he himself says, "will not return to me empty, but will accomplish what I desire and achieve the purpose for which I sent it" (Isa. 55:11), irrespective of opposition from human beings or from demons, despite natural phenomena or historical circumstances.

The Christian, then, ought not use past historical factors or present cultural circumstances to prejudge the prospects for future gospel success. Rather, he or she should evaluate its possibilities solely on the basis of the revelation of God in Scripture—for the success of the gospel is "not by might nor by power, but by my Spirit" (Zech. 4:6). *Thus, the postmillennialist's ultimate confidence is in the sovereign God.*

God's Blessed Provision

In addition, the Lord of lords amply equips his church for the task of world evangelistic success. Among the abundant divine provisions for the church are the following:

---

[30]Ps. 24:1; cf. Ex. 9:29; 19:5; Lev. 25:23; Deut. 10:14; 1 Sam. 2:8; 1 Chron. 29:11, 14; Job 41:11; Ps. 50:12; 89:11; 115:16; 1 Cor. 10:26, 28 (NKJV).

(1) We have the very presence of the risen Christ with us.[31] He is the One who commands us to "go and make disciples of all nations," while promising to be with us to the end (Matt. 28:19–20). We can therefore be "confident of this, that he who began a good work in you will carry it on to completion until the day of Christ Jesus" (Phil. 1:6).

(2) We are indwelt by the Holy Spirit from on high.[32] Thus, we believe that "the one who is in you is greater than the one who is in the world" (1 John 4:4b). Among his many ministries he causes the new birth, empowers believers for righteous living, and blesses their gospel proclamation in bringing sinners to salvation.[33]

(3) The Father delights in saving sinners.[34] In fact, the Father "did not send his Son into the world to condemn the world, but to save the world through him" (John 3:17).

(4) We have the gospel, which is the very "power of God" unto salvation.[35] We also wield the powerful Word of God as our spiritual weapon: "The weapons we fight with are not the weapons of the world. On the contrary, they have divine power to demolish strongholds. We demolish arguments and every pretension that sets itself up against the knowledge of God, and we take captive every thought to make it obedient to Christ" (2 Cor. 10:4–5).[36]

(5) To undergird and empower us to gospel victory, we have full access to God in prayer[37] through Jesus' name.[38] Christ even directs us to pray to the Father: "Your kingdom come, your will be done on earth as it is in heaven" (Matt. 6:10).

(6) Though we have supernatural opposition in Satan, he is a defeated foe as a result of the first advent of Christ. "Since the children have flesh and blood, he too shared in their humanity so that by his death he might destroy him who holds the power of death—that is, the devil" (Heb. 2:14).[39] Consequently, we can

---

[31] John 6:56; 14:16–20, 23; 15:4–5; 17:23, 26; Rom. 8:10; Gal. 2:20; 4:19; Eph. 3:17; Col. 1:27; 1 John 4:4.

[32] John 7:39; 14:16–18; Rom. 8:9; 1 Cor. 3:16; 2 Cor. 6:16.

[33] John 3:3–8; 1 Cor. 6:11; Titus 3:5; 1 Peter 1:11–12, 22.

[34] Ezek. 18:23; 33:11; Luke 15:10; 2 Cor. 5:19; 1 Tim. 1:15; 2:5.

[35] Rom. 1:16; cf. 15:19; 16:25; 1 Cor. 1:18, 24; 1 Thess. 1:5.

[36] Cf. also 2 Cor. 6:7; Eph. 6:17; 1 Thess. 2:13; Heb. 4:12.

[37] Matt. 7:7–11; 21:22; Eph. 2:18; Phil. 4:6; Heb. 4:16; 10:19–22; 1 John 3:22; 5:14–15.

[38] John 14:13–14; 15:7, 16; 16:23–24, 26; 1 John 3:22; 5:14–15.

[39] Matt. 12:28–29; Luke 10:18; John 12:31; 16:11; 17:15; Acts 26:18; Rom. 16:20; Col. 2:15; 1 John 3:8; 4:3–4; 5:18.

so resist him that he will flee from us (James 4:7; 1 Peter 5:9); we can crush him under our feet (Rom. 16:20). Indeed, our God-given mission is to turn humanity "from darkness to light, and from the power of Satan to God" (Acts 26:18). *Thus, the church's ample equipment is given by a gracious Savior.*

Therefore, since God creates the world for his glory, governs it by his almighty power, and equips his people to overcome the enemy, the postmillennialist asks: "If God be for us, who can be against us?" (Rom. 8:31). Our confidence is in the service of the Lord Jesus Christ, "the ruler of the kings of the earth" (Rev. 1:5). He sits at God's "right hand in the heavenly realms, far above all rule and authority, power and dominion, and every title that can be given, not only in the present age but also in the one to come. And God placed all things under his feet and appointed him to be head over everything for the church" (Eph. 1:20–22). We have confidence that the resurrection of Christ is more powerful than the fall of Adam.

Of course, all of this does not *prove* God wills to win the world through gospel victory. But it should dispel any premature, casual dismissals of postmillennialism as a viable evangelical option, thereby paving the way for reconsidering the case for our evangelistic hope. The question now becomes: Is the postmillennial hope rooted in God's inspired and inerrant Word? Let us now consider this topic.

THE REDEMPTIVE-HISTORICAL FLOW OF POSTMILLENNIALISM

In the major section following this one, I will provide brief exegetical notations on several prominent texts for postmillennialism. But having just erected the general theological framework within which postmillennialism develops, I now would like to trace its redemptive-historical flow in broad strokes.

Creation and Edenic Covenants

The God of creation is a God of covenant. Scripture structures God's relationship to and rule over both humankind and creation in covenantal terms.

Though the term "covenant" (Heb.: *berîth*) does not appear in Genesis 1, the constitutive elements of a covenant are there.

Jeremiah does use the word "covenant" of creation. In Jeremiah 33:24–25 the creation covenant that secures the regularity of the days and seasons serves as a ground of hope in God's covenantal faithfulness to his people in the world: "This is what the LORD says: 'If I have not established my covenant with day and night and the fixed laws of heaven and earth, then I will reject the descendants of Jacob and David my servant and will not choose one of his sons to rule over the descendants of Abraham, Isaac and Jacob. For I will restore their fortunes and have compassion on them.'"[40] Hosea 6:7 also indicates a covenantal framework for Adam's Edenic experience: "Like Adam, they have broken the covenant—they were unfaithful to me there."

In the creation covenant, God appoints humanity as his vice-regent over the earth. The Lord creates human beings in his image and places all creation under them to be developed to God's glory.[41] Although a rich constellation of ideas cluster around the image of God, textually we know that at least one major concept involves humankind's *rule* over the earth:

> Then God said, "Let us make man in our *image*, in our likeness, and let them *rule* over the fish of the sea and the birds of the air, over the livestock, over all the earth, and over all the creatures that move along the ground. . . ." God blessed them and said to them, "Be fruitful and increase in number; fill the earth and subdue it. *Rule* over the fish of the sea and the birds of the air and over every living creature that moves on the ground." (Gen. 1:26, 28, emphasis added)

As the image of God under covenantal obligation, Adam and Eve must develop human culture to his glory, exercising righteous dominion over all the earth. This, of course, cannot be done by Adam and Eve alone, so God blesses and commands them to "be fruitful and increase in number" and to "fill the

---

[40]See O. Palmer Robertson, *The Christ of the Covenants* (Phillipsburg, N.J.: Presbyterian and Reformed, 1980), ch. 5; Willem VanGemeren, *The Progress of Redemption: The Story of Salvation from Creation to the New Jerusalem* (Grand Rapids: Zondervan, 1988), Part I.

[41]Gary North, *The Dominion Covenant: Genesis* (Tyler, Tex.: Institute for Christian Economics, 1982); Kenneth L. Gentry Jr., *The Greatness of the Great Commission: The Christian Enterprise in a Fallen World*, 2d ed. (Tyler, Tex.: Institute for Christian Economics, 1993), chs. 1–2.

earth," so that they might obediently "subdue it" (Gen. 1:28a). The empowerment to dominion (the "image of God") for humanity's good ("God blessed them") is followed up with the authorization ("let them rule") and the obligation ("God ... said to them ... 'Rule'") to dominion.

And because human culture is the sum deposit of humankind's normative activities in the world, this necessitates the *corporate* activity of human beings working in *concert*. This requires social order and civil polity to promote the development of civilization and the progress of culture. Contrary to humanistic evolutionary assumptions the Bible infallibly records early human development of culture. In fact, it proceeds at a remarkably rapid pace: human beings begin cattle farming, create musical instruments, and work with metals while Adam is still living (Gen. 4:17–22). This is humanity's holy calling, the God-ordained, creational drive: "Man *must* exercise dominion. It is part of his nature to do so."[42] Tragically, however, sin enters the world so that

> as a result of the fall ... man's urge to dominion is now a perverted one, no longer an exercise of power under God and to his glory, but a desire to be God. This was precisely the temptation of Satan, that every man should be his own god, deciding for himself what constitutes right and wrong (Gen. 3:5).[43]

In response to humanity's rebellious treason, God, who creates the world for his own glory, acts in sovereign mercy to initiate covenantal redemption in order to effect reconciliation with his fallen creature. In the historical context of the Fall God promises redemption and pledges to crush Satan, who sparks humankind's rebellion. To the serpent used by and representative of Satan, God says (Gen. 3:15):

> And I will put enmity
> > between you and the woman,
> > and between your offspring and hers;
> he will crush your head,
> > and you will strike his heel.

---

[42]North, *Dominion Covenant*, 29.

[43]Rousas J. Rushdoony, *The Institutes of Biblical Law* (Vallecito, Calif.: Ross House, 1973), 448. This is a common temptation to civil rulers throughout history. See: Isa.

This is the Edenic covenant, which is the foundation of redemption and supplements the creation covenant.

Here we have the protoevangelium, the first promise of the gospel. This passage anticipates struggle in history: the seeds of the representative participants in the Fall will engage in mortal conflict. Ultimately, this is a cosmic struggle between Christ and Satan, a contest played out *on earth and in time* between the city of humanity (under the dominion of Satan) and the city of God. Its historical nature is crucial to grasp: the Fall occurs in history; the struggle ensues in history; the focal seed of the woman appears in history (the historical Christ, who is the incarnation of the transcendent Creator, John 1:1–3, 14).

Significantly for the eschatological debate, this historical struggle ends in historical victory: the seed of the woman (Christ) crushes the seed of the serpent (Satan). We know from the New Testament's evidence that the historical crucifixion and resurrection of Christ legally effected Satan's ruin: "And having disarmed the powers and authorities, he made a public spectacle of them, triumphing over them by the cross" (Col. 2:15). Indeed, this is a fundamental motive to his incarnation, for "the reason the Son of God appeared was to destroy the devil's work" (1 John 3:8b; cf. Heb. 2:14). We further learn that Christ's redemptive labor will have consequences in history: "Now is the time for judgment on this world; now the prince of this world will be driven out. But I, when I am lifted up from the earth, will draw all men to myself" (John 12:31–32). Christ's historical lifting up, on which his victory is predicated, occurs either at his crucifixion, resurrection, or ascension—or most probably all three considered as a redemptive unit.

Postmillennialists emphasize the covenantal crushing of Satan in history at Christ's first advent, with its results being progressively worked out in history on the plane of Adam's original rebellion, Satan's consequent struggle, and Christ's incarnational intrusion. The protoevangelium promises in seed form (no pun intended) the victory of Christ in history, just as the Fall and its effects are in history. The first Adam's fall will be overcome by the second Adam's lifting up. God does not abandon history.

14:4, 12–17; Ezek. 28:2, 6–10; Matt. 22:20–21; Rev. 13. Hegel expresses the modern concept: "The State is the divine idea as it exists on earth.... The march of God in the world, that is what the State is."

Abrahamic Covenant

Although there are several redemptively significant covenants in Scripture, space forbids my highlighting each one. I will, however, turn to the Abrahamic covenant, a major redemptive covenant. The essence of the Abrahamic covenant appears in Genesis 12:2–3 (though later revelation develops it further; cf. 15:5–7):

> I will make you into a great nation
>> and I will bless you;
> I will make your name great,
>> and you will be a blessing.
> I will bless those who bless you,
>> and whoever curses you I will curse;
> and all peoples on earth
>> will be blessed through you.

Here the revelation of the covenant seed focuses more narrowly, moving from the general "seed of the woman" (i.e., he will be a human) to a more specifically defined family seed (i.e., he will be from Abraham's family). Ultimately, of course, the seed line will narrow to an individual: Jesus Christ, "the son of David, the son of Abraham" (Matt. 1:1; cf. John 8:56; Gal. 3:16, 19).

For my present purpose, note that "all peoples on earth will be blessed through" Abraham. The New Testament explains this for us:

> The Scripture foresaw that God would justify the *Gentiles* by faith, and announced the gospel in advance to Abraham: "All nations will be blessed through you. . . ." The promises were spoken to Abraham and to his seed. The Scripture does not say "and to seeds," meaning many people, but "and to your seed," meaning one person, who is Christ. (Gal. 3:8, 16, emphasis added)

Or, as Paul relates it elsewhere, "the promise" to Abraham is "that he would be heir of the world" (Rom. 4:13).

This supports the postmillennialist's historical optimism. Abraham's cosmic heirship develops by means of the spread of the gospel. The historical prospects of gospel victory bringing blessing on all nations comes *by gradualistic conversion*, not catastrophic imposition (as in premillennialism) or apocalyptic conclusion (as in amillennialism). This *modus operandi* has long been the method of God and the experience of God's people in Scripture. God gives Israel the Promised Land through process: "The LORD your God will drive out those nations before you, little by little. You will not be allowed to eliminate them all at once, or the wild animals will multiply around you" (Deut. 7:22; cf. Ex. 23:29–30). Prophecy also expects the incremental progress of redemptive victory among all nations: We see the water of life flowing gradually deeper (Ezek. 47:1–12), and the kingdom of heaven slowly growing larger (Dan. 2:35) and taller (Ezek. 17:22–24; Matt. 13:31–32), permeating more fully (Matt. 13:33), and producing more fruitfully (Mark 4:1–8, 26–28).

The historical goal of the Abrahamic covenant shines through clearly in the Psalms and the prophets (see later discussion). Let me now jump ahead to the conclusive new covenant.

New Covenant

Jeremiah 31:31–34 prophesies a coming new covenant, which also anticipates a time of great covenant glory:

"The time is coming," declares the LORD,
    "when I will make a new covenant
with the house of Israel
    and with the house of Judah.
It will not be like the covenant
    I made with their forefathers
when I took them by the hand
    to lead them out of Egypt,
because they broke my covenant,
    though I was a husband to them," declares
       the LORD.
"This is the covenant I will make with the house
      of Israel
    after that time," declares the LORD.
"I will put my law in their minds
    and write it on their hearts.
I will be their God,
    and they will be my people.
No longer will a man teach his neighbor,
    or a man his brother, saying, 'Know the LORD,'

because they will all know me,
    from the least of them to the greatest," declares
    the LORD.
"For I will forgive their wickedness
    and will remember their sins no more."

Because of the towering influence of the Abrahamic covenant and the historical circumstances of his audience, Jeremiah orients the covenant to "the house of Israel and the house of Judah." But since the Abrahamic covenant contains blessings for "all peoples on earth" (Gen. 12:3), we may expect the new covenant to do likewise. In fact, in the first century Christ establishes this new covenant in his death and commemorates it in the Lord's Supper (Luke 22:20; 1 Cor. 11:25; 2 Cor. 3:6; Heb. 8:8; 9:15; 12:24), which orthodox Christianity recognizes is for *all* of God's people, Jew and Gentile alike. All who trust in Christ, consequently, are as "Abraham's offspring" (Rom. 4:16; cf. Gal. 3:7, 9, 14, 29), because we are in Christ, and he is the ultimate issue of Abraham (Gal. 3:16). In short, Christians are presently partakers of the new covenant.

This new covenant will be more glorious by far than the old covenant: It will ensure a deeper and surer keeping of the righteous directives of God's law (Jer. 31:33b), a firmer and fuller spiritual relation to God (v. 33c), and a more powerful and extensive knowledge of God (v. 34). Thus, we may expect a wondrous exhibition of God's rule in history through this glorious covenant.

EXEGETICAL EVIDENCE
FOR POSTMILLENNIALISM

Let me now turn to some specific passages undergirding and illustrating this glorious expectation. Contrary to some complaints, postmillennialism is not a theological construct lacking exegetical foundations.[44] It is not rooted solely in a few carefully selected proof texts,[45] nor is it primarily an Old Testament-dependent

---

[44]H. Wayne House and Thomas D. Ice, *Dominion Theology: Blessing or Curse?* (Portland, Ore.: Multnomah, 1988), 9–10. For a Reconstructionist response, see Greg L. Bahnsen and Kenneth L. Gentry Jr., *House Divided: The Break-up of Dispensational Theology,* 2d. ed. (Tyler, Tex.: Institute for Christian Economics, 1996).

[45]Millard J. Erickson, *Contemporary Options in Eschatology: A Study of the Millennium* (Grand Rapids: Baker, 1977), 72.

system without New Testament support.[46] Numerous passages in both Testaments support the postmillennial system so that the Scripture as a whole breathes the optimistic air of hope.[47] Of course, because of space constraints, I will only be able to highlight a few of these.

Particularly significant in the eschatological debate are the messianic psalms. The postmillennialist derives great encouragement for his or her historical optimism from these glorious prophetic hymns. For instance, Psalm 22:27 anticipates a time when "all the ends of the earth will remember and turn to the LORD, and all the families of the nations will bow down before him"—apparently on the basis of evangelistic persuasion rather than Armageddon imposition. Other psalms follow suit: His salvation is to be known among all nations (67:2); all the ends of the earth will fear him (67:7); all nations will come and worship (86:9); renowned enemies will be converted (87:4); all kings will revere him (102:15). In fact, Messiah will be seated in heaven until his enemies become his footstool (110:1)—a theme verse that becomes the most cited Old Testament verse in the New Testament.[48]

In Psalm 72 messianic victory is tied to preconsummative history, before the renovation of the present universe and the establishment of the eternal new heavens and earth:

He will endure *as long as the sun,*
    as long as the moon, throughout all generations.
He will be like rain falling on a mown field,
    like showers watering the earth.
In his days the righteous will flourish,
    prosperity will abound till the moon is no more.
He will rule from sea to sea,
    and from the River to the ends of the earth.
        (Ps. 72:5–8, emphasis mine)

---

[46]George Murray, *Millennial Studies: A Search for Truth* (Grand Rapids: Baker, 1948), 86; Richard Gaffin, "Theonomy and Eschatology: Reflections on Postmillennialism," in Barker and Godfrey, *Theonomy: A Reformed Critique*, 217; David J. Englesma, "A Defense of (Reformed) Amillennialism," *The Standard Bearer* (Aug. 1, 1996): 437.

[47]For a fuller presentation, see my *He Shall Have Dominion*, chs. 9–13.

[48]Quotations include: Matt. 22:44; 26:64; Mark 12:36; 14:62; Luke 20:42–43; 22:69; Acts 2:34–35; Heb. 1:13. Allusions may be found in: 1 Cor. 15:24; Eph. 1:20–22; Phil. 2:9–11; Heb. 1:3; 8:1; 10:12, 13; 1 Peter 3:22; Rev. 3:21.

Psalm 2

But let me focus on Psalm 2, a particularly instructive psalm. The glorious vision contained in this psalm provides us with another inspired interpretation of human history.[49] It relates the cosmic turmoil among the nations and the prophetic assurance of its glorious outcome. Thus, it follows the pattern of the protoevangelium (Gen. 3:15), showing temporal struggle followed by historical victory.

The psalm opens with the nations noisily raging "against the LORD and against his Anointed One" (vv. 1–3). Ultimately considered, all world turmoil is rooted in opposition to God's authority, which opposition is the essence of all sin (Gen. 3:5; Rom. 1:18–21). The nations of the world are seeking to free themselves from the sovereign rule of the Lord and his Anointed: "Let us break *their* chains" (v. 3, emphasis added).

Their rage is not only evil but pathetically futile, for the Lord sits serenely enthroned in transcendent majesty above: "The One enthroned in heaven laughs; the Lord scoffs at them" (v. 4). Here the psalmist bitingly portrays God's confidence in his laughing mockery of his enemies' opposition against him and his "Anointed One" (v. 2). The term *Anointed One* here (Heb. *meshîach*) designates the great Deliverer and King, whom the Jews long expected (see John 1:20, 24–25, 41, 49; cf. Mark 15:32; Luke 24:19–21). He is our Lord and Savior, Jesus Christ (Mark 8:29–30; 14:61–62).

The New Testament interprets this psalm messianically, with the rage of the nations especially coming to expression in the crucifixion (Acts 4:25–27):

> "You spoke by the Holy Spirit through the mouth of your servant, our father David:
>
> > 'Why do the nations rage
> > and the peoples plot in vain?
> > The kings of the earth take their stand
> > and the rulers gather together
> > against the Lord
> > and against his Anointed One.'

---

[49]For the theonomic implications of Psalm 2, see Greg L. Bahnsen, "The Theonomic Position," in Smith, *God and Politics*, 28–30.

Indeed Herod and Pontius Pilate met together with the
Gentiles and the people of Israel in this city to conspire
against your holy servant Jesus, whom you anointed."

In the crucifixion this psalm "attained its height, but was not
finally exhausted or fulfilled," in that the cosmic battle rages on.[50]

In verse 5 the long-suffering confidence of God gives way to
his righteous indignation: "Then he rebukes them in his anger and
terrifies them in his wrath." In fact, in Psalm 2 David borrows several Hebrew words from Exodus 15 (*ʾaz, nibhᵉlû, yōshēb*), where a
celebration song recounts the routing of Egypt and anticipates the
terror of Israel's Canaanite enemies. Messiah will vanquish the raging nations of the world as surely as God conquers Israel's Canaanite foes. Alexander comments: "[That such folly] is often suffered to
proceed long with impunity is only, in the figurative language of
this passage, because God first laughs at human folly, and then
smites it."[51] But, of course, providence moves slowly, in that "with
the Lord ... a thousand years are like a day" (2 Peter 3:8).

In contrast to the nations' raging futility, God sovereignly
declares: "I [emphatic personal pronoun in the Hebrew] have
installed my King on Zion" (v. 6). God does not speak of this
installed one as "a king" or "the king," but as "*my* King." Verse
7 expands our understanding of this installation, showing the
Messiah himself speaking: "I will proclaim the decree of the
LORD: He said to me, 'You are my Son; today I have become your
Father.'" The "decree" is a pledge of adoption by God, a holy
coronation rite establishing this King's legitimacy (see 2 Sam.
7:13–14; Ps. 89:26–27).

The word "today" suggests a formal moment at which the
title becomes associated with the new Ruler. Rather than occurring at Christ's Second Advent, as many assume, the New Testament relates it once again to the first century—at the exaltation
of Christ, beginning with his resurrection. "[God] has fulfilled
this for us, their children, by raising up Jesus. As it is written in
the second Psalm: 'You are My Son, today I have become your
Father'" (Acts 13:33; cf. Rom. 1:4). Since the resurrection/ascen-
sion Christ has been installed as the King (Rom. 1:4), ruling from
God's right hand (Rom. 14:9–11; Eph. 1:20–22; Col. 1:18; 1 Peter

---

[50]J. A. Alexander, *The Psalms: Translated and Explained* (Grand Rapids: Baker,
rep. 1977 [1873]), 14.

[51]Ibid., 15.

3:22; Rev. 17:14; 19:16). The Great Commission speaks of Christ's being "given" all authority—apparently at his resurrection (Matt. 28:18; cf. the aorist tense in Phil. 2:9).

But what of this installation "on Zion"? Zion was a historical site, to be sure—a Jebusite fortress David captured and renamed the "City of David" (2 Sam. 5:6–9). When David brought the ark to Zion, the hill became sacred (2 Sam. 6:10–12). Because of its holy significance, then, the name "Zion" was gradually applied beyond the historical site to include Mount Moriah, where Solomon built the temple (Isa. 8:18; Joel 3:17; Mic. 4:7)—and eventually to all of Jerusalem (2 Kings 19:21; Ps. 48:2, 11–13; 69:35; Isa. 1:8). "Zion became in Hebrew tradition the central symbol of God's rule, the kingdom of God, a realm of justice, righteousness, and peace."[52] As such it even represents the whole Jewish nation (Isa. 40:9; Zech. 9:13). In the New Testament Zion/Jerusalem transcends Old Testament realities, reaching to heaven itself (Gal. 4:25–26; Heb. 12:22; Rev. 14:1). Thus, the center of theocratic rule has been transferred to heaven, where Christ presently rules over his kingdom (John 18:36; Rev. 1:5).

Now all that the enthroned Messiah needs do is: "Ask of me, and I will make the nations your inheritance, the ends of the earth your possession" (Ps. 2:8). Remarkably, this securing of "the nations" is the very task he assigns to his followers in the Great Commission: "Go and make disciples of all nations" (Matt. 28:19a; see discussion below). He will rule over them with his rod and dash in pieces those who refuse to submit (Ps. 2:9). This he does by his mighty Word and under his controlling providence (Heb. 1:3, 8–13; cf. Matt. 21:43–44). Because of this ultimate hope, the raging nations receive warning (Ps. 2:10–12):

> Therefore, you kings, be wise;
>   be warned, you rulers of the earth.
> Serve the LORD with fear
>   and rejoice with trembling.
> Kiss the Son, lest he be angry
>   and you be destroyed in your way,
> for his wrath can flare up in a moment.
>   Blessed are all who take refuge in him.

---

[52]Lamontte M. Luker, "Zion" in Watson E. Mills, ed., *Mercer Dictionary of the Bible* (Macon, Ga.: Mercer Univ. Press, 1991), 986.

This psalm continues developing the redemptive-historical theme of struggle and victory that began with the protoevangelium. It throbs with historical optimism and serves virtually as a postmillennial tract. Let me now turn to a sample from the prophets.

Isaiah 2:2–4

In Isaiah 2:2–4 (and Mic. 4:1–3) we learn that the "last days" will witness the universal attractive influence of the worship of God, which requires the international dispersion and influence of Christianity. This will issue forth in righteous living on a personal and social level and international peace on the cultural and political level. Isaiah indicates the "last days" will be the era witnessing these things—not some era *after* the last days: "*in* the last days" (v. 2) means "during." According to the New Testament the "last days" begin with the coming of Christ in the first century.[53] They cover the remaining days of temporal history until the second coming of Christ, which will be "the end" (1 Cor. 15:24; cf. Matt. 13:39–40, 49). Hence, they are the *last* days—with none to follow.

"Judah and Jerusalem" (Isa. 2:1) represent the whole of the people of God, just as "Israel and Judah" do in Jeremiah 31:31, where the new covenant specifically applies to the international church in the New Testament (see previous discussion). The references to the "mountain," the "house of the God of Jacob," and "Zion" refer to the church. According to the revelation of the New Testament, the church is the focal point (but not the totality) of the kingdom of God (Matt. 16:18–19); she becomes the temple and house of God.[54] She is the earthly manifestation of the city of God (Gal. 4:25–26; Heb. 12:22; 1 Peter 2:6; Rev. 21:2) and sits on a hill to influence the world (Matt. 5:14; Heb. 12:22; Rev. 14:1; 21:10). Historical Jerusalem is where Christ effected redemption (Acts 10:39; Rom. 9:33; 1 Peter 2:6) and where Christianity began (Luke 24:47, 52; Acts 1:8; 2:1ff.). The historical "city

---

[53]Acts 2:16–17, 24; 1 Cor. 10:11; Gal. 4:4; Heb. 1:1–2; 9:26; James 5:3; 1 Peter 1:20; 1 John 2:18; Jude 18.

[54]The church is the "temple of God" in 1 Cor. 3:16; 6:19; 2 Cor. 6:16; Eph. 2:19–22; 1 Peter 2:5. She is specifically designated "the house of God" in 1 Tim. 3:15; Heb. 3:6; 1 Peter 4:17.

of peace" stands as a symbol of the transnational, suprahistorical city of God, from whence the peace of God ultimately flows.[55]

Isaiah says that Christ's church will be "established" (Heb. *kûn*) in "the top of the mountains," indicating she will be "permanently fixed, rendered permanently visible."[56] After the introductory phrase "last days," Isaiah has placed the word "established" first for emphasis. In Old Testament eschatological portrayals this house is gigantic (Ezek. 40:2); Jerusalem expands her borders (Isa. 54:1–5) and towers over a plain (Zech. 14:10). Thus, the church is so firmly established as to tower over the world. She is a permanent, life-giving fixture in the earth; the "gates of Hades" cannot prevail against her (Matt. 16:18), nor may she "be shaken" (Heb. 12:28).[57] In both Isaiah 2:2 and Micah 4:1 the Hebrew niphal participle

> must be understood of an enduring condition, and the same is implied in the representation in verses 3, 4 of Jehovah's teaching function, of his judging between nations and of the state of peace and security prevailing, every man sitting under his vine and fig-tree and none of them afraid (the last in Micah only).[58]

"All nations will stream" (Isa. 2:2) into the church to worship the Lord, who saves them. Political force does not compel them; rather, the grace of God constrains them. There they will be discipled in his ways and from his law (v. 3). Christianity will become the agent of gracious redemptive influence in the world. The swelling river of people urging others to "come, let us go" to the house of God (v. 3) portrays successful evangelism leading to gospel prosperity.

With overwhelming numbers converting to Christ and being discipled in God's law, great socio-political transformation naturally follows (Isa. 2:4):

---

[55]See David E. Holwerda, *Jesus and Israel: One Covenant or Two?* (Grand Rapids: Eerdmans, 1995), 96–99; Larry R. Helyer, "Luke and the Restoration of Israel," *Journal of the Evangelical Theological Society* 36 (1993): 317–29.

[56]J. A. Alexander, *Commentary on the Prophecies of Isaiah* (Grand Rapids: Zondervan, rep. 1977 [1887]), 1:97.

[57]Matt. 7:24–27; 1 Cor. 3:11; Eph. 2:20; 2 Tim. 2:19; Rev. 21:9ff.

[58]Geerhardus Vos, *The Pauline Eschatology* (Phillipsburg, N.J.: Presbyterian and Reformed, rep. 1991 [1930]), 7.

He will judge between the nations
    and will settle disputes for many peoples.
They will beat their swords into plowshares
    and their spears into pruning hooks.
Nation will not take up sword against nation,
    nor will they train for war anymore.[59]

Peace with God (vv. 2–3) gives rise to peace among human beings (v. 4); adoption overcomes alienation. This prophecy must be the goal of our prayer lives: "Your kingdom come, your will be done on earth as it is in heaven" (Matt. 6:10).

Matthew 13

On entering the New Testament we find the prophesied eschatological kingdom flowing into history. The birth narratives freely reflect on the covenantal and hope-filled promises of the Old Testament with great expectancy (Luke 1–2). The kingdom comes "near" (Gk. *engys*) in the early ministry of Christ, because the time was fulfilled (Mark 1:14–15; cf. Gal. 4:4). Christ's power over demons and Satan's kingdom shows the kingdom as coming in during his earthly ministry (Matt. 12:28). The kingdom does not await some future, catastrophic, visible coming (Luke 17:20–21). Consequently, although Christ resists attempts to make him a political king (John 6:15), he accepts adulation as a redemptive king (Luke 18:38–40) and claims to be king while on earth (John 18:36–37). He is formally enthroned as king following his resurrection/ascension (Acts 2:30–36). From then on we hear of his being in a royal position "at the right hand of God."[60]

Because of this, first-century Christians proclaimed him king (Acts 5:31; 17:7; Rev. 1:5) with regal dignity, authority, and power (Eph. 1:22; Phil. 2:9). Since that time Christ translates us into his kingdom at our conversion (Col. 1:12–13; 4:11; 1 Thess. 2:12), organizes us as a kingdom (1 Peter 2:9; Rev. 1:6, 9), and mystically seats us with him in rulership (1 Cor. 3:21–22; Eph. 1:3; 2:6; Col. 3:1).

---

[59]See Gentry, *Greatness of the Great Commission* and Gary North, *Millennialism and Social Theory* (Tyler, Tex.: Institute for Christian Economics, 1990).

[60]Mark 16:19; Luke 22:69; Acts 2:33; 5:31; 7:55–56; Rom. 8:34; 14:11; Eph. 1:20–23; Col. 1:18; 3:1; Heb. 1:3, 13; 8:1; 10:12; 12:2; 1 Peter 3:22; Rev. 17:14; 19:16.

In his kingdom parables of Matthew 13 the Lord sketches some of the basic aspects of his spiritual kingdom, two of which are particularly helpful for postmillennialism's optimistic gradualism and deserve our attention. But I will quickly first note the others since the kingdom parables compose a unit.

In the parable of the sower (Matt. 13:3–23) Christ identifies the righteous citizens of his kingdom: those who rightly receive the Word of God. In keeping with postmillennial expectations—and with the covenants of Genesis 1:26–31; 3:15; 12:2–3 and the prophecies of Psalm 2:8 and Isaiah 2:3—their numbers will greatly increase: thirty, sixty, and a hundredfold (Matt. 13:8; cf. God's blessing on Isaac in Gen. 26:12).

The parables of the weeds (Matt. 13:24–30, 36–43) and the net (13:47–50) warn that despite the incredible growth of its citizenry, the historical manifestation of the kingdom will always include a mixture of both the righteous and the unrighteous. These will not be separated absolutely until the resurrection at the history-ending Second Advent. The kingdom will never be perfect while on earth.

The parables of the hidden treasure (Matt. 13:44) and the pearl of great price (13:45–46) speak of the priceless value and blessings of the kingdom. The parables of the mustard seed (13:31–32) and the yeast (or leaven) (13:33) instruct us as to both the gradual development and the ultimate outcome of the kingdom in history. I will focus a little more closely on the developmental outcome of the kingdom as revealed in these last two parables.

The parable of the mustard seed reads: "The kingdom of heaven is like a mustard seed, which a man took and planted in his field. Though it is the smallest of all your seeds, yet when it grows, it is the largest of garden plants and becomes a tree, so that the birds of the air come and perch in its branches" (Matt. 13:31–32). The imagery relates something magnificent beyond comprehension: A minuscule seed gives rise to a tree in which birds may nest their young. Birds singing among the branches symbolize peaceful serenity (Ps. 104:12, 17). In Daniel 4:12 and Ezekiel 31:3, 6 the greatness of Babylon and Assyria (which God providentially grants, Jer. 27:5–8; Ezek. 31:3, 9) appears as massive trees wherein birds nest: Daniel portrays the gracious provision of food for all; Ezekiel symbolizes the kingdom's greatness. That is, these are great kingdoms, which for a time secure provisions and shelter for human beings.

Christ teaches us that God has a kingdom that also will grow up to be a great tree providing nesting places for the birds and their young. Ezekiel 17:22–24a further informs Christ's imagery:

> This is what the Sovereign LORD says: I myself will take a shoot from the very top of a cedar and plant it; I will break off a tender sprig from its topmost shoots and plant it on a high and lofty mountain. On the mountain heights of Israel I will plant it; it will produce branches and bear fruit and become a splendid cedar. Birds of every kind will nest in it; they will find shelter in the shade of its branches. All the trees of the field will know that I the LORD bring down the tall tree and make the low tree grow tall. I dry up the green tree and make the dry tree flourish.

This passage speaks of the universal magnificence and glorious exaltation of the kingdom of heaven, which, when fully grown, will graciously provide shelter for all. Both Ezekiel's prophecy and Christ's parables point to the growth and dominance of Christ's kingdom: the shoot on a high mountain grows above all the trees; the mustard seed becomes the largest plant in the garden. Thus, the parable of the mustard seed speaks of the gradual *extension* of the kingdom in the world.

The parable of the yeast reads: "The kingdom of heaven is like yeast that a woman took and mixed into a large amount of flour until it worked all through the dough" (Matt. 13:33).[61] Whereas the previous parable speaks of extensive expansion, this one speaks of the kingdom's intensive penetration.

Yeast is a penetrative agent that diffuses itself throughout its host from within (cf. the internal nature of the kingdom, Luke 17:20–21;[62] John 3:3; Rom. 14:17). Contrary to popular miscon-

---

[61]For an excellent postmillennial treatment of this parable, see O. T. Allis, "The Parable of the Leaven," *The Evangelical Quarterly* 19 (October 1947): 254–73.

[62]"*Within you* (*entos hymōn*). This is the obvious, and, as I think, the necessary meaning of *entos*. . . . The only other instance of *entos* in the N.T. (Matt. 23:26) necessarily means 'within' ('the inside of the cup')" (A. T. Robertson, *Word Pictures in the New Testament* [Nashville: Broadman, 1930], 2:229). Cf. Josephus, *Antiquities*, 5:107. Moule observes: "In a careful review of the evidence up to that date, P. M. S. Allen shows that the Xenophon passages usually quoted for *among* really support *within*; that the LXX evidence supports *within*; and that even a few examples from Symmachus which appear at first to support *among* are not valid as an argument since the words are such as to make the meanings interchangeable" (C. F. D. Moule, *An Idiom-Book of New Testament Greek* [Cambridge: Cambridge Univ. Press, 1959], 84).

ception yeast does not *always* represent evil, for it is found in God-ordained offerings in Leviticus 7:13; 23:17; Amos 4:5. Of course, when associated with immoral qualifiers, it speaks of evil (e.g., "yeast of malice"). But here in Matthew 13:33 yeast symbolizes the "kingdom of heaven." This kingdom is so spiritually glorious that those who are "poor in spirit" and "persecuted because of righteousness" receive it as a blessing (Matt. 5:3, 10; Luke 6:20). Actually, yeast's subtle penetrative power is the source of its legendary interest (Gal. 5:9). In analogy it may signify the penetrative influence of *either* good or evil.

Christ emphatically teaches, in other words, that the kingdom will thoroughly suffuse itself in the whole world (cf. Matt. 13:38). The glorious expectations for the kingdom of heaven are clear: The kingdom will penetrate all (13:33), will produce up to a hundredfold return (13:8), will grow to great stature (13:31–32), and will dominate the field/world (having sown the wheat seed in the world, that world to which Christ returns will be a wheat field, not a weed field, 13:30). The kingdom's gracious and righteous influence will totally penetrate the world system.

The kingdom parables, then, comport well with the victory expectations of the Old Testament. The kingdom of the God of heaven (Dan. 2:44), which Christ urgently preaches (Mark 1:15) and which is a joyous treasure (Matt. 13:44), will grow to a position of dominance in the world.

John 12:31–32

In John 12:31–32 Christ powerfully and confidently asserts: "Now is the time for judgment on this world; now the prince of this world will be driven out. But I, when I am lifted up from the earth, will draw all men to myself." Ironically, the moment of his greatest weakness (his crucifixion) becomes the key to his great victory (cf. Col. 2:14–15), which includes the "judgment" of the world, the casting out of Satan, and the drawing of all humanity. And this moment is about to occur: it "now is" (v. 31).

Calvin's comments on the word "judgment" (Gk. *krisis*) here are helpful. He focuses on the broader meaning of the Hebrew backdrop (which forms the cultural framework within which Christ's hearers reason):

The word *judgment* is taken as "reformation" by some and "condemnation" by others. I agree rather with the former, who expound it that the world must be restored to due order. For the Hebrew word *mishpat* which is translated as *judgment* means a well-ordered constitution.... Now we know that outside Christ there is nothing but confusion in the world. And although Christ had already begun to set up the kingdom of God, it was His death that was the true beginning of a properly-ordered state and the complete restoration of the world.[63]

The rectifying of the evil and chaos Satan has brought into the world is about to begin. Tasker writes:

By His own forthcoming conflict with evil in His passion, the situation created by the fall of Adam will be reversed. It was because of disobedience that man was driven by God out of the garden of Eden for having submitted to *the prince of this world* (31); now by the perfect obedience of Jesus on the cross the prince of this world will be deposed from his present ascendancy.[64]

The Lord immediately appends the means of this restoration: Christ will cast out the great tempter of human beings and will begin redemptively drawing everyone to himself. The massive influence of Christ's reconciling death will operate in history through the age-long drawing of all men (cf. Isa. 2:2; Matt. 28:20), resulting in the world-as-a-system returning to God. He will not accomplish this catastrophically by external political imposition, but gradually by internal personal transformation.[65] Redemptively transformed people generate a righteously transformed world.

God's gracious drawing finally results in a massive, systemic conversion of the vast majority of humankind. This universal drawing leads to a redeemed world, as other Scriptures demand: God seeks the redemption of the world as a created

---

[63]John Calvin, *The Gospel According to St. John*, in David W. Torrance and Thomas F. Torrance, eds., *Calvin's New Testament Commentaries* (Grand Rapids: Eerdmans, 1961), 2:42.

[64]R. V. G. Tasker, *The Gospel According to St. John*, Tyndale New Testament Commentaries (Grand Rapids: Eerdmans, 1960), 150.

[65]Matt. 13:33; Luke 17:20–21; John 18:36–38; cf. Rom. 12:1–2; 2 Cor. 5:17; Col. 3:5–11.

system of men and things—the world that he has created (Gen. 1), claims (Ps. 24:1), and loves (John 3:16). The word "world" in Greek is *kosmos*, which speaks of an orderly arrangement, a system. Numerous passages speak of the worldwide scope of redemption and are instructive in their eschatological implications. These passages clearly present Christ in his redemptive labors—and just as expressly speak of the divinely assured worldwide effect of his redemption.[66]

In 1 John 4:14 we discover the divinely covenanted goal of God's sending his Son: He is to be "the Savior of the *world*." Thus, John 3:17 explicitly states that "God did not send the Son into the world to condemn the world, but to *save* the *world* through him." John 1:29 views him as in process of actually saving the world: "the Lamb of God, who *takes away the sin* of the *world*." Even more strongly put is 1 John 2:2, where Jesus Christ becomes "the *atoning sacrifice* for our sins, and not only for ours but also for the sins of the *whole world*" (emphasis added in all above quotes). Paul applies the "reconciling" work of Christ to the world (Rom. 11:15; 2 Cor. 5:19).

In each of these passages we see God's sure provision for full and free salvation. Consequently, when they speak of God's actions in Christ as in the process of taking "away the sin of the world" (John 1:29), as setting forth Christ as "the Savior of the world" (1 John 4:14), as intended to "save" the world rather than to "condemn" it (John 3:17), as being "the atoning sacrifice for the sins of the world" (1 John 2:2), as "reconciling the world to himself" (2 Cor. 5:19; cf. Rom. 11:15), the idea must be protensive, that is, stretched out over time. That is, Christ's labors will eventually effect the redemption of the created system of humanity and things. That redemptive hope is legally secured in the past, progresses gradually through time, and results in a redeemed world system in the future, a world that operates on the basis of righteousness as God originally intended it.

These passages do not teach an "each-and-every universalism"; at the end "weeds" are in the wheat field (Matt. 13:25). Rather, they set forth the divinely assured prospect of a coming day in which the world *as a system* (a *kosmos* rather than a *chaos*)—

---

[66]See Benjamin B. Warfield, "Christ the Propitiation for the Sins of the World," in John E. Meeter, ed., *Selected Shorter Writings of Benjamin B. Warfield*, vol. 1 (Phillipsburg, N.J.: Presbyterian and Reformed, 1970), ch. 23.

involving the vast majority of humanity and things, in all their cultural relations—will be redeemed. In that day Christianity will be the rule rather than the exception; righteousness will prevail and evil will be reduced to negligible proportions. The world system will operate on a Christian ethico-redemptive basis. Christ's providential application of his redemption will gradually bring in a time of universal worship, peace, and prosperity longed for by the prophets of the Old Testament (Matt. 13:17; 1 Peter 1:10–12). As John explains to the first-century Christians undergoing various tribulations: Christ is the propitiation not only for their sins as a little flock (cf. Luke 12:32), but for the sins of the world as such (1 John 2:2). This is the covenantal expectation for history; this is the postmillennial hope.

This grand design for the world leads Christ to call his disciples to pursue the Great Commission, to which I now turn.

Matthew 28:18–20

The Great Commission is widely known and loved, but little understood. Properly considered it is truly a *Great* Commission and a foundational element of the postmillennial hope.[67] Christ prefixes the actual commission with a bold—and necessary—claim: "All authority in heaven and on earth has been given to me." This prefatory declaration reveals a dramatic contrast to Christ's previous humility. No longer does he speak as during his state of humiliation: "The Son can do nothing by himself" (John 5:19; cf. 5:30; 8:28). But what happens in his ministry? When is this authority given?

Both the position and the tense of the word "given" in Christ's declaration (Matt. 28:18) are instructive. This verb appears in the emphatic first position, and its aorist indicative form *edothe* signifies point action in past time. The point when this occurs is obviously at Jesus' resurrection. The historical circumstances of the Great Commission not only suggest this (Christ utters the commission shortly after his resurrection), but so do other passages. For example, Romans 1:4 states of Christ: He "was declared with power to be the Son of God by his resurrection from the dead."[68]

---

[67]Gentry, *Greatness of the Great Commission.*

[68]Of course, it is true in terms of his essential deity that this "all authority given" was "not as a new gift, but a confirmation and practical realisation of the

Philippians 2:8–9 uses the same tense[69] in pointing to the resurrection as that time when Christ is "bestowed" authority: "He humbled himself and became obedient to death—even death on a cross! Therefore God exalted him to the highest place and gave him the name that is above every name." As noted earlier, this grant of kingly authority fulfills Psalm 2:6–7. The resurrection, then, followed shortly by the ascension, establishes Christ as the King, possessing "all authority."

Acts 2:30–31 agrees that the resurrection of Christ is to kingly authority: "But he [David] was a prophet and knew that God had promised him on oath that he would place one of his descendants on his throne. Seeing what was ahead, he spoke of the resurrection of the Christ." Then Peter, making reference to Psalm 110, adds: "For David did not ascend to heaven, and yet he said, 'The Lord said to my Lord: "Sit at my right hand until I make your enemies a footstool for your feet"'" (Acts 2:34b–35).

Matthew 28:18 indicates that something new occurs at his resurrection. He is *now* given "all authority." The spoils of victory are his—victory over sin, death, and the devil belong to him (Col. 2:14–15; Heb. 2:13–14; 10:12–14). His new-found authority entails *universal* dominion, encompassing "heaven and earth." Thus, it is identical with that of God the Father (Gen. 14:19; Matt. 11:25), who possesses unbounded lordship. As Kuiper observes: "The Great Commission is usually thought of as a missionary command. It is that and far more than that. Its theme is *The Sovereign Christ*. It is a glorious declaration of his sovereignty."[70]

Not only is his authority above all other, but it penetrates every realm. It is not just in the spiritual arena (the innerpersonal realm), but in all spheres of life. It universally and comprehensively serves as the basis for a truly Christian worldview. The "all" that defines "authority" is here used in the *distributive* sense. A. B. Bruce notes that Christ claims "every form of authority; command of all means necessary for the advancement of the

---

power over all things, which had been delivered unto Him by the Father" as regards his human existence (F. C. Cook, ed., *New Testament; Vol. 1: St. Matthew—St. Mark—St. Luke*, in *The Holy Bible According to the Authorized Version A.D.[1619], With an Explanatory and Critical Commentary and a Revision of the Translation* [New York: Charles Scribner's Sons, 1901], 196).

[69]In Phil. 2:9, however, the word *echarisato* is used for "given" (from *charizomai*).

[70]R. B. Kuiper, *God-Centered Evangelism* (Grand Rapids: Baker, 1961), 60.

Kingdom of God."[71] Each and every realm of thought and activity is under his authoritative command: ecclesiastical, familial, and personal—as well as ethical, social, political, economic, and so on. Consequently, we are to "demolish arguments and every pretension that sets itself up against the knowledge of God, and we take captive every thought to make it obedient to Christ" (2 Cor. 10:5). The rich reward of his redemptive labor is sovereign lordship over all (Eph. 1:19–23; Phil. 2:9–10; Col. 1:18; 1 Peter 3:21–22; Rev. 1:5; 17:14; 19:16).

After triumphantly securing universal lordship, Christ sets in gear the machinery he will employ toward the goal of exercising his dominion. He entrusts the extension of his kingdom influence to his Spirit-blessed people, whom he indwells and leads: "Therefore go and make disciples of *all nations*" (Matt. 28:19, emphasis added). This fits well with all that I note above: The Great Commission is world-encompassing. The ascended Christ mandates an expanded church. Would he assert his sovereign lordship so vigorously and command his disciples so majestically were it not his intention that they fulfill his obligation?

With these words Christ does not merely send "forth his disciples *into* all nations" (Adams) to be a "witness" (Feinberg), providing a "testimony" that "calls for a decision" (Hoekema). Nor does he simply commission them "to proclaim a message to the ends of the earth" (Pentecost), "to preach the gospel unto all nations" (den Hartog), or "to urge universal proclamation of the gospel" (Hoyt) in order to draw "out a people from among the peoples or nations of the world" (Ice).[72] According to the clear words of the Great Commission, Christ commands his disciples actually to "make disciples of all the nations."

The essential precondition to the evangelical postmillennial

---

[71]A. B. Bruce, "Matthew" in W. Robertson Nicoll, *The Expositor's Greek New Testament*, vol. 1 (Grand Rapids: Eerdmans, 1951 [rep.]), 339.

[72]Adams, *The Time Is at Hand*, 44 (emphasis mine); Charles Lee Feinberg, "The Jew After the Rapture," in Feinberg, ed., *Prophecy and the Seventies* (Chicago: Moody, 1971), 182; Anthony A. Hoekema, *The Bible and the Future* (Grand Rapids: Eerdmans, 1979), 138; J. Dwight Pentecost, *Thy Kingdom Come* (Wheaton, Ill.: Victor, 1990), 221; Arie den Hartog, "Hope and the Protestant Reformed Churches' Mission Calling," *The Standard Bearer* 66 (Jan. 1, 1990): 166; Herman A. Hoyt, "A Dispensational Premillennial Response," in Robert G. Clouse, ed., *The Meaning of the Millennium: Four Views* (Downers Grove, Ill.: InterVarsity Press, 1977), 145; House and Ice, *Dominion Theology*, 159.

hope[73] is evangelism leading to the new birth. After all, "no one can see the kingdom of God unless he is born again" (John 3:3b). Hence, Christ commands our marking out people as his own through baptism. The expansion of his kingdom comes not through evolutionary forces, human wisdom, or political strategy; it comes through obedient service to Christ while proclaiming the gospel, which "is the power of God" unto salvation (Rom. 1:16b; cf. 1 Cor. 1:18, 24).

Though earlier he limits their ministry to Israel (Matt. 10:5–6; 15:24), Christ now commissions his followers to disciple "all nations." Acts, which takes up the history of the Christian faith where the Gospels leave off, traces the nascent progress of the gospel among the nations. It opens with Christ's commanding the same few disciples to promote his message "in Jerusalem, and in all Judea and Samaria, and to the ends of the earth" (Acts 1:8); it ends with Paul in Rome, boldly preaching the gospel (Acts 28:16, 31). This progress from Jerusalem to Rome witnesses thousands of conversions, testifying to the dramatic power in Christianity.[74]

A great number of scholars recognize the Great Commission to be "a clear reference to the prophecy in Daniel 7:14, not only as to the fact but in the words themselves."[75] Daniel's passage provides that after Christ *ascends to* the Ancient of Days (not: returns to earth, v. 13), "he was given authority, glory and sovereign power; all peoples, nations and men of every language worshiped him" (7:14). This is precisely what the Great Commission expects, that all nations will be discipled under his universal authority, resulting in their baptism into the glorious name of the Triune God.

---

[73]It is important to understand that, by definition, there can be *no* liberal postmillennialism. That is, by definition postmillennialism believes *Christ will return* after the Millennium. What liberal theologian believes in the return of Christ to end history?

[74]Acts 2:41; 4:4; 5:14; 9:35, 42; 11:24–26; 17:4; 18:8, 10; 19:18, 26.

[75]Herman Ridderbos, *The Coming of the Kingdom* (Philadelphia: Presbyterian and Reformed, 1962), 467. Matthew 28:18–20 "has been formulated quite consciously in terms of" Daniel 7:13–14 (Lloyd Gaston, *No Stone on Another: Studies in the Significance of the Fall of Jerusalem in the Synoptic Gospels* [Leiden: E. J. Brill, 1970], 385). See, for example, the comments of the following scholars: D. A. Carson, Frank E. Gaebelein, Henry Alford, R. T. France, W. F. Albright, C. S. Mann, B. T. D. Smith, Frank Stagg, R. H. Fuller, W. C. Allen, John A. Broadus. For bibliographic data, see my *Greatness of the Great Commission*, 44, n.15.

What is more, not only does Jesus authoritatively command the apostles to disciple all nations, but he even promises he will be with them (and all his people) "always" (Gk. *pasas tas hēmeras*, Matt. 28:20). That is, he will be with them through the many days until the end to oversee the successful completing of the task.[76] This is the postmillennial hope.

1 Corinthians 15:20–28

Along with the kingdom parables and the Great Commission, Paul's resurrection discourse in 1 Corinthians 15 provides us with strong New Testament evidence for the postmillennial hope. Here Paul speaks forthrightly of Christ's present enthronement and insists he is confidently ruling with a view to subduing his enemies in history.

First Corinthians 15:20–22 outlines the fundamental order of the eschatological resurrection: "But Christ has indeed been raised from the dead, the firstfruits of those who have fallen asleep" (v. 20). In the first century Christ experiences the eschatological resurrection; because of this, he is the firstfruits guarantee of our own future resurrection.

In verses 23–24 we have more detail regarding the order and events associated with the resurrection: "But each in his own turn:[77] Christ, the firstfruits; then, when he comes, those who belong to him. Then the end will come." As Paul is then in the first century, so are we now in our day awaiting the eschatological coming of Christ and our resurrection. According to Paul Christ's coming marks "the end" (Gk. *telos*). At his second coming history is over in that the resurrection occurs at "the end"; there will be no millennial age on the present earth to follow.[78]

---

[76]The New Testament suggests long "seasons" pass before Christ returns (Matt. 25:5, 19; Acts 1:7; 2 Tim. 3:1; 2 Peter 3:4–9). Postmillennialism does not hold to the imminency of Christ's return. The fulfillment of great prophecies remain: the conversion of the Jews (Rom. 11) and the dominant victory of Christianity (Isa. 2:2–4). For a discussion of the implications of this denial of imminence, see: Gentry, *He Shall Have Dominion*, ch. 14.

[77]For a discussion of the Greek word *tagma* ("turn") see Benjamin B. Warfield, "The Prophecies of St. Paul," in *Biblical and Theological Studies* (Philadelphia, N.J.: Presbyterian and Reformed, rep. 1952 [1886]), 484.

[78]For helpful discussions of this prohibition against an intervening kingdom (*Zwischenreich*) era prior to the end, see C. K. Barrett, *From First Adam to Last* (Lon-

The resurrection is a general resurrection of both the righteous and unrighteous (Dan. 12:2; John 5:28–29; Acts 24:15), which will occur on the "last day" (John 6:39–40, 44, 54; 11:24; 12:48).[79]

There is more: "The end will come, when he hands over the kingdom to God the Father" (v. 24). That is, the end of earth history arrives "whenever" (Gk. *hotan*) Christ "hands over" the kingdom to the Father. In the syntactical construction before us, the handing over of the kingdom must occur in conjunction with "the end."[80] The Greek for "hands over" here is *paradidō*, which is a present subjunctive. When the present subjunctive follows *hotan*, it indicates a present contingency relative to the main clause, which here is that "the end will come." So the contingency regards the date of the end: "whenever" it may be that he delivers up the kingdom.

Associated with the predestined end here is the promise that Christ will not deliver up his kingdom to the Father until "*after* he has destroyed all dominion, authority and power" (emphasis added). In the Greek text the aorist subjunctive of the verb *katargēsē* ("has destroyed") follows *hotan*. Such a construction indicates that the action of the subordinate clause ("he has destroyed") *precedes* that of the main clause ("the end will come").[81] Not only so, but the very context demands this: How could Christ hand over an unsubdued kingdom?

Gathering this exegetical data together we see that the end is contingent; it will come at the unrevealed, unknown time when Christ delivers up the kingdom to the Father. But this will not occur until "after he has destroyed all dominion, authority and power." Consequently, the end will not occur, Christ will not turn the kingdom over to the Father, until *after* he abolishes his opposition prior to his return. This harmonizes perfectly with

---

don: Black, 1962), 101; Vos, *The Pauline Eschatology*, 238–58; Herman Ridderbos, *Paul: An Outline of His Theology* (Grand Rapids: Eerdmans, 1975), 556–59; W. D. Davies, *Paul and Rabbinic Judaism* (New York: Harper, 1967), 291–98. See also A. T. Robertson, *Word Pictures in the New Testament* (Nashville: Broadman, 1930), 4:191.

[79]Of course, Paul only mentions the resurrection of those "in Christ" (vv. 20, 23) because their future is his overriding concern in the present passage.

[80]William F. Arndt, F. Wilbur Gingrich, and Frederick W. Danker, eds., Walter Bauer, *A Greek-English Lexicon of the New Testament and Other Early Christian Literature*, 2d ed. (Chicago: Univ. of Chicago Press, 1979), 588, 1a.

[81]Ibid., 588, 1b.

the Old Testament covenantal and prophetic expectations—and with the postmillennial hope.

Furthermore, we learn that "he [Christ] must [Gk. *dei*] reign until he has put all his enemies under his feet" (v. 25). Here the present infinitive for "reign" (Gk. *basileuein*) indicates he is presently reigning. Christ is now actively "the ruler of the kings of the earth" and "has made us to be a kingdom of priests to serve his God and Father—to him be glory and power for ever and ever" (Rev. 1:5, 6). Here in 1 Corinthians 15:25 we learn that he must continue to reign, he must continue to put his enemies under his feet. In verse 24 the end is awaiting the abolishing of "all dominion, authority and power"; here it is delayed until "he has put all his enemies under his feet." Clearly, Paul expects Christ's conquering of all opposition before history ends. The last enemy he will subdue is death itself—at the eschatological resurrection. But the subduing of his other enemies occurs before this, before the resurrection and during the outworking of history under his reign.

In verse 27 Christ clearly has the title to rule, for the Father has "put everything under his feet." This is the Pauline expression (borrowed from Ps. 8:6) equivalent to Christ's declaration that "all authority in heaven and earth has been given to me." Christ has both the *promise* of victory and the *right* to victory.

Paul's glorious teaching in 1 Corinthians 15 virtually demands a postmillennial interpretation. Christ is presently ruling until his rule subdues all of his enemies—in time and on earth.

Revelation 20

I would prefer to leave Revelation 20 out of my presentation.[82] It plays too prominent a role in the eschatological debate, overshadowing much clearer passages and bringing confusion into the debate. James L. Blevins complains that "the millennium becomes 'the tail that wags the dog.'"[83] After presenting his exposition of Revelation 20 in defense of premillennialism,

[82]I deal with this passage in the larger context of defending a preterist approach to Revelation in Pate, *Four Views on the Book of Revelation*, esp. 82–86.

[83]James L. Blevins, "Revelation, Book of," in Mills, ed., *Mercer Dictionary of the Bible*, 761.

George E. Ladd confesses: "There are admittedly serious theological problems with the doctrine of a millennium."[84] B. B. Warfield is surely correct when he laments: "Nothing, indeed, seems to have been more common in all ages of the Church than to frame an eschatological scheme from this passage, imperfectly understood, and then to impose this scheme on the rest of Scripture *vi et armis*."[85]

Postmillennialist Loraine Boettner receives criticism, however, for omitting Revelation 20 in an earlier eschatological debate.[86] So, as does Berkhof, I reluctantly engage this much disputed text: "While this idea is not an integral part of Reformed theology, it nevertheless deserves consideration here, since it has become rather popular in many circles."[87]

But before doing so, we must bear in mind two important considerations. (1) The only place in all of Scripture associating a period of one thousand years with the reign of Christ is the first half of this single chapter. If a literal earthly Millennium is such an important and glorious era in redemptive history (as premillennialists argue), then it is odd that reference to the thousand years should appear in only one passage in all of Scripture. (It is also remarkable that it is absent from 1 Corinthians 15 and 1 Thessalonians 4, where the premillennialist should expect it.)

(2) This becomes even more significant in that it occurs in the most figurative book in all of Scripture. Revelation prophesies through symbolic imagery.[88] If the thousand years serve as a literal time frame, why is it only mentioned in one highly symbolic book?

What, then, does the postmillennialist make of this passage? The thousand years in Revelation 20 seem to function as a symbolic value, not strictly limited to a literal thousand year period. After all, (1) this is clearly a vision in that it opens: "and I saw" (Rev. 20:1a); (2) the perfectly rounded and exact numerical value seems more compatible with a figurative interpretation; (3) the

---

[84]George E. Ladd, in Clouse, *The Meaning of the Millennium*, 40.

[85]B. B. Warfield, "The Millennium and the Apocalypse," *The Princeton Theological Review* 2 (October 1904), 3.

[86]Anthony Hoekema, in Clouse, *The Meaning of the Millennium*, 150.

[87]Louis Berkhof, *Systematic Theology*, 708.

[88]John notes upon his opening: "The revelation of Jesus Christ, which God gave him to show his servants what must soon take place. He made it *known* [Gk. *sēmainō* from *sēmeion*, sign, token] by sending his angel to his servant John" (Rev. 1:1).

first event in the vision is the binding of Satan with a chain, which surely is not literal (see below).

But of what is the "thousand" a symbol? One thousand is the cube of ten (10 x 10 x 10); ten is the number of quantitative perfection (apparently because it is the full complement of digits on a person's hands or feet). The "thousand years," then, serve as John's symbolic portrayal of the long-lasting glory of the kingdom Christ established at his first coming. The numerical value is no more literal than that which affirms God's ownership of the cattle on a thousand hills (Ps. 50:10), promises that Israel will be a thousand times more numerous (Deut. 1:11), measures God's love to a thousand generations (7:9), expresses the desire for a thousand years in God's courts (Ps. 84:10), or compares a thousand years of our time to God's day (90:4; 2 Peter 3:8).

In Revelation 20:1–3 John portrays the negative implications of Christ's triumph over Satan, when "the dragon, that ancient serpent, who is the devil, or Satan" (v. 2) is spiritually bound (Gk. *deō*). This binding restricts him from successfully accomplishing his evil design in history. The angel from heaven who binds him evidently is Christ himself. (1) Christ appears under angelic imagery elsewhere in Revelation (cf. Rev. 10:1 with 1:13–15). (2) The struggle of the ages is ultimately between Satan and Christ (Gen. 3:15; Matt. 4:1–11; John 12:31–32; Acts 26:15–18), making it most appropriate for Christ to bind Satan. (3) Matthew 12:28–29 informs us of Christ's "binding" of Satan during his ministry and in relation to the struggle between Christ's and Satan's kingdoms: "If I drive out demons by the Spirit of God, then the kingdom of God has come upon you. Or again, how can anyone enter a strong man's house and carry off his possessions unless he first ties up [Gk. *deō*, same word as in Rev. 20:2] the strong man? Then he can rob his house" (Matt. 12:28–29; see preceding context for reference to Satan's kingdom).

Christ accomplishes Satan's binding judicially in the first century; the binding increasingly constricts Satan throughout the Christian era (i.e., the "one thousand years"), except for a brief period just prior to the Second Advent (Rev. 20:2–3, 7–9). This binding does not result in the *total inactivity* of Satan; rather, it restrains his power by Christ's. The context specifically qualifies the purpose of the binding: in order that (Gk. *hina*) Satan not "deceive the nations." Before the coming of Christ, all nations beyond the borders of Israel were under the dominion of Satan.[89] Israel alone of all the peoples of the earth was an oasis in a sin-parched world; only they knew the true God and salvation.[90] But with the coming of Christ and the spread of "the gospel of the kingdom" (Matt 24:14; cf. 4:17, 23; Mark 10:25, 29; Luke 9:2, 6) beyond the borders of Israel (Matt. 28:19; Acts 1:8; 13:47; 26:20), Satan began losing his dominion over the Gentiles.

In Revelation 20:4–6 we see the positive implications of Christ's kingdom. While Satan is bound, Christ rules and his redeemed people participate with him in that rule (Rev. 20:4). These participants include both the quick and the dead: the martyred saints in heaven ("those who had been beheaded because of their testimony for Jesus and because of the word of God") and the persevering saints on earth ("and those who [Gk. *hoitines*] had not worshiped the beast" [NASB]).[91] Christ's kingdom rule involves all those who suffer for him and enter heaven above, as well as those who live for him during their earthly sojourn—after all, he has "all authority in heaven and on earth" (Matt. 28:18).

According to John the "first resurrection" secures the participation of the saints (both dead and living) in the rule of Christ (Rev. 20:4–6). This refers to the spiritual resurrection of those born again by God's grace: "We know that we have passed from death to life, because we love our brothers. He who does not love remains in death" (1 John 3:14). "Now if we died with Christ, we believe that we will also live with him" (Rom. 6:8). "But because of his great love for us, God, who is rich in mercy, made us alive with Christ even when we were dead in transgressions—it is by grace you have been saved. And God raised us up with Christ and seated us with him in the heavenly realms in Christ Jesus" (Eph. 2:4–6). "When you were dead in your sins and in the uncircumcision of your sinful nature, God made you alive with Christ. He forgave us all our sins" (Col. 2:13).

In fact, in his Gospel the author of Revelation parallels the spiritual resurrection of soteriology with the physical resurrection

---

[89]2 Kings 17:29; Ps. 96:3–5 [cf. 1 Cor. 10:20]; Luke 4:6; Acts 14:16; 17:30; 26:17–18.

[90]Deut. 7:6ff; Ps. 147:19–20; Amos 3:2; Rom. 3:1–2.

[91]We must note that "*kai hoitines* introduces a second class of persons, 'confessors...'" (Henry Barclay Swete, *Commentary on Revelation* [Grand Rapids: Kregel, rep. 1977 (1906)], 262).

of eschatology, just as he does in Revelation 20 (see fuller discussion below):

> I tell you the truth, whoever hears my word and believes him who sent me has eternal life and will not be condemned; he has *crossed over from death to life*. I tell you the truth, *a time is coming and has now come when the dead will hear the voice of the Son of God and those who hear will live*. For as the Father has life in himself, so he has granted the Son to have life in himself. And he has given him authority to judge because he is the Son of Man.
>
> Do not be amazed at this, for *a time is coming when all who are in their graves will hear his voice and come out—* those who have done good will rise to live, and those who have done evil will rise to be condemned. (John 5:24–29, emphasis added)

Having been spiritually resurrected, the saints (whether in heaven or on earth) are spiritually enthroned. Revelation 20:4–6 speaks of the saints living and reigning with Christ, which elsewhere refers to a spiritual reality in the present experience of God's people: "God raised us up with Christ and seated us with him in the heavenly realms in Christ Jesus" (Eph. 2:6). "So then, no more boasting about men! All things are yours, whether Paul or Apollos or Cephas or the world or life or death or the present or the future—all are yours" (1 Cor. 3:21–22). "Since, then, you have been raised with Christ, set your hearts on things above, where Christ is seated at the right hand of God. Set your minds on things above, not on earthly things" (Col. 3:1–2).

This is a redemptive reign in that they (and we today) are priests and kings: "Blessed and holy are those who have part in the first resurrection. The second death has no power over them, but they will be priests of God and of Christ and will reign with him for a thousand years" (Rev. 20:6). John informs his original audience early in Revelation that Christ "has made us to be a kingdom and priests to serve his God and Father" (1:6). Peter tells the first-century Christians (and us): "You are a chosen people, a royal priesthood, a holy nation, a people belonging to God, that you may declare the praises of him who called you out of darkness into his wonderful light" (1 Peter 2:9).

Thus, the saints' reigning "with Christ" on thrones while Satan is bound beautifully pictures his redemptive kingdom already established: Christ brings his kingdom into the world to battle with Satan during his earthly ministry (Matt. 4:1–11; 12:28–29); God formally bestows kingly authority on him at his resurrection/ascension (Matt. 28:18; Rom. 1:4); and Christ promises continuing growth in history until the end (Matt. 13:31–33; 1 Cor. 15:25). The King of kings possessing all authority, commissions his servants to bring others into his kingdom, promising all the while to be with them and to bless them in their labor (Matt. 28:18–20; Phil. 4:13). Christians are overcomers (cf. 1 John 2:13–14; 4:4; 5:4–5) and are seated with Christ who presently rules: "To him who overcomes, I will give the right to sit with me on my throne, just as I overcame and sat down with my Father on his throne" (Rev. 3:21). The "millennial" era has already lasted almost two thousand years; it may continue another thousand or ten thousand more, for all we know.

The "rest of the [spiritually] dead" do not participate in this spiritual resurrection. In fact, they do "not come to life until the thousand years" is finished (Rev. 20:5). At that time they are physically resurrected (implied) in order to be subjected by "the second death" (eternal torment), which is brought about at Judgment Day (20:11–15). At that time, of course, God will resurrect all humanity physically (Job 19:23–27; Isa. 26:19; John 5:28–29; Acts 24:15; Rom. 8:11, 23; Phil. 3:20; 1 Thess. 4:16).

John's symbolic portrayal of Christ's kingdom and rule depicts the transcendent glory of Christianity in the world. As his rule expands through the preaching of the gospel, righteousness, tranquillity, and prosperity will eventually come to majestic expression. We do not know when his kingdom will reach its height or how long it will prevail, but John's grand vision encourages us to understand that we will participate for a long time in its growth as we worship and serve King Jesus.

CONCLUSION

The case for the postmillennial hope begins at creation, develops by means of redemption, and is assured by revelation. From Genesis to Revelation earth history is the focal point of the universe in the outworking of God's marvelous plan for his own glory and the good of his highest creature, the human race. Providence is slow. History is long. We are impatient. But God's will shall "be done on earth as it is in heaven" through the gospel that he ordains as the "power of God for the salvation of everyone who believes" (Rom. 1:16).

The slow and deliberate nature of the providential advance of the kingdom reminds us of the little child who plays at his grandmother's feet as she cross-stitches a decorative wall hanging. All he can see from his perspective below is the chaotic pattern of clipped threads and jumbled colors. But from her perspective above she sees a developing work of art following a sure pattern. Once she skillfully completes the project, the child sees its beauty causing his wonder to vanish in delight.

We now see but a little stream of hope. But this stream, flowing continuously in history, will become a river of life and will one day overflow its banks:

> The man brought me back to the entrance of the temple, and I saw water coming out from under the threshold of the temple toward the east (for the temple faced east). The water was coming down from under the south side of the temple, south of the altar. He then brought me out through the north gate and led me around the outside to the outer gate facing east, and the water was flowing from the south side.
>
> As the man went eastward with a measuring line in his hand, he measured off a thousand cubits and then led me through water that was ankle-deep. He measured off another thousand cubits and led me through water that was knee-deep. He measured off another thousand and led me through water that was up to the waist. He measured off another thousand, but now it was a river that I could not cross, because the water had risen and was deep enough to swim in—a river that no one could cross. He asked me, "Son of man, do you see this?"
>
> Then he led me back to the bank of the river. When I arrived there, I saw a great number of trees on each side of the river. He said to me, "This water flows toward the eastern region and goes down into the Arabah, where it enters the Sea. When it empties into the Sea, the water there becomes fresh. Swarms of living creatures will live wherever the river flows. There will be large numbers of fish, because this water flows there and makes the salt water fresh; so where the river flows everything will live.

Fishermen will stand along the shore; from En Gedi to En Eglaim there will be places for spreading nets. The fish will be of many kinds—like the fish of the Great Sea. But the swamps and marshes will not become fresh; they will be left for salt. Fruit trees of all kinds will grow on both banks of the river. Their leaves will not wither, nor will their fruit fail. Every month they will bear, because the water from the sanctuary flows to them. Their fruit will serve for food and their leaves for healing." (Ezek. 47:1–12)

AN AMILLENNIAL RESPONSE TO KENNETH L. GENTRY JR.

Robert B. Strimple

I express appreciation for Pastor Gentry's attempt to establish his postmillennial eschatology on a biblical basis. Surely he has laid to rest the charge (too often heard in the past) that the kind of evangelical postmillennialism he advocates rests on liberal, humanist, evolutionist presuppositions; as he rightly notes in his note 73, when terms are used correctly "there can be *no* liberal postmillennialism ... by definition postmillennialism believes *Christ will return* after the Millennium. What liberal theologian believes in the return of Christ to end history?" The question remains, however, whether his attempt to present a biblical argument for postmillennialism is successful.

Mr. Gentry espouses a particular form of postmillennialism, namely, "theonomic postmillennialism." The contemporary theology known as theonomy (also Christian Reconstructionism or dominion theology) raises its own difficulties with regard to biblical exegesis, theology, and ethics.[1] But since the distinctives of *theonomic* postmillennialism are not emphasized in Gentry's essay, they will not be addressed in this response. One contention, however, must be challenged—that "the Westminster Standards endorse the theonomic outlook" (note 24). Theonomy insists that all the Mosaic judicial laws, along with the particular

---

[1]The reader is referred to two studies in particular: *Theonomy: A Reformed Critique*, ed. William S. Barker and W. Robert Godfrey (Grand Rapids: Zondervan, 1990); and Meredith G. Kline, "Comments on an Old/New Error," *Westminster Theological Journal* 41:1 (1978): 172–89.

penalties for their transgression (including capital punishment not only for murder but also for such crimes as adultery, homosexual acts, blasphemy, and incorrigible and physical rebellion in children) continue to be binding today and should be applied by the civil government. Is that the teaching of the Westminster Confession of Faith?

Chapter XIX of the Westminster Confession deals with the law of God. It makes the traditional threefold distinction of moral, ceremonial, and judicial law.[2] After affirming (1) that the *moral* law (which was given originally to Adam and later delivered on Mount Sinai in the Ten Commandments) continues to be God's perfect rule of righteousness, containing our duty toward God and other human beings, and (2) that the *ceremonial* laws "prefigured" Christ and "are now abrogated, under the new testament," the Confession goes on to affirm (3) with regard to the *judicial* laws:

> To them [the people of Israel] also, as a body politic, He [God] gave sundry judicial laws, which *expired* together with the State of that people; not obliging any other now, further than the general equity thereof may require. (emphasis added)

As Sinclair Ferguson has noted, this statement of the Westminster Confession

> is not the *natural* way of expressing a *theonomic* view. It is certainly not the way contemporary theonomists express their position. For the Confession, the governing principle is that the Mosaic judicial laws have *expired* (whatever else may be said to clarify their relevance), whereas for theonomists the governing principle is that the Mosaic judicials *have not expired* but are still in force; Christ has confirmed them and they are all perpetually binding.[3]

---

[2]Theonomy commonly replaces this threefold division with a twofold one, regarding the Mosaic judicial laws as simply concrete expressions of the moral law, which are therefore (like the moral law) of permanent moral obligation. See Sherman Isbell, "The Divine Law of Political Israel Expired, Part I: General Equity," *The Presbyterian Reformed Magazine* 12:2 (1997): 63–83, an excellent study showing the important "points of variance between theonomy and the doctrine of the Westminster Confession of Faith" (p. 66).

[3]Sinclair B. Ferguson, "An Assembly of Theonomists? The Teaching of the Westminster Divines on the Law of God," in *Theonomy: A Reformed Critique*, 326–27.

Gentry claims that the Confession's endorsement of theonomy is evident from its proof texts and from the writings of its framers. Ferguson examines both, concludes that "at important points the exegesis of the Divines and the exegesis of theonomists differ," and then affirms: " . . . we must conclude that the Westminster Confession cannot be appealed to as an expression of theonomy in its contemporary form."[4] The 1997 General Assembly of the Free Church of Scotland had good grounds, I believe, for declaring that "the teachings commonly known as Theonomy or Reconstructionism contradict the [Westminster] Confession of Faith and are inconsistent with the Bible."[5]

Early in his essay Pastor Gentry offers the following definition of postmillennialism:

> *Postmillennialism expects the proclaiming of the Spirit-blessed gospel of Jesus Christ to win the vast majority of human beings to salvation in the present age. Increasing gospel success will gradually produce a time in history prior to Christ's return in which faith, righteousness, peace, and prosperity will prevail in the affairs of people and of nations. After an extensive era of such conditions the Lord will return visibly, bodily, and in great glory, ending history with the general resurrection and the great judgment of all humankind.*

The New Testament, however, presents a different picture of the character of this age between Christ's ascension and his second coming and of what Christ's church may look forward to before her Lord returns. Christ Jesus, who was delivered over to death for our sins, has been raised to life for our justification (Rom. 4:25). He has been exalted and seated at God's right hand in heaven (Heb. 1:3). "And God placed all things under his feet and appointed him to be head over everything for the church, which is his body, the fullness of him who fills everything in every way" (Eph. 1:22–23). Christ is King *now!* He is not waiting to begin exercising his dominion at some future day. Thus, Christians have every reason to be bold and confident in their faithful service of the King and the proclamation of his glorious gospel throughout the world.

---

[4]Ibid., 338, 346.
[5]*The Monthly Record of the Free Church of Scotland* (June-July, 1997), 130.

But what is the nature of Christ's present kingdom? Because Gentry has defined the victory Christ seeks in the present age in terms of "the vast majority of human beings" being saved and then coming to exercise political, judicial, social, and economic control over "the world-as-a-system,"[6] thus inaugurating "a time of universal worship, peace, and prosperity," he must view Christ's kingly reign as a *failure* so far—a failure for these now two thousand years since his ascension. We must be careful not to substitute for God's sure promises expectations that may seem "reasonable" to us. If we do, we may begin to devalue the blessings Christ is pouring out on his church *now* by his Spirit, and we may fail to appreciate the eschatological nature of the kingdom *already* inaugurated by Christ's resurrection and exaltation, and by the Pentecostal outpouring of the Holy Spirit. And as we do, we may find ourselves insisting that the consummation arrive before its time.

True, God has promised "a time of universal worship, peace, and prosperity"; but the consistent witness of the New Testament is that that time will come only when our Lord Jesus Christ himself has come "a second time . . . to bring salvation to those who are waiting for him" (Heb. 9:28). Gentry repeatedly emphasizes that the struggle between Christ and Satan is a "historical struggle [that] ends in historical victory." This is true. And it will end in total and perfect victory at "the end" of history (Gk. *to telos,* 1 Cor. 15:24; 1 Peter 4:7), the end of "this age," which will come when Christ comes—that is, when both God's people and God's created cosmos enter into total and perfect deliverance from sin and all its consequences (Rom. 8:18–23), when the present earth and heavens will give way "to a new heaven and a new earth, the home of righteousness" (2 Peter 3:13). God's "creational purpose" will be fulfilled in the *new* creation, which is not to be understood as a *second* creation *ex nihilo* but rather as a renewal, a re-creation of God's original creation. (Compare the renewal of the cosmos with the *resurrection* that will fulfill God's redemptive purpose for his people, Rom. 8:23.)

Later in his essay Gentry makes the startling statement that the "redeemed world system in the future" (still future but *before* Christ's coming and the consummation) will operate "on the

---

[6]Surely this is an untenable definition of the Greek word *kosmos* in John 1:29; 3:16–17; 1 John 4:14.

basis of righteousness *as God originally intended it.* .... Righteousness will prevail and evil will be reduced to negligible proportions" (emphasis added). Is God's original intention for his creation simply that evil should be "reduced to negligible proportions"?! If this is "the postmillennial hope," it contrasts poorly with the amillennial hope.

When we ask concerning God's purpose and the church's mandate for this present time, we are reminded of our Lord's commission (Matt. 28:16–20) and the apostle's statement of the reason behind the apparent "delay" in the promised coming: "He is patient with you, not wanting anyone to perish, but everyone to come to repentance" (2 Peter 3:9). Berkouwer writes:

> If missions is in fact closely connected with the eschatological expectation, it is important to note that the community of believers on its way to the future assumes a very central and meaningful place. The church receives a mandate in this darkness, a mandate that will be fulfilled by the Lord Himself.... Why is there a "not yet" instead of a radical, triumphant consummation? Because Christ gives the reconciled creature *time* and *space* in order that he may participate in the harvest, not only as mere spectator, but as co-worker.[7]

When Gentry writes that Christ "will be with [his people] through the many days until the end to oversee the successful completing of the task. This is the postmillennial hope," he implies that only the postmillennialist believes that the task given the church by her risen Lord will be successfully completed. Not so. Amillennialists (and premillennialists) certainly believe that this age will not end until the Lord's purposes are fulfilled. But Gentry has failed to establish that making disciples of all nations, baptizing them, and teaching them require that that fulfillment be in postmillennial terms. Our Lord has promised that "this gospel of the kingdom will be preached in the whole world as a testimony to all nations, and then the end will come" (Matt. 24:14); but only God knows when the church's ministry among the nations will have achieved its goal, when the elect church will have been gathered from every nation (Rev. 5:9) and his Son will return.

---

[7]G. C. Berkouwer, *The Return of Christ*, trans. James Van Oosterom (Grand Rapids: Eerdmans, 1972), 132, 135.

God the Father "has blessed us in the heavenly realms with every spiritual blessing in Christ" (Eph. 1:3). The Lord Jesus Christ "gave himself for our sins to rescue us from the present evil age" (Gal. 1:4), so that in a blessed sense the powers of the age to come have broken in *now* for those who are united to the risen Christ by faith. Yet it remains true that the church continues to live in *this* age, the *present* age, this *evil* age, and will do so until Christ comes again. And that fact speaks volumes as to what the church may expect in the years ahead before her Savior returns. Think, for example, of what the Lord Jesus himself has taught us. Our Lord knows of only *two* ages, the present age and the age to come.[8] He tells his disciples that in this present age they cannot expect anything other than oppression and persecution and must forsake all things for his sake.

Jesus nowhere predicts a glorious future on earth before the end of the world, as postmillennialists posit. On the contrary, the things he himself experienced are the things his church will experience. A disciple is not above the teacher or a slave above the master. Only in the age to come will our Lord's disciples receive everything back along with eternal life (Matt. 19:27–30; cf. 5:3–12; 8:19–20; 10:16–42; 16:24–27; John 16:2, 33; 17:14–15; etc.).[9]

And with this teaching of Jesus the rest of the New Testament is uniformly consistent. When the apostle Paul thinks of this present time, he thinks of *sufferings* as its characteristic mark (Rom. 8:18;[10] see also John 16:33; Acts 14:22; Rom. 8:36; 2 Cor. 1:5–10; Phil. 1:29; 3:10; 1 Peter 4:12–19). Gentry appeals to Deuteronomy 7:22 and the conquest of Canaan as the model for God's working to conquer the world through the church at the present time. But when the New Testament locates the church in the history of redemption, the paradigm to which it points is not the Canaan occupation but the *desert* experience (Heb. 3:7–19). Christ's church today remains the church in the desert, and gradual worldwide dominion does not occur in the desert. Canaan

---

[8]Note this well. Postmillennialism seems to posit *three* ages: the present evil age, a future "golden" age (see Gentry's definition reference to "a time in history prior to Christ's return in which . . ."), and the "age to come," of which the New Testament speaks.

[9]Herman Bavinck, *The Last Things*, ed. John Bolt, trans. John Vriend (Grand Rapids: Baker, 1996), 109.

[10]In my essay I comment on the NIV's misleading translation of Romans 8:18.

and rest still lie ahead. Like father Abraham, believers remain "aliens and strangers on earth" (11:13), who have no enduring city here but look for one to come (13:14).

And not only is it true that the church still lives in the present age, it is also true (according to the New Testament) that the church lives in the "last days" of this present age. There is every reason to think that the Bible views "this age" as having begun with the very beginning of history, while from the New Testament perspective the "last days" began with the advent of Christ. Thus the two concepts coincide to this extent, that the last days are the last lap of this present age. As John Murray has observed, "This explains a common characteristic of both. This age is evil, the last days are characterized by many evils. In them scoffers abound and perilous times come."[11]

The apostle Paul wrote, by the inspiration of the Spirit: "In fact, everyone who wants to live a godly life in Christ Jesus will be persecuted, while evil men and impostors will go from bad to worse, deceiving and being deceived" (2 Tim. 3:12–13). Persecution, apostasy, Antichrist—these find no place in the postmillennial vision, but they are essential elements in the New Testament picture of the last days. By means of his preterist reading of the Olivet Discourse (Matt. 24 and parallels), 2 Thessalonians 2, and the book of Revelation, Gentry tries to assure Christians that the worst days of persecution, apostasy, and the Antichrist are past (except for the brief Satan-led rebellion just before Christ's second coming, which Rev. 20:7–9 seems to require as an undigested surd in the postmillennial scheme).

Preterism would require a response chapter of its own, but I submit three things here. (1) In the Olivet Discourse the destruction of the temple is viewed as a proleptic, typological fulfillment of that final judgment of God; final deliverance of the elect will occur only at Christ's coming and the end of the age (Matt. 24:3), while tribulation, wars, famines, and earthquakes are "represented as characterizing the interadventual period as a whole."[12] (2) Nero cannot be "the lawless one," whom the Lord

[11]John Murray, "Structural Strands in New Testament Eschatology," in *Papers Read at the Seventh Annual Meeting of the Evangelical Theological Society* (December 29–30, 1954), ed. John F. Walvoord, 8.

[12]John Murray, "The Interadventual Period and the Advent: Matthew 24 and 25," in *Collected Writings of John Murray*, vol. 2 (Edinburgh: Banner of Truth, 1977), 389. See also Calvin's *Commentary on a Harmony of the Evangelists, Matthew, Mark, and*

Jesus will "destroy by the splendor of his coming" (2 Thess. 2:8). (3) Neither can Nero be the beast of Revelation, who will be destroyed only after his defeat by the rider on the white horse in the final battle, the battle of Armageddon (Rev. 19).[13]

The idea of the Antichrist in general and that of the apostasy in particular reminds us that we may not expect an uninterrupted progress of the Christianization of the world until the Parousia. As the reign of truth will be extended, so the forces of evil will gather strength, especially toward the end. The universal sway of the kingdom of God cannot be expected from missionary effort alone; it requires the eschatological interposition of God.[14]

The New Testament everywhere makes clear that *the focus of the believer's hope is to be the second coming of Christ*. Many texts, of course, immediately come to mind:

> 1 Thess. 1:9–10: "You turned to God from idols to serve the living and true God, and to wait for his Son from heaven, whom he raised from the dead—Jesus, who rescues us from the coming wrath."
> Titus 2:12–13: "... and to live self-controlled, upright and godly lives in this present age, while we wait for the

---

Luke, where Calvin speaks of the "blending" in this discourse of the destruction of Jerusalem and the end of the age as figure and final fulfillment.

[13]Gentry presents his suggestion that Nero is the man of lawlessness of 2 Thess. 2 and the beast of Revelation in *He Shall Have Dominion*, (Tyler, Tex.: Institute for Christian Economics, 1992), 383–93. He there insists that 2 Thess. 2:1 ("Concerning the coming of our Lord Jesus Christ and our being gathered to him") refers to Jesus' coming in destruction on Jerusalem and the resulting "gathering together" of Christians "in a *separate* and *distinct* assembly." (So much for literalism!) In an unpublished paper on *The Date and Setting of the Book of Revelation*, Charles E. Hill observes (p. 8): "One might ask, if it is so obvious that 666 referred to Nero, why this truth did not even occur to Irenaeus, who discusses several options for its interpretation, but does not even mention this possibility?" With regard to the preterist reading of Revelation he writes (pp. 21–22): "I am struck over and over with the fact that Revelation is not essentially about Israel. It is about Christ's kingship and lordship over all.... The rebellion against him is worldwide and the redemption he effects is worldwide. A constraining of the focus to the old covenant people of Israel, even with the accompanying shift of attention to the church, does not seem to comport with the grand scope of the book."

[14]Geerhardus Vos, *Redemptive History and Biblical Interpretation: The Shorter Writings of Geerhardus Vos*, ed. Richard B. Gaffin Jr. (Phillipsburg, N.J.: Presbyterian and Reformed, 1980), 41.

blessed hope—the glorious appearing of our great
God and Savior, Jesus Christ."

Heb. 9:28: "He will appear a second time, not to bear sin,
but to bring salvation to those who are waiting for
him."

James 5:7: "Be patient, then, brothers, until the Lord's
coming."

1 Peter 1:13: "Set your hope fully on the grace to be given
you when Jesus Christ is revealed."

2 Peter 3:11–12: "You ought to live holy and godly lives as
you look forward to the day of God and speed its
coming."

The contrast between the New Testament hope and the
postmillennial hope seems to be clear and undeniable. As Cornelis Venema has observed,

> Postmillennialism *alters the focus* of the believer's hope
> for the future. Whereas the New Testament depicts the
> church in this present age as a church continually participating in the sufferings of Christ and eagerly awaiting
> the return of Christ at the end of the age, the postmillennial view encourages an outlook for the future that is
> focused on an anticipated period of largely undisturbed
> blessedness in the millennial kingdom.... The golden age
> postmillennialist has his sights fixed upon the coming
> golden age rather than the return of Christ at the end of
> the age.[15]

The New Testament permits no "date-setting" with regard
to Christ's second coming. No, not even in the broad general
terms demanded by postmillennialism. By definition (look at
Gentry's definition again) postmillennialism looks forward to "*a
time in history prior to Christ's return*"—and that is "*an extensive
era*"—"*in which faith, righteousness, peace, and prosperity will prevail
in the affairs of people and of nations.*" How can that hope not take
our eyes off the "blessed hope" of Christ's appearing? Compare
the following two statements regarding the believer's expectation: The first is written by a theonomic postmillennialist; the second is the last sentence in the Westminster Confession of Faith:

---

[15]Cornelis P. Venema, "Evaluating Post-millennialism (II)," *The Outlook* (January 1998), 22.

Every day brings us closer to the realization of the knowledge of God covering the entire world. . . .[16] God promises [Deut. 7:9] that He will bless His people for one thousand generations. By the analogy of Scripture, then, this means that a figure of forty thousand years is a bare *minimum*. This world has tens of thousands, perhaps hundreds of thousands of years of increasing godliness ahead of it, before the Second Coming of Christ.[17]

As Christ would have us to be certainly persuaded that there shall be a day of judgment, both to deter all men from sin; and for the greater consolation of the godly in their adversity: so will He have that day unknown to men, that they may shake off all carnal security, and be always watchful, because they know not at what hour the Lord will come; and may be ever prepared to say, Come Lord Jesus, come quickly. Amen.[18]

Up to this point I have concentrated on showing why I believe the postmillennial vision of the nature of Christ's present kingdom and of the believer's hope is out of harmony with the New Testament revelation. The question comes then: On what basis does Gentry put forward his postmillennial eschatology? Because there are so few pages left of the maximum number allotted for this response, my comments can only be sketchy pointers in certain directions.

Pastor Gentry begins with a fairly lengthy history of postmillennialism. In this regard I would simply caution the reader to do the necessary research and evaluate for himself or herself the eschatological statements of each of the theologians cited as

---

[16]Note by way of contrast the focus of the apostle's hope: "Our *salvation* is nearer now than when we first believed" (Rom. 13:11). John Murray reminds us that "the usage of the New Testament . . . would point to the conclusion that when this term [salvation] is used with reference to the future it denotes the consummation of salvation to be realized at the advent of Christ" (*The Epistle to the Romans*, vol. 2 [Grand Rapids: Eerdmans, 1965], 165).

[17]David Chilton, *Paradise Restored* (Fort Worth: Dominion, 1985), 221–22. Chilton goes on to write in the next sentence: "I am not interested in setting dates. I am not going to try to figure out the date of the Second Coming." Surely this reveals a strange understanding of what it means not to try to set the date of the Parousia!

[18]Westminster Confession of Faith (33.3). Compare the similar statements of the believer's hope in the continental Reformed creeds: Heidelberg Catechism question and answer 52 and Belgic Confession, article 37.

either nascent or full-blown postmillennialists before accepting that characterization of their position. For example, the documentation cited for Athanasius in Gentry's earlier book, *He Shall Have Dominion*, consists entirely of statements by Athanasius showing that "the great progress of the gospel is expected."[19] On the basis of *that* criterion virtually every Christian theologian could be claimed as a postmillennialist! Another example: Gentry lists John Calvin as "an incipient postmillennialist." This will surely come as a surprise to Calvin scholars, who have viewed the Second Helvetic Confession (1566) as echoing the teaching of all the leading Reformers, and of Calvin in particular, in article 11 (cf. art. 27):[20]

> We further condemn Jewish dreams that there will be a golden age on earth before the Day of Judgment, and that the pious, having subdued all their godless enemies, will possess all the kingdoms of the earth. For evangelical truth in Matt. chs. 24 and 25, and Luke, ch. 18, and apostolic teaching in II Thess., ch. 2, and II Tim., chs. 3 and 4, present something quite different.

Gentry's section, "Theological Foundations of Postmillennialism," presents no doctrines that are distinctive of postmillennialism. Certainly amillennialists (and premillennialists) also affirm God's "creational purpose," "sovereign power," and "blessed provision." Thus, this section contributes nothing to the defense of postmillennialism's fundamental specific contention (that Christ will win "the vast majority of men to salvation in the present age"). At the end of the section Gentry himself recognizes this.

In the next section, "Redemptive-Historical Flow of Postmillennialism," Gentry continues to paint with a broad brush, citing biblical passages that speak of the creation covenant, the Abrahamic covenant, and the new covenant, but which at no

---

[19]Kenneth L. Gentry Jr., *He Shall Have Dominion*, 85.

[20]Compare Calvin in the *Institutes*, 3.25.5, and the Augsburg Confession, article 17. Typical of Calvin's eschatological focus is his comment on 2 Peter 4:7 ("The end of all things is near"): "We must remember this principle, that from the time when Christ once appeared there is nothing left for the faithful except to look forward to His second coming with minds alert" (*Calvin's Commentaries: The Epistle of Paul the Apostle to the Hebrews and The First and Second Epistles of St. Peter*, trans. William B. Johnston [Grand Rapids: Eerdmans, 1963], 303).

point establish the specifics of the postmillennial vision. For example, as noted above, postmillennialists are not the only Christians who believe that "Christ's redemptive labor will have consequences in history." Gentry's accent on the historical and temporal "this world" realism of redemptive history makes a telling and helpful point against Platonism or Barthianism, but is irrelevant as an argument against amillennialism or premillennialism.

Gentry titles the final section of his essay "Exegetical Evidence for Postmillennialism." Even *this* section, however, Gentry introduces as follows: "Let me turn to some specific passages *undergirding* and *illustrating* the glorious expectation" (emphasis added). The reader is left looking in vain for the specific biblical passages that *teach* it, that *prove* it! This continues to be my most fundamental objection to postmillennialism: that postmillennialism is simply not taught—clearly, explicitly—in any passage of Scripture. It is always presented by its exponents by way of inference or implication. Gentry can say that "contrary to some complaints postmillennialism is not a theological construct lacking exegetical foundations," but he has not demonstrated this. Herman Hanko is correct, I believe, in concluding that "the Scriptural proof for postmillennialism simply does not exist."[21]

In this section, as in the previous sections, Gentry begins from the perspective of the Old Testament, interpreted according to a literalistic hermeneutic (applied less consistently, however, than by dispensationalists), and then tries to read his conclusions into the New Testament. This is a fundamental methodological, hermeneutical error. Please review the first section of my own essay, where I argue that the New Testament—the post-resurrection, post-Pentecost revelation given to the church there—must be our only authoritative, infallible guide in all things, including our interpretation of the Old Testament.

> It is a question [of] what the Spirit of Christ who was in them [the Old Testament prophets] wished to declare and reveal by them. And *that* is decided by the New Testament, which is the completion, fulfillment, and therefore interpretation of the Old.[22]

---

[21]Herman Hanko, "An Exegetical Refutation of Postmillennialism," in *Protestant Reformed Theological Journal* 11 (April 1978): 36.

[22]Herman Bavinck, *The Last Things*, 96.

The New Testament certainly does not encourage us to read the Old Testament in postmillennial terms. In all the major eschatological texts of the New Testament—texts where the entire sweep of the age between the first and second comings of Christ is described and foretold in detail by the inspiration of the Holy Spirit (e.g., the Olivet Discourse; 1 Cor. 15; 2 Peter 3; the entire book of Revelation!)—no mention is made of a golden age prior to Christ's second coming.[23] None of the Old Testament messianic psalms or prophetic passages is ever applied to such a golden age by the New Testament writers.

I have said that the reader searches in vain for even *one* biblical text that explicitly sets forth the postmillennial vision of a golden age to come before Christ comes again. It might have been assumed that Revelation 20, since it is the only passage in the Bible that speaks of a millennial reign of Christ, is that text. Stanley Grentz has written that "of course, it [postmillennialism] builds its primary case from a futurist interpretation of John's vision";[24] but this is not true. Indeed, Gentry says that he "would prefer to leave Revelation 20 out of [his] presentation," and he addresses this text only "reluctantly." He states that "if a literal earthly millennium is such an important and glorious era in redemptive history (as premillennialists argue), then it is odd that reference to the thousand years should appear in only one passage in all of Scripture."[25] I would suggest that it is even more odd that the postmillennialist Millennium does not appear even in that one millennial passage!

Gentry does try to see in Revelation 20:1–6 the postmillennialist hope of Christ's visible kingdom *gradually* being established *on this present earth* by simply inserting these thoughts, even though they appear nowhere in the text. He says that the binding will "increasingly" constrict Satan, who "*began* losing his dominion over the Gentiles" with the coming of Christ (emphasis added). He says that "the first resurrection" refers *both* to those who die in the Lord and reign in heaven with him *and* to those who live and reign with him on this earth. (I point

[23]See Lee Irons's home page: http://members.aol.com/ironslee.

[24]Stanley J. Grentz, *The Millennial Maze* (Downers Grove, Ill.: InterVarsity, 1992), 72.

[25]Gentry focuses on denying that "the thousand years serve as a literal time frame," but the literalness of the number is not the premillennialist's primary concern. He or she is often willing to consider its "symbolic value."

out in my essay the indications in the text that a *heavenly* scene is in view, and the reference in v. 5 to "the rest of the dead" who "did not come to life until the thousand years had ended" confirms that it is believers who have *died* who experience the first resurrection.) And he concludes: "As his rule expands through the preaching of the gospel, righteousness, tranquillity, and prosperity will eventually come to majestic expression." (I ask again: Where does this teaching appear in the text?)

But Gentry acknowledges that the Millennium spoken of in this text refers to the entire "Christian era." He says that "the 'millennial' era has already lasted almost two thousand years; it may continue another thousand or ten thousand more, for all we know." This raises a final problem. If the "Millennium" in the Bible refers to the entire era between Christ's first and second comings, on what biblical basis does Gentry use that word to refer to a separate and distinct "time in history prior to Christ's return," a time of unprecedented blessing and prosperity? If the "Millennium" in the Bible refers to the entire Christian era, the "millennial conditions" that must prevail before Christ returns would seem to be those conditions that prevail *now*.

A PREMILLENNIAL RESPONSE TO KENNETH L. GENTRY JR.

Craig A. Blaising

Kenneth Gentry first offers us a definition and history of the idea of postmillennialism, then an explanation of how postmillennial thought fits within the broad themes of biblical theology, and finally a list of passages that he believes gives support to postmillennial eschatology. My response will generally address the first and last aspects of his presentation (since I agree with him that his survey of general themes is not conclusive for the millennial issue). Because of editorial constraints, my remarks must be brief and selective.

I have five comments on Gentry's historical definition of postmillennialism. (1) Gentry adheres to the spiritual vision model of the eternal state. This is consistent with his tracing the structure of postmillennial thought back to Origen, Eusebius, and Augustine. Throughout his exposition of biblical texts, Gentry postulates that the Second Advent will bring about the end of history. In his view the eternal state is so radically different from present conditions that promises of a messianic kingdom could have no fulfillment there.[1] He wants to find a fulfillment for those promises in an earthly, time-sequenced context, so he relates them to the current period before the return of Christ. However, this brings him into conflict with many passages that describe that eschatological kingdom as *everlasting*.

---

[1]Despite his occasional reference to the new heavens and new earth, Gentry consistently contrasts the kingdom on earth and in history to the eternal state. The contrast is typical of the spiritual vision model of eternity.

(2) In Gentry's definition of postmillennialism, he asserts the well-known postmillennial claim that through the work of evangelism there will gradually come "a time in history prior to Christ's return"—even "an extensive era"—of "[Christian] faith, righteousness, peace, and prosperity." This is the Millennium of postmillennialism. A short time later, however, he introduces what he calls "generic" postmillennialism, in which that "extensive era" is missing from the definition and in which the Millennium is defined as the entire interadvent period. Nevertheless, Gentry later speaks of "the victory of Christ in history," "a wondrous exhibition of God's rule in history," "an enduring condition . . . of the state of peace and security prevailing," a "great socio-political transformation" that comes through conversion to Christ and discipleship of "overwhelming numbers," the final result of "a massive, systemic conversion of the vast majority of humankind," and "a redeemed world" that is "the divinely assured worldwide effect of his redemption."

Gentry's thought seems most clearly expressed when he speaks of the gradual progress of redemption through the age until there results a redeemed world system that fulfills the prophetic predictions of a worldwide kingdom of God. Gentry has a "Millennium," but he doesn't call it a millennium, nor does he relate it to John's millennial vision. He follows a traditional amillennial interpretation of relating Revelation 20:1–6 to the interadvent age. However, this leaves him without any textual basis for *a period in the future of the interadvent age in which kingdom conditions will attain to a systemic and universal level not yet seen*. As will be noted below, none of the texts he advances unequivocally supports this view, and by taking an amillennial interpretation of Revelation 20, he has eliminated what older postmillennialists believed was their anchor text.[2]

(3) Gentry advocates a preterist approach "to a number of the great judgment passages of the New Testament." He does

---

[2]On the importance of Revelation 20 to earlier postmillennialists, see for example, Robert E. Lerner, "Joachim of Fiore's Breakthrough to Chiliasm," *Cristianesimo nella storia* 6 (1985): 489–512. Also see the discussion of postmillennial writers in Peter Toon, ed., *Puritans, the Millennium and the Future of Israel: Puritan Eschatology 1600 to 1660* (Cambridge: Jas. Clarke, 1970). Toon's remark on Brightman is typical: "The latter-day glory of the saints of Christ on earth, and how this would come to be, Brightman found clearly described in [Revelation] chapters 20 to 22" (ibid., 29).

not defend this view here, referring the reader instead to other published works. This preterist approach is faulty. It ignores the way the Day of the Lord functions typologically in biblical eschatology.[3] From the Old Testament to the New, the Day of the Lord has referred to various events (a locust plague in Joel, the Assyrian invasion in Amos, the Babylonian invasion in several texts). But each time the pattern is amplified and projected into the future typologically of an ultimate Day of the Lord, in which God "will punish the world for its evil, the wicked for their sins" (Isa. 13:11). This is ultimately manifest in the final judgment.

Two observations missed by Gentry should be noted. (a) Throughout biblical theology, the eschatological kingdom is seen as coming in its fullness through a Day of the Lord. (b) Throughout the New Testament, the second coming of Jesus is the coming of the Day of the Lord. However much of the pattern of New Testament prediction was manifest in the destruction of Jerusalem in the first century, Jesus' second coming did not occur then. Consequently, *the pattern of judgment on an unrepentant world projects forward to describe the world conditions into which Jesus will return*. Gentry himself admits that Satan will stir up a world rebellion prior to the return of Jesus. As premillennialists have often pointed out, this is inconsistent with postmillennialist expectations of world progress. The point is that the Second Coming is consistently presented in the New Testament in this hostile context. It is the coming of Christ in the Day of the Lord that brings in the future fulfillment of the eschatological kingdom both in its millennial and final forms.

(4) Gentry has often used the word "optimism" in his description of postmillennialism. Does this mean that premillennialists are pessimists? Some premillennialists seem to teach that every aspect of life in this world is irreversibly declining until the return of Christ, and some postmillennialists seem to believe that the world has the ability to better itself and will better itself so as to bring in the golden age. But the idea that premillennialism per se is pessimistic is a stereotype. Premillennialists do not know when Christ will return. In the past two thousand years revivals have come, gone, and been followed by others. Christianity has had varying degrees of influence on cultural and political formation

---

[3]In this regard, it is interesting to me that in Gentry's survey of the major themes of biblical theology, no mention is made of the Day of the Lord.

and reformation. The harvest is plentiful and the world is large. There is no reason to preclude limits on what might be accomplished in any given generation.

But there will be no lasting or permanent establishment of the kingdom until Christ returns. That is why Scripture repeatedly tells us that our hope is to be fully set on Christ's coming and the grace that comes with him (1 Peter 1:13), that is, on "his appearing and his kingdom" (2 Tim. 4:1; cf. Titus 2:13). Surely, we will give an account of our work during the interadvent age. But the glory of the kingdom in its prophetic form is never something that we achieve prior to his coming but always something we look for at his coming and something in expectation of which we serve him in the present.

(5) By virtue of its insistence that the interadvent kingdom will necessarily progress and advance to the level of a worldwide Christian order, postmillennialism owes us an explanation of the history of the last two thousand years. Nineteenth-century postmillennialists (and even Loraine Boettner in the twentieth century[4]) were happy to oblige us, so confident were they that the progress of which they spoke *could be seen* even as their theology required that it *must be seen*. Gentry, however, is strangely silent on this issue. Is this acceptable? He tells us that the Millennium in Revelation is symbolical—it is not necessarily a thousand years in length. Then he tells us that the Millennium stands for the whole interadvent age, so that its actual duration turns out to be almost (and may be more than) *twice* its "literal" meaning! He also tells us that the kingdom is gradually advancing through this age and will reach worldwide conditions. After almost two thousand years, should we not be able to see this progress?

Furthermore, should we not have the right, on Gentry's theory, to expect that those portions of the world where Christianity was first introduced would already be well on their way to this final order—completely Christianized societies, whose inhabitants are almost completely Christian, guided by Christian principles into a political and social experience of righteousness, peace, and prosperity? And should we not expect this phenomenon to show evidence of spreading, ever gradually yet

---

[4]See Loraine Boettner, "Postmillennialism," in *The Meaning of the Millennium: Four Views*, ed. Robert G. Clouse (Downers Grove, Ill: InterVarsity, 1977), 117–41.

irreversibly, into the rest of the world? Or is our experience more in keeping with a premillennial expectation that world conditions may shift and change throughout this interadvent age, and that we always face the task of evangelism and discipleship directed to all nations until the Lord comes, stops the activity of the devil, and brings those kingdom promises into their final stages of fulfillment?

I come now to specific texts that Gentry exposits in support of postmillennialism. As he has noted, many features of Psalm 2 are cited by the New Testament with respect to Christ's resurrection and ascension. These are inaugurated aspects of the eschatological kingdom, which are manifest in the interadvent period. Gentry does not do well, however, in explaining how the themes of rebellion and subjugation by force in this psalm find their fulfillment at this time. Is the preaching of the gospel the fulfillment of dashing to pieces those who refuse to submit to him (cf. Ps. 2:9)? He should observe how this psalm is applied in the New Testament to various phases of Jesus' history: the baptism (Matt. 3:17), the resurrection and ascension (as Gentry has noted), but also the Second Coming. Revelation 19:15 describes our Lord's smiting the nations at his return and proceeding to rule them with an iron rod. Paul's description of the Second Coming in 2 Thessalonians 1:6–12 reinforces this image. Matthew 25:31–46 also presents Christ as ruling and judging the nations from an enthroned position after his return. These texts see the final fulfillment of Psalm 2's regal language in a kingdom that ensues from that Second Coming.

Isaiah 2:2–4 does not support Gentry's postmillennialism. It does not speak of a gradually developing situation but, as Alexander noted (cited approvingly by Gentry), of a situation "permanently fixed, rendered permanently visible." Furthermore, the description is indeed one of permanence. There is no thought at all in this passage that these are temporary conditions to be replaced by some timeless spiritual order. A literary, contextual interpretation of the kingdom theme in Isaiah shows that the establishment of this kingdom will follow the judgments of the Day of the Lord, will be presided over by the Messiah, and is described in two ways—mortal and immortal.

Like other postmillennialists, Gentry claims support from the kingdom parables of Matthew 13. He calls our attention primarily to the parable of the mustard seed and the parable of the yeast in the bread dough. These parables contrast the beginning of the kingdom, inaugurated by Christ at his ascension, and the final manifestation of the kingdom, which shows its worldwide extent in keeping with prophetic promise. The inaugural aspect is the new revelation about the kingdom, which is being set in complementary fashion alongside what was previously revealed (see the parable of the householder). However, these parables do not say anything about "the gradual development" of the kingdom. They only contrast the beginning with the end. We may infer that the beginning and the end are "organically" connected, but except for the parable of the wheat and the weeds (and possibly the sower), the parables make no statement about "how" the process moves from beginning to end.

When we turn to the wheat and the weeds parable, Gentry is forced to acknowledge that "the historical manifestation of the kingdom will always include a mixture of both the righteous and the unrighteous." He tries to play down the size of this unrighteous element, for clearly it goes against his postmillennial expectations. But the Lord describes both the wheat and the weeds as growing together until the harvest. Many kingdom parables warn of judgment on those who are not prepared to receive the Lord at his coming.

The parable of the sower also works against Gentry's expectation, because contrary to his exposition, it is not the seed but the soils that represent people who hear and respond. The seed in that parable represents the Word of God (13:18–23). The bountiful harvest is the fruition of that Word in a person's life, not a great number of people who respond to Christ. If the parable of the soils represents how gospel preaching will be received in this age, then it shows that only about one in four truly respond—not good news for a postmillennialist.

Finally, we must note that in the parable of the wheat and the weeds, the Lord speaks of transition between two phases of the kingdom at his coming. In Matthew 13:41, tares are gathered out of his kingdom at the coming of the Lord. Then, in 13:43, the wheat goes on to shine forth in the kingdom of their Father. The first phase of kingdom speaks of interadvent conditions—both good and evil will be present. There will be no new phase of the kingdom, certainly not one in which the devil's activity of sowing tares has ceased, until Christ returns.

John 12:31–32, in which the Lord declares that he will draw all to himself when he is lifted up, is a precious text. But the Lord does not say that prior to his return human beings and human culture will become more and more Christian, eventually reaching "a time of universal worship, peace, and prosperity longed for by the prophets of the Old Testament."

Matthew 28:18–20 also proclaims the universal authority of the Lord and commands us to disciple the nations. But once again, the Lord makes no promise that before his coming the nations will be thoroughly discipled, experiencing the fulfillment of kingdom promises.

Gentry is right to turn us to Acts to see how this discipling mandate was pursued. Certainly, the preaching of the kingdom is carried forward right to the end of the book (Acts 28:16, 31). Curiously, Gentry makes no mention of Acts 1:6, where after a forty-day discussion on the kingdom of God (1:3), the disciples asked Jesus, "Lord, are you at this time going to restore the kingdom to Israel?" The reference to Israel is important for Israel has no place in Gentry's postmillennialism. Yet this notion of a restoration of the kingdom to Israel is completely in line with the Old Testament prophets' descriptions of the future eschatological kingdom (such as Isa. 2). The question is strategically placed at the beginning of Acts. The Lord's answer has to do with the time, not the nature, of the kingdom.

That point of time is further expounded by Peter in Acts 3. The ascended Lord will remain in heaven *until the time of the restoration of all things about which God spoke by the mouths of his holy prophets from ancient time.* The prophets spoke of the coming eschatological kingdom. They spoke of the restoration of the kingdom to Israel. Jesus at his ascension teaches that this will be fulfilled at a later time. Peter, his apostle, teaches that this will happen after the Second Coming. There is no thought that this in any way contradicts the Great Commission. Rather, it puts it in perspective within the overall kingdom plan of God, a plan that has nothing to do with postmillennialism.

First Corinthians 15:20–28 does not provide any support for postmillennialism. Gentry makes an exegetical mistake when he says, "according to Paul, Christ's coming marks 'the end.'" Actually, in verses 23–34, Paul sets up a sequence: Christ, the firstfruits, *then* [*epeita*, the next stage in the sequence] those who are Christ's at his coming, *then* [*eita*, the next stage in the sequence] the end. Christ's coming marks the second stage, not the third (in which the end occurs). How long a time will pass between the second and third stages? Almost two thousand years have passed between the first and second stages; thus, one should not preclude the possibility that some period of time may pass between the second and third stages as well.

Gentry is more helpful in analyzing the two "when" clauses and the explanatory "for" that follow and explain "the end" in 1 Corinthians 15:24–25. Christ will reign, subjugating his enemies up to "the end." There is nothing here that speaks of a gradual, progressive spread of kingdom conditions until they reach a time when those conditions will prevail to characterize the world—and all this prior to the return of Christ![5]

I find Gentry's treatment of Revelation 20 the most disappointing part of his article. The book of Revelation was written as a message from the ascended Lord, Jesus Christ, to the churches (1:1; 22:16). It should not be treated in a cavalier manner, but with respect. As we do so, let us seek a grammatical, historical, and literary understanding of the text, in a manner befitting an evangelical commitment to the authority of Scripture.

I want to emphasize that it is not odd that only here does the Lord give us the truth of a millennial kingdom between the Second Coming and the Judgment Day; rather, this is consistent with the fact of progressive revelation. No doubt there are many other things the Lord has yet to reveal to us when he comes. It so happens that at the end of canonical revelation, the Lord has revealed this added feature to the prophetic scenario. It is not our place to contend with him over the issue because he had not chosen to reveal it earlier!

That Revelation is filled with symbols and figures is not a reason for refusing what it teaches when that teaching can be discerned in a grammatical, literary, and contextual fashion. I find it strange that Gentry complains that Revelation's literary genre is an unsuitable basis for premillennialism when he in turn attempts to base postmillennialism on the parables of Jesus and Old Testament prophecies, which he interprets in a symbolical

---

[5]Once again, I refer the reader to Wilber B. Wallis, "The Problem of an Intermediate Kingdom in 1 Corinthians 15:20–28," *Journal of the Evangelical Theological Society* 18 (1975): 229–42.

manner (and not always consistently; cf. his interpretation of Zion in Isa. 2 and Ps. 2).

The fact is, Gentry does not interpret the text of Revelation 20:1–6 in a literary, grammatical, contextual manner. He largely repeats a traditional Augustinian interpretation. I refer the reader to my article in this book for a critique of this approach. I would add several comments. (1) Gentry's claim that the angel who binds the devil in 20:1 is Christ is not supported by the literary context. The angel in 10:1 is not a clear reference to Christ in spite of some common features with John's vision in chapter 1. Christ is presented in this book as the Lamb and as the Son of Man. He is never called an angel but is rather the Lord, who communicates to John by his angel (1:1; 22:16). Revelation 10:1 fits the pattern of *angelic* messengers, and 20:1–3 fits the pattern of *angelic* action (see 12:7–9).

(2) There is nothing in Revelation 20:1–3 that supports the idea that the binding is an "increasing" phenomenon, taking place throughout the age.

(3) Revelation does not speak anywhere else about dead saints *reigning* with Christ, and chapter 20 does not speak of a reign by the dead but by those who have risen from the dead.

(4) Gentry repeats the traditional view that "came to life" in Revelation 20:4–5 means regeneration, but his view fails for grammatical, syntactical, and contextual reasons (see my article). His claim that the word "resurrection" means spiritual rebirth is without contextual support in the Bible and leaves the book of Revelation without any clear statement on the actual resurrection of believers.

In conclusion, Kenneth Gentry's argument for postmillennialism is not compelling. Crucial evidence for a limited period of universal peace and righteousness prior to the return of Christ is absent from the texts he has presented. And the Lord's final word to his churches, in which he reveals a transitional millennial kingdom between his return and the final judgment, has not received the careful attention it deserves.

Chapter Two

AMILLENNIALISM

Robert B. Strimple

AMILLENNIALISM

Robert B. Strimple

Although Christians today may think of the designations pre-, post-, and amillennialism as traditional, they are actually of fairly recent origin when measured by the broad sweep of church history. The term *amillennialism* has been widely current since sometime in the 1930s, although when it was first used remains a mystery. But as Louis Berkhof has noted, while "the name is new indeed ... the view to which it is applied is as old as Christianity."[1] In this chapter we will concentrate not on church history but on the biblical considerations that have caused many Christians throughout the ages to reject millennialism, whether of the premillennial or the postmillennial type.

Our English word "eschatology" comes from the Greek words for "last things" (*eschatos*) and "word, study" (*logos*), but we must recognize that in the view of the New Testament writers the "last days" of redemptive history were inaugurated by Christ's resurrection and exaltation and the Pentecostal outpouring of the Holy Spirit (Acts 2:16–21, "the last days"; 1 Cor. 10:11, "the fulfillment [end] of the ages"; Heb. 1:1–2, "in these last days"; 1 Peter 1:20, "in these last times"). The whole of God's redemptive revelation is structured in terms of promise (Old Testament) and fulfillment (New Testament), and therefore a fully adequate summary of biblical eschatology must consider the teaching of the entire Bible!

---

[1]Louis Berkhof, *Systematic Theology*, 4th ed. (Grand Rapids: Eerdmans, 1962), 708. See the comments of R. B. Gaffin Jr. in *Theonomy: A Reformed Critique*, ed. W. S. Barker and W. Robert Godfrey (Grand Rapids: Zondervan, 1990), 197–202.

In this chapter we will simply focus on two crucial factors: (1) the instruction we receive from the New Testament regarding the proper interpretation of Old Testament prophecy, and (2) the teaching of the New Testament regarding the second coming of Christ and the events that will accompany that coming. On that background, we will then look at two passages often considered to be of special significance: Romans 11 and Revelation 20:1–10.

CHRIST: THE THEME OF OLD TESTAMENT PROPHECY

In the Old Testament are passages that speak of a coming time of worldwide peace and righteousness, a time when the *temple* will be rebuilt, the *priesthood* will be restored, and *sacrifices* will again be offered (e.g., Ps. 72:7–11; Isa. 60:10–14; Ezek. 37:24–28; 40–48). Premillennialists insist that such passages are to be taken "literally" (exactly what that requires at every point is a matter debated among premillennialists), and that they refer to conditions in the *Millennium*, that thousand-year kingdom that Christ will establish on this earth at his second coming, with his capital at Jerusalem, the temple rebuilt, the priesthood reestablished,[2] animal sacrifices again offered, and the throne of David again erected. Each Sabbath Christ the prince will enter the temple by the eastern gate while the priests sacrifice the burnt offering of six spotless male lambs and a ram, as well as the fellowship offerings (Ezek. 46). The people will once again be taught to distinguish between the unclean and the clean, and circumcision of the flesh as well as the heart will again be required (Ezek. 44:23, 9). Thus the worship of the messianic kingdom will see a return to those elements that were central under the old covenant.

But is it correct to interpret such Old Testament prophecies as descriptions of a future millennial kingdom that Christ will establish on this earth at his second coming? To answer that, the crucial question the Christian must ask, of course, is this: How does the *New Testament* teach us to interpret such passages? In

---

[2]Various attempts are made by premillennialists to harmonize the differing pictures given in the prophets regarding those from whom the restored priesthood will be chosen, whether from the Levites (Jer. 33:18), the sons of Zadok only (Ezek. 40:46; 43:19; 44:15), or all the nations (Isa. 66:20–1).

the New Testament Christ's church has been given, by the inspiration of the Holy Spirit, that post-resurrection, post-Pentecost revelation that is absolutely authoritative, her infallible guide in all matters of faith and life, including this vitally important matter of how to interpret Old Testament prophecy.

As we read the New Testament, we come to understand that the Old Testament prophets spoke of the glories of the messianic age that was coming—that age inaugurated by Christ in which the church now lives—in terms of their own age and the religious blessings of God's people in that old covenant age. Central to those blessings were the concepts of the people of Israel, the land of Canaan, the city of Jerusalem, the temple, the sacrifices, and the throne of David.

It is a necessary feature of effective communication, which we have all experienced and understand, that when we wish to describe to a friend something that he or she has not yet experienced, we do so by appeals to what our friend has already experienced. In order to communicate to God's people still living under the old covenant, the prophets by the Spirit's inspiration spoke of the blessings God would pour out under the new covenant in terms of the typological images so familiar to the old covenant saints.[3]

---

[3]For discussions of this principle, see the classic works of Patrick Fairbairn: *The Interpretation of Prophecy* (London: Banner of Truth Trust, rep. 1964 [1856]); *The Typology of Scripture* (Grand Rapids: Zondervan, 1975); *An Exposition of Ezekiel* (Wilmington, Del.: National Foundation for Christian Education, 1969). An interesting little volume is entitled *The Prophetic Prospects of the Jews or Fairbairn vs. Fairbairn* (Grand Rapids: Eerdmans, 1930), which consists of two lectures delivered by Patrick Fairbairn twenty-five years apart. In Part I (1839) the earlier Fairbairn argues the case for a strict literalism in interpreting Old Testament prophecy (it is the literalism of *post*millennialism, however, rather than premillennialism). Regarding Hosea 1, for example, Fairbairn insists that "there is no possible room for mistaking who are the proper subjects of the prophecy, as they are spoken of under the names of 'the children of Judah and the children of Israel,' the two distinctive branches of the Jewish nation" (p. 21). In a footnote he calls the references in 1 Peter 2:10 and Romans 9:24–26 to *Gentile* converts as fulfillment of Hosea's prophecy "an extension of its meaning beyond the literal and primary import." In Part II (1864), however, Fairbairn recognizes how arbitrary and unsubmissive to the instruction of the New Testament such a statement is. He now calls the insistence that prophecy is to be read "simply as history written beforehand" (and thus according to strict literalism) "the Jewish [as opposed to Christian] principle of prophetical interpretation" (pp. 91–92).

Surprisingly, *The New Scofield Reference Bible* (New York: Oxford University Press, 1967) suggests that Ezekiel's prophecy of sacrifices again offered in the New

For a zealous Jew who has not received the Christ, and for whom therefore the veil remains unlifted whenever the old covenant is read (2 Cor. 3:14), such a principle of prophetic interpretation as the premillennialist one that says we are to interpret Old Testament prophecy "literally whenever possible" is understandable. Sadly the Jewish Zionist, for example, has no other meaningful principle of interpretation with which to operate. But Christian believers live in the full light of the New Testament revelation, the revelation of the Christ of God, and are we not to take advantage of this? Are we not to see that what is in the Old Testament concealed is in the New Testament revealed (as Augustine put it)? That what is in the Old Testament contained is in the New Testament explained? Was not the apostle Paul by the inspiration of the Holy Spirit telling us something important when he said that we read the Old Testament with a veil over our understanding until we read the Old Testament in the light of the fulfillment revelation that has come in Jesus Christ?

All evangelical Christians are accustomed to viewing the Old Testament sacrifices and feasts and ceremonies as being types, that is, teaching tools pointing forward to the work of Christ. Why then should the elements that we will consider now—the land of Canaan, the city of Jerusalem, the temple, the throne of David, the nation Israel itself—not be understood using the same interpretive insight that we use in interpreting the sacrifices and ceremonies?

But it is not merely that this may seem logical to us. The fact is that our authoritative New Testament teaches us that this is precisely how we *should* understand such elements in the Old Testament prophecies. And with regard to any type—whether it be sacrifice, feast, temple, or land—when the reality is introduced, the shadow passes away. And it does not pass away in order to be at some future restored; it passes away because in Jesus Christ it has been fulfilled! We do not speak of this as a "spiritualizing" interpretation of the Old Testament sacrifices or

_____

Temple "is not to be taken literally . . . but is rather to be regarded as a presentation of the worship of the redeemed in Israel . . . using the terms with which the Jews were familiar in Ezekiel's day" (p. 888). Fairbairn could not have said it better! Anthony A. Hoekema asks the obvious question: "If the sacrifices are not to be taken literally, why should we take the temple literally? . . . a crucial foundation stone for the entire dispensational system has here been set aside." *The Bible and the Future* (Grand Rapids: Eerdmans, 1979), 204.

rituals, using that term in a negative sense as somehow denying their reality. We see this as a fulfilling of that of which the sacrifices and ceremonies spoke. Why should it be considered any different with regard to these five elements that we now look at? In the New Testament we see the true meaning of all these Old Testament types, and the central figure in biblical prophecy is the Lord Jesus Christ. It is Christ, not the Hebrew people, who is the subject of the Old Testament prophets.[4]

The True Israel

The true Israel is Christ. *He* is the suffering Servant of the Lord, this one who is—wonder of wonders—the Lord himself! Turn, for example, to Isaiah 41. Surely the Old Testament saint, as he or she studied the "Servant Songs" of Isaiah, had to be puzzled. Jewish commentators to this day are puzzled. Here Israel is called by God his chosen one (41:8–9). But as we go to 42:1–7, the Lord says:

> Here is my servant, whom I uphold,
>   my chosen one in whom I delight;
> I will put my Spirit on him
>   and he will bring justice to the nations.
> He will not shout or cry out . . .
> I will keep you and will make you
>   to be a covenant for the people
> and a light for the Gentiles,
>   to open eyes that are blind,
> to free captives from prison
>   and to release from the dungeon those who
>   sit in darkness.

Is it still the nation that is in view as the Lord's Servant, or is this now an individual, the Messiah?

We know how these verses from Isaiah 42 are interpreted in the Gospels—they are seen as fulfilled in Jesus Christ. But notice how Isaiah goes on to speak in 44:1–2, 21; 45:4:

> But now listen, O Jacob, my servant,
>   Israel, whom I have chosen.

---

[4]George L. Murray, *Millennial Studies* (Grand Rapids: Baker, 1948), 57.

> This is what the Lord says—
> > he who made you, who formed you in the womb,
> and who will help you. Do not be afraid, O Jacob,
> > my servant,
> > Jeshurun, whom I have chosen. . . .
> Remember these things, O Jacob,
> > for you are my servant, O Israel. . . .
> For the sake of Jacob my servant,
> > of Israel my chosen,
> I summon you [Cyrus, see preceding and following
> > verses] by name. . . .

If we were to go on reading here in Isaiah, we would see the movement back and forth, and the cause for puzzlement—clear statements that the nation Israel is the Lord's Servant, but also veiled hints that the Servant is an individual. Perhaps even Isaiah himself was puzzled. Remember how Peter spoke of the prophets "trying to find out the time and circumstances to which the Spirit of Christ in them was pointing . . ." (1 Peter 1:10–12).[5]

How could the answer be clear before the birth of Christ? Yes, Israel was called to be God's Servant, a light to enlighten the nations and to glorify God's name. But since Israel was unfaithful to her calling and failed to fulfill the purposes of her divine election, the Lord brought forth his Elect One, his Servant, his true Israel.

In Matthew 2:15 the Evangelist sees Hosea 11:1 fulfilled in the flight of the holy family to Egypt and their eventual return: "Out of Egypt I called my son." Some critics consider this to be a completely arbitrary and baseless allegorical exegesis on Matthew's part, that Matthew takes a reference which in Hosea is clearly a reference to the nation Israel (and it is, of course; read the context in Hos. 11) and applies that text to Christ. That is obviously a totally fanciful use of that Scripture, says the critic. But the Christian should know better, because the Christian knows that Christ *is* the true Israel of God, the one in whom Israel's history is recapitulated and God's purposes for Israel come to fulfillment.

Since Christ is the true Israel, the true seed of Abraham, we who are *in Christ* by faith and the working of his Spirit are the

---

[5]Remember too the perplexity of the Ethiopian eunuch, who asked Philip, "Tell me, please, who is the prophet talking about, himself or someone else?" (Acts 8:34).

true Israel, the Israel of faith, not of mere natural descent. Paul writes in Galatians 3:7–9, 26–27, 29:

> Understand, then, that those who believe are children of Abraham. The Scriptures foresaw that God would justify the Gentiles by faith, and announced the gospel in advance to Abraham: "All nations will be blessed through you." So those who have faith are blessed along with Abraham, the man of faith....
>
> You are all sons of God through faith in Christ Jesus, for all of you who were baptized into Christ have clothed yourselves with Christ.... If you belong to Christ, then you are Abraham's seed, and heirs according to the promise.

Too often in meditating on this wonderful truth, we omit the all-important link in the chain of redemption that Christ himself is. We say: "Yes, the nation of Israel was the people of God in the old covenant. Now in the new covenant the believing church is the people of God." And thus we quickly run past (or we miss the blessed point entirely) the fact that we Christians are the Israel of God, Abraham's seed, and the heirs of the promises, only because by faith we are united to him who is alone the true Israel, Abraham's *one* seed (note Paul's emphasis on the singular in Gal. 3:16). We believers get in on the blessings promised to Israel only because by God's grace we are in him who is God's elect Israel, and by God's grace those blessings are extended to those who are united to Christ by faith.[6]

Hebrews 8 and 10 have presented great difficulty for premillennialist interpreters (leading to a variety of explanations), because the writer here quotes the new covenant prophecy of Jeremiah 31:31–34 and seems clearly to say that the new covenant prophesied through Jeremiah is that better covenant founded on better promises of which our Lord Jesus Christ is the mediator (8:6), and which is in force *now*, bringing blessing to both Jews and Gentiles. Many premillennialists have insisted,

---

[6]An example of the failure to make this all-important link clear is found in Stanley Grenz's statement of the amillennial position: "On the basis of the hermeneutical principle of the priority of the New Testament, amillennialists conclude that promises originally given to Israel are fulfilled in the church" (*The Millennial Maze* [Downers Grove, Ill.: InterVarsity, 1992], 155). We must recognize that the promises are fulfilled *in Christ* and thus in those who are in union with him by faith.

however, that this new covenant is not fulfilled (at least not fully fulfilled) as God's covenant with his church now, but rather will be fulfilled during the Millennium. Why? Because God says in Jeremiah (and it is quoted in Heb. 8:8) that this new covenant is one that he will make "with the house of Israel and with the house of Judah"; and clearly the Jews, for the most part, are not enjoying the benefits of this covenant now.

But there is no good reason for us to stumble over this passage. Yes, the new covenant *is* made "with the house of Israel and with the house of Judah." Praise God that in union with God's Son, the true Israel, we are members of that house. The apostle Paul writes in Philippians 3:3: "For it is we who are the circumcision, we who worship by the Spirit of God, who glory in Christ Jesus, and who put no confidence in the flesh."

Canaan, the Land of Promise

In the New Testament we also learn that Canaan, the land of promise, was but a type of that fuller and richer inheritance that is to be Abraham's and all his children's in Christ: the whole world, heaven and earth, renewed and restored in righteousness (2 Peter 3:13) as the home of God's new race of men and women in Christ Jesus, the second Adam.

In Romans 4:13, for example, we read: "It was not through law that Abraham and his offspring received the promise that he would be heir of the world [Gk. *kosmos*], but through the righteousness that comes by faith." Where in the Old Testament do you find the promise that Paul refers to here? *Nowhere*, if you insist on strict literalism. But you find it in Genesis 17:8 ("The whole land of Canaan ... I will give as an everlasting possession to you and your descendants after you") if you see that this is inspired apostolic *interpretation* of the Old Testament promise that Paul is giving us here. The point to remember always is that it is inspired apostolic interpretation that is authoritative and normative for us.[7]

Hebrews 11 (esp. vv. 10–16) also reflects on Abraham's promised inheritance. This passage speaks of that which is *heav-*

---

[7]In the light of Romans 4:13, it may be significant that when Paul quotes Exodus 20:12 in Ephesians 6:3, he omits the specific reference to Canaan ("that the Lord your God is giving you"), thus enlarging the promise.

enly. But this must not cause us to deny that Abraham's inheritance is also *earthly*; as such it is not promised to Abraham and his children for a thousand years only. Isaiah, Peter, and John all speak of that inheritance in terms of "a new heaven *and* a new earth." The future home of Christ and his people will be earthly as well as heavenly.

Amillennialism is often charged with ignoring the fact that there are prophecies regarding the restoration and renewal of the earth that are yet to be fulfilled. But amillennialism does not ignore such prophecies. It simply recognizes that they are to be understood (in the light of Isa. 65:17; 66:22; 2 Peter 3:13; Rev. 21:1) in terms of a *new* heaven and a *new* earth. They picture that which will indeed be earthly, but *eternal*—not merely for a thousand years. The scope of Christ's redemptive accomplishment will be truly *cosmic*, and it will be as complete and as perfect for humankind's environment as it will be for human beings themselves.

The Holy City of Jerusalem

When we think about what the New Testament says regarding the holy city of Jerusalem, Hebrews 12:18–24 immediately comes to mind. "You have not come to a mountain that can be touched. . . . But you have come to Mount Zion, to the heavenly Jerusalem, the city of the living God. . . ." Perhaps we have read verses 18–21 in this chapter, paused, breathed a deep sigh of relief, and thought: "Oh my, am I ever glad I haven't come to a mountain like that! I couldn't take that. That was serious business. That was an awesome scene. Fire, darkness, gloom and storm, the trumpet blast, the very voice of God as it were, death for one misstep. Moses himself, the leader with whom God had spoken face to face, was trembling with fear."

But if we respond that way, we have missed the whole point of the writer's argument. As we continue to read (vv. 22–29), his point is that if the reality of the experience inaugurating the old covenant was an awesome experience, and the penalty for taking it lightly and disregarding the warnings of the God who spoke to them from Sinai was serious indeed, how much more awesome is the new covenant believer's experience. How much greater will be the eternal consequences of turning away from the God who reveals himself so much more fully and clearly in his Son, the mediator of the new covenant. We have not come to a *created* mountain—and that is all that Mount Sinai was, even on that fearsome occasion of the giving of the old covenant. We have not come to the Most Holy Place in the tabernacle or in the earthly temple. We have come to the true Most Holy Place, to the presence of God himself! We have come to the heavenly throne of God, the true and eternal Mount Zion.

Now, in one sense we are still waiting for the heavenly Jerusalem. "We are looking for the city that is to come" (Heb. 13:14). Consummation day, the full manifestation of the heavenly Jerusalem, still lies ahead (Rev. 21). But we thank God that in a preliminary but real sense we have already arrived at that city. "You *have come* to Mount Zion, to the heavenly Jerusalem, the city of the living God" (Heb. 12:22, emphasis added).

The biblical distinction between the earthly Jerusalem and the heavenly Jerusalem is not the distinction between the "literal" and the "spiritual," using "spiritual" in the sense of the nonliteral. It is the distinction between the copy and the real thing. Think of Hebrews 9:23–24, where we read that the elements in the earthly tabernacle of Moses were simply copies of the heavenly sanctuary of God's own presence. The heavenly is the true, the genuine article.

Think of John's emphasis on the "true" in his Gospel. Jesus is the true vine, the true light, the true bread. Jesus is the reality to which the vine on the temple wall, the light of the lampstand, and the consecrated bread in the sanctuary all pointed.

Perhaps we can use the terms that Paul uses in 1 Corinthians 15:44–46, *natural* and *spiritual*, where the historical order of the first man (Adam) and the second man (Christ) also highlights a general principle: "The spiritual did not come first, but the natural, and after that the spiritual." Spiritual realities are just as "literal," just as real as natural phenomena. The believer's resurrection body, for example, is called "a spiritual body" in verse 44, not to suggest that it will lack reality or substance, but rather to emphasize that it will no longer be weak, mortal, and perishable, because it will be the body raised by and perfectly fashioned and controlled by the Spirit of the risen and never-to-die-again Christ.

Think too of how Paul speaks of the true Jerusalem in Galatians 4:25–26: "Now Hagar stands for Mount Sinai in Arabia and corresponds to the present city of Jerusalem, because she is in slavery with her children. But the Jerusalem that is above is free, and she is our mother."

In Revelation 14:1 John sees the Lamb "standing on Mount Zion." The ancient prophecies of Isaiah 2:2–4 and Micah 4:1–3 of "many peoples" from "all nations" streaming to Jerusalem will not be fulfilled during a future Millennium by terrestrial pilgrimages to an earthly city. Praise God, that blessed prophecy is being fulfilled *now* as men and women of every tribe on the face of the earth call upon the name of Zion's King and become citizens of "the Jerusalem that is above," the mother of all who are in Christ by faith.

Thus, it is significant that Jesus does not direct the woman whom he met at the well to go from Mount Gerizim (where the Samaritans worshiped) to Jerusalem (where the Jews worshiped). Rather, Jesus directs her to *himself*.[8] Notice again the emphasis on the "true" here in John 4:23–26:

> "Yet a time is coming and has now come when the true worshipers will worship the Father in spirit and truth, for they are the kind of worshipers the Father seeks. God is spirit, and his worshipers must worship in spirit and in truth."
>
> The woman said, "I know that Messiah" (called Christ) "is coming. When he comes, he will explain everything to us."
>
> Then Jesus declared, "I who speak to you am he."

The true temple of the true Jerusalem gives the true and living water. The prophet Ezekiel (Ezek. 47:1) had been given the vision of that water tumbling from the temple from south of the altar so that "where the river flows everything will live" (47:9). The woman of Samaria, however, received not the vision or the picture; she received the reality. Jesus says (John 4:10, 14):

> "If you knew the gift of God and who it is that asks you for a drink, you would have asked him and he would have given you living water.

---

[8]Edmund P. Clowney, "The Final Temple," in *Studying the New Testament Today*, ed. John H. Skilton (Philadelphia: Presbyterian and Reformed, 1974), 118. This eloquent and comprehensive study can also be found in the *Westminster Theological Journal* 35 (Winter 1973): 156–89.

> ... whoever drinks the water I give him will never thirst. Indeed, the water I give him will become in him a spring of water welling up to eternal life."

When we think of the significance of Jerusalem as the divinely chosen capital of God's covenant people, we think also of the throne of David and of the temple.

The Kingdom of David

With regard to the promises to David, we may first note the way in which Luke presents the coming of Jesus as the fulfillment of those promises (Luke 1:30–33):

> But the angel said to her, "Do not be afraid, Mary, you have found favor with God. You will be with child and give birth to a son, and you are to give him the name Jesus. He will be great and will be called the Son of the Most High. The Lord God will give him the throne of his father David, and he will reign over the house of Jacob forever; his kingdom will never end."

The kingdom of David's greater Son is to be an *eternal* kingdom, as promised in 2 Samuel 7:16 and Isaiah 9:6. Just as the promise to Abraham of a land forever cannot be fulfilled on this present, sin-cursed earth, so also the promise to David of a throne forever cannot be fulfilled in any mortal human being.

Continue to read the rest of Luke 1 and you will be struck by the stirring images in which Mary (vv. 46–55) and Zechariah (vv. 67–79) sing their praise to God for his redeeming work. Note, for example Luke 1:52–55, 69–73:

> He has brought down rulers from their thrones
>   but has lifted up the humble.
> He has filled the hungry with good things
>   but has sent the rich away empty.
> He has helped his servant Israel,
>   remembering to be merciful
> to Abraham and his descendants forever,
>   even as he said to our fathers....
> He has raised up a horn of salvation for us
>   in the house of his servant David
> (as he said through his holy prophets of long ago),

> salvation from our enemies
> > and from the hand of all who hate us—
> to show mercy to our fathers
> > and to remember his holy covenant,
> > > the oath he swore to our father Abraham. . . .

The songs sound like passages from the Psalms or from one of the Old Testament prophets. Why do Mary and Zechariah speak that way? Is it because (as classic dispensationalism has explained it) this Messiah came with the sincere intention of fulfilling the covenant and the oath sworn to Abraham and the promise given to David; but, because of the unbelief of the Jewish people, that offered kingdom had to be postponed until the future Millennium, and the fulfillment of the promises to Abraham and to David had to be postponed until then? Is that the explanation?

The rest of Luke's two-volume work (Luke-Acts) makes it clear that this is not the answer. Mary and Zechariah speak as they do here because they are old covenant saints, and this is the Spirit-inspired language of their old covenant piety. They are like the prophets before John the Baptist, and we would not expect them to speak in the language of the apostle Paul. Although there are, of course, similarities in the imagery of the later apostles, there is an unmistakable Old Testament tinge to the songs of Luke 1. What an eloquent testimony to the authenticity of Luke's record! And what helpful light is shed on the nature of Old Testament prophetic imagery.

As we turn to the book of Acts, how does the apostle Peter see the promise of 2 Samuel 7:16 fulfilled? By the resurrection of Jesus (see Acts 2:30–31):

> "But he [David] was a prophet and knew that God had promised him on oath that he would place one of his descendants on his throne. Seeing what was ahead, he spoke of the resurrection of the Christ. . . ."

That climactic redemptive event is seen as the fulfillment also of Psalm 2:7; 16:10; and Isaiah 55:3 (see Acts 13:32–37):

> "We tell you the good news: What God promised our fathers he has fulfilled for us, their children, by raising up Jesus. As it is written in the second Psalm:
> > "'You are my Son;
> > > today I have become your Father.'

The fact that God raised him from the dead, never to decay, is stated in these words:

    "'I will give you the holy and sure blessings promised to David.'

So it is stated elsewhere:

    "'You will not let your Holy One see decay.'"

Again, it is the inspired interpretation of Old Testament prophecy by the New Testament apostles that is the authoritative guide for our interpretation. How instructive in this regard is the record of the Jerusalem Council in Acts 15. Here we read of the missionary report that Paul and Barnabas gave as they traveled through Phoenicia and Samaria and as they spoke to the council of apostles and elders at Jerusalem (15:3–4)—an amazing account of Gentiles being converted through their preaching. Peter then reminds the assembly that his ministry also has seen Gentiles as well as Jews saved "by faith ... through the grace of our Lord Jesus" (15:9–11). When James then speaks (15:13–21), he points to the prophecy of Amos 9:11–12 as the key to understanding this amazing grace phenomenon.

To see the sharp contrast between the interpretive principles of James and the interpretive principles of classic dispensational premillennialism, it is helpful to read the note on pp. 1169–1170 of the original *Scofield Reference Bible*[9] alongside James's speech. In order to maintain his principle of "literal wherever possible," Scofield must understand Amos's words as a prophecy of what will happen *after* the end of "the present, or church-age" (characterized by Peter as a taking out from among the Gentiles of a people for God's name) when God will "re-establish the Davidic rule over Israel" and at last fulfill the Davidic covenant, with Gentiles at that time also seeking God.

But such a "literal" interpretation of this passage cannot be correct. If this had been the burden of James's appeal to Amos, it would have made James's argument irrelevant to the issue at hand. On this interpretation James declared to the council that they should not be puzzled or disturbed by Simon Peter's report of Gentiles being brought to God, because the prophets had foretold that this is exactly what would happen *during the Millennium.*

---

[9]C. I. Scofield, ed., *The Scofield Reference Bible* (New York: Oxford Univ. Press, 1909).

An elder present at the council might well have responded: "That's all well and good, James, but what we are seeking now is a scriptural understanding of what is happening in the church right now."

And that is exactly what James gives them, and us, by the Spirit. James sees Amos 9:11–12 being fulfilled right before his eyes, so to speak. The introductory words "after this" must be understood from the prophet's perspective; in the Amos context the reference is to what God will accomplish by his redemptive grace after the time of the Exile. In his note Scofield calls James's speech "dispensationally ... the most important passage in the N.T." From the standpoint of the insight provided us for the proper interpretation of Old Testament prophecy, this passage is indeed most important, for note well what is happening here:

> James's application of the prophecy finds the fulfilment of its first part (the rebuilding of the tabernacle of David) in the resurrection and exaltation of Christ, the Son of David, and the reconstitution of His disciples as the new Israel, and the fulfilment of its second part in the presence of believing Gentiles as well as believing Jews in the Church.[10]

Are we to say that James, the brother of our Lord and the leading elder in the Jerusalem church, was here "spiritualizing" Old Testament prophecy in some unhealthy or dangerous way? Of course not. Then how can such a charge be rightly made against amillennialists when they seek to understand Old Testament prophecy in precisely the same Christ-centered way that James does?

The Temple of God

A final typologically rich image in the old covenant tapestry is that of the temple of God. At this point we can only be brief. The major theme in the prophetic picture of what God promised to do in the days of the Messiah is the fact that he would perfectly restore for his people their former blessings. But that is not the whole story. Not only in the New Testament but already in

---

[10]F. F. Bruce, *Commentary on the Book of the Acts* (NICNT; Grand Rapids: Eerdmans, 1981), 310.

the Old Testament prophets themselves, it is revealed that the blessings of the new covenant fulfillment will far transcend what God's people had known at the highest point of the old covenant foretaste.

> It is not only the reunited remnant of both Israel and Judah that are to be redeemed (Isa. 11:13; Ezek. 37:15–22; Hos. 1:11; 3:5). The Gentiles are included (Isa. 2:2–4; Micah 4:1–3). The outcasts of other nations are gathered with the captivity of Israel (Isa. 56:6–8) and their sacrifices will be accepted on God's altar (Zech. 14:16–19). From the ingathered Gentiles God will choose priests and Levites (Isa. 66:21).[11]

The key to the fulfillment of such wonderful promises is the coming of Christ. Jesus himself declared: "One greater than the temple is here" (Matt. 12:6). Jesus spoke of raising up the temple after three days (John 2:19–22), and John tells us that Jesus was referring to himself.

Perhaps that passage in John 2 is so familiar to us that we read it too quickly and pass by it without appreciating its full significance. We might think: "Isn't that an interesting figure of speech? Jesus refers to his body as the temple. Jesus certainly has a gift for picturesque speech. We can learn a lot from him regarding the use of concrete images." If so, we miss the point completely. Jesus speaks of his resurrection as the raising up of the temple not because anybody's body might be pictured as a temple, but because he *is* the true temple of God.

> All that the temple means, then, is fulfilled in Jesus Christ: the dwelling of God's glory in the sanctuary; the provision of atoning sacrifice at the gate; the meeting of fellowship where the praises and prayers of Israel ascend from the holy feast; the flowing water of life that comes forth from the threshold of the house—all are realities in Christ.[12]

Why should it be considered by any evangelical Christian to be "liberal-leaning spiritualization" to affirm that all these prophecies are fulfilled in Christ, in whom all the promises of

---

[11]Clowney, "The Final Temple," 105.
[12]Ibid., 119.

God are "Yes"—and we say "Amen" to the glory of God (2 Cor. 1:20). We know it is not to "spiritualize away" the sin offering to say that it is forever fulfilled by Christ. Why should it be considered dangerous spiritualization to affirm the same truth about the temple, the gate, and the altar that we affirm about the sacrifice once-for-all offered there?

Since Christ is the *true* temple, we are to look for no other. When the apostle John is given that climactic vision of a new heaven and a new earth, and of "the Holy City, the new Jerusalem, coming down out of heaven from God, prepared as a bride beautifully dressed for her husband" (Rev. 21:2), he reports: "I did not see a temple in the city, because the Lord God Almighty and the Lamb are its temple" (21:22).

If the Jews should succeed some day in building a new temple on the rock in Jerusalem, that would not be in fulfillment of God's Word but in denial of it and his work, a denial of the Lord's Christ—as John would call it, a synagogue of Satan (Rev. 2:9; 3:9). No other foundation can anyone lay than the one already laid (1 Cor. 3:11). No other temple can be erected on that foundation than that which is being erected, in which all the saints of God, Jew and Gentile, are being built as living stones (Eph. 2:19–22; 1 Peter 2:5).

Premillennialists have often raised the question: "But what about 'the hope of Israel'? Does not the amillennialist understanding of biblical revelation rob Israel of her hope?" No, the "hope of Israel" is that which the elect of Israel (as well as the elect of the Gentiles) have obtained. That is the clear teaching of the apostle Paul in Romans 11:7—"What Israel sought so earnestly it did not obtain, but the elect did." And that is nothing less than the fullness of God's salvation in Jesus Christ, in whom the Immanuel promise of the covenant is preeminently and finally fulfilled: "I will be their God and they will be my people" (Jer. 31:33).

Perhaps a simple illustration will help highlight the point that the fulfillment may transcend the terms in which a promise is presented. Consider a young man looking forward to entering a local college in the fall. In appreciation for his good work in high school, his father promises that he will give him "wheels" for his upcoming birthday so that the boy will have transportation as a commuting student. The son is overjoyed, thinking that

Dad is going to buy him a motorbike! Birthday morning arrives, and Dad asks him whether he has been out in the driveway yet. The son hurries outside, but there is no motorbike there! Now, there *is* a $200,000 Ferrari sports car parked in the driveway, but there is no motorbike. Does the son come back to his father crying: "You have robbed me of my hope"? Obviously not. This is a rather materialistic illustration; but surely with regard to the reality of our spiritual blessings in Christ, the fulfillment by God's grace (both now and in the day of the consummation and the eternal state) far transcends the terms in which the promise has been revealed.

THE SECOND COMING OF CHRIST: THE GRAND FINALE OF REDEMPTIVE HISTORY

The Old Testament does not teach a future millennial kingdom of Christ. Uniformly the Old Testament prophets speak of the Messiah's *everlasting* kingdom and its *everlasting* blessings.[13] With regard to the New Testament revelation concerning the future, however, we must say even more than that. Not only does the New Testament not teach a future millennial kingdom, in what it teaches us about Christ's second coming, the New Testament *rules out* an earthly millennial kingdom following Christ's return, because the New Testament reveals clearly that the following events are all concurrent; that is, all will occur together in one cluster of end-time events, one grand dramatic finale of redemptive history: the second coming of Christ, the resurrection of believers (and the "change" of living believers, 1 Cor. 15:51), the resurrection of the unjust, judgment for all, the end, the new heaven and new earth, and the inauguration of the final kingdom of God, the blessed eternal state of the redeemed.

Because this is so, Scripture has to be forced into artificial interpretations in order to fit in a millennial period after Christ's return, separating the resurrection of unbelievers from that of believers, separating their judgment from Christ's coming and the judgment of believers, and separating the cosmic renewal (a

---

[13]See, for example, Gen. 17:7–8; 48:4; 2 Sam. 23:5; 1 Chron. 16:17–18; Ps. 105:10–11; Isa. 45:17; 55:3; 61:7–8; Jer. 32:40; 50:4–5; Ezek. 16:60; 37:26; Dan. 4:3, 34; 7:14, 27; 12:2.

new heaven and a new earth) from Christ's coming. In our study of several New Testament passages below, that is the primary point we will be making, namely, the concurrence of all these awesome end-time events. We will have to examine many details to make that point, but it will be important not to miss the forest for the trees.

When the concurrence of all these end-time events is recognized, the resulting eschatological picture is a simple one. Some see this simplicity as a weakness of amillennialism. But we must never confuse simplicity with superficiality or complexity with profundity. We have space to consider only a sampling of the New Testament revelation.[14]

John 5:28–29

Listen to what our Lord says:

> Do not be amazed at this, for a time is coming when all who are in their graves will hear his voice and come out—those who have done good will rise to live, and those who have done evil will rise to be condemned.

Stanley Grenz calls the doctrine of two bodily resurrections, with a thousand-year period intervening between them, "the linchpin of premillennialism."[15] But not only is there no hint of this notion in our Lord's declaration, his statement appears clearly contrary to it. From the Greek word translated "a time" in the NIV of John 5:28 we get our English word "hour." An hour is coming, our Lord says, in which *all* the dead will be raised.

The apostle Paul presents the same teaching when he tells Felix, the governor, that he has the same hope in God as his Jewish accusers, "that there will be a resurrection of both the righteous and the wicked" (Acts 24:15). Note the singular: "a resurrection." Later we will consider 1 Corinthians 15:22–24 and Revelation 20:5 to determine whether those texts require us to seek an alternative to the natural reading of these affirmations of our Lord and of his apostle.

---

[14]With regard to the arguments presented in this section, I am indebted to insights presented by Professor John Murray in his classroom lectures at Westminster Theological Seminary in 1958 (unpublished).

[15]Grenz, *The Millennial Maze*, 128.

2 Thessalonians 1:5–10

In this passage the apostle Paul addresses these words of comfort and encouragement to the church:

> All this is evidence that God's judgment is right, and as a result you will be counted worthy of the kingdom of God, for which you are suffering. God is just: He will pay back trouble to those who trouble you and give relief to you who are troubled, and to us as well. This will happen when the Lord Jesus is revealed from heaven in blazing fire with his powerful angels. He will punish those who do not know God and do not obey the gospel of our Lord Jesus. They will be punished with everlasting destruction and shut out from the presence of the Lord and from the majesty of his power on the day he comes to be glorified in his holy people and to be marveled at among all those who have believed.

Is this graphic picture compatible with the premillennial concept of a divided future judgment? Note that it will be *at one and the same time* that (1) God will "pay back trouble to those who trouble" the Thessalonian believers, and "will punish those who do not know God and do not obey the gospel of our Lord Jesus," and that (2) God will "give relief to you who are troubled, and to us as well."[16]

It is typical of biblical references to this wondrous consummation event that it is spoken of here in various ways, alerting us to the fact that the New Testament often describes the same event, or cluster of events, from different points of view. (1) This twofold judgment will be meted out by God "when the Lord Jesus is revealed from heaven in blazing fire with his powerful angels." Thus we learn that the believers' relief will be received at the visible return of Christ.[17]

(2) This will occur when Christ "comes to be glorified in his holy people and to be marveled at among all those who have

---

[16]"The great consummating day of the Lord, which will bring this final age to its conclusion, will be a day of salvation for some and a day of destruction for others: it is, clearly, one and the same day" (Philip E. Hughes, *Interpreting Prophecy* [Grand Rapids: Eerdmans, 1980], 37).

[17]The language is similar to that used in the Synoptic Gospels to describe the Parousia, which classic dispensationalism has taught is a reference to the secret rapture.

believed." The time when Christ will be glorified in his saints and marveled at among all believers will surely be when he comes to raise to life those who have died in him and to take away all believers to meet him in the air so that we will be with him forever (1 Thess. 4:15–18).

(3) All this will take place "in that day." In the Greek text this phrase stands alone at the end of verse 10 as a shortened reference to a special day in biblical prophecy: the Day of the Lord, the Day of Judgment.

This twofold judgment can thus be spoken of as occurring at the coming of Christ *for* his saints, at his *visible revelation* from heaven, on that *Day*. It cannot be maintained, therefore, that that coming [*parousia*], that revelation [*apokalypsis*], and that day [*hēmera*] will occur at different times.

The judgment executed by God at the coming of Christ will be twofold: blessing for God's people, punishment for unbelievers. It will not do to suggest that this passage speaks only of the *temporal* punishment (death) received by the ungodly living on this earth when Christ returns and that *final* judgment will be executed a millennium later. The apostle's language is generally inclusive. He speaks not only of those troubling the Thessalonians but also of all "those who do not know God and do not obey the gospel of our Lord Jesus." To say that ungodly men and women must be living at the time of Christ's return in order to suffer punishment at that time is no more tenable than to say that believers must be living at Christ's return in order to receive final relief and blessing then. If the judgment threatened here is one that will fall only on those alive at Christ's return, the threat will fail to be fulfilled with regard to the persecutors of the Thessalonians, because they died long ago.

This passage speaks of the final and eternal damnation— "everlasting destruction ... shut out from the presence of the Lord"—that will be administered by God, the holy judge, not after the resurrection of the ungodly at the end of the Millennium, but at the return of Christ.

Romans 8:17–23

Now if we are children, then we are heirs—heirs of God and co-heirs with Christ, if indeed we share in his sufferings in order that we may also share in his glory.

> I consider that our present sufferings are not worth comparing with the glory that will be revealed in us. The creation waits in eager expectation for the sons of God to be revealed. For the creation was subjected to frustration, not by its own choice, but by the will of the one who subjected it, in hope that the creation itself will be liberated from its bondage to decay and brought into the glorious freedom of the children of God.
>
> We know that the whole creation has been groaning as in the pains of childbirth right up to the present time. Not only so, but we ourselves, who have the firstfruits of the Spirit, groan inwardly as we wait eagerly for our adoption as sons, the redemption of our bodies.

Here the apostle speaks of the ardent longing of both believers in Christ and the whole creation for the promised coming glory. He also speaks of the sufferings of this present time and the glory that will be revealed to us. The NIV translation "our present sufferings" obscures, perhaps, the thrust of the apostle's contrast, which is "not [a contrast] between the sufferings endured by a believer in this life prior to death and the bliss upon which he enters at death."[18] The phrase "this present time" is another way of referring to the period that Paul speaks of elsewhere as "this age" or "the present age" (Rom. 12:2; Gal. 1:4; Eph. 1:21). The contrast, in other words, is between the sufferings that characterize *this* age and the glory that will characterize the *next* age, the coming age.

In speaking of "the whole creation," the apostle uses the figure of speech called "personification"; that is, he speaks of the material cosmos as though it were a thinking, feeling, willing person. Not only are believers "groaning" in "eager expectation" of the coming glory, but "the whole creation" also. The creation has been subjected to the fruitlessness, deterioration, and decay involved in the curse pronounced in Eden because of Adam's sin (Gen. 3:17–18). The one who subjected it "in hope" (Rom. 8:20) was God. And the "hope" Paul speaks of is the hope of the cosmic renewal promised elsewhere in Scripture: "the renewal [regeneration] of all things" (Matt. 19:28); "the time ... for God to restore everything" (Acts 3:21); the "new heaven and a new earth" (2 Peter 3:13; Rev. 21:1; cf. Isa. 65:17; 66:22).

---

[18]John Murray, *The Epistle to the Romans* (Grand Rapids: Eerdmans, 1959), 1:300.

In other words, these are "the pains of childbirth" that Paul speaks of in Romans 8:22; they are not death pains. This world is going to be renewed, not annihilated. Otherwise Paul could not have said that it was subjected "in hope" (8:24–25). This is why we should speak of cosmic renewal rather than of cosmic destruction. Think of the parallel Peter draws between the future judgment and the past judgment of the Flood: "The world of that time was ... destroyed," but it was certainly not annihilated (2 Peter 3:6). Compare Paul's picture of the Christian as a "new man" (Eph. 4:24; Col. 3:10, KJV) and as a "new creation" (Gal. 6:15). The new being is the old being made new.

The Christian is not a new person in the absolute sense, as though God had chosen to create a people for himself out of thin air or out of the stones by the roadside. Jesus said that God could do that (Matt. 3:9), but God has not chosen to do that. Rather, he has chosen to make lost sinners new by the power of Christ's Spirit. The renewal of the cosmos is comparable to the resurrection of the body. How new that body will be—as different from our present body as the grain that appears is from the seed that is sown (1 Cor. 15:35–44). Yet Paul indicates that there will remain a connection (mysterious though this must seem to our minds) to our present bodies. Otherwise this miracle could not be spoken of as a "resurrection" of our bodies.

As Paul vividly portrays the eager desire of both believers and the whole creation, he rejoices in the fact that that desire will be satisfied; both will know a sure and complete deliverance.

Paul expresses this future deliverance of God's people in various ways. He speaks of glorification with Christ (Rom. 8:17), "the glory that will be revealed in us" (v. 18), the revealing of the sons of God (v. 19), "the glorious freedom of the children of God" (v. 21), "our adoption as sons, the redemption of our bodies" (v. 23). All these terms speak of complete deliverance from sin and the wonderful results of that deliverance.

Paul tells us here when this total deliverance will be ours—at the resurrection. He calls this "the redemption of our bodies," that great goal for which believers have received the seal of the Holy Spirit as the deposit "guaranteeing our inheritance until the redemption of those who are God's possession" (Eph. 1:14). Paul also refers to this as "our adoption," because not until then will the full implications of the blessed adoption that we already enjoy in union with God's Son be realized. And, as we will see, Paul clearly teaches in 1 Corinthians 15:23 that the resurrection of those who belong to Christ occurs at Christ's coming [*parousia*].

Paul describes the deliverance of creation as creation's liberation "from its bondage to decay . . . into the glorious freedom of the children of God" (Rom. 8:21). Thus, the deliverance of creation itself from all the corrupting consequences of human sin as they have affected the creation will be as complete and as final as the deliverance from sin and its consequences are for God's people.

Here again the apostle directs our attention to when this deliverance will be achieved: when "the sons of God [are] revealed" (Rom. 8:19). That day of their "revelation" [*apokalypsis*] as God's children is the glorious goal of the believers' expectation, and it is the goal of the creation's expectation also. At that time the creation itself "will be liberated from its bondage to decay and brought into the glorious freedom of the children of God" (v. 21). The "revealing of the sons of God" and "the glorious freedom of the children of God" cannot be postponed beyond the coming of Christ and the resurrection, nor can the deliverance of creation be postponed beyond that great day.

This is put beyond any doubt by verses 22–23, where we see both believers and the whole creation groaning together and waiting together for the adoption that is here defined as "the redemption of our bodies." That marvelous event, the resurrection, is thus revealed to be the end-point of the creation's groaning also.

Therefore, the significance of this passage with regard to the so-called "millennial issue" is clear. The apostle Paul, by the inspiration of the Holy Spirit, teaches us that the resurrection glory of the children of God will mark the resurrection glory of creation as well. At Christ's coming, not a millennium later, "the creation itself will be liberated from its bondage to decay" and come to enjoy a glory that is likened to "the glorious freedom of the children of God."

2 Peter 3:3–14

A careful reading of this passage will reveal that Peter here presents a picture of what will happen when our Lord returns in entire harmony with Paul's teaching in Romans 8:17–23.

Peter is responding to the scoffers who will ask: "Where is this 'coming' he promised?" (2 Peter 3:4) by declaring that "the day of the Lord will come" (v. 10). Clearly that "coming" [*parousia*] of Christ and that "day of the Lord" refer to the same event. Otherwise Peter's affirmation in verse 10 would not be relevant as an answer to the mocking question of verse 4. In verses 7, 10, 11, 12, and 13, Peter speaks of what can be called the "cosmic renewal"—that is, the destruction of the present heaven and earth by fire so that a new heaven and a new earth, "the home of righteousness," may appear. This will take place, Peter says, at "the day of judgment and destruction of ungodly men" (v. 7).

Premillennialists have often responded that this concurrence of the ungodly being judged and the world being burned with fire presents no problem for their view since premillennialism sees both occurring at the end of the Millennium. But it is not simply that in this passage the cosmic renewal is placed within "the day of the Lord" (v. 10; "the day of God," v. 12)—as if we might conceive of the Day of the Lord as a long period of time, with the judgment of the ungodly and the cosmic renewal taking place at the end of that Day. Rather, it is the *coming* (*parousia*) of the day of the Lord that is identified with the disappearance of the present heavens and earth.

This interpretation of verse 10 is confirmed by verse 12. Unfortunately, the NIV here refers merely to "the day of God." The Greek text speaks of "the *coming* [*parousia*] of the day of God." Thus the NASB translates verse 12: "looking for and hastening the coming of the day of God." Again, it is the coming of the day of God that is to be marked by the melting of the elements in the heat. Notice that Peter here gives believers the same exhortation to watchfulness and holiness of life in view of the coming disintegration of the present heavens and earth (vv. 11, 13, and 14) that is given elsewhere in the New Testament in view of the coming of Christ himself. Both Christ's coming and the transformation of the cosmos are presented as the goal of the Christian's watchful waiting, for both will occur together.

In other words, the picture presented by the Spirit through Peter does not allow for a thousand years intervening between the second coming of Christ and the coming of the day of divine judgment and cosmic renewal.

1 Corinthians 15:20–26

Premillennialists have often viewed this passage from Paul as not merely compatible with premillennial doctrine but as presenting positive support for that doctrine:

> But Christ has indeed been raised from the dead, the firstfruits of those who have fallen asleep. For since death came through a man, the resurrection of the dead comes also through a man. For as in Adam all die, so in Christ all will be made alive. But each in his own turn: Christ, the firstfruits; then, when he comes, those who belong to him. Then the end will come, when he hands over the kingdom to God the Father after he has destroyed all dominion, authority and power. For he must reign until he has put all his enemies under his feet. The last enemy to be destroyed is death.

Some argue that since the apostle in verse 22 refers to a general resurrection—that is, a resurrection of the unjust as well as the just—we would expect him to speak of the resurrection of the unjust in verses 23–24 as well. Thus, Paul's reference to "the end" in verse 24 must be interpreted as pointing to another stage, the final, after-the-Millennium stage of the resurrection: "Then the end [*of the resurrection*] will come." But the fact is that there is no reference to a general resurrection in verse 22.

Those who argue that Paul speaks here of the resurrection of all humankind insist that the word "all" in the second clause ("all will be made alive") must be as all-inclusive as the term "all" in the first clause ("all die"). Elsewhere, however, the apostle uses the word "all" when his reference is not all-inclusive, and he can even use that word in both clauses of the same sentence when in only one of those clauses is the reference all-inclusive. We think immediately of Romans 5:18, where Paul's language is so strikingly parallel to 1 Corinthians 15:22: "Consequently, just as the result of one trespass was condemnation for all men, so also the result of one act of righteousness was justification that brings life for all men." Although the "all men" in that first clause is all-inclusive (excluding only our sinless Savior), the "all men" in the second clause cannot be all-inclusive, because the context is clear that Paul is here speaking of that justification that is unto everlasting life; and it is contrary to Paul's theology to say that all men and women receive that justification whether or not they trust in Christ.[19]

Similarly, in 1 Corinthians 15:22 when Paul speaks of being "made alive in Christ," both that verb and that prepositional phrase are used so consistently in the New Testament to refer to the highest conceivable salvation blessings that we must insist that the resurrection Paul has in view in verse 22 is that resurrection that is resurrection to life eternal. Nowhere in 1 Corinthians 15 does the resurrection of the unjust enter the picture.

The foundation of the premillennial interpretation of verses 23–24 rests on the appearance here of two adverbs (*epeita* and *eita*), "adverbs of time, denoting sequence"[20]—both translated "then" in the NIV. It is argued that just as "an unidentified interval" has intervened between the resurrection of Christ and the resurrection of those who belong to Christ (an interval marked by the Greek adverb *epeita* in v. 23), so too "a second undefined interval" will intervene between the resurrection of believers at Christ's coming and "the end" (an interval marked by the Greek adverb *eita* in v. 24).[21] This interval is the millennial reign of Christ, Christ's kingdom as distinguished from the Father's kingdom. George Ladd writes:

> One may reason, therefore, that the "end" is to take place at a considerable period after the Parousia of Christ, at which time (at the end) he will deliver the kingdom to the Father when, by means of his reign during the intervening period, he has completed the task of subduing all enemies.[22]

In response it must be granted that the adverb *eita* can mark a long interval, just as the adverb *epeita* does indicate a long interval here in verse 23. But either of these "adverbs of sequence" can also be used in the sense of *immediate* sequence:

---

[19]In the previous section of this letter to the Romans (3:21–5:11) the apostle has clearly taught that sinners are justified "by faith" (note esp. 3:21, 26, 30; 4:5, 13; 5:1–2). It is not simply that by faith we come to realize that we have been justified; rather, as Paul puts it in his letter to the Galatians, "we have put our faith in Christ Jesus that we may be justified" (Gal. 2:16).

[20]George Eldon Ladd, *Crucial Questions About the Kingdom of God* (Grand Rapids: Eerdmans, 1952), 178.

[21]George Eldon Ladd, "Historic Premillennialism," in *The Meaning of the Millennium: Four Views*, ed. Robert G. Clouse (Downers Grove, Ill.: InterVarsity, 1977), 39.

[22]Ladd, *Crucial Questions*, 179.

for example, *epeita* in Luke 16:7; *eita* in John 20:27. Not the adverb itself, in other words, but only the context can determine for us the length of the interval marked by the adverb. The adverb alone cannot carry the entire weight of the premillennial construction suspended on it. Berkouwer observes:

> The train of thought in 1 Corinthians 15:23f. is not the series: Christ's resurrection followed by the resurrection of *believers*, and finally by the general resurrection. The emphasis is on being in Christ and the power of His resurrection. The interpretation of the sequence *epeita ... eita ...* as a Pauline reference to a millennium smacks of being too much influenced by Revelation 20.[23]

What, then, can we learn from the context that will answer the question of how long an interval is marked by the second "then," the "then" at the beginning of verse 24? (1) The broader context of Paul's letters (and the New Testament generally) shows us that "the end" cannot be separated from the second coming of Christ. Notice, for example, how the apostle earlier in this same letter to the Corinthians brings together the revelation (*apokalypsis*) of our Lord Jesus Christ, the end, and the Day of our Lord Jesus Christ: ". . . as you eagerly wait for our Lord Jesus Christ to be revealed. He will keep you strong to the end, so that you will be blameless on the day of our Lord Jesus Christ" (1 Cor. 1:7–8).

(2) Looking more closely at 1 Corinthians 15, in verses 24–26 we learn that Christ will destroy death, "the last enemy," at "the end." That will be the last act Christ will accomplish as he puts all enemies under his feet and "hands over the kingdom to God the Father." But notice that in verses 54–55, the apostle Paul once again speaks of the coming victory over death.

> . . . then the saying that is written will come true: "Death has been swallowed up in victory."
>
> "Where, O death, is your victory?
> Where, O death, is your sting?"

The adverb "then" (*tote*) in the middle of verse 54 tells us when this victory over death will be accomplished. And that "then" points us back to what Paul has been describing for several verses here: *the resurrection of believers*.

---

[23]G. C. Berkouwer, *The Return of Christ* (Grand Rapids: Eerdmans, 1972), 302.

Therefore, we must conclude that victory over death will occur at the resurrection of believers (v. 54), which occurs at the coming of Christ (v. 23), and that this victory occurs at "the end" (vv. 24–26). Thus, once again "the end" cannot be separated from the second coming of Christ. Therefore the force of the "then" in verse 24 *must* be that of "immediately then."

Premillennialism responds that Paul speaks of *two* victories over death in this chapter: a preliminary one at Christ's coming and the resurrection of believers (vv. 54–55), and a final one after the Millennium at the resurrection and judgment of unbelievers (vv. 24–26). There is nothing in the apostle's language to support this, however. Paul himself does not introduce a distinction between death for believers and death for unbelievers. In both these sections he speaks simply of "death" absolutely, without further qualification. Indeed there is no evidence that Paul has the resurrection of the wicked in view in *either* of these passages when he speaks of the destruction of death, the last enemy. Would it not be rather strange for Paul to rejoice in the resurrection, judgment, and final punishment of the unjust as the acts in which death is finally destroyed? The fact is that death is never destroyed as far as the wicked are concerned. For them the resurrection of the body is merely the prelude to final judgment and what the Bible speaks of as "the second death" (Rev. 20:6).

The mediatorial reign of Christ reaches its climactic end when he destroys the last enemy, death, by raising to life his people (vv. 54–55) at his coming (v. 23). Now if "the end" is reached at the coming of Christ, when did Christ's mediatorial reign begin? The New Testament clearly points us to the resurrection and exaltation of Christ as the beginning of that reign (see Acts 2:36; Eph. 1:20–23; Phil. 2:9–11; Heb. 1:3; 10:12–13; 1 Peter 3:21–22). In Ephesians 1:21 Paul uses the same Greek words he uses in 1 Corinthians 15:24 (*archē, exousia, dynamis*), and in the same order: "exalted far above all dominion and authority and power." That Ephesians passage also tells us that it was "when he raised him from the dead" (v. 20) that God exalted Christ to begin that lordship and that reign.

In 1 Corinthians 15:24–27 the apostle rejoices in the mediatorial dominion that Christ is now exercising with the goal of putting all his enemies under his feet. That reign will be completed when Christ comes and "the last trumpet" signals the resurrection day for Christ's people (15:52).[24] That resurrection change will make it possible for us to inherit the kingdom of God—that final and eternal kingdom of God that is here contrasted with the mediatorial kingdom of Christ.[25]

Clearly when Paul says that Christ will one day hand over the kingdom to God the Father (v. 24) "so that God may be all in all" (v. 28), he is not contradicting Peter, who speaks of "the eternal kingdom of our Lord and Savior Jesus Christ" (2 Peter 1:11). We must remember that it is specifically Christ's reign of conquest over his enemies that Paul has in view here in 1 Corinthians 15. When that conquest is complete and every enemy has been destroyed, that particular *kind* of reign will have reached its end. Redemptive history will have reached its dramatic conclusion; every divine purpose will have been fulfilled; and the Son will hand over to the Father that mediatorial dominion given him for the purpose of achieving that perfect righteousness and peace, the eternal *shalom* of God.

TWO PASSAGES CONSIDERED CRUCIAL BY MILLENNIALISTS

Romans 11

Both premillennialists and postmillennialists have appealed to this passage as providing significant support for their positions. George Ladd, for example, insists that "there are two passages in the New Testament which cannot be avoided,"[26] passages that clearly point to a premillennial perspective, one of which is Romans 11:26. John Murray, on the other hand, has often been viewed as a "one-text" *post*millennialist on the basis of his interpretation of the phrase "life from the dead" in Romans 11:15 as a figurative expression that speaks of "an

---

[24]Paul here uses the Greek adjective from which our word "eschatology" comes: *eschatos*, "last." We ought to appreciate the full significance of that designation. It would seem strange if the "last" trumpet sounds at the resurrection of believers if Christ's mediatorial reign only begins then and if another resurrection occurs after a lengthy period of time.

[25]According to the premillennial interpretation, the resurrection ushers believers into the millennial kingdom of Christ, as distinguished from the final kingdom of God. Paul's language in 1 Cor. 15:50, however, does not fit that construction.

[26]Ladd, "Historic Premillennialism," 27.

unprecedented quickening for the world in the expansion and success of the gospel," resulting from "the reception of Israel again into the favour and blessing of God."[27]

It should be emphasized, however, that the conclusion that Paul in Romans 11 predicts a future mass conversion of ethnic Israel prior to Christ's return does not, by itself, prove the correctness of any particular millennial position. After all, that interpretation has been presented not only by both premillennialists and postmillennialists, but by some leading amillennialists as well. For example, Geerhardus Vos sees the apostle speaking in this chapter of "the receiving back of the unbelieving majority of the Jews into favor," a national conversion "on the largest of scales at the predetermined point in the future."[28] More recently, Stanley Grenz has insisted that "the apostle clearly anticipates a future conversion of Israel on a grand scale, an event that would usher in a glorious day for the entire world." But Grenz notes that such a hope does not "require an earthly millennial reign of Christ, for the conversion of Israel could just as easily prepare for the inauguration of the eternal state as for an earthly golden age."[29]

Grenz's contention that in Romans 11 the apostle "clearly" predicts a future national conversion of Israel is debatable, as we will see. But what is undeniably clear is that in this entire section of the letter in which Paul especially focuses on the question of the place of the Jews in God's salvation plan (chs. 9–11), he says not a word about a return of the Jews to the Promised Land or about a millennial kingdom in which Christ will reign from his throne in Jerusalem—nor is there any clear reference to a "golden age" prior to Christ's return in which this world will be largely Christianized. The amillennialist can "relax" as he or she studies this passage, knowing that millennial positions are not at stake.

But we must ask whether it is indeed Paul's intention in Romans 11 to predict a future conversion of national Israel. Before considering that question, we must recall the context in which the argument of this chapter appears.

---

[27]John Murray, *The Epistle to the Romans*, vol. 2 (Grand Rapids: Eerdmans, 1965), 84, 81.

[28]Geerhardus Vos, *The Pauline Eschatology* (Phillipsburg, N.J.: Presbyterian and Reformed, rep. 1991 [1930]), 87, 88.

[29]Grenz, *The Millennial Maze*, 171.

In Romans 1 the apostle had spoken of the gospel as the power of God for salvation to everyone who believes, "first for the Jew ..." (1:16). But Paul was sensitive to the fact that that claim might seem to be contradicted by the large-scale unbelief of the Jews. He well knew the objection: "If the coming of the Messiah was to mark an age of great blessing for Israel, how can it be that the Jews have rejected this one whom you call the Messiah, Paul? The Jews do not seem to have been blessed by him." As Calvin expressed this objection: "Either ... there is no truth in the divine promise, or ... Jesus, whom Paul preached, is not the Lord's Christ who had been peculiarly promised to the Jews."[30] That is the "apologetic problem" that Paul faces squarely in chapters 9–11.

In 9:1–5 Paul begins his answer by acknowledging that Israel was indeed specially chosen by God and thus the possessor of the highest spiritual blessings, and by acknowledging with great sorrow that his fellow Jews (for the most part) are not now enjoying the blessing of salvation in Christ. But beginning in verse 6, he rejects the implication falsely drawn from that fact: "It is not as though God's word had failed. For not all who are descended from Israel are Israel."

How could God reject a nation whom he had elected? Paul's answer: Election and nationality are not equally inclusive. That Israel would be blessed did not necessarily mean that the whole nation would be blessed. The true Israel consists of the children of the promise, the election of grace; and they have been blessed. Paul then gives a series of illustrations to show that mere physical descent from Abraham did not guarantee the possession of the blessings promised to Abraham.

Beginning at 9:30 the focus of Paul's argument shifts from the electing grace of God to the response of men and women—whether of faith, which looks to the righteousness God provides, or of unbelief, which seeks to establish its own righteousness. The Jew will be received by God on the same basis as the Gentile (10:11–13); and the Jews' problem is not that they have not had the gospel preached to them; rather, they have not believed the gospel (10:16–21).

---

[30]John Calvin, *The Epistles of Paul the Apostle to the Romans and to the Thessalonians*, trans. Ross MacKenzie (Grand Rapids: Eerdmans, 1960), 190.

As chapter 11 begins, the apostle repeats the argument of chapter 9. God has his true Israel, his elect, but that election is not coextensive with the whole nation. Paul himself is an example of an elect Jew (11:1). Even as Elijah learned that the elect remnant numbered seven thousand in his day, "so too, at the present time there is a remnant chosen by grace" (11:5). "What then?" Paul concludes in verse 7. "What Israel sought so earnestly it did not obtain, but the elect did. The others were hardened...."

Many commentators, however—and not only millennialist ones, as we have noted—see Paul's argument taking a new turn at verse 11. Often chapter 11 is outlined this way: Paul answers the question asked in verse 1 ("Did God reject his people?") by stating that the rejection of the Jews is neither total (vv. 1–10) nor final (vv. 11–32). But the fact is that Paul consistently presents just *one* answer in chapters 9–11, namely, that the rejection of Israel is not total and that not all are Israel who are of Israel. Romans 11 deals with the place of Israel in the redemptive purposes of God at the present time, not at some future time.

Obviously, the kind of careful step-by-step analysis of chapter 11 required to establish this conclusion cannot be attempted here.[31] Only two or three crucial points can be briefly noted.

As already indicated, Paul answers the question raised in verse 1 ("Did God reject his people?") not by pointing to a future time when God's grace will at last reach the Jews but rather by pointing to the present, to himself as "Exhibit A" of God's saving grace (v. 1), to the Jewish remnant "at the present time" (v. 5), and—in the verses that come after the alleged "turning-point" in his argument (v. 11)—to his own present ministry to the Gentiles and its effect of arousing Jews to jealousy (see esp. vv. 11, 13–14, 23). It is this process (which has been graphically described as "a wave motion") that is the unifying theme of verses 11–32, so that throughout the entire time before Christ's return the waters of God's salvation continually crash against the dam of the Gentiles and return to the Jews.[32]

---

[31]An especially helpful analysis is presented by O. Palmer Robertson in *Perspectives on Evangelical Theology*, ed. Kenneth S. Kantzer and Stanley N. Gundry (Grand Rapids: Baker, 1979), ch. 16, "Is There a Distinctive Future for Ethnic Israel in Romans 11?"

[32]See Herman Ridderbos, *Paul*, trans. John Richard de Witt (Grand Rapids: Eerdmans, 1975), 354–61.

At the beginning of this section, in giving a negative answer to the question posed in verse 11, Paul announces the true purpose of the stumbling of Israel, and in doing so he outlines in one sentence the teaching of the remainder of the chapter: "Again I ask: Did they stumble so as to fall beyond recovery? Not at all! Rather, because of their transgression, salvation has come to the Gentiles to make Israel envious" (vv. 11–12). That summarizes Paul's entire argument in verses 11–32: Don't try to complicate it!

At the climactic conclusion of this section, as Paul sums up his argument in verses 30–31, he again refers to that divine "wave motion." Note especially the three times the word "now" appears in these verses:[33]

> Just as you who were at one time disobedient to God have *now* received mercy as a result of their disobedience, so they too have *now* become disobedient in order that they too may *now* receive mercy as a result of God's mercy to you.

This summary statement makes it clear that the apostle's concern in chapter 11 is not to predict the future but to explain the motive and the purpose of his present ministry.

It is this "wave motion" process that is the "mystery" that Paul alludes to in verse 25.[34] It is that process that is in view when Paul writes in verse 26, "and so ..." (lit., "and in this way ..."). The combination of Greek words Paul uses here (*kai houtōs*) is never used to refer to temporal sequence ("and then ...") but

---

[33]There are early manuscripts that do not include the third "now" (though the text of the most important of these, p^{46}, is not altogether certain). But the combination of Sinaiticus, Vaticanus, and the original Greek hand of Claromontanus, all including the third "now," is significant external evidence. Considered from the standpoint of internal evidence, it seems more likely that "now" was omitted by a scribe who felt that it hardly fit the fact of the Jews' present unbelief than that it was accidentally inserted as a repetition of the preceding "now." (The word *hysteron*, "later," was inserted at this point in some manuscripts that are clearly much later— an indication of the difficulty some later scribe had with the apostolic statement before him.) There seems to be good reason, therefore, for seeing the third "now" as part of the original text, as do the UBS Greek New Testament, the NIV, and the NASB.

[34]Thomas Schreiner asks ("The Church as the New Israel and the Future of Ethnic Israel in Paul," *Studia Biblica et Theologica* 13 [April 1983]: 26), "How is the salvation of all the elect of Israel's history a mystery?" But the mystery is not the fact of their salvation but the mode, the method God is using to save them.

always to refer to either a logical relationship or the manner by which something is done.

Paul's statement in verse 25 that "Israel has experienced a hardening in part until the full number of the Gentiles has come in" has often been understood as teaching that *after* the fullness of the Gentiles has been realized, the hardening in part that has fallen on Israel will be lifted, and Israel nationally will be converted. But there is nothing in the Greek word "until" to indicate this idea of a national conversion for Israel in the future. That idea would have to be explicitly taught somewhere in the context for us to bring it in here. It cannot simply be read into the "until" phrase itself. As a matter of fact, in accordance with its common usage, the concern in that "until" phrase is not with a new situation that will exist after the end of the present age but rather with the situation that will exist before the end, *and all the way up to* the end of the present age. As Joachim Jeremias notes: "Actually, in the New Testament [this Greek phrase] regularly introduces a reference to reaching the eschatological goal."

In this regard, note Revelation 2:25–26: "Only hold on to what you have *until* I come. To him who overcomes and does my will *to the end,* I will give authority over the nations" (emphasis added; cf. also Luke 21:24; 1 Cor. 11:26; 15:25). As Palmer Robertson has written:

> "Hardening ... until" too frequently has been understood as marking the beginning of a new state of things with regard to Israel. It hardly has been considered that "hardening ... until" more naturally should be interpreted as eschatologically terminating in its significance. The phrase implies not a new beginning after a termination point in time, but instead the continuation of a prevailing circumstance for Israel until the end of time.[35]

What the apostle Paul teaches in Romans 11:25 is that hardening on the part of ethnic Israel will continue right up until the full number of the Gentiles has come in.

We have emphasized that Paul's theme in this chapter is the "wave motion" process by which salvation is coming to both Gentiles and Jews throughout this gospel age. Although this is a process that is now under way, it *is* a process. When Paul

---

[35]Robertson, "Is There a Distinctive Future for Ethnic Israel in Romans 11?" 220.

speaks of the "fullness" of Israel (v. 11), "all Israel" (v. 26), and the "fullness" of the Gentiles (v. 25), he looks to the completion of that process and its result. According to the apostle, the glorious blessing that will be the result of both the full number of elect Gentiles and the full number of elect Jews having been brought into God's family by faith will be nothing less than "life from the dead" (v. 15). That is, Resurrection Day will have arrived!

Against the postmillennial suggestion that "life from the dead" in Romans 11:15 refers to a "golden age" to be ushered in following the national conversion of Israel[36] stands what would seem to be an insuperable objection. How can such an age follow after both the fullness of the Gentiles and the fullness of Israel have come in? We must take that term "fullness" (Gk. *plē-rōma*) in its fullest sense. For Paul it is a term filled with full and rich consummation significance. With the bringing in of the fullness of both Israel and the Gentiles, God's redemptive purposes will be accomplished. There will then be no further period of history to delay the consummation of redemption's blessings.

Revelation 20:1–10

Obviously this passage, the one place in the Bible where reference to "the thousand years" appears, is a most significant one for our discussion. George Ladd has written:

> ... even if the rest of the Bible were entirely silent on this point, that fact would not militate against the belief in a millennium if the exegesis of the Apocalypse [Revelation] required it.... It might well be that in the Apocalypse, elements of a new revelation were imparted to John by the Lord, to the effect that there should be a millennial interregnum.[37]

Many Christians agree with Ladd here. Some have acknowledged themselves to be "one-text premillennialists," with Revelation 20:1–10 as that one text on which their premillennialism rests.

---

[36]See the comment from John Murray quoted earlier in this section. This is the interpretation given in the commentaries on Romans by David Brown, Frederick Godet, Robert Haldane, Charles Hodge, and William G. T. Shedd. See Iain H. Murray, *The Puritan Hope* (Edinburgh: Banner of Truth, 1971), for an index to pages in that volume where this interpretation of Romans 11:15 by Puritan writers may be found.

[37]Ladd, *Crucial Questions*, 181–82.

But we should quickly correct one serious misunderstanding that Ladd's statement might cause. It might be thought that amillennialists insist that Revelation 20 cannot teach an earthly millennial kingdom after Christ's coming because the rest of the Bible is silent on this point. That seems to be what Ladd is suggesting. But this is not true. Amillennialists would agree that if a truth is taught with unmistakable clarity in Scripture, it is to be believed—even if it is taught in just one verse. But what must be made clear is that amillennialists believe that Scripture is not merely silent on this point. Scripture speaks to this matter, and in doing so rules out such an earthly kingdom intervening between the second coming of Christ and the Final Judgment and the new heaven and new earth. This was the point we were making in the second section of this essay, and it is the amillennialist's insistence that Scripture does not contradict Scripture.

Amillennialists want to interpret Revelation 20 in a way that is consistent with the rest of the Scriptures. Ladd insists that this is a false approach: "The exegetical approach must always precede the theological. . . . One cannot come to the Scriptures with a system of eschatology and fit the records into one's system."[38] Ladd means that we should not come to Revelation 20 with certain preconceptions. Rather, interpret the chapter first; then worry about how it fits in with the rest of the Bible's teaching. Certainly we must agree that this is a sound approach to any biblical passage. But we ask two questions: (1) Are premillennialists themselves true to this principle in their interpretation of Scripture? We believe Warfield was correct in his judgment that

> there has been much less tendency-interpretation [biased interpretation] of Revelation 20 in the interest of preconceived theory, than there has been tendency-interpretation of the rest of the Scripture in the interest of questions derived from misunderstandings of this obscure passage.[39]

(2) Is it not a valid principle of biblical interpretation that less clear, more difficult portions of the Bible are to be interpreted in the light of the more clear portions, the poetry in the light of the prose, the figurative in the light of the literal? This is

---

[38]Ibid., 135.

[39]Benjamin B. Warfield, *Biblical Doctrines* (New York: Oxford, 1929), 643.

not to say that the premillennial interpretation of Revelation 20 is perfectly straightforward and without any exegetical problems. But it is to question whether we should be willing to set aside the entire New Testament, or force it into artificial interpretations, on the basis of one brief passage in an apocalypse that is admittedly highly figurative, rich in symbols, and therefore somewhat difficult.

Ladd concludes his book with this statement: "The basic question remains: What does the exegesis of Revelation 20 require? All other considerations must be subservient to the exegesis of this passage."[40] Surely that is an astonishing statement! Are we to bring all the rest of the Bible to Revelation 20 and push it, squeeze it, and make it fit in? I suggest that is a false approach to the interpretation of biblical prophecy. As Archibald Hughes has written: "It is a very precarious foundation, in a book of symbolical visions, to take such a phrase as 'a thousand years' and make it a foundation to carry the superstructure of a complete system of interpretation."[41]

In presenting now a brief interpretation of Revelation 20:1–10, a seven-point outline may be helpful. (1) Note that there is nothing in this passage to give any hint that it is to be connected with those Old Testament prophecies that speak of a coming era of national glory for Israel (see the first section of this essay). Those passages talk about the inheritance of earthly Canaan and glory for earthly Jerusalem. There is nothing about that in Revelation 20. Rather, it talks about a thousand-year kingdom, whereas the Old Testament prophecies talk about an everlasting kingdom. At first glance, therefore, it might appear that the present passage and those Old Testament prophecies are not speaking of the same subject. At the very least, there is nothing in the Revelation passage itself to clearly link them.

(2) The order in which the visions appear in the book of Revelation is not necessarily the order of fulfillment. It seems that the end of chapter 19 brings us right down to the end of the age, the second coming of Christ, the great final battle, judgment on the beast and false prophet. It does not follow that chapter 20 necessarily speaks of what will happen next. Its visions may take

---

[40]Ladd, *Crucial Questions*, 183.

[41]Archibald Hughes, *A New Heaven and A New Earth* (Philadelphia: Presbyterian and Reformed, 1958), 56.

us back to the first coming of Christ and the beginning of the present gospel age.

If so, this would not be a unique phenomenon in this book. Perhaps the clearest example of an abrupt return to the beginning of the church age is found in chapter 12. In 11:18 we read that "the time has come for judging the dead." We have been brought down to the end of the age at the end of chapter 11. With chapter 12, however, we return to the beginning of the New Testament period with a figurative vision of the birth of Christ and of his ascension to the throne of God. If this can happen in chapters 11 and 12, we cannot rule out the possibility that with chapters 19 and 20 also we are first brought in vision to the second coming of Christ and then taken back to his first coming. We must not simply assume that chapter 20 must be describing events that occur after the events described in chapter 19.

(3) There are two visions in Revelation 20:1–10, linked together by the phrase "a thousand years." Thus, we may well conclude that the two are contemporaneous. Nevertheless, they are separate visions. Verses 1–3 and 7–10 go together. They speak about Satan: Satan bound and Satan released. The three verses in between (vv. 4–6) are somewhat parenthetical and give us a separate vision of souls and thrones and reigning. We suggest that the one vision relates to certain events on earth, while the other vision is a door opened on the situation in heaven.

(4) How are we to interpret the symbol of Satan being "bound"? Chapter 12 has already spoken of a certain restraint on the dragon, Satan, after Christ's ascension. Satan is not able to accomplish his purpose. He wants to destroy the woman and her offspring, but he cannot do it. He is restrained by God. Does chapter 20 have in view another phase of Satan's being restrained, something independent of what had been described in chapter 12? Or is this an example of the kind of restatement in somewhat different terms and different symbols that is characteristic of Revelation? Perhaps 20:1–3 is speaking of another aspect of that restraint placed on Satan as a consequence of Christ's redemptive work and triumphant exaltation.

We must keep in mind the eschatological teaching of the New Testament as a whole, which is set forth in terms of not one but two great climactic points: the first coming of Christ and the second coming of Christ. With the second coming of Christ there will be full and complete consummation. But already at the first coming of Christ, we have what we might call *anticipatory* consummation. We have the decisive battle fought and the great victory won. In a real sense the kingdom of God has come, and Christ has dealt decisively with Satan.

It is important to recall how the work of Christ at his first coming is described in the New Testament with regard to its relation to Satan. In Matthew 12:28–29 our Lord says:

> But if I drive out demons by the Spirit of God, then the kingdom of God has come upon you.
> Or again, how can anyone enter a strong man's house and carry off his possessions unless he first ties up the strong man? Then he can rob his house.

This is a great eschatological event: The kingdom of God has come! To explain this event our Lord gives a brief parable. How does one go about taking away a strong man's possessions, possessions that he has gained no doubt by illegal means? The way to do it is first to tie up the strong man (the Greek verb here is the same one translated "bound" by the NIV in Rev. 20:2); then you can proceed to carry off his possessions. Jesus clearly gives this parable to describe the mission he had come to accomplish.

In John 12:31, as our Lord speaks of the significance of his approaching death, he says: "Now is the time for judgment on this world; now the prince of this world will be driven out." Judgment day has arrived, and the prince of this world (Satan) will be cast out (the Greek verb here is the same one translated "threw" in Rev. 20:3, with addition of the prefix "out"). "Now," Jesus says, through his atoning work, this will happen (read the entire context, John 12:20–33).

In Colossians 2:15 the apostle Paul vividly describes Christ's victory over the demonic powers at the cross: "And having disarmed the powers and authorities, he made a public spectacle of them, triumphing over them by the cross." Christ has disarmed Satan's hosts. What a great victory!

Hebrews 2:14–15 speaks of Christ's assuming our humanity "so that by his death he might destroy him who holds the power of death—that is, the devil—and free those who all their lives were held in slavery by their fear of death." Astonishingly strong language, we may think—the devil destroyed! (The

Greek verb is the same one Paul uses in 1 Cor. 15:26 with reference to Christ's destroying death, the last enemy, at the resurrection.) Does not this same New Testament tell us that "your enemy the devil prowls around like a roaring lion looking for someone to devour" (1 Peter 5:8)? Yes, it does; and what Peter says is true. But notice the kind of language the writer to the Hebrews uses to describe Christ's victory over Satan at the cross, so eternally significant does he see that victory to be.

In 1 John 3:8 we read that "the reason the Son of God appeared was to destroy the devil's work." In the context John is saying that if you are doing the devil's works, then you are showing yourself to be on the side of a defeated enemy. Christ is the conqueror. If you are truly Christ's, you will not be engaged in the devil's works.

In other words, the New Testament emphasizes two climactic points in Christ's victory over Satan: victory at the cross, and victory at his second coming. We must ask, then: Is that two-climax structure preserved in Revelation 20:1–10? Or do we have introduced here a new feature that requires a significant revision of that basic New Testament perspective? Are we now to adopt an outlook that sees *three* climactic focal points: (1) victory at the cross and the resurrection; (2) victory at Christ's second coming and the inauguration of his millennial reign; and (3) a final victory at the end of the Millennium?

As we examine the passage, we find good reason to suggest that Revelation 20 does not present such a modification of the consistent New Testament perspective. Rather, Revelation 20:1–10 is a figurative representation of Christ's victory over Satan at each of the two climactic points.

At the cross Satan is bound—but not absolutely. Revelation 20:2–3 does not say that Satan is bound, period. He is bound in one respect only, namely, "to keep him from deceiving the nations [the Gentiles] anymore." The age of salvation for the Gentiles has arrived. Prior to Christ's ministry Israel was the one nation called out from all the nations of the world to know God's blessings and to serve him. There were exceptions, of course—those who came to know God's grace even though they were not of the children of Abraham after the flesh. But essentially all the nations on this earth were in darkness, under Satan's deception. But then, praise God! Christ came and accomplished his redemptive work. On the day of Pentecost the Holy Spirit was poured out "on all people" (Acts 2:17), signifying the fact that the gospel of Christ is a gospel for all the nations, not just the Jewish people. The age of world missions had begun, and Satan's deceptive work on that grand scale over so many centuries had come to an end. The risen Lord himself gave his apostle this commission (Acts 26:17–18):

> I am sending you to them [the Gentiles] to open their eyes and turn them from darkness to light, and from the power of Satan to God, so that they may receive forgiveness of sins and a place among those who are sanctified by faith in me.

Before leaving the reference in Revelation 20 to the binding of Satan, there is one additional text worth noting. Many Christians sincerely believe that to say that Christ bound Satan at the cross, in any sense, is inconsistent with Satan's present and real activity. But consider the picture presented in Jude 6 (cf. 2 Peter 2:4):

> And the angels who did not keep their positions of authority but abandoned their own home—these he has kept in darkness, bound with everlasting chains for judgment on the great Day.

What does this mean? Does it mean that all Paul's language about our wrestling against the forces of demonic darkness (Eph. 6:11–12) is so much rhetorical window dressing? The demons are in chains, after all. There is no real struggle for the Christian in this life, right? Wrong! Jude's statement does not mean that at all. It does not mean that these fallen angels are not active. It means that they are active within the scope of God's permission, and it means that their final destiny is assured.

We might well ask, then: If Jude, by the Spirit's inspiration, can describe all of these demonic beings as in everlasting chains now, why should it be thought that to interpret Satan's being bound as a reference to what is true now is somehow inconsistent with Satan's present activity? This is scriptural language, no more contradictory of Satan's present activity than Jude 6 is contradictory of the present activity of the whole host of fallen angels.

(5) In Revelation 20:8 we have a reference to "the battle." The Greek text has the definite article ("the"), and it is impor-

tant not to lose that, because we read about "the battle" at other points in the book of Revelation. In 16:14, for example, we read: "They are spirits of demons performing miraculous signs, and they go out to the kings of the whole world, to gather them for the battle on the great day of God Almighty." And in 19:19: "Then I saw the beast and the kings of the earth and their armies gathered together to make war [in the Greek text the noun with the definite article appears here, lit., 'the battle'] against the rider on the horse and his army."

In 16:14 kings are called forth to *the battle*. In 19:19 the beast and the kings of the earth come forth to *the battle*. In 20:8 Satan leads his host up to *the battle*. It seems clear that these three texts describe not three battles but one. The new point revealed in 20:8 (because Revelation never repeats itself merely for the sake of repetition; something new is revealed each time) is what happens to Satan as a result of this battle. Chapter 19 records what will happen to the beast and the false prophet as a result of their defeat in this battle. Here in 20:10 we learn what will happen to Satan. The verses in between 19:19 and 20:10 take us back to the first coming of Christ and to the binding of Satan resulting from his redemptive work.

(6) We come now to the parenthetical scene of verses 4–6 about the reign of the saints, where the veil separating heaven from earth is drawn back, and we are given a glimpse of the saints of God reigning with Christ. Note that there is no reference in these verses, directly or indirectly, to earthly things or earthly affairs. As a matter of fact, in terms of its vocabulary this vision is most similar to the other heavenly visions in Revelation.

Let me explain. In 20:4 is a reference to "the souls" (*psychai*). That word can be used in the New Testament to refer simply to "people." In the Greek text of Acts 2:41, for example, we read that three thousand *psychai* were saved on the day of Pentecost. In such a statement there is no emphasis on the "soul" aspect as opposed to the "body" aspect of the human person. But in the context of Revelation 20:4, where John sees "the souls of those who had been beheaded because of their testimony," a contrast between soul and body does seem to be intended.

There is also reference here to thrones. Throughout Revelation the throne of Christ and his people is always in heaven.[42] In

---

[42]See 1:4; 3:21; 4:5; 6:16; 7:9ff.; 8:3; 12:5; 14:3; 16:17; 19:4–5; 20:4, 11; 21:5; 22:1, 3.

3:21 this specific promise is given: "To him who overcomes, I will give the right to sit with me on my throne, just as I overcame and sat down with my Father on his throne." Revelation 20:4 pictures the fulfillment of that blessed promise.

Verses 4–6 are a vision of the reign of Christians with their Savior after they depart this life and as they await Christ's second coming, the resurrection, and eternal bliss. The saints are pictured as martyrs for their Lord. Perhaps this picture represents all God's people. In the visions of Revelation "all are either ideal saints or ideal sinners."[43] Note that in verse 5 the martyrs are contrasted with "the rest of the dead"—those who will know "the second death." In other words, they are contrasted with *all* unbelievers.

In verse 5 we read that "the rest of the dead did not come to life until the thousand years were ended." The point John is making is not that they will live then. Rather, he is emphasizing that the unbelieving will not enjoy this wonderful blessing that the saints enjoy, the wonderful blessing of living and reigning with Christ throughout the thousand years. Remember what we said earlier, when we were considering Romans 11:25, about the eschatologically terminating force of that "until" phrase. Remember also what we said, when considering 1 Corinthians 15:22, about the rich salvation significance of life in Christ, that life that is life indeed. As our Lord told us in John 5:29, only "those who have done good will rise *to live* ... those who have done evil will rise *to be condemned*" (emphasis added).

We are told in Revelation 20:6 and 14 that the only thing awaiting these dead after the thousand years is "the second death." It is not that John denies that they will be resurrected bodily to face the judgment (v. 13). But he never describes the unbelieving as "the living" or as "the resurrected." Their names are simply not written in "the book of *life*" (v. 15, emphasis added). Even as they stand before the great white throne in judgment, they are described as "the dead" (v. 12).

In other words, John's picture is not that believers live at Christ's coming and unbelievers live at the end of the Millennium. The unbelievers *never truly live*. Believers live and reign with Christ for a thousand years. The rest of the dead, John says,

---

[43]William John Dey, *The Message of the Book of Revelation* (London: Oxford Univ. Press, 1924), 10.

do not enjoy this wonderful blessing. They do not experience life throughout these thousand years. What will they experience instead? The second death.

In verses 5–6 John speaks of "the first resurrection." Clearly this phrase implies a second resurrection. But does this mean that premillennialism is correct after all, that there will be two resurrections, the resurrection of believers at Christ's coming and the resurrection of unbelievers a millennium later? Not at all. The reference to the first resurrection implies a second, true—a second resurrection for the same people! Similarly, "the second death" (v. 6) implies a first death—but also for the same people, the unbelievers.

We might say that the believer in Christ will experience one death and two resurrections. The first resurrection occurs when he or she departs this life and is immediately ushered into the presence of Christ to reign with him. The second resurrection will be bodily at Christ's second coming, when believers are made ready for the eternal state (1 Cor. 15:50). Unbelievers, by contrast, will experience just one resurrection—and that a resurrection unto condemnation—but they will know two deaths. The first death is psycho-physical on this earth. The second death will be eternal, following the judgment.

The apostle John, however, does not speak of the believer knowing death at all!—or of the unbeliever knowing resurrection. As Meredith G. Kline notes:

> Just as the resurrection of the unjust is paradoxically identified as "the second death" so the death of the Christian is paradoxically identified as "the first resurrection." ... What for others is the first death is for the Christian a veritable resurrection.[44]

(7) Revelation 20, then, presents a broad panorama of the gospel age, God's purposes on earth and the blessing of his people in heaven, followed by a vivid account of the Last Judgment and the consummation. But what is the significance of the number "one thousand"? We may readily assume that the number is symbolic, for numbers are used symbolically throughout Revelation. But what is the meaning of the symbol? It is impossible to be

---

[44]Meredith G. Kline, "The First Resurrection," *Westminster Theological Journal* 37 (Spring 1975): 371.

dogmatic on such a matter, but the suggestion of Geerhardus Vos is certainly an interesting one:

> The symbolism of the one thousand years consists in this, that it contrasts the glorious state of the martyrs on the one hand with the brief season of the tribulation passed here on earth, and on the other hand with the eternal life of the consummation.[45]

John's vision is given by the Spirit for the edification and strengthening of God's people in all ages. By it Christians are encouraged to fight the good fight (2 Tim. 4:7), having every assurance that in Christ they will overcome the evil one to reign with their Savior.

God's people in every age have been saved "in hope" (Rom. 8:24). The hope of the old covenant saints was oriented to the coming of God's promised Redeemer. The riches of the Messiah's person and his saving work were graphically portrayed to them in terms of the central elements in their religious experience: the land of Canaan, the city of Jerusalem, the throne of David, the temple, and the nation of Israel itself.

Because he is God incarnate, truly God and truly man, in Jesus the two principal lines of Old Testament messianic expectation converge: (1) the promise that the Lord himself will come and reveal himself as Lord (e.g., the prophecy of Isa. 40:3 of a voice calling in the desert to "prepare the way for the LORD" is fulfilled in the ministry of John the Baptist preparing the way for Jesus [Matt. 3:1–3]); and (2) the promise that the Lord will send his anointed Servant. In Jesus both lines of eschatological expectation converge. He who is "the Lord's Christ" (Luke 2:26) is at the same time "Christ the Lord" (Luke 2:11).

As those "on whom the fulfillment of the ages has come" (1 Cor. 10:11), we Christians now have the inestimable privilege of knowing the fulfillment of that Old Testament hope. Because of the finished work of the crucified and risen Lord Jesus Christ and the ministry of the Holy Spirit he poured out on the church at Pentecost, we experience all the wonderful blessings of life in union with Christ.

---

[45]Geerhardus Vos, "Eschatology," *The International Standard Bible Encyclopedia* (Chicago: Howard-Severance, 1915), 987.

But we continue to walk by faith and to live in hope. Consummation day still lies ahead. Perfection of blessing for Christ's people will come only when Christ himself appears "a second time, not to bear sin, but to bring salvation to those who are waiting for him" (Heb. 9:28). That "glorious appearing of our great God and Savior, Jesus Christ" (Titus 2:13) will initiate the grand finale of redemptive history: the resurrection of believers, the resurrection of the unbelieving, judgment for all, the new heaven and new earth, and the inauguration of the final kingdom of God, the blessed eternal state of the redeemed. This is "the blessed hope" of the church, and by that hope we are sustained to serve our God in love and in joy through every trial until all our hope is fulfilled at the return of our Savior.

A POSTMILLENNIAL RESPONSE TO ROBERT B. STRIMPLE

Kenneth L. Gentry Jr.

COMMENDATION AND APPRECIATION

I would like to begin my response to Dr. Strimple by expressing my appreciation for his fine chapter in our study. His insightful theological analysis and lucid writing style furnish us with a succinct and cogent case for amillennialism—*much of which I as a postmillennialist affirm.* In fact, since we are both from the Reformed theological tradition, we agree on a great number of issues. I was particularly impressed with his presentation of Christ as the fulfillment of the typology of Israel, the land, Jerusalem, David, and the temple. He is surely correct when he observes that "the proper interpretation of Old Testament prophecy" is a "crucial factor" in the eschatological debate.

In the short space available I will offer a two-pronged postmillennial response.

GENERAL DIFFERENCES AND SHORTCOMINGS

As I reflect upon Strimple's presentation I wonder if the "already/not yet" hermeneutical principle should have as its theological corollary: "almost/but not quite." So much of his analysis is right on target—*as far as it goes.* But he stops short of what I believe to be logical conclusions. And these conclusions define the differences between Strimple's amillennialism and my postmillennialism. I will provide a few illustrative samples, then focus on a fundamental disagreement with his presentation.[1]

Because of his overlooking their original contexts, Strimple, like Blaising, runs into trouble with Isaiah 65:17 and Revelation 21:1. As I note in my response to Blaising, the new heavens and new earth that Isaiah and John have in mind are *present* realities consequent upon the first advent of Christ.[2] After all, Isaiah speaks of the presence of sin and death (Isa. 65:20), while John demands the temporal nearness of his new creation (Rev. 22:6). In speaking of a *present* "new creation," these texts expect a cosmic-revolutionary impact for Christ's redeeming work; they expect postmillennial gospel success.[3]

Were Strimple to follow his own exegetical direction, he would become a postmillennialist on his view of Isaiah 2. He notes that Isaiah 2:2–4 "is being fulfilled *now*." My exposition of Isaiah 2 notes that Isaiah strongly projects the worldwide dominance of redemption: Christianity will be "established" and "raised" above its competitors (v. 2), "all nations will stream to it" (v. 2), and universal peace will prevail because of it (v. 4).

Were Strimple to follow his own exegetical direction, he would become a postmillennialist on his view of Ezekiel 47. He understands Ezekiel's temple with its ever-deepening water flowing from the altar as *a present reality*. He even quotes a portion of 47:9: "where the river flows everything will live." This powerfully underscores the postmillennial hope, as I mention in my closing paragraph in my chapter above.

Were Strimple to follow his own exegetical direction, he would become a postmillennialist on his view of Psalm 2. He sees the beginning of the fulfillment of Psalm 2 in the first century. My exposition of Psalm 2 notes that David strongly projects

---

[1] I refer the reader to my original postmillennial presentation, which emphasizes several of the biblical texts Strimple mentions, and to my response to Blaising, which alludes to some of Strimple's other passages.

[2] We discover revelation on the *consummational* new creation in 2 Peter 3. See my *He Shall Have Dominion: A Postmillennial Eschatology*, 2d. ed. (Tyler, Tex.: Institute for Christian Economics, 1997), 308–15.

[3] For more detail, see ibid., 373–78. See also John Jefferson Davis, *Christ's Victorious Reign: Postmillennialism Reconsidered* (Grand Rapids: Baker, 1986), 37–38; John Calvin, *Commentaries on the Book of the Prophet Isaiah*, trans. William Pringle (Grand Rapids: Eerdmans, 1948), 4:397–401; E. W. Hengstenberg, *Christology of the Old Testament* (McLean, Va.: MacDonald, rep. n.d.), 2:392–400.

the worldwide dominance of redemption: the nations will be his "inheritance" (v. 8); the Lord will "dash" his opposition "to pieces like pottery" (v. 9); world kings and judges are therefore warned to "serve the LORD with fear" (vv. 10–11).

Were Strimple to follow out his own exegetical direction, he would become a postmillennialist on his view of 1 Corinthians 15. He argues for the sequential fulfillment of the data here. My exposition of this passage notes that Paul strongly projects the worldwide dominance of redemption: Christ now reigns and "must reign until he has put *all* of his enemies under his feet" (v. 25, emphasis added). Only then will he hand "over the kingdom to God the Father" (v. 24).

In each of these four examples of what I call "differences and shortcomings," Strimple effectively *begins* a postmillennial exposition, but then he cuts short his exegetical inquiry before realizing the force of the glorious historical hope expressed therein.

As I have noted elsewhere,[4] the contemporary-historical nature of postmillennialism's optimistic hope sets it apart from premillennialism and amillennialism. Both of these pessimistic alternatives lack relevant contemporary-historical hope in three different aspects. (1) As systems of gospel proclamation each teaches the gospel of Christ will not exercise any majority influence in the world before Christ's return. (2) As systems of historical understanding each holds that the Bible teaches there are prophetically determined, irresistible trends downward toward chaos in the outworking and development of history. (3) Therefore, as systems for the promotion of Christian discipleship each dissuades the church from anticipating and laboring for wide-scale success in influencing the world for Christ during this age.

SPECIFIC DISAGREEMENT AND RESPONSE

In his most important section Strimple provides an amillennial exposition of Romans 11 and Revelation 20. Since I deal with Revelation 20 in both my original presentation and (in more detail) in my response to Blaising, I will concentrate here on his exposition of Romans 11.

---

[4]Kenneth L. Gentry Jr., *The Greatness of the Great Commission: The Christian Enterprise in a Fallen World*, 2d. ed. (Tyler, Tex.: Institute for Christian Economics, 1993), 147.

Initial Observations

Strimple notes that both postmillennialism and premillennialism see Romans 11 as prophesying a future mass conversion of Israel. Indeed, in his footnote 36 he lists several noted postmillennial commentators promoting this view (Hodge, Godet, Haldane, Shedd, and Murray). He observes that such an exposition "by itself" is not contra-indicative to amillennialism, in that many amillennialists hold this view (e.g., Vos and Grenz).

Furthermore, he (correctly, I believe) notes that Paul "says not a word about a return of the Jews to the Promised Land or about a millennial kingdom in which Christ will reign from his throne in Jerusalem." These omissions certainly seem damaging to Blaising's dispensational schema; they are tantamount to Sherlock Holmes's dog that did not bark. What better place for Paul to mention the millennial reign from Jerusalem? But Paul is deafeningly silent.

Crucial Observations

I will summarize, then briefly respond to what I deem to be five key points made by Strimple in his exposition of Romans 11.

(1) Strimple argues that "Romans 11 deals with the place of Israel in the redemptive purposes of God at the present time, not at some future time." Paul is *not* "pointing to a future time" at all but rather "to the present." He urges us to "note especially the three times the word 'now' appears in" verses 30–31, which indicates "the apostle's concern in chapter 11 is not to predict the future but to explain the motive and the purpose of his present ministry." Indeed, "the amillennialist can 'relax' as he or she studies this passage, knowing that millennial positions are not at stake."

Response: (a) Strimple contradicts himself. How can he claim that "millennial positions are not at stake" when he presents Romans 11 as an "insuperable objection" against postmillennialism? If true, millennial positions *are* at stake. Moreover, despite his vigorous denial of the future orientation of Romans 11, he notes that Paul's use of *plērōma* (vv. 12, 25) "is a term with full and rich consummation significance," and that Paul's "until" phrase stretches *all the way up to* the end of the present age," thereby "reaching the eschatological goal." These clearly future-oriented observations contradict Strimple's present-only limitation.

Interestingly, the future prospect is strong enough in Romans 11 that in an amillennial work cited by Strimple himself, Ridderbos chastises another amillennialist for downplaying it: "It seems to me that Berkouwer, in *The Return of Christ*, takes altogether too little account of the future element in Paul's pronouncements."[5]

(b) Strimple misunderstands Paul's use of *nyn* ("now"). Paul sets "now" in contrast to the past ("at one time," *pote*, Rom. 11:30), not the future. As Cullmann reminds us, Christ is the center point of history, dividing it into two parts.[6] Paul's contrast is between the B.C. era and the A.D. era, between the past (before Christ's incarnation) and the present (after his incarnation). Our eschatological future up to the Second Advent is continually unfolding in the present era—the "now" time.[7] No additional redemptive-historical era remains (such as the premillennialist's Millennium) for the temporal fulfillment of prophecy; the "now" time will witness the fulfillment of all remaining temporal prophecies (see my postmillennial chart in my response to Blaising). Before Christ came, the Gentiles were "without hope" (Eph. 2:12), but "now" he has come to save them (Eph. 2:13–18). So naturally Paul speaks of his "now" ministry, his ministry in the final, preconsummational, redemptive-historical age, as Romans 11:30 makes clear. Thus, contrary to Strimple, Paul *is* pointing to the future—though it is a part of the "now" time.

(c) Strimple misses an implication of Paul's structure. Paul hints at sequencing in his use of "now."[8] The presently operating

[5]Herman Ridderbos, *Paul*, trans. John Richard de Witt (Grand Rapids: Eerdmans, 1975), 359, n. 71.

[6]Oscar Cullmann, *Christ and Time: The Primitive Christian Conception of Time and History*, trans. Floyd V. Filson, 3d ed. (Philadelphia: Westminster, 1964), 17.

[7]Paul refers to this "now" time elsewhere in such a way as to include *all* of the present era up to the end, not just his own day: "For he says, 'In the time of my favor I heard you, and in the day of salvation I helped you.' I tell you, now is the time of God's favor, now is the day of salvation" (2 Cor. 6:2; cf. Eph. 2:3; 2 Tim. 1:10; Heb. 9:26). The "now" time is also the "last days" (Acts 2:16–17, 24; 1 Cor. 10:11; 2 Tim. 3:1; Heb. 1:1–2; 9:26; 1 Peter 1:20; 1 John 2:18), the fullness of time (cf. Mark 1:15; Gal. 4:4).

[8]Though not crucial to the debate, I disagree with Strimple's argument for including the third *nyn* in the text (see his footnote 33). The UBS text includes the third *nyn* in brackets and with a C rating in its textual-critical apparatus. This rating indicates "the Committee had difficulty in deciding which variant to place in the text." In fact, bracketed words are not "completely certain" (Kurt Aland et al., eds., *The Greek New Testament*, 4th ed. [New York: United Bible Societies, 1994]). The Tasker text omits the third *nyn*.

"now" time witnesses Jewish disobedience and Gentile conversion; the remaining future portion of the "now" time will eventually witness the return of Israel to God. Paul does not know the *duration* of the present Jewish "hardening," though he anticipates its conclusion in the "now" period. It may be prolonged, as suggested in his settling for saving only "some" (v. 14) in his lifetime. Admittedly, Paul is relating his present ministry concerns, but he does so in a context informed by the past (vv. 2–4) and oriented to the future. We find the future tense in Romans 11:26, one of the verses of special interest: "And so all Israel *will* be saved."[9]

(2) Strimple insists that Paul is not setting up a future-oriented temporal sequencing of events running from Israel's fall, then to the conversion of the Gentiles, and then to Israel's conversion. He insists that *kai houtōs* ("and so" in the statement "and so all Israel will be saved," v. 26) does *not* refer "to temporal sequence": "The combination of Greek words Paul uses here [*kai houtōs*] is never used to refer to temporal sequence ('and then . . .') but always to refer to either a logical relationship or the manner by which something is done." In other words, Romans 11 does not teach that "*after* the fullness of the Gentiles has been realized," then Israel "will be converted."

Response: Strimple overstates his exegetical case. Despite his universal negation ("never") and affirmation ("always"), *houtōs* clearly can suggest temporal sequence, even though this is not its fundamental meaning. (a) As competent a Greek scholar as Bruce declares: "It should suffice to point out the well attested use of Gk. *houtōs* ('so,' 'thus') in a temporal sense."[10] Indeed, many noted commentators accept the outright temporal significance of the term (M. Stuart, C. K. Barrett, E. Käsemann, B. Corley), while others allow its temporal nuance here (O. Michel, J. D. G. Dunn, R. Schmitt, A. Feuillet).[11]

---

[9]On Strimple's amillennial present-time, nonsequential analysis (see below), we should expect Paul to use a present participle rather than the future passive indicative (*sōthēsetai*).

[10]F. F. Bruce, *The Epistle of Paul to the Romans*, Tyndale New Testament Commentaries (Grand Rapids: Eerdmans, 1963), 222. H. A. W. Meyer, *Critical and Exegetical Handbook to the Epistles to the Corinthians* (Edinburgh: T. & T. Clark, 1877), ad. loc., lists the following examples from classical writings: Thucydides 3.96.2; Xenophon, *Anabasis* 3.5.6; Democritus 644.18; 802.20.

[11]Noted in Douglas Moo, *The Epistle to the Romans* (Grand Rapids: Eerdmans, 1996), 719, n. 38.

(b) In 1 Corinthians 11:28 Paul writes: "But let a man examine himself, and so [*kai houtōs*] let him eat of the bread and drink of the cup" (NASB). Indeed, some major versions translate this usage temporally: "A man ought to examine himself *before* he eats of the bread and drinks of the cup" (NIV). "Examine yourselves, and *only then* eat of the bread and drink of the cup" (NRSV).[12] Temporal sequence likewise seems clear in other texts (Acts 17:33; 20:11; 1 Cor. 14:25).

(c) In Romans 11 *houtōs* (v. 26) obviously correlates with *achri* ("until," v. 25), suggesting a temporal function: "Israel has experienced a hardening in part *until* the full number of the Gentiles has come in. And *so* all Israel will be saved" (pers. trans.). The linking of these two particles suggests a temporal connotation for *kai houtōs* (see comments below on *achri*).

(d) Though denotatively the modal character of *houtōs* means "in this manner," connotatively *in this context* it implies a succession of time. Regarding Israel, Paul is satisfied to "save *some* of them" (v. 14, emphasis added) while recognizing that *eventually* "all Israel will be saved" (v. 26). Though admittedly the Greek term *houtōs* does not reflect bare temporality, yet here it bespeaks a remarkable temporally conditioned means of development: Israel's falling, then the Gentiles' arising, and finally Israel's return (see below). Even Strimple notes: "It is this process (which has been graphically described as 'a wave motion') that is the unifying theme of verses 11–32." In other words, a "process" leads to "all Israel" being saved (whatever that means), thus requiring a temporal flavor for *houtōs*. After all, the antecedent hardening of Israel gives rise to the Gentile mission. Since the salvation of the Gentiles provokes envy (v. 14) in Israel, that which "provokes" necessarily precedes what is provoked. Consequently, Paul's whole scenario in this chapter is temporally conditioned: *first*, Israel's fall and hardening, *then* the Gentiles' salvation, *then* Israel's saving. It is "because of their transgression [that] salvation has come to the Gentiles" (v. 11), which will eventually work to the salvation of "all Israel" (v. 26).

(3) When Paul writes: "Israel has experienced a hardening in part *until* the full number of the Gentiles has come in" (v. 25),

---

[12]See also *The New Testament in Modern English* (Phillips), *The New Testament in the Language of Today* (Beck), *The New English Bible*, and *The New Testament in Modern Speech* (Weymouth).

Strimple writes that the word "until" does *not* speak of "a new situation that will exist after the end of the present age but rather with the situation that will exist before the end, *and all the way up to* the end of the present age," which reaches to "the eschatological goal." This "hardening until" is an "eschatologically terminating" experience, so that "the hardening on the part of ethnic Israel will continue right up until the full number of the Gentiles has come in."

Response: (a) Let me begin by noting that at this point a major difference arises between Strimple's amillennialism on the one hand, and both premillennialism and postmillennialism on the other.[13] Strimple denies any further hope of salvation to Israel as a corporate mass; their hardening "will exist . . . all the way up to the end." This seems anticontextual in that Paul concludes his argument by praising God (11: 33–36) after noting in verse 32 that "God has bound all men over to disobedience *so that he may have mercy on them all*" (i.e., Jew and Gentile, emphasis added). This simply restates his earlier principle: "There is no difference between Jew and Gentile—the same Lord is Lord of all and richly blesses all who call on him" (10:12). Strimple allows salvation to the Gentiles, but only divine hardening on Israel as such—up to the very end of history. On his analysis, it would seem that in God's eyes, there *is* a difference between Jew and Gentile.

(b) Strimple overstates his case for the phrase *achri hou* ("until," v. 25). For one thing, he implies (surely by accident) that postmillennialists assert Israel's conversion on the basis that it may "simply be read into the 'until' phrase itself." Postmillennialism does not "simply read" into this phrase Israel's conversion; rather, postmillennialism considers the whole contextual flow (e.g., vv. 11–12, 15) in light of Paul's concluding declaration "and so all Israel will be saved" (v. 26). Strimple well knows this for he deals at length with verse 26.

---

[13]Allis provides a helpful eschatological sorting device for us to understand millennial positions. To classify a position we need to know both the *nature* and the *chronology* of the millennial period. If its nature involves massive cultural influence, then the position may be either premillennial or postmillennial. If its chronology has Christ returning *after* the millennium, it may be either amillennial or postmillennial. Once these two questions are resolved, we can properly classify one's millennial view (O. T. Allis, *Prophecy and the Church* [Phillipsburg, N.J.: Presbyterian and Reformed, 1945], 4).

(c) Strimple argues that the "common usage" of *achri hou* "is not with a new situation that will exist" afterward but with the situation that will exist "*all the way up to* the end of the present age" as an "eschatological goal." This seems more a theological assertion than an exegetical observation. Actually, the New Testament phrase *achri hou* often implies a change of circumstances that have nothing to do with eschatology, his four samples notwithstanding.[14] Notice the implied change of circumstances in four noneschatological samples of *achri hou*:

> Luke 1:20 (NRSV): "But now, because you did not believe my words, which will be fulfilled in their time, you will become mute, unable to speak, *until* the day these things occur."
>
> Luke 17:27: "People were eating, drinking, marrying and being given in marriage, *up to* the day Noah entered the ark. Then the flood came and destroyed them all."
>
> Acts 1:1–2: "In my former book, Theophilus, I wrote about all that Jesus began to do and to teach *until* the day he was taken up to heaven, after giving instructions through the Holy Spirit to the apostles he had chosen."
>
> Acts 27:33: "And *just before* dawn, Paul urged them all to eat. 'For the last fourtenn days,' he said, 'you have been in constant suspense and have gone without food—you haven't eaten anything.'"

Clearly, *achri hou* can imply temporal succession leading to changed circumstances. Indeed, when Paul mentions Israel's "fullness" (vv. 12, 25) and "all Israel" (v. 26), these references, according to Strimple, look "to the completion of that process and its result." Morris even uses this phrase as evidence of the *temporary* nature of Israel's hardening.[15]

(4) According to Strimple, when Paul mentions Israel's "fullness" (vv. 12, 25) and "all Israel" (v. 26), he is merely looking "to the completion of that process and its result," not predicting "a future conversion of national Israel." Rather, Paul's

---

[14]Indeed, Moo (*Romans*, 71, n. 30) notes that twenty-five of the forty-eight appearances of *achri* end with a reversal of circumstances.

[15]Leon Morris, *The Epistle to the Romans* (Grand Rapids: Eerdmans, 1988), 420.

concern is different; he is answering the "apologetic problem" of Jewish unbelief in light of their sovereign divine election. The apostle resolves this problem by explaining that "election and nationality are not equally inclusive." He does so by giving "a series of illustrations to show that mere physical descent from Abraham did not guarantee the possession of the blessings promised to Abraham."

Response: Here, of course, we come upon a fundamental disagreement between postmillennialism and amillennialism. (a) Certainly *part* of Paul's resolution to this "apologetic problem" notes that individual Israelites cannot claim convenantal protection irrespective of personal disbelief. Paul's warning involves a serious call to faith. *But this is not the whole of Paul's answer.*

(b) Were Paul simply speaking of the fullness of the number of the elect, as per Strimple, his argument would be tautological: All the elect will be saved, which is to say all the elect are elect. Where is the "mystery" (v. 25) in this? Furthermore, the meaning of "Israel" would shift its meaning between verse 25b (where it clearly means the whole people) and verse 26a (where Strimple suggests it means only the elect among the whole people).

(c) As Paul concludes his treatment of Jewish unbelief, he carefully structures his climax with a twofold crescendo implying double resolution to the apologetic problem. He argues that Israel's fall is neither *complete* (there is a present remnant, vv. 1–10) nor *final* (there is a future hope, vv. 11–32). Notice the distinct units of thought in Romans 11: Both sections begin with *legō oun* (vv. 1a, 11a; lit., "I say therefore"). Both are followed by a question expecting a negative answer (introduced by *mē*, vv. 1b, 11b). Both potentialities are emphatically denied (*mē genoito*, vv. 1c, 11c). Both end with a collection of Old Testament passages (vv. 8–10, 26–27).

Paul's fundamental apologetic concern regards Israel as a whole: "his people" (v. 1), "his people, whom he foreknew" (v. 2). The Old Testament clearly assumes the whole of Israel as God's people.[16] If Paul's answer was that God would save only a remnant, then he could not emphatically declare God's promise continues intact to "his people." Why would Paul change his

---

[16]Deut. 4:37; 7:7–8; 10:15; 14:2; 1 Kings 3:8; Ps. 33:12; 105:6, 43; Isa. 41:8, 9; 44:1; Amos 3:2.

concern—from the whole people to the remnant of the people—at the very point where he offers a direct denial of the failure of God's promise to his people?

The question opening the second section is: "Again I ask: Did they stumble so as to fall beyond recovery? Not at all!" (v. 11a). The purpose of Israel's fall was emphatically not to reduce Israel's numbers before God, but "rather, because of their transgression, salvation has come to the Gentiles to make Israel envious" (v. 11b). Strimple's view is that the second phase simply continues the argument of the first phase, despite Paul's careful exhibition of a twofold argument. If verse 26 ("all Israel will be saved") is simply saying the same thing, then Paul's climax is anticlimatic: "There is a remnant."

(d) Paul expresses a clear interest in Israel as a whole, that is, in her numerical fullness,[17] for he refers to Israel as "his people" (v. 1), clearly speaking of the corporate people as such. In its context Paul sets the phrase "all Israel" (v. 26) over against the "remnant" (v. 5), "others" (v. 7), "some" (v. 17), and "part" (v. 25). He also parallels it with "fullness" (*plērōma*, v. 12). It is Israel's rejection as a whole that Paul contrasts to her "acceptance" (v. 15). These contextual observations strongly suggest the numerical reversal of Israel's fortunes in redemptive history. Since Paul's concern is that the race of Israel is failing of the promise in his day, it would seem the race of Israel must also return. Interestingly, ancient Jewish thought in Paul's day uses the phrase "all Israel" to designate the numerical mass of Israel, minus certain disreputable classes (*Mishnah*, Sanhedrin 10:1).

(e) In verse 28 Paul implies that the promise for Israel is for the whole of Israel, which eventually will include even "the rest" though currently in unbelief: "As far as the gospel is concerned, they are *enemies* on your account; but as far as election is concerned, *they are loved* on account of the patriarchs" (emphasis added). Thus, the people as a whole relate to the patriarchal promises, though currently they stand in rebellion. Indeed, the "stumbling" (v. 11a), "transgression" (vv. 11b, 12a), and "loss"

---

[17]Hodge informs us that the view he presents (and I am defending) is the view "generally received in every age of the church, with the exception of" the Reformation; the Reformation shift was due to "extravagances of the millenarians" (Charles Hodge, *Commentary on the Epistle to the Romans* [Grand Rapids: Eerdmans, rep. 1955 (1886)], 371).

(v. 12b) are the nation's as a whole. By parity of reasoning, then, so must be her "fullness": "But if their transgression means riches for the world, and their loss means riches for the Gentiles, how much greater riches will their fullness bring!" (v. 12). Paul even argues that if the first part is "holy" ("set apart"), then so must be the whole (v. 16). To properly draw the antithesis, we must reckon with the numerical contrasts and implications.

(f) In verse 12 Paul refers back to the "hardened" mass of Israel (vv. 7–10), showing that *their* hardening will not be forever: "But if *their transgression* means riches for the world, and their loss means riches for the Gentiles, how much greater riches will *their fullness* bring!" (emphasis added).

(g) By all appearance Paul's argument is a fortiori. If something bad like Israel's fall leads to the good of Gentile conversions, how much greater, then, will be Israel's conversion! If the negative brings positive blessing, how much more will the positive bring even more positive blessing! To expect Israel's continued hardening until the end undercuts Paul's dramatic presentation.

(5) Strimple confidently observes that this process explanation presents "an insuperable objection" against postmillennialism when we consider the question: "How can such an age follow after both the fullness of the Gentiles and the fullness of Israel have come in?" This is because "with the bringing in of the fullness of both Israel and the Gentiles, God's redemptive purposes will be accomplished." In fact, on the basis of Romans 11:15 Strimple notes of the saving of "all Israel" (v. 26) that, when it occurs, "Resurrection Day will have arrived!"

Response: Strimple asks how an age can follow after the fullness of both the Gentiles and Israel. The answer appears simple: The state of affairs in the first century (and even to the present) has the majority of both Gentiles and Israel in opposition to God. But once the Gentiles are saved in full number (in this continuing age), then the Jews will return to God in full number;[18] upon completing this "wave action" the world as such will be saved.

This does not, however, entail an each-and-every universalism. Consequently, a threefold task remains: (a) Continue proclaiming the gospel to the lost, though they are now a minority.

---

[18]Paul's reference to the Gentiles' coming in (v. 25) seems a clear example of entering the kingdom of God, entering salvation: cf. Matt. 5:20; 7:13, 21; 18:3; 19:23; 23:13; Mark 9:43, 45, 47; 10:15, 23–25; Luke 13:34; 18:17, 24; John 3:5; Acts 14:22.

(b) Sustain the majoritarian influence of Christianity on succeeding generations through family nurture, Christian education, and gospel proclamation. (c) Develop the cultural implications of the Christian worldview in all of life on a scale theretofore unknown. History no more has to end simply because the race is saved than we must die when we are saved. Strimple's view is tantamount to arguing that once you are saved, there is nothing left to do.

Though Strimple interprets verse 15 as referring to the eschatological resurrection, most scholars see it as a metaphor for radical spiritual transformation. It refers to the enormous spiritual-moral transformation occurring in the world as mass revival sweeps the bulk of the human race into the kingdom of God. After all, Ezekiel portrays Israel's spiritual renewal and return from captivity as a resurrection (Ezek. 37);[19] the Lord relates the recovery of the prodigal son to his family as a resurrection (Luke 15:24). In fact, our individual salvation is likened to a resurrection (John 5:24; 1 John 3:14). Indeed, Paul frequently refers to "life" or "being alive" as the new life in Christ,[20] just as he also speaks of "death" as a spiritual condition.[21] Now think of the implications of millions of conversions throughout the world!

---

[19]Many commentators agree, such as Reformed commentators Raymond B. Dillard and Tremper Longman III: "Ezekiel clearly looked for a new exodus, a return from exile, a new covenant, and a new heart and spirit for the restoration community (36). The revival of the nation would be like the resurrection of the dead (37)" (*An Introduction to the Old Testament* [Grand Rapids: Zondervan, 1994], 324). Edward J. Young speaks of "the vision of the dry bones and the glorious statement that the children of Israel shall be returned to their land" (*Introduction to the Old Testament* [Grand Rapids: Eerdmans, rev. 1964], 246). See also John B. Taylor, *Ezekiel: An Introduction and Commentary*, Tyndale Old Testament Commentaries (Downers Grove, Ill.: InterVarsity, 1969), 234–36. Of Ezekiel 37:1–14 dispensationalist John F. Walvoord comments: "God promised to restore Israel, and in the strongest possible terms indicated that He would bring new life to her, that she would be restored as a nation, that she would be indwelt by the Holy Spirit, and she would settle in her own land in safety" (*Prophecy Knowledge Handbook* [Wheaton, Ill.: Victor, 1990], 186). Charles Dyer agrees: "The reviving of the dry bones signified Israel's national restoration" ("Ezekiel," in John F. Walvoord and Roy B. Zuck, eds., *The Bible Knowledge Commentary: Old Testament* [Wheaton, Ill.: Victor, 1985], 1298).

[20]Rom. 5:18; 6:4, 10–11, 13; 8:6, 12–13; 10:5; 2 Cor. 2:16; 5:15; Eph. 4:18; Phil. 2:16.

[21]Rom. 6:11, 13; Eph. 2:1, 5; Col. 2:13.

A PREMILLENNIAL RESPONSE TO ROBERT B. STRIMPLE

Craig A. Blaising

I appreciate the work that Robert Strimple has done in presenting us with an argument for amillennialism. I wish to comment on several points and draw a general conclusion.

At the outset, let us note that Strimple appears to confuse premillennialism with classical dispensationalism. I have shown in my article that while classical dispensationalism is one form of premillennialism, the two terms cannot be simply equated. For the sake of the reader, let me point out that premillennialism per se does not teach that the future intermediate kingdom will be characterized by a return to old covenant conditions including the Levitical sacrificial system. In fact, it is hard to find present-day dispensationalists who teach this. Why? Because of the progress of divine revelation given in Christ to the effect that his priesthood and his sacrifice abolish the former system.[1] This principle of progressive revelation is crucial to premillennialism, but it is one that Strimple's amillennialism does not fully accept.

In the first section of his article, Strimple argues that the New Testament interprets Old Testament eschatological realities in such a way as to exclude premillennialism. But his argument is confused and unconvincing for several reasons.

(1) Strimple uses an argument that in its traditional form presupposes a spiritual-vision view of eschatological reality. The

---

[1]See, for example, Mark F. Rooker, "Evidence From Ezekiel," in Donald K. Campbell and Jeffrey L. Townsend, eds. *A Case for Premillennialism: A New Consensus* (Chicago: Moody, 1992), 119–34, esp. 132–34.

argument is this: The New Testament interprets the earthly and national features of Old Testament eschatology as spiritual realities. Premillennialism, which requires an earthly fulfillment of these hopes, is thereby precluded by the very hermeneutic that the New Testament employs. Strimple's version of this argument echoes many of its common themes. For example, he refers to the earthly features of Old Testament covenant and promise as "images," "shadows," and "copies" that will disappear when the "reality" they signify is revealed. Elsewhere, however, Strimple uses the language of new creation eschatology, which I have shown is not incompatible with premillennialism. His vacillation between these two eschatological models weakens his argument against premillennialism and leaves his actual view on the final state unclear.

(2) A historical, grammatical, literary, and contextual study of the texts Strimple presents fails to support his argument. Certainly, the New Testament uses the Old Testament in many interesting ways. These have been analyzed in many works on the subject. But, the New Testament does not "transcendentalize" Old Testament eschatology. It reaffirms the reality and basic structure of Old Testament eschatology even as it gives new revelation about the Messiah, about an inaugural fulfillment of certain features of that eschatology, and about additional features of the eschatological pattern.

For example, Strimple argues that in Romans 4:13, when Paul says that Abraham and his descendant(s) will inherit the world, this shows that the fulfillment of the land promise to Israel transcends the literal terms of that promise. But a closer examination of Romans 4 shows that this is not the case. Paul does not refer to the land promise when he says that Abraham and his descendant(s) will inherit the world, but rather to the promise given in Genesis 17:5 that Abraham would be the father of many nations. (Genesis informs us that Abraham literally was the father of many Gentile nations.)

Furthermore, the logic of Paul's argument takes in the point that Abraham's descendants would be as numerous as the stars in the sky and the dust of the earth. The great multitude and cosmic reference apparently led Paul to the point that Abraham and his descendant(s) would inherit the world. But there is no thought that the specific land promised in Genesis 13, 15, and so on will be missing from that world. Rather than "transcending" the promise, New Testament revelation complements it in such a way as is compatible with the structure of the Old Testament text itself. Finally, note that there is nothing in this discussion of the nature of the inheritance that Abraham and his descendant(s) will receive that precludes premillennialism.

Strimple cites texts from Hebrews to show that the language of Old Testament promise is transcended by a heavenly fulfillment. However, he fails to appreciate fully Hebrews' futurist eschatology. While Strimple recognizes that the heavenly city to which we are now related (Heb. 12:22–24) is "coming" in the future (13:14), he does not observe that Hebrews also speaks of a coming world (2:5). The coming of the city is not the coming of heaven as a final fulfillment of promises that the Old Testament placed on the earth, but the coming of the eschatological city from heaven to the future world, just as John also foresaw in Revelation 21. And this fully harmonizes with Paul's statements about our present relationship to a heavenly city (Gal. 4:26; Phil. 3:20) on the one hand and about a renewed creation in which our resurrection glory will be manifest (Rom. 8:18–25) on the other.

For its part, the Old Testament also predicts a future Jerusalem of great glory in a new creation (Isa. 60; 65). The New Testament adds to this the fact that since our King, Messiah Jesus, has ascended into heaven, his present heavenly dwelling is our present capital city. But in the future, just as Jesus will come to earth for the final fulfillment of his kingdom (Acts 1:11), so the city that is now in heaven likewise will come to that eschatological world. The New Testament does not "transcend" Old Testament expectation of a glorified Jerusalem in the future kingdom of glory on this earth, and there is nothing here that is inimical to premillennialism.

I agree with Strimple that the New Testament presents Christ as Israel, but not in a way that "transcends" or removes the idea of corporate, ethnic, national Israel. Israel is not just a "shadow" of the Christ that is done away with once the true reality of his presence arrives. I must be brief, but I believe a careful study of Scripture demonstrates this truth. (1) The New Testament presentation of Christ as Israel flows from the structure of the covenants. The Davidic covenant organized the seed of Abraham into a monarchy and concentrated the roles of Israel as Yahweh's Son and Israel as the mediator of blessing especially in the person of the anointed king (2 Sam. 7:8–16; 1 Chron. 17:4–14; Ps. 2; 72; Luke 1:68–79; Gal. 3:14). It hardly seems necessary to say that never is there any thought that this kind of structure will somehow eliminate the reality of the nation itself.

(2) The oracles of Isaiah, rather than leaving a confused picture about the national versus individual identities of the Servant of Yahweh, actually present the solution within themselves, although Strimple makes no reference to it. Isaiah 49 shows that the servant "Israel" will bring national Israel back to God and also extend Yahweh's salvation to the ends of the earth (49:5–6). Isaiah 53 teaches that "he" (the Servant) bears "our" (Israel's) iniquities. The point in both passages is the restoration and salvation of the corporate Servant by the action of the individual Servant.

(3) The New Testament presents Jesus as the Christ, the King of Israel, in whom Israel's history is "recapitulated" (as Strimple has said), and as the Servant who bears the sins of many. But there is no thought that Israel as a national entity has disappeared from God's eschatological plan. Jesus preaches the kingdom to Israel and ascends with the promise that he will restore the kingdom to Israel at his return (cf. Acts 1:3, 6–7; 3:19–21 [cf. 3:18–26]).

Many studies have noted that the term *Israel* is consistently used in the New Testament in an ethnic, national sense.[2] "Israel" is never used of the church per se despite the application of Israel typology to the church in many passages. Hence, Strimple's expositional use of the phrase *true Israel* is technically incorrect and misleading. True, Galatians 3:29 says that all of us in Christ, Gentile believers included, are Abraham's descendants. Remember that Paul in Romans 4 traced the Abrahamic paternity of Gentile believers to the Genesis 17 promise that Abraham would be the father of many nations. In Galatians 3, he develops his argument from the promise that "all nations will be

---

[2]R. Meyer is typical in his remark: "Israel (17 times) [in Pauline literature] stands for either the historic people or the eschatological whole Israel but significantly not for Paul's own community" ("Israel ...," in *The New International Dictionary of New Testament Theology*, ed. Colin Brown [Grand Rapids: Zondervan, 1976], 2:315).

blessed through you" (3:8), and from the particular way in which "in you" refers to the Messiah. The Old Testament itself develops the covenant theme of mediation ("in you") in terms of the Davidic king (the Anointed One or Messiah; cf. Gen. 22:18 with Ps. 72:17). Paul does not develop the idea of Gentile paternity in Abraham from "through Isaac . . . your offspring will be reckoned" as he does for "Israel" in Romans 9. When Paul used the phrase "Israel of God" in Galatians 6:16, he did not refer to Jews *and Gentiles* in Christ, but (as G. C. Berkouwer has admitted) to Jewish Christians.[3] This fits Paul's use of "Israel" in Romans 9–11.

A consideration of Roman 11 must be brief. Many recent studies have been published on Romans 9–11 confirming the point that Paul speaks of the future of national Israel.[4] Contrariwise, Strimple's exposition follows what S. Lewis Johnson Jr. has termed "the Dutch interpretation," found in the works of G. C. Berkouwer, Herman Ridderbos, and William Hendriksen.[5] Basically, the Dutch view argues that Romans 9–11 deals not with the salvation of national Israel in the future but with the salvation of a Jewish remnant in the present.

This Dutch interpretation contrasts two things that in Paul are intimately connected. Note first of all that Strimple admits that "[the true] Israel" in Romans 9:6 refers to believing Jews as a subset within "Israel" and not to a combination of Gentile and Jewish believers. It is these Jewish believers whom Paul takes back to the covenant promise, "through Isaac . . . your offspring will be reckoned." Then let us observe, as Strimple does not, that from this point on Paul uses the term *Israel* consistently of the nation as a whole. The nation is composed of two parts, the elect remnant and the rest, who are hardened, who have stumbled. The nation as a whole failed to attain to the promised blessing because of the extent of the partial hardening. What Strimple and the Dutch interpretation fail to note is the theme of the *reversal* of the national condition. Israel as a whole has fallen from

---

[3]G. C. Berkouwer, *The Return of Christ*, trans. Jas. Van Oosterom (Grand Rapids: Eerdmans, 1972), 344.

[4]J. Lanier Burns cites many of these studies in his detailed article, "The Future of Ethnic Israel in Romans 11," in C. Blaising and D. Bock, eds., *Dispensationalism, Israel and the Church: The Search for Definition* (Grand Rapids: Zondervan, 1992), 188–229.

[5]S. Lewis Johnson Jr., "Evidences From Romans 9–11," in *A Case for Premillennialism*, 211–12, 214–15, 217–19.

favor because a partial hardening has set in. But the promise of an elect remnant points to a time when "all Israel will be saved."[6]

This reversal theme begins in Romans 11 with the observation that God's preservation of a remnant of Jewish believers indicates that he has not rejected "his people." The Old Testament prophetic context for this discussion relates the promise of future national blessing to the presence of a believing remnant during the time of exile and judgment. The presence of the remnant does not eliminate or fulfill in some transcendental way the promise of national blessing made by covenant. Rather, the remnant's existence is tied to the hope of a *return* of God's favor to the *nation*.

Likewise, Paul moves from the idea of the present existence of a remnant of faith to the future salvation of all Israel in accordance with covenant promise. Whereas in his present ministry he seeks the salvation of "some of them" (Rom. 11:13–14), provoked by the jealousy of Gentile salvation, he also foresees their "fullness" (11:12). Whereas a partial hardening has occurred, "all Israel will be saved" (11:25–26). The *all* stands in contrast to the part such that when the all are saved, there will be no large part that is hardened. Usage tells us that the expression *all Israel* means national Israel as a whole.[7] The future tense in "will be saved" points to this salvation as a future reality. The "and so" (which as Strimple notes is most likely taken in the sense of "in this manner") in 11:26 indicates *how* this will come about. That *how* looks in two directions: the immediately preceding point (11:25) of the fullness of the Gentiles coming in (*not* the remote idea of a part of Israel being saved in the present) and the immediately following explanation—"as it is written"—of the fulfillment of covenant promises to Israel at the future coming of Christ.

Consequently, Paul uses the term *Israel* to refer to ethnic Jews, a believing remnant of which anticipates the salvation of the nation as a whole at the return of Christ. He does not "transcend" Old Testament prophecy but reaffirms its expectations even as he adds to it the new revelation of mysteries relating to the interadvent period (cf. also Eph. 3:1–13). Finally, there is

---

[6]Johnson agues this case effectively (ibid., 199–223).

[7]Meyer, "Israel," 2:312–13; Johnson, "Evidences From Romans 9–11," 215; Burns, "The Future of Ethnic Israel in Romans 11," 212–13.

nothing here that by nature excludes a millennial phase of Christ's eschatological kingdom.

In his second section, Strimple claims that the New Testament, minus the book of Revelation, does not teach a millennial kingdom and definitely rules out the possibility of a millennial kingdom. The first point is not surprising. Most premillennialists have argued that only in the book of Revelation is the millennial kingdom *explicitly* revealed. But by his second point, Strimple seeks to preclude the possibility that even Revelation teaches premillennialism. Scripture cannot contradict Scripture. If previous Scripture teaches that premillennialism is impossible, then no reading of Revelation can teach premillennialism.

But is it true that the simple descriptive pattern of Second Coming events in New Testament eschatology rules out the possibility of a multiple-stage fulfillment? No! Why? First of all, because it has happened before. Think of what the Lord told Moses in Exodus 3:17: "I have promised to bring you up out of ... Egypt into the land of the Canaanites...." Are we to think that because no forty-year interval appears between "out of Egypt" and "to the land of the Canaanites" that therefore such an interval is impossible? With respect to Christ, the prophets predicted that a Messiah would be born, grow up, and rule over a glorious kingdom forever (see Isa. 9:6–7; 11:1–10). Should we assume that those simple and singular descriptions make an interadvent period of more than two thousand years impossible?

In 2 Samuel 7:12–13, the Lord promised David that after his death, he would raise up David's son and establish his kingdom forever. Was it clear at that time, as Scripture later tells us, that this promise relates to a line of kings descended from David?[8] Was it possible within the language of that promise for the line to be interrupted and the kingdom of David's son to be absent from the earth for a time? Was it possible within the language of that promise for the kingdom to be inaugurated centuries later with the resurrection and ascension of one of David's descendants and yet be fulfilled in an everlasting sense only after a couple of millennia? If all of this is possible in the language of that simple promise to raise up David's son and give him an everlasting kingdom, is it impossible that that kingdom might come not just in two stages (inaugural and final) but three (inaugural, millennial, final)?

---

[8]See 1 Kings 8:20–24; 15:4–5; 2 Kings 8:19; 2 Chron. 13:5; 21:7; 23:3.

We could cite many more examples of this, but the point is that the pattern of prophetic fulfillment should alert us to the possibility that simple promises may be fulfilled through some complex temporal sequence. In 1 Peter 1:10–12, it was not the *nature* of prophetic promises that puzzled the prophets, as amillennialists would have us believe. Rather, it was the specific identity of the Messiah and the *time* of prophetic fulfillment. We need to be open to the Lord's own revelation as to how he will fulfill his promises in time and not impose restrictions of our own devising before the canon is closed.

If we turn specifically to the texts Strimple cites, we can see that the possibility of sequenced fulfillment lies within a contextual understanding of each passage. John 5:28–29 speaks of the *hora* ("hour") in which all will be resurrected. But 1 John 2:18 says that it is *now* the last hour. If the eschatological hour can be extended over two thousand years, it is not impossible that a thousand years might transpire between the resurrection of the just and the resurrection of the unjust.

Second Thessalonians 1:5–10 speaks of several events that will happen "in that day." But the Day of the Lord is not an instantaneous event in Scripture. As to the possibility that the punishment meted out by Christ could take place in two stages separated by time, we need only to remember the pattern revealed in Isaiah, that while in Isaiah 2 the punishment appears in the singular, in Isaiah 24 the punishment consists of immediate destruction for some and imprisonment for others with punishment following "after many days." I have already drawn attention to how Revelation 19–21 follows the pattern of Isaiah 24–25.

All the events of 1 Thessalonians 1 are likewise included within the sequence given in John's visions. Briefly, we should note that there is nothing in Romans 8 that prevents the glorification of creation from taking place in stages (cf. Isa. 25 and 65). As for 2 Peter 3:10, 12, the syntax does not require Strimple's claim that everything happens at the inception of the Day of the Lord.

In 1 Corinthians 15, Strimple admits that the *epeita . . . eita* sequence ("then . . . then") in verses 23–24 can mark a sequence of long intervals. It is therefore not the case that a Millennium is impossible here. But his conclusion that in these verses the "end," the resurrection of believers, and the Second Coming are all simultaneous misses some features of the text. (1) The word "end" (*telos*) in 1 Corinthians does not necessarily mean the moment of the Second Coming, as we can see in 10:11.

(2) The language of victory over death at the resurrection of believers in 1 Corinthians 15:54–56 does not preclude a subsequent resurrection for unbelievers since this language is applicable to each stage of resurrection (as 2 Tim. 1:10 shows us in the case of Christ's own resurrection). Strimple does not see this because he is misled by Berkouwer into overlooking the logical and structural significance of "but each in his own turn" in verse 23—*stages* of resurrection *are* a point of emphasis in this text.

(3) Strimple misses the significance of 1 Corinthians 15:25–28 for the meaning of the making of *all* alive in stages. These verses grammatically explain "the end" as the last stage of resurrection. The end must be the resurrection of unbelievers since at the "end" death is completely abolished. (Even Strimple acknowledges that the resurrection of believers at the second stage leaves the resurrection of unbelievers unaccounted for.) The complete abolishment of death must logically entail a reversal of state for those who are dead at that time. Since the first two stages have been separated as events in history, it is not impossible that the second and third stages may be temporally separated as well.[9]

Finally, we come to Revelation 20. Contrary to Strimple, earlier revelation has not ruled out in advance a millennial kingdom. Ironically, Strimple has fallen into the very trap in which he thinks dispensationalists have been snared—he has failed to allow later revelation to add to and clarify the hope previously revealed. Confident that he already knows that an intermediate kingdom is impossible for God, he "squeezes" and "forces" John's revelation to fit a predetermined pattern.

But, we ask, is this proper? Moreover, considering that this book is a late revelation from the Lord himself to the churches

---

[9]An excellent analysis of this text can be found in Wilber B. Wallis, "The Problem of an Intermediate Kingdom in 1 Corinthians 15:20–28," *Journal of the Evangelical Theological Society* 18 (1975): 229–42. Also see D. Edmond Hiebert, "Evidence from 1 Corinthins 15," in *A Case for Premillennialism*, 225–34. We also need to note that a distinction in the stages of resurrection is also indicated in Paul's characteristic expression "resurrection *from* the dead" (see Phil. 3:11, emphasis added). This expression implies the notion that some are raised from the dead while others are left in a state of death. Jürgen Moltmann sees this as a key feature in biblical millennialism (*The Coming of God: Christian Eschatology*, trans. Margaret Kohl [Minneapolis: Fortress, 1996], 195–99).

(Rev. 1:1; 22:16), with the admonition that the words are "faithful and true" (22:6), we ask, is this wise? Should not one be open to what the Lord himself says about how (i.e., the manner and time) he will fulfill those things that he has previously revealed, especially as it is the most detailed explanation given on the topic?

My exposition of Revelation 20 provides the critique of Strimple's interpretation. The reader is directed to those remarks. For the sake of brevity, let me just note two things. (1) With respect to the judgment on Satan in Revelation 20:1–10, contextual interpretation shows that John's vision is *not* about the binding of the devil at the time of Jesus' crucificion but about an imprisonment at the Second Advent, which halts his activity of deceiving the nations. Revelation 20:1–3 cannot be skipped in trying to determine what happens to the devil at the Second Coming. The battle of 20:8 should not be identified with the battle of 19:19 on the basis of the Greek article to the exclusion of the literary context as a whole. The context tells us that the devil was imprisoned at the Second Advent; then, after a thousand years, he was expelled into hell.

(2) Strimple's view of the saints' coming to life and reigning with Christ is problematic. (a) Strimple has ignored Revelation 5:10, which promises a future reign on the earth. (b) It is *not* true that dead saints are enthroned in heaven elsewhere in John's visions. (c) Strimple's approach leaves Revelation with only a reference to the bodily resurrection of unbelievers (he sees this in 20:13). In his view, the book has no clear statement on the bodily resurrection of believers (he goes to 1 Cor. 15:50 for the resurrection of believers). (d) There is no basis in Scripture for speaking of "resurrection" in the way Strimple does.[10] Scripture knows of no "making alive" of believers subsequent to regeneration and prior to bodily resurrection. Certainly, Scripture says that believers will "depart and be with Christ" at death (Phil. 1:23), but nowhere in Scripture is the death of the believer

---

[10]Strimple uses the phrase "resurrection of the [*or* our] body." This usage is congenial to his idea that there is a resurrection of the soul (after regeneration and at death) that is distinguishable from the resurrection of the body. But this is not biblical language. Scripture never speaks of *resurrection* of the body but rather of "resurrection of the dead" or "resurrection from the dead." The redemption of our bodies (Rom. 8:23) occurs at our resurrection from the dead. To distinguish for the dead a resurrection of the body from a resurrection of the soul is not biblical.

described as a "coming to life." Such an interpretation should cause us concern, for it moves dangerously in the direction of denying the bodily resurrection altogether.

In summary, I find Strimple's argument for amillennialism unconvincing. The issues he raises (i.e., the New Testament interpretation of the Old Testament, the express teachings of New Testament eschatology, and key texts such as Romans 11 and 1 Corinthians 15) are not incompatible with the later revelation of a millennial kingdom between the Second Coming and the Final Judgment. And Strimple has not offered compelling reasons for disregarding the grammatical, literary, and contextual interpretation of John's vision in Revelation 20 that discloses that millennial kingdom in the divine plan.

Chapter Three

PREMILLENNIALISM

Craig A. Blaising

PREMILLENNIALISM

Craig A. Blaising

A BRIEF DEFINITION
OF PREMILLENNIALISM

The two most central convictions of premillennialists about the future can be stated in relation to the word *premillennial*. The foremost conviction is that Jesus is coming back. All hopes and expectations for the future are focused on his return. His coming will be *pre-*, that is, *prior to*, a millennial kingdom.

Obviously, then, the second central conviction has to do with the *millennial* part of *premillennial*. This is the belief that after Jesus comes, he will establish and rule over a kingdom on this earth for a millennium, that is, for a thousand years.

We can fill in the picture of premillennialists' beliefs about the future by asking how they relate the resurrection of the dead, the Final Judgment, and the eternal destinies of the saved and the lost to the Second Coming and the Millennium. Premillennialists believe that when Jesus comes, he will raise the dead in two stages. First, he will raise some to participate with him in the millennial kingdom. After the Millennium (the thousand-year period) is over, he will raise the rest of the dead and institute the Final Judgment. Then will come the final and eternal destinies of the saved and the lost.These future expectations are common to all premillennialists. They can be diagrammed as shown on the following page.

One major difference among premillennialists today concerns the doctrine of the Rapture. This doctrine is taught in

PREMILLENNIALISM

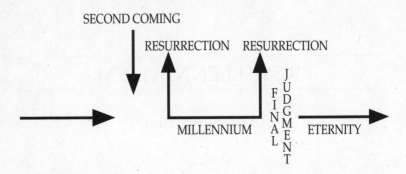

1 Thessalonians 4:13–18, to the effect that when Christ comes, he will resurrect believers who have died and will "catch up" those believers who are still alive (apparently transforming them into glorified bodies; cf. 1 Cor. 15:51–58) to meet him in the air. Being caught up with the Lord per se is not a matter of dispute among evangelicals. The issue has to do with whether the Rapture is temporally distinct from, or is a temporal phase of, the Second Coming.

Only certain premillennialists make this distinction. There are two such positions—(1) *pretribulationism* and (2) *midtribulationism*—which hold that the Rapture will take place either (1) before or (2) in the midst of a period of apocalyptic woe and distress prior to the second coming of Jesus (a period known as the Tribulation). Since all premillennialists believe that Christ's second coming will occur after the tribulation, pretribulationists and midtribulationists necessarily affirm two comings or two stages of the one second coming of Christ. *Posttribulationists* are premillennialists who believe that the Rapture and the Second Coming are not distinguishable temporally. They believe that both occur in the one event of Christ's second coming, which will transpire at the end of the Tribulation. These tribulational views can be illustrated as shown in the chart on the following page.

The rationale for these different tribulational views has been stated elsewhere.[1] It is not possible to review that discus-

---

[1]Much has been written on the various tribulational views. A helpful presentation and critical interaction can be found in Richard R. Reiter et. al., *The Rapture: Pre-, Mid-, or Post-Tribulational?* (Grand Rapids: Zondervan, 1984).

TRIBULATIONIST POSITIONS

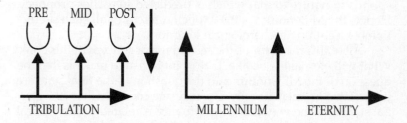

sion here. In what follows, I will focus on the Millennium and the eternal state of the saved.

As we will see, the basic structure of premillennial belief is taken from John's vision of the return of Jesus and a Millennium subsequent to that return in the book of Revelation. The premillennial view focuses especially on the sequence of Christ's return followed by a millennial kingdom as well as the exegetical meaning of that Millennium (including its before and afterwards resurrections), which John describes in his visions recorded in Revelation 19:11–20:10. The premillennial interpretation of these verses is well known; I will later attempt to present it with some detail and in the context of an overall interpretation of Revelation.

Most premillennialists are quick to acknowledge that a thousand-year kingdom transpiring between the coming of Christ and the Final Judgment is explicitly found only in Revelation 20. Nevertheless, they would argue that the Millennium is compatible with or an aspect of the broadly based biblical theme of a coming eschatological kingdom of God. As a matter of progressive revelation, the Millennium adds to and helps to harmonize the broader biblical teaching. Some premillennialists, however, have argued that earlier canonical teaching about a coming eschatological kingdom refers precisely to the millennial kingdom John envisioned.

The difference between these two positions lies in an understanding of the eternal state. The former argument identifies the eternal state with the final fulfillment of the eschatological kingdom of God predicted throughout the Bible. Such an interpretation is consistent with the repeated prediction of that kingdom as being everlasting. The latter argument relates all such prophecy to the Millennium because it believes that the eternal state is radically different from the nature of the eschatological kingdom as that kingdom is set forth in Scripture. Only the Millennium corresponds in nature to that which is predicted in earlier prophecy. Hence, the Millennium is the explicit referent of all such predictions of a coming eschatological kingdom.

All of this raises for us the second major concern of this book: What will eternal life be like? The point I wish to make is that the question of the Millennium and the question of the final state are interrelated hermeneutically. The way one conceptualizes the eternal state and the way that conceptuality is related to the biblical teaching on a coming eschatological kingdom conditions how one will look at John's prophecy of a coming Millennium. Amillennial and postmillennial rejections of premillennialism traditionally have had more to do with a preunderstanding of what is "proper," "fitting," or "plausible" in relation to their traditional expectations about eternal life than with any specific biblical teaching contradicting the premillennial coming of Christ.

In what follows, I intend to examine two models for conceptualizing eternal life. Then, I intend to explore how these models have functioned in the history of interpretation and what role they have played both in the demise of premillennialism in the patristic era and the emergence of modern premillennialism in post-Reformation Protestantism. Following that, I will attempt to demonstrate the harmony of premillennialism with a biblical theology of the kingdom of God and the necessity of premillennialism from the standpoint of a literary and grammatical interpretation of the book of Revelation.

TWO MODELS OF ETERNAL LIFE

There are a number of variations on the common Christian belief that those whom Christ redeems will receive eternal life. As to where eternal life will be "lived" and as to what it will be like, the views can be grouped into two basic models, which I call the *spiritual vision* model and the *new creation* model.[2] I will

---

[2]An interpretive model is a heuristic device for comprehending complex views. Models are used to study theological views on a number of doctrinal issues. The spiritual vision and new creation typology I have chosen is consistent with many analyses of Christian eschatology. Finer distinctions can be drawn beyond what I have presented here. The reader might want to compare my categories to those of Colleen McDannell and Bernhard Lang, *Heaven: A History* (New Haven: Yale Univ.

describe these models first, and then we will see how they have arisen and what traditional bearing they have in Christian thought.

The Spiritual Vision Model

The *spiritual vision model* of eternity emphasizes biblical texts promising that believers will see God or receive full knowledge in the future state of blessing. It notes that Paul speaks of the Christian life in terms of its heavenly orientation, and adds to this the biblical description of heaven as the dwelling place of God, as the present enthroned position of Christ, and as the destiny of the believing dead prior to their resurrection.

In the history of the church, many Christian theologians have claimed that the final state of the resurrected will be in heaven. The way in which they have described it draws not only on biblical themes such as we have mentioned but also on cultural ideas common to the classical philosophical tradition. That tradition has contributed to the spiritual vision model in three basic convictions: (1) a basic contrast between spirit and matter; (2) an identification of spirit with mind or intellect; and (3) a belief that eternal perfection entails the absence of change. Central to all three of these is the classical tradition's notion of an ontological hierarchy in which spirit is located at the top of a descending order of being. Elemental matter occupies the lowest place.

In the spiritual vision model of eternity, heaven is the highest level of ontological reality. It is the realm of spirit as opposed to base matter. This is the destiny of the saved, who will exist in that nonearthly, spiritual place as spiritual beings engaged eternally in spiritual activity.

The perfection of heaven in the spiritual vision model means that it is free of all change. This changelessness is contrasted with life on the material earth. While changelessness means freedom from death and decay, it also means the absence of development or growth. It means freedom from temporal and historical

---

Press, 1988); and H. Paul Santmire, *The Travail of Nature* (Philadelphia: Fortress, 1985). Comparison should also be made to the typologies of Christian conceptions of the kingdom of God given in Benedict T. Viviano, *The Kingdom of God in History* (Wilmington, Del.: Michael Glazier, 1988); and Howard A. Snyder, *Models of the Kingdom* (Nashville: Abingdon, 1991). Snyder (15–24) offers a helpful overview of the idea of models and their use in theology for those who desire further introduction to them.

change, such that the arrival of eternity (or better, one's arrival in eternity) is characterized as the end of time and history.

Following the classical tradition's identification of spirit with mind or intellect, the spiritual model views eternal life primarily as cognitive, meditative, or contemplative. With this point of emphasis, the place or realm of eternal life is really a secondary or even inconsequential matter. In its essential reality, eternal life is a state of knowing. Knowing what? Knowing God, of course—and this in a perfect way, which means in a changeless manner. Perfect spiritual knowledge is not a discursive or developmental knowledge but a complete perception of the whole. The Platonic tradition spoke of it as a direct, full, and unbroken *vision* of true being, absolute good, and unsurpassed beauty. Following the biblical promise that the saints will see God, the Christian tradition has spoken of eternal life as the *beatific vision* of God—an unbroken, unchanging contemplation of the infinite reality of God.

New Creation Model

The *new creation model* of eternal life draws on biblical texts that speak of a future everlasting kingdom, of a new earth and the renewal of life on it, of bodily resurrection (especially of the physical nature of Christ's resurrection body), of social and even political concourse among the redeemed. The new creation model expects that the ontological order and scope of eternal life is essentially continuous with that of present earthly life except for the absence of sin and death. Eternal life for redeemed human beings will be an embodied life on earth (whether the present earth or a wholly new earth), set within a cosmic structure such as we have presently. It is not a timeless, static existence but rather an unending sequence of life and lived experiences. It does not reject physicality or materiality, but affirms them as essential both to a holistic anthropology and to the biblical idea of a redeemed creation. This is what is meant by the "creation" part of the label for this model.

While eternal life is essentially continuous with present existence, it is not simply an unending extension of present conditions. To be sure, there will be a significant difference in the quality of eternal life. Those who share that life will be immortal, having been freed from death through resurrection or translation. Sin will not exist. The saints will be confirmed and glorified in a holy character by the Spirit of God. As such, they will enjoy communion with God as well as with one another in the new creation. This is the "spirituality" of eternal life in the new creation model—not the absence of materiality but the full effect of the Holy Spirit's indwelling the resurrected physical bodies of the redeemed. (This is also the meaning of "spiritual bodies" in 1 Cor. 15—material bodies indwelt by and glorified by the Holy Spirit.)

Following the language of Isaiah 25, 65, and 66, of Revelation 21, and of Romans 8, the new creation model expects the earth and the cosmic order to be renewed and made everlasting through the same creating power that grants immortal and resurrection life to the saints. The nonhuman aspects of creation, both animate and inanimate, will be greatly blessed beyond the state of things prior to the transgression of Adam and Eve. This is the "new" in the "new creation" view of eternity.

While these two models are fundamentally different, they are not exact opposites. The spiritual vision model separates and contrasts the realms of spiritual and physical reality and understands the final state of blessing in terms of the former alone. The new creation model rejects the dichotomy that is crucial to the spiritual vision model and sees eternal life in a holistic spiritual and material sense. Note that we are speaking of *models* of eternal or everlasting life. The new creation model does not deny that the dead in Christ are with him now in heaven. The issue has to do with the nature of resurrection life, which the spiritual vision model sees as essentially identical with the present state of the believing dead. The new creation model, by contrast, sees the resurrection state as significantly different—as different as life is from death!

Moreover, the new creation model should not be understood as denying the hope that the saved will see God. Whereas the believing dead are in the presence of Christ now, this model expects that their vision of and fellowship with God will be enriched within the fullness of life in a new creation. The key point is that whereas the spiritual vision model abstracts spirit from matter, hierarchicalizes it ontologically, and sees perfection in a changeless, atemporal state, the new creation model affirms a future holistic creation blessed with the perfection of righteousness and everlasting life.

HERMENEUTICS AND THE TWO MODELS IN CHRISTIAN THOUGHT

Having sketched out these models, two general comments can be made about the ways in which Christians have thought about them. (1) The spiritual vision model was the dominant view of eternal life from roughly the third century to the early modern period.[3] With some variation, it still exercises considerable influence today. Ideas that we have associated with the new creation model can be found in apocalyptic and rabbinic Judaism and in second-century Christian writers such as Irenaeus of Lyons.[4] They would appear in Christian thought occasionally after the third century, but it was not until the modern era that they began to receive a broader hearing as a conceptuality that actually belongs to Scripture, and a conceptuality that is actually worthy of theological affirmation.

The long dominance of the spiritual vision model has conditioned the way Christians traditionally and habitually think and converse about eternal life. These ideas are already present in the mind of one who begins to research and study what the Bible teaches on the subject. In hermeneutics, this phenomenon is called *preunderstanding*—the understanding one has about a subject before researching it, or the understanding one has about what a text is probably saying before one begins to study it.[5] The spiritual vision model functions as the preunderstanding with which many Christians begin to study or investigate biblical teaching about our future hope.

This in itself does not mean that the spiritual vision model is wrong. Many times we find that our preunderstanding about what Scripture teaches on a subject is confirmed, deepened, and strengthened through further research and study in God's Word. But what if that preunderstanding is wrong? The problem is that

---

[3]Besides the works listed earlier, one should also note Jeffrey Burton Russell, *A History of Heaven: The Singing Silence* (Princeton: Princeton Univ. Press, 1997).

[4]Brian Daley, *The Hope of the Early Church: A Handbook of Patristic Eschatology* (New York: Cambridge Univ. Press, 1991), 5–32; Santmire, *The Travail of Nature*, 35–44.

[5]See William W. Klein, Craig L. Blomberg, and Robert L. Hubbard Jr., *Introduction to Biblical Interpretation* (Dallas: Word, 1993), 99–116.

we are inclined to favor our preunderstanding. In so doing, we are apt to pass over contrary signals in the text and try to harmonize something of what it says with our predisposed way of viewing it. When we are done, we may falsely declare our view as supported by the text, even bolstered by the illusion that we have grown in our understanding of the matter.

Is it possible to correct a false preunderstanding? Of course! But it does require a willingness to submit one's convictions to reformulation by the Scriptures. It also requires a commitment to hermeneutical practices that are conducive to that reformulation rather than insulate one from it.

(2) There are many today who believe that the spiritual vision model is neither discoverable by nor sustainable by the historical, grammatical, and literary methods of interpretation that most evangelicals consider normative. Whereas biblical terms, phrases, and patterns may be employed by the model (as we have noted in the descriptions given above), nevertheless, the essential claim about the final state of the redeemed and the descriptions of the same are found to be imported into the reading of Scripture rather than exegeted from its text.[6]

When we examine the history of Christian thought, we find that the spiritual vision model was intimately connected with practices of "spiritual interpretation" that were openly acknowledged to be contrary to the literal meaning of the words being interpreted. The long term practice of reading Scripture in this way so conditioned the Christian mind that by the late Middle Ages, the spiritual vision model had become an accepted fact of the Christian worldview. Hermeneutical justification was unnecessary. Reasonable persons (and even unreasonable ones) simply *knew* that ultimate salvation was spiritual in essence, consisting in the eternal beatific vision. The pilgrim character of life for those who wanted to be saved involved an assent to God in which the world must progressively be left behind and spiritual realities come ever clearer in view.

The fact that many evangelicals today argue for a new creation eschatology on the basis of a proper literary-grammatical

---

[6]See the helpful discussion by G. B. Caird, "The Language of Eschatology," in his *The Language and Imagery of the Bible* (Philadelphia: Westminster, 1980), 243–71. Also see Caird's argument for a new creation eschatology in his "The Christological Basis of Christian Hope," in *The Christian Hope*, by G. B. Caird et al. (London: SPCK, 1970), 21–24.

interpretation of Scripture has required nothing less than a revolution in Christian thought—a revolution that can be traced back to the Reformation. Even then, changes in Christian thinking about the future hope have occasioned piecemeal results in a number of alternative scenarios.

The variety of opinions that evangelicals hold on the Millennium also derives from the history of this hermeneutical conflict. In order to explain why evangelicals believe what they do about "the Millennium and beyond," some account must be given of the historical and hermeneutical struggle to conceptualize eternal life and harmonize the millennial vision of Revelation 20 with it.

In what follows, we will look at the hermeneutics of the spiritual vision model as it became dominant in Christian culture and also at how the Reformation introduced factors that would lead to the hermeneutical challenge of this model. We will see how the adoption of the spiritual vision model of eternal life affected the interpretation of the Millennium in Revelation 20 and how premillennialism was able to reemerge in post-Reformation thought in response to the same hermeneutical influences that also led to a new creation model of eschatology.

From Spiritual Interpretation to Christian Worldview— The Spiritual Vision Model of Eternal Life in Classical Christian Thought

The emergence of the spiritual vision model into a dominant position in Christian thought can be traced back to the profound influence of Origen of Alexandria. Origen ministered in the early third century when the church was beginning to spread more broadly into Greco-Roman society. Three features of his work were particularly attractive: (1) He affirmed the churches' basic rule of faith against Jews, pagans, and Gnostics; (2) he affirmed the metaphysical sensibilities of Middle Platonic culture, making his theology more attractive to educated classes than the new creation theology of Irenaeus; and (3) he produced extensive commentaries and homilies showing how to exposit his theology from the Scriptures.[7]

---

[7]For a general study of Origen, see Henri Crouzel, *Origen: The Life and Thought of the First Great Theologian*, trans. A. S. Worrall (San Franscisco: Harper & Row, 1989);

In his biblical studies, Origen carried forward the typology by which earlier Christians had argued that Jesus and his ministry was the fulfillment of the program and plan of God in the Old Testament. This gave his hermeneutic a traditional feel, which the church immediately recognized. However, Origen added to his typology a vertical element, which oriented the entire structure of biblical narrative to heavenly spiritual realities.[8] Typology and the literal sense by itself might lead one to new creation expectations, but the vertical allegory transcended these hopes. Origen believed that Christians needed to read Scripture in this spiritual manner, and his commentaries demonstrated how to do so from words, names, narrative relationships, and even the shapes of Hebrew letters. Furthermore, spiritual interpretation was not only supposed to reveal the spiritual vision model of salvation, it was also intended to mediate a present experience of it and thereby assist a redeemed soul in its spiritual ascent. In this way, spiritual interpretation with its spiritual vision model of final salvation was integrated into the spirituality that defined the Christian life.[9]

We can measure the response to Origen's method in the example of Augustine. In his *Confessions*, Augustine tells us that he had been embarrassed in his earlier years by what he thought

and Joseph Wilson Trigg, *Origen: The Bible and Philosophy in the Third-Century Church* (Atlanta: John Knox, 1983).

[8]On a general introduction to Origen's hermeneutic within the Alexandrian tradition see Manlio Simonetti, *Biblical Interpretation in the Early Church: An Historical Introduction to Patristic Exegesis*, trans. John A. Hughes (Edinburgh: T. & T. Clark, 1994), 34–52; Robert Grant and David Tracy, *A Short History of the Interpretation of the Bible*, 2d ed. (Philadelphia: Fortress, 1984), 52–62; and M. F. Wiles, "Origen as Biblical Scholar," in *The Cambridge History of the Bible; Vol. 1: From the Beginnings to Jerome*, ed. P. R. Ackroyd and C. F. Evans (Cambridge: Cambridge Univ. Press, 1970), 454–89. Also see the section on Origen in G. E. Lampe, "The Exposition and Exegesis of Scripture: 1. To Gregory the Great," in *The Cambridge History of the Bible; Vol. 2: The West From the Fathers to the Reformation*, ed. G. E. Lampe (Cambridge: Cambridge Univ. Press, 1969), 173–77. An excellent study on allegory in the Alexandrian tradition prior to Origen can be found in David Dawson, *Allegorical Readers and Cultural Revision in Ancient Alexandria* (Berkeley: Univ. of California Press, 1992).

[9]For a more detailed study of Origen's hermeneutics and its relationship to his understanding of spirituality, see Karen Jo Torjesen, *Hermeneutical Procedure and Theological Method in Origen's Exegesis* (Berlin: Walter De Gruyter, 1986). To put all of this in the context of eschatology, see Daley, *The Hope of the Early Church*, 44–64; Santmire, *The Travail of Nature*, 44–53; and Viviano, *The Kingdom of God in History*, 38–45.

was the literal reading of the Bible (actually a caricature formed through childhood impressions and Manichean polemics).[10] He was developing an interest in Neo-Platonism as an alternative to Manichean Gnosticism when he heard the Origenistic preaching of Ambrose.[11] It helped him to see Christianity in a completely new light, and soon he became a Christian. The spiritual vision model of eternal life he contemplated through spiritual interpretation was, he believed, confirmed in his own typically Neo-Platonic mystical visions.[12] After he became a bishop, his writings affirmed the spiritual vision model, and his homilies and commentaries promoted the practice of allegorical interpretation.[13]

In the Middle Ages, spiritual interpretation was developed and classified into various types. The vertical element of which we have been speaking was identified as anagogy (from *anagogē*, which means ascent, elevation, or a lifting up). By means of anagogy, one was supposed to contemplate heavenly realities (defined in terms of our spiritual vision model).[14]

In the sixth century, a corpus of writings attributed to Dionysius the Areopagite, promoted anagogy as part of a Christianized Neo-Platonic worldview. These writings exercised a profound influence on the medieval mind.[15] Here, anagogy was not limited to the text of Scripture. Practically anything in one's range of experience could be a starting point for anagogical contemplation. The goal was to transcend mentally the lower orders

---

[10]See esp. *Confessions*, 7.

[11]On Ambrose, see esp. Bernard McGinn, *Foundations of Mysticism* (New York: Crossroad, 1991), 202–16.

[12]On the mysticism of Augustine, see ibid., 228–62.

[13]Simonetti, *Biblical Interpretation in the Early Church*, 103–8. Santmire sees some development in Augustine's attitude toward material creation in his latter thought (*The Travail of Nature*, 55–73). Also see McDannell and Lang, *Heaven: A History*, 54–68; Daley, *The Hope of the Early Church*, 131–50.

[14]Anagogy was one of the four senses of Scripture promoted in the Middle Ages: literal, tropological, allegorical, and anagogical. The last three develop what was known as the spiritual sense. The tropological sense was the moral sense of the text. Allegory was specifically used in reference to doctrinal teachings, the rule of faith. Anagogy was the eschatological meaning of the text. See Grant and Tracy, *A Short History of the Interpretation of the Bible*, 85; Simonetti, *Biblical Interpretation in the Early Church*, 119.

[15]McGinn, *Foundations of Mysticism*, 157–82. Also see his *Growth of Mysticism* (New York: Crossroad, 1994), 80–118.

of the cosmic hierarchy and come into a mystical, ecstatic union with God. To ascend in this contemplation, one needed to negate all thoughts of known or experienced reality.[16] By its very practice, the new creation descriptions of biblical eschatology and their ontological continuity with present creation and salvation history had to be denied.

The broader practice of anagogy indicates that the spiritual vision model no longer required the support of biblical hermeneutics. It had become a fixed, accepted feature of the Christian worldview. This explains why in the thirteenth century when Aquinas and others criticized the practice of spiritual interpretation, the spiritual vision model remained unaffected.[17]

Medieval reason recognized the same hierarchy of being that previous generations found revealed to them in the spiritual sense of the Bible. Just like anagogy, reason was expected to lead one in an ascent up the ontological hierarchy to contemplate God. By an analogy of being (which incorporated a positive element missing from apophaticism) one was supposed to reason from lower orders of being to the higher order, from natural things to spiritual things, from earth to heaven. Thus, reason harmonized the spiritual vision model with literal interpretation. When literal interpretation rendered to the reader a historical narrative of God's actions with regard to earthly people, reason would take the narrative and draw a vertical correspondence to spiritual realities in heaven. When literal interpretation confronted the reader with a final state set upon a new earth, the spiritual vision model, secure in the rationality of Christian culture, controlled the observation.

The final state of blessing in that new creation could only be contemplative. If there was going to be a new earth, and even if one was to go so far with literal interpretation as to acknowledge the existence of various life forms on that new earth, reason had to say (because it accepted the spiritual vision model as a matter of principle) that their only possible purpose would be to mediate the vision of God. Redeemed humanity would

---

[16]This is what is known as apophatic theology. See Vladimir Lossky, *The Mystical Theology of the Eastern Church* (Cresswood, N.Y.: St. Vladimir's Seminary Press, 1976), 25ff.

[17]On Aquinas's critique of spiritual interpretation, see Grant and Tracy, *A Short History of the Interpretation of the Bible*, 83–91.

simply and changelessly contemplate God through those new earthly realities.[18]

Millennial Possibilities in a Spiritual Vision Eschatology

Ancient Christian premillennialism weakened to the point of disappearance when the spiritual vision model of eternity became dominant in the church.[19] A future kingdom on earth simply did not fit well in an eschatology that stressed personal ascent to a spiritual realm. Furthermore, the practice of spiritual interpretation left little to support millennialism. Old Testament promise and prophecy was converted wholesale into mystical anagogy. New Testament references to heaven were made to teach the spiritual vision model, and spiritual interpretation forced New Testament new creation language to harmonize with it. Only the book of Revelation was left as a premillennial hold-out along with certain Old Testament apocalyptic texts echoed in John's visions.[20]

With little supportive context, the book of Revelation was a conceptual anomaly on the altered landscape of Christian thought. The cognitive dissonance was so great that Dionysius, bishop of Alexandria (c. 200–c. 264), professed that he had no idea what the book was saying. A literal reading made no sense to him at all, and he hoped that soon a spiritual interpretation could be found[21]—quite a contrast from only a half century earlier, when Irenaeus, bishop of Lyons (c. 130–c. 200), expounded a canonically integrated premillennial theology stressing Revelation's own testimony that its words were faithful and true.[22]

Some tried to extend the book's isolation by excluding it from the canon altogether.[23] Most, however, were willing to work

---

[18]McDannell and Lang, *Heaven: A History*, 80–93; Santmire, *The Travail of Nature*, 84–95.

[19]On early Christian millenarianism, see Jean Daniélou, *The Theology of Jewish Christianity*, trans. John A. Baker (Philadelphia: Westminster, 1964), 377–404.

[20]On the history of interpretation of the book of Revelation, see Arthur W. Wainwright, *Mysterious Apocalypse: Interpreting the Book of Revelation* (Nashville: Abingdon, 1993).

[21]Eusebius, *Historia Ecclesiastica*, 7.24–25.

[22]Irenaeus, *Adversus Haereses*, 5.35.2.

[23]Wainwright, *Mysterious Apocalypse*, 30–34.

with it. But how could Revelation and its Millennium be made to fit conceptually with the new spiritual vision eschatology?

One alternative was simply to convert the book of Revelation into a thoroughgoing allegory of the soul's spiritual struggle and final advent to the vision of God. One might even retain premillennialism if one could convert the Millennium into a wholly contemplative state. Augustine toyed with this form of premillennialism for a while before discarding it in favor of his well-known amillennial view.[24]

A wholly spiritual reading of Revelation was not attractive to the church because it had become used to reading the book in a realistic manner. They saw their own day-to-day experiences of living for Christ in a hostile world in John's visions of conflict, death, disasters, persecution, and martyrdom. They recognized in the sequence of visions their own hope that world conditions would change. This change would come prior to the Final Judgment. It would be ushered in by the coming of Christ. He would bind the devil, who was provoking the present suffering, cast the emperor who was inflicting it into the lake of fire, raise the martyrs back to life, and reign with his saints on the earth for a thousand years before instituting the Final Judgment. The Millennium to which they looked belonged to the same order of reality as the visions of trouble and trial.[25]

The break for revisionists, however, came in the fourth century with the "Christianization" of the Roman Empire. It was now possible to argue that Christian experience had taken on a "millennial" character, thus removing the anomaly of a future Millennium from Christian hope. With the anomaly removed, nothing stood in the way of a full conversion of Christian eschatology to the spiritual vision model.

There were two ways in which the Millennium could be said to have been realized in present experience. One was the Constantinian or later Byzantine model, which saw millennial fulfillment in the imperial political order.[26] Taking this approach, one could still read John's visions in a sequential fashion, the only difference from earlier tradition being that what had been read as a sequence from the present to the future was now seen as a movement to the present from the past.

---

[24]Augustine, *City of God*, 20.7.

[25]Wainwright, *Mysterious Apocalypse*, 22–23.

[26]See Viviano, *The Kingdom of God in History*, 45–50.

Many believed that the new Christian imperial order was the fulfillment of the Millennium. And this order functioned as a type of eternal spiritual reality.[27] The trials and sufferings that in the text appear prior to the Millennium denoted the experiences of Christians under the old pagan Roman Empire. All that was past; the empire was now Christian. No future Millennium should be expected. Rather, Christians should fix their eschatological hopes completely on the beatitude of seeing God and Christ in heaven.[28]

Of course, the plausibility of this interpretation depended on whether Christian experience in the Christian empire *was actually conceivable* in terms of millennial description. The reader of the book of Revelation was obliged to compare his or her present experience with the millennial description in the text and agree that John's predictions had been fulfilled. Even if the claim seemed plausible, there was the matter of certain structural features in Revelation 19–20 that would prevent a reader from adopting the proposed interpretation—features such as the coming of Christ, the imprisonment of the devil, and a resurrection of the dead, all before the Millennium. These had to be given satisfactory explanation. But this could be done through spiritual interpretation, which would be excused by a church that was now becoming accustomed to the practice generally and was satisfied that an overall realistic interpretation—an overall interpretation in terms of Christian experience in real world conditions—had been achieved.

The other way in which the Millennium could be seen as realized in present Christian experience can be labeled the Augustinian or ecclesiastical view. In this interpretation the millennial reality was identified with the institutional church. The church now reigns with Christ and exercises power on the earth in the administration of grace.[29] Augustine put forth this view in the early fifth century as political order in the West crumbled. The advantages of his form of realized millennialism over the Constantinian view were clearly evident. The church offered a

---

[27]D. M. Nicol, "Byzantine Political Thought," in *The Cambridge History of Medieval Political Thought, c.350–c.1450*, ed. J. H. Burns (Cambridge: Cambridge Univ. Press, 1988), 52–53.

[28]Wainwright, *Mysterious Apocalypse*, 44–46.

[29]Viviano, *The Kingdom of God in History*, 51–56.

more stable institutional reality than the empire for the fulfillment of John's millennial vision.

But Augustine's view also required a more radical reading
of the book of Revelation. If the institutional church was the fulfillment of the millennial vision in Revelation 20, then the Millennium must have begun when the church first came into
existence. This means that John could not have been speaking
about a reality that was future to him when he recorded his
vision of the millennial kingdom. Yet, it seemed undeniable that
the earlier visions in John's book described real suffering and
conflict, which the church had faced prior to the conversion of
Constantine—and still faces as events since that time have
proven. How were these observations to be reconciled?

They were reconciled by rejecting the narrative-historical
sequence in John's visions. The church had not been wrong in
reading Revelation realistically; it was simply mistaken in its sup-
position that John intended a sequence in his visions leading to
a future Millennium. The correct interpretation understands that
these visions recapitulate the same events.[30] Understood this way,
Revelation presents a dialectical Christian experience that is both
persecuted and suffering, and "millennially" blessed *at the same
time*. Augustine interpreted the two cities of Revelation 17 and
21 as concurrent realities. The church is the city of God, and it fulfills John's millennial vision in Revelation 20. But the church suffers from the hostility of the world, the city of the devil, and in
that respect it experiences what John envisioned prior to Revelation 20. Because the millennial experience is now present, readers are not supposed to expect any future Millennium. They are
to focus completely on a spiritual visionary hope. Their spiritual
journey starts now in the church, the millennial blessing, and is
supposed to move to the future blessing of the beatific vision,
assisted by various mystical glimpses along the upward way.[31]

Of course, the plausibility of the Augustinian ecclesiastical
interpretation depended on convincing Christians that their present experience in the church actually is the millennial experience John envisioned, and on providing a double hermeneutical
movement that (1) rendered as simultaneous what the text

---

[30]The principle of recapitulation had appeared earlier in Victorinus. Tyconius
and Augustine popularized it (see Wainwright, *Mysterious Apocalypse*, 29).

[31]Ibid., 34–39; Daley, *The Hope of the Early Church*, 128–31, 133–34.

seems to present in terms of narrative-historical sequence, and (2) reinterpreted inconvenient textual features such as we have already mentioned—the coming of Christ, the imprisonment of the devil, and a resurrection of the dead. The latter part of this hermeneutical procedure would be accomplished by spiritual interpretation, which, as has already been noted, interiorized those aspects of the text. The first part would be achieved by proposing an overall structural interpretation in which the millennial vision is made simultaneous with its preceding visions.

The Reformation Challenge and the Possibility of New Creation Eschatology

The Reformation precipitated a revolution in Christian culture. Although the Reformers themselves did not directly challenge the spiritual vision model, they did unleash powerful currents of thought that led to both the reemergence of new creation eschatology and the reconsideration of millennialism. (1) The Reformation presented a systemic challenge to the medieval consensus of Christian thought. The challenge centered in the understanding of grace and its reception. However, a revisionary impulse was set loose that raised questions across the board. Not all of these questions manifested themselves in the sixteenth century. Rather, they surfaced in various ways down to our own time.

(2) Most important, the Reformation emphasized the authority of the Bible's literal sense in theological expression.[32] Combined with the revisionary impulse, the stress on biblical authority helped to propel an intensive program of studies in both Old and New Testament. After the Reformation, the meaning of literal interpretation developed through these studies as attention came to bear on the philological, historical, literary, and grammatical aspects of the canonical writings. This in turn has

---

[32] A brief overview of Reformation hermeneutics can be found in Grant and Tracy, *A Short History of the Interpretation of the Bible*, 92–99. Also see Roland H. Bainton, "The Bible in the Reformation," in *The Cambridge History of the Bible: The West from the Reformation to the Present Day*, ed. S. L. Greenslade (Cambridge: Cambridge Univ. Press, 1963), 1–37. Also see James S. Preus, *From Shadow to Promise* (Cambridge, Mass.: Belknap Press, 1969); Hans W. Frei, *The Eclipse of Biblical Narrative* (New Haven: Yale Univ. Press, 1974), 17–37; and David L. Puckett, *John Calvin's Exegesis of the Old Testament* (Louisville: Westminster, 1995).

led to the study of biblical theology, which focuses on theological terms and categories indigenous to and developed in the biblical texts—a corrective to cultural, philosophical ways of thought that may intrude into systematic theology and become hardened by tradition to the detriment of biblical authority.

(3) The Reformation triggered a more acute sense of the historical nature of human life. The Reformers and their successors viewed their struggle with the papacy as part of the unfolding fulfillment of biblical apocalyptic. The sense of the historical moment and its place in the flow of history was different from the symbolic view of time in medieval thought. This sense of history and the prospect of future earthly conditions different from the past came to dominate the modern mind. Most important, however, the Reformation and post-Reformation sense of historical identity was defined in relationship to *biblical* history. This at the same time reinforced the idea that biblical history was significant in its literal sense aside from allegorically symbolizing immobile heavenly realities. Furthermore, identification with the apocalyptic portion of biblical history naturally led to an explosion of studies on the book of Revelation, beginning in the seventeenth century and continuing down to the present.[33]

(4) We should not overlook the importance of the rise of modern science in the sixteenth century. The Copernican revolution and further developments by Galileo, Newton, and Boyle discredited medieval chemistry and cosmology, which undergirded doctrines about ethereal bodies and an immobile, empyrean heaven.[34] The spiritual vision model survived these assaults by rendering heaven and spiritual bodies wholly transcendent to our

---

[33]The historical reading of the visions of Revelation goes back to the early church, but it was reemphasized by Joachim of Fiore (1145–1202). The Reformation reinvigorated this approach as part of their critique of the institutional church. See Wainwright, *Mysterious Apocalypse*, 55–61. Bebbington notes the importance of the apocalyptic tradition for a Christian notion of history; see D. W. Bebbington, *Patterns in History: A Christian View* (Downers Grove, Ill.: InterVarsity, 1979),43–67. On the development of the ideas of time and history in conjunction with the reemphasis of apocalyptic in Reformation thought, see esp. Robin Bruce Barnes, *Prophecy and Gnosis: Apocalypticism in the Wake of the Lutheran Reformation* (Stanford: Stanford Univ. Press, 1988), 100–140.

[34]The empyrean heaven was thought to be a part of the cosmos, the highest level, the realm of pure light, in which the resurrected would dwell forever beholding God (who yet transcends this highest level) (see McDannell and Lang, *Heaven: A History*, 80–93).

present cosmology and physics. Heaven, as God's dwelling place, must in fact be understood as transcendent. However, the scientific revolution helped raise the possibility that biblical descriptions of the final state of the saved might be understood in a more literal manner than that which the spiritual vision model had allowed.

Developing scientific knowledge brought a greater understanding of biological life. Obviously, some of these developments brought conflict with post-Reformation orthodoxy. Moreover, they have not always been beneficial to the health and survival of the earthly life being investigated. But in spite of these conflicts, Christian as well an non-Christian worldviews have gained a greater knowledge of and greater appreciation for earthly life.

I do not have the space available to trace in more detail the modern developments of the themes of history, nature, and the literal study of Scripture. One should certainly not think that their development from the Reformation to today has been linear. Nevertheless, the history of biblical and theological study has led us to a situation today in which a new creation model is much more widely affirmed than at any time in Christian thought since the early patristic era. Also, we must note that the same factors that have led to a new creation view have contributed significantly to the rise of millennialism in the modern era.

The Reemergence of Premillennialism
in Post-Reformation Protestantism

There are two basic reasons why premillennialism reemerged in Protestant Christianity: (1) the failure of the millennial claims of Western Christendom, which opened up new options for interpreting John's millennial vision, and (2) the recovery of the literal sense of Revelation 20, along with the broader supportive context of biblical eschatology.

The Reformers rejected the millennial claims of church and state. The Pope and the institutional church were morally and spiritually corrupt, the mortal enemy of true believers. The Reformers could not in any way see them as the kingdom of Christ but rather as Antichrist. From the Reformation view of things, readers of Revelation had two choices: (1) They could decide that the Millennium had passed in an earlier period of church history and that they were living in Revelation 20:7–10, the satanically precipitated trouble just before the Final Judgment; or (2) they could reason that the Millennium had not yet come. The Reformers themselves took the former option, whereas many of their successors took the latter. But this latter option would involve a major change in the traditional way the book of Revelation had been read. For if the Millennium was indeed future, then it would have to be future within the structure of the book of Revelation itself. And that would mean that the traditional recapitulatory reading of the book would have to be significantly modified or abandoned altogether.

The millennial question was being thrown open just at the time that newly emerging Protestant scholarship was developing the Renaissance practice of reading a work in its full, literary context. With confirmation from rabbinic sources, Protestant scholars began to recover the literal sense of Old Testament narrative and prophecy, and with it, the realistic themes of a new creation eschatology—themes of material, political, and social, as well as spiritual blessing on nations, peoples, and the earth itself. A new interest in Israel—nationally and corporately—began to form in Christian eschatological thought, encouraged by the new literary understanding of the Old Testament and the discovery that Paul in Romans 11 actually predicted Israel's future salvation.

By the early seventeenth century practically all millennialists expressed the hope for the future salvation of the Jews and the renewal of Israel's national blessing. Hand in hand with this belief came the hope that national, political, and social blessings would be given to all nations. Gradually a more holistic understanding of the kingdom of God in accordance with biblical eschatology began to take shape.[35]

The idea of a future Millennium was the immediate beneficiary of this new knowledge. Features of the eschatological

---

[35]See Peter Toon, *Puritans, the Millennium and the Future of Israel: Puritan Eschatology 1600 to 1660* (Cambridge: James Clarke & Co., 1970), 23–26. Interest in the future of the Jews can also be traced in James West Davidson, *The Logic of Millennial Thought: Eighteenth-Century New England* (New Haven: Yale Univ. Press, 1977). See also Christopher Hill, "Till the Conversion of the Jews," in *Millenarianism and Messianism in English Literature and Thought 1650–1800*, ed. Richard H. Popkin (Leiden: E. J. Brill, 1988), 12–36.

kingdom in Old and New Testament theology were directly transferred to it. These features, particularly the existence of a nation of converted ethnic Jews, helped in turn to underscore the *futurity* of the Millennium (for obviously, no such nation of Christian Jews had ever yet existed). Furthermore, by relating new covenant themes to the Millennium, Protestant theologians could explore the Bible's new creation eschatology while delaying the more fundamental assessment of whether the traditional understanding of the final state needed to be revised.

Christian history had severely challenged the traditional recapitulatory reading of John's visions, and hermeneutical advances made a future Millennium a conceptual possibility. But for premillennialism, the crucial hermeneutical question had to do with those features in Revelation 19–20 that set the Millennium apart from all preceding visions—namely, the coming of Christ, the binding of the devil, and the resurrection of martyrs to reign with Christ in the millennial kingdom. Even those who preferred a sequential rather than a recapitulatory reading of John's visions tended to accept Augustine's interpretation of these features.

There were two ways that those who believed in a future Millennium could go on this question, and they constitute the two options of *postmillennialism* and *premillennialism*. The postmillennial option was to maintain as much of the traditional interpretation of Revelation 19–20 as was possible for futurism. The coming of Christ was the coming of the gospel message; the binding of the devil was his restraint, subjugation, and defeat in human lives by the gospel message; and the resurrection of martyrs was the spiritual birth that the gospel message brings. This interpretation could be accommodated to a future Millennium by postulating a future conversion of earth's inhabitants that would be different in extent from the partial results we have seen up to now. Early postmillennialists differed on whether Protestant military forces were a necessary accompaniment to Protestant preaching for the inauguration of the Millennium.

After debacles such as the Anabaptist rebellions of the sixteenth century and the English Fifth Monarchy movement of the seventeenth century, most postmillennialists opted for the gospel message alone as the means for introducing the millennial age (although we still see the more militaristic side in postmillennial interpretations of Western colonialism and of various military conflicts, such as the American Civil War). Daniel Whitby and Jonathan Edwards both popularized the idea that the Millennium would arrive by means of a great revival.[36]

Twelve centuries of reading the features of Revelation 19–20 as inner spiritual realities certainly favored the postmillennial option. But there was a deeper philosophical problem anchoring this favoritism—Augustine's classic distinction between time and eternity. The demarcation between these two was absolute. When it came to the features of Revelation 20, Augustine insisted that the bodily resurrection belonged by necessity to eternity. By definition, it could not, except in the special case of the Lord prior to his glorification, subsist in time. Thus, it was impossible for the resurrection to occur prior to the end of time. It could not be a resurrection to life on this earth as we know it. By definition, it had to be a "heavenly" existence. That, of course, meant that premillennialism was metaphysically unthinkable.[37]

Biblical eschatology, however, made it thinkable. Perhaps the resurrection appearances of Christ had greater implication than Augustine imagined. Ezekiel 37 spoke of a kingdom of the resurrected on earth. Certainly, Isaiah and Jeremiah expected Messiah to rule the nations in an eschatological kingdom. The revelation of a resurrection to Daniel also seemed to anticipate the future establishment of the earthly kingdom of God.

In 1627, Johann Alsted, a German Reformed theologian, dared to propose that Revelation 20 should be read literally. Alsted, who was thoroughly familiar with Old Testament prophecies of an eschatological messianic kingdom on earth, was living in the midst of the Thirty Years War. The realism of Old Testament kingdom prophecies regarding nations living on the earth in peace joined with his observation that Revelation 20 literally predicted the binding of the devil in national relationships. Furthermore, the literal reading clearly taught a bodily resurrection of martyrs for the purpose of reigning in that kingdom. The issue could not be spiritual resurrection since spiritual

---

[36]On post-Reformation postmillennialism see Richard Bauckham, *Tudor Apocalypse* (Oxford: Sutton Courtenay, 1978), 208–32; Toon, *Puritans, the Millennium and the Future of Israel*, 26–41. On the revivalist postmillennialism of Whitby and Edwards, see Davidson, *The Logic of Millennial Thought*, 141–75.

[37]Daley, *The Hope of the Early Church*, 131–32.

death was not in view in those verses. The bodily resurrection of those who were put to death physically for their testimony to Christ was a reward, a blessing, granted in the text to those who were faithful to him. Consequently, Alsted concluded that in Revelation 20, John actually envisioned a future kingdom on earth free from the influence of Satan, in which resurrected Christian martyrs would reign with Christ.[38]

In the same year, Joseph Mede, fellow of Christ College, Oxford, published his *Clavis Apocalyptica*, that is, *The Key of the Revelation*, as rendered in its English translation of 1642.[39] The key to understanding the book, according to Mede, was the synchronic structures that coordinated certain visions. Alsted had proposed a thoroughly sequential, chronological reading of Revelation. Mede argued that recapitulation was a feature of the book. However, contrary to Augustine, this recapitulation had to be established on literary rather than theological grounds. When that recapitulation was properly observed, it could be seen to form itself around a basic narrative sequence.

Working within the structure of John's visions, Mede came to the conclusion that the millennial kingdom had to be a future period both from John's standpoint and from that of the history of the church up to Mede's own day. The appearing of Christ in Revelation 19 had to be understood as a visible appearing prior in time to the Final Judgment of 20:11–15, one that ushers in the millennial reign of 20:1–7. The judgment of the beast and false prophet between the appearing of Christ and the millennial kingdom indicated that the millennial kingdom must follow "the times of Antichrist" rather than run concurrent with it. Furthermore, Mede argued that the resurrection of 20:4–6 could only be understood contextually as a bodily rather than spiritual resurrection. Since the purpose of the first such resurrection in those verses is to reign with Christ in the millennial kingdom, that resurrection further confirms the future nature of the millennial period.

Between 1627 and 1629, Mede refined his interpretations as he grappled on the one hand with a theological preunderstand-

---

[38]See Toon, *Puritans, the Millennium and the Future of Israel*, 42–56.

[39]On Joseph Mede, see Toon, 56–61. Also see, Katharine R. Firth, *The Apocalyptic Tradition in Reformation Britain 1530—1645* (Oxford: Oxford Univ. Press, 1979), 214–28; Davidson, *The Logic of Millennial Thought*, 43–47; James E. Bear, "Historic Premillennialism," *Union Seminary Review* 55 (1944): 201–7.

ing informed by a spiritual vision eschatology, and on the other with premillennial observations that pointed in the direction of a new creation model. He acknowledged his difficulty in accepting the fact that John actually envisioned a bodily resurrection prior to the Final Judgment. Nevertheless, a grammatical and literary interpretation clearly indicated this to be the case. Still, he tried to accommodate the idea by postulating the reign of the resurrected in heaven during the millennial period. However, further study convinced him that a reign of the resurrected on earth was precisely what was revealed to John.[40] Theology had to yield in this matter to the authority of biblical revelation. That, however, was as far as Mede got. The final state, for him, was still seen in the traditional spiritual manner.

We see in the case of Mede that two issues are vital to the position of premillennialism. One is the literary, contextual understanding of John's millennial vision. The other is the broader contextual issue of new creation eschatology. The latter gives the interpreter a contextual conceptuality in which to interpret the former. Within this framework, Revelation 19–20, interpreted in a grammatical, lexical, and literary contextual manner, gives the crucial sequence of premillennial eschatology.

But does new creation eschatology concern only the Millennium? Or does it present a holistic future hope of which the Millennium forms one part? A difference of opinion here has contributed to the variety of premillennialisms in the modern era. We now turn to this variety.

VARIETIES OF PREMILLENNIALISM

As we have noted, the recovery of premillennialism took place within the hermeneutical struggle between a traditional spiritual vision eschatology and a literary-grammatically derived new creation eschatology. At stake in this conflict was not only the possibility and nature of a post-Advent millennial kingdom, but also the nature of the final state. As the two eschatological models vied with one another in the mind of evangelical Christianity, a variety of premillennial options were proposed. Other differences—distinctive interpretations that constitute the unique contributions of individual expositors—

---

[40]Bear, "Historic Premillennialism," 204–5.

add to this variety as well. It is not possible within the confines of this chapter to comment on all of them. However, it may be helpful to outline a general typology of premillennial views such as is commonly acknowledged today.

Dispensational Premillennialism

One of the most distinctive forms of premillennialism is that of *classical dispensationalism*, which developed in the context of nineteenth-century premillennial prophecy conferences. Its key ideas were first formulated by John Nelson Darby, an early leader in the Brethren movement. From Brethren writings, its ideas spread into American premillennialism to the point that it became the dominant form of premillennialism at the time of the fundamentalist-modernist controversy. Representative expressions of classical dispensationalism can be found in the notes of the *Scofield Reference Bible* and especially in the *Systematic Theology* of Lewis Sperry Chafer. In the 1960s, dispensational theologians began to modify some important features. Nevertheless, classical dispensationalism has remained a powerful influence in evangelical eschatological thought.[41]

As a comprehensive approach to Scripture, dispensationalism concerns many more issues than premillennialism per se. It is not possible to address all of these issues here. Consequently, and in keeping with our purpose in this chapter, we will focus our attention on how classical dispensationalists understood the Millennium and the final state.

Classical dispensationalism sought to resolve the tensions between new creation and spiritual vision eschatologies by affirming two coexisting eternal realms of salvation, one heav-

---

[41]On the history of dispensationalism see C. Bass, *Backgrounds to Dispensationalism: Its Historical Genesis and Ecclesiastical Implications* (Grand Rapids: Eerdmans, 1960); E. Sandeen, *The Roots of Fundamentalism: British and American Millenarianism 1800–1930* (Chicago: Chicago Univ. Press, 1970); T. Weber, *Living in the Shadow of the Second Coming* (New York: Oxford, 1979); C. Norman Kraus, *Dispensationalism in America: Its Rise and Development* (Richmond: John Knox, 1958); Craig A. Blaising, "Dispensationalism: The Search for Definition," in *Dispensationalism, Israel and the Church: The Search for Definition*, ed. Craig A. Blaising and Darrell L. Bock (Grand Rapids: Zondervan, 1992). Also see Craig A. Blaising, "The Extent and Varieties of Dispensationalism," in *Progressive Dispensationalism*, by Craig A. Blaising and Darrell L. Bock (Wheaton, Ill.: Victor, 1993), 9–75.

enly and one earthly. The earthly eschatology, dispensationalists believed, was clearly derived from literary historical studies of Old Testament prophecy; it corroborated Protestant millennialism's growing interest in Israel. At the same time, the early dispensationalists promoted a highly mystical form of Christian spirituality that drew heavily on the traditional spiritual vision model of heaven as the final destiny for Christian believers. Dispensationalists solved the tension between these two concerns by postulating two coexisting forms of ultimate salvation—one eternal in heaven for the church and one everlasting on the new earth for Israel.

It appears that dispensationalists developed the earthly side of this dual eschatology as a polar opposite to the spiritual side. This indicates that the primary metaphysical scheme in classical dispensational thought was that of the traditional spiritual vision model, which postulates just this kind of opposition (spiritual vs. material, heavenly vs. earthly). Advocates of spiritual vision eschatology had often complained that a literal interpretation of Old Testament prophecy would lead to a completely earthly, material, and particularly "Jewish" eschatology. Moreover, such a view was incompatible with the New Testament revelation of spiritual blessings in Christ. Dispensationalists accepted this complaint as true. But unlike traditional Christian thought, they found a place for this kind of earthly eschatology in the future plan of God. Having affirmed the preunderstanding of what a literal interpretation must lead to, dispensationalists freely developed the earthly side of their eschatology in the most "Jewish" sense possible.

How did this dualist eschatology affect premillennialism? Actually, classical dispensationalism maintains two different premillennialisms conjoined together. The church looks forward to a spiritual millennial experience. Much as Joseph Mede had suggested in his earlier writing on this subject, classical dispensationalists expected that the church would be in heaven with Christ during the millennial period. One can see this as a form of the spiritual contemplative premillennialism that Augustine had once thought possible. Certainly, this expectation was in keeping with the spiritual vision orientation of the church. After the Millennium, the church would remain in heaven for a final state, much as the spiritual vision model had traditionally predicted.

During the same millennial period, however, Israel and Gentile nations would be on the earth, experiencing an earthly, physical, and political millennial kingdom that correlates with a literal interpretation of Old Testament eschatology. After the Millennium, these peoples would be brought into an eternal enjoyment of those blessings as the earth was being renewed.

Classical dispensationalism engendered a number of unique and interesting interpretations of Scripture that are beyond the scope of this essay.[42] But perhaps something should be said about the use of the word *dispensation*. Prior to the rise of historical criticism, biblical studies often made use of the term *dispensation* to periodize biblical history. Dispensationalists, however, divided the dispensations of biblical history between their two eschatologies. This meant that whereas one period of biblical history was to be understood within the framework of earthly blessings, a succeeding dispensation was placed within the framework of spiritual blessings. Christian interpretation had traditionally done something like this in relating the Old and New Testaments. But it had also argued that the spiritual dispensation replaced or fulfilled the earthly. Dispensationalists, however, argued that the present spiritual dispensation could not be seen as a fulfillment of earlier earthly dispensations but that all dispensations should be kept separated and oriented to two different eschatologies, one earthly and one spiritual.

One benefit from this was that dispensationalism encouraged readers to take seriously some of the diversity that actually exists in biblical theology. Later evangelical biblical scholars who differed with classical dispensationalism's dualist eschatology nevertheless benefited from the sanctioning of recognized complexity in the biblical text. Within this complexity, dispensationalism helped to underscore the importance of the earthly, material, and political aspects of biblical prophecy, which should not be simply "spiritualized" in prophetic fulfillment. Most important, dispensationalists from John Darby to John Walvoord emphasized the irrevocable place of Israel in the plan of God.[43] Except for the dualism in which dispensationalism pre-

---

[42]For the implications of the central dualism for dispensational interpretation, see Craig A. Blaising, "The Extent and Varieties of Dispensationalism," 23–31.

[43]All dispensationalists have emphasized the future of Israel, but perhaps no one more than John F. Walvoord, whose prodigious works have always kept this as

sented this view, the future of Israel is a truth that is being recognized more widely today, even if its acceptance comes begrudgingly on the part of some.[44]

Of course, dispensationalists are also known for their emphasis on a pretribulational Rapture. In this doctrine, they adapted certain seventeenth-century experimental distinctions between the appearing and the coming of Christ in a new way, that is, to distinguish between two tribulational visitations of Christ. The pretribulational Rapture became, for classical dispensationalism, the spiritual coming of Christ in the spiritual eschatology of the church, whereas the posttribulational descent of Christ to the earth became the glorious coming of Messiah to fulfill the earthly eschatology of Israel. The separation of the two in time—the pretribulational Rapture and posttribulational descent to the earth—allowed the two eschatologies to separate without conflict prior to their respective millennial fulfillments.

Beginning in the late 1950s, some dispensationalists began to abandon classical dispensationalism's dualism of heavenly and earthly eternal states.[45] This meant that a choice had to be made in favor of either a spiritual vision model or a more earthly model of eternity. Some (such as Charles Ryrie and John Walvoord) chose the former, believing that all the redeemed would share an eternal destiny that was spiritual in nature (even though the

---

a central theme. See his *The Millennial Kingdom* (Grand Rapids: Zondervan, 1959); *Israel in Prophecy* (Grand Rapids: Zondervan, 1962); *The Prophecy Knowledge Handbook* (Wheaton, Ill.: Victor, 1990); and *Major Bible Prophecies* (Grand Rapids: Zondervan, 1991).

[44]Much attention has been drawn to Romans 9–11 by Karl Barth. See his treatment of election in *Church Dogmatics* II.2, trans. G. W. Bromiley et. al. (Edinburgh: T. & T. Clark, 1957), 195–305. See also C. E. B. Cranfield, *A Critical and Exegetical Commentary on The Epistle to the Romans*, 2 vols. (Edinburgh: T. & T. Clark, 1979), 2:445–592; Markus Barth, *The People of God* (Sheffield: JSOT Press, 1983). Two recent studies on Romans 9–11 by premillennialists should be noted here: J. Lanier Burns, "The Future of Ethnic Israel in Romans 11," in Blaising and Bock, eds., *Dispensationalism, Israel and the Church*, 188–229; S. Lewis Johnson Jr., "Evidence from Romans 9–11," in Donald K. Campbell and Jeffrey L. Townsend, eds., *A Case For Premillennialism: A New Consensus* (Chicago: Moody, 1992), 199–223.

[45]For more information on the revision of dispensationalism beginning in the late 1950s, see Craig A. Blaising, "Development of Dispensationalism by Contemporary Dispensationalists," *Bibliotheca Sacra* 145 (1988): 254–80; "Dispensationalism: The Search for Definition," 23–30; "The Extent and Varieties of Dispensationalism," 31–46.

redeemed would be segregated between Israel and the church).[46] Others (such as Alva J. McClain and J. Dwight Pentecost) believed that eternity for all the redeemed of all dispensations would be on the new earth in a new creation experience of final salvation (still segregated, however, as Israel versus the church).[47]

However, these revised dispensationalisms maintained the effects of the dualist approach in their reading of the history of dispensations leading up to eternity (where one dispensation of an earthly character is replaced with a spiritual one, and vice versa). Most maintained dual millennial spheres of blessing— one spiritual for the church and one earthly for Israel. As a result, many unique dispensational interpretations were maintained but without the support of the final dualism for these dispensational differences.

Beginning in the late 1980s, publications began to appear marking the complete abandonment of classical dispensationalism's systemic dualism for a holistic approach. This approach, known as *progressive dispensationalism*, has preserved many valuable insights from traditional dispensational readings of Scripture, recognizing spiritual, material, political, and ethnic purposes in the divine plan yet without bifurcating them into irreconcilable programs.[48]

Historic Premillennialism

In spite of its widespread popularity, not all premillennialists became dispensationalists. By the mid-twentieth century,

---

[46]Charles Ryrie, *Dispensationalism Today* (Chicago: Moody, 1965), 147. Walvoord stresses the fact of a future new earth, but presents it as essentially discontinuous with the present. Hence, his views are classified with the spiritual vision model of eternity. Walvoord, *Major Bible Prophecies*, 413–14; also see his *Prophecy: 14 Essential Keys to Understanding the Final Drama* (Nashville: Nelson, 1993), 167–75; cf. 74–79.

[47]J. Dwight Pentecost, *Things to Come: A Study in Biblical Eschatology* (Grand Rapids: Zondervan, 1958), 562; Alva J. McClain, *The Greatness of the Kingdom* (Winona Lake, Ind.: BMH Books, 1959), 510–11.

[48]See Blaising and Bock, eds., *Dispensationalism, Israel and the Church*; Blaising and Bock, *Progressive Dispensationalism*; Robert Saucy, *The Case for Progressive Dispensationalism* (Grand Rapids: Zondervan, 1993); John S. Feinberg, ed., *Continuity and Discontinuity: Perspectives on the Relationship Between the Old and New Testaments* (Westchester, Ill.: Crossway, 1988). For responses to progressive dispensationalism, see Wesley R. Willis and John R. Master, eds., *Issues in Dispensationalism* (Chicago: Moody, 1994); Charles Ryrie, *Dispensationalism* (Chicago: Moody, 1995).

some premillennialists (such as George E. Ladd) sought to distinguish themselves from classical dispensationalism by using the label *historic premillennialism*.[49] Ladd was concerned that many people simply assumed that premillennialism was the same thing as classical dispensationalism. In fact, premillennialists of the patristic and early modern eras did not share classical dispensationalism's dualist approach to eschatology. Historic premillennialism, then, was intended to indicate the other form of premillennialism, which was not dispensational.

But the label *historic premillennialism* is just as likely to be misleading, since it gives the impression that there are no differences among premillennial views other than those that have to do with dispensationalism. Actually, other than the absence of classical dispensationalism's dualist approach to biblical eschatology, the only positive features that unify premillennial views ancient and modern are those that dispensational premillennialism affirms as well—a millennial kingdom in which Satan is bound, instituted after the visible coming of Christ, and a partial resurrection of the dead but prior to the Final Judgment.

Other than dispensationalism's experiment with dualist eschatologies, premillennialists throughout history have sought to present their views as one unfolding salvation narrative. In doing so, they had to face the question as to whether and to what extent they were willing to accommodate the cultural and traditional idea of a spiritual vision eschatology. All premillennialists recognized features of a new creation eschatology in the biblical text, and they easily related these features to the millennial kingdom that they expected on the basis of a literal reading

---

[49]We have already noted the use of the term *historic premillennialism* in the 1944 article by James Bear. Concern for distinguishing between premillennialism and dispensationalism began to appear in the pages of *The Presbyterian Guardian* in 1936 (e.g., the issues of May 4, August 3, and November 14, 1936; March 13, 1937). Ladd's position was clarified in G. E. Ladd, *Crucial Questions About the Kingdom of God* (Grand Rapids: Eerdmans, 1952); *The Gospel of the Kingdom* (Grand Rapids: Eerdmans, 1959); *Jesus and the Kingdom* (New York: Harper and Row, 1964), republished as *The Presence of the Future* (Grand Rapids: Eerdmans, 1974). His most direct protest against dispensationalism was his criticism of pretribulationism in his *The Blessed Hope: A Biblical Study of the Second Advent and the Rapture* (Grand Rapids: Eerdmans, 1956). He presented the position of "historic premillennialism" as opposed to dispensational premillennialism in R. G. Clouse, ed., *The Meaning of the Millennium: Four Views* (Downers Grove, Ill.: InterVarsity, 1977).

of Revelation 20. But when it came to the final state, some were more inclined to affirm a traditional spiritual vision model of eternity. As a consequence, they developed premillennial views that might be called *reductionist premillennialism*. That is, they reduced the scope of new creation eschatological fulfillment to the millennial period alone. Some reductionist premillennialisms can be found in the patristic period, as exemplified by Tertullian,[50] as well as in the early modern recovery of premillennialism, as exemplified in the seventeenth-century scholars Joseph Mede and Thomas Goodwin.[51]

Other premillennialists were willing to adopt a more thoroughgoing new creation eschatology. The Millennium that they anticipated was compatible and consistent with the new creation order of the final state. We can see this in the patristic era in Irenaeus of Lyons,[52] and in modern times in the work of many well-known nineteenth-century premillennialists, such as Nathaniel West, W. J. Erdman, A. J. Gordon, and Samuel Kellogg.[53] This

---

[50]Tertullian, *Adversus Marcionem* 3.24: "For we do profess that even on earth a kingdom is promised us: but this is before we come to heaven, and in a different polity ... after [the millennial kingdom] ... we shall be changed in a moment into angelic substance ... and be translated into that heavenly kingdom ..." (trans. Ernest Evans [Oxford: Clarendon Press, 1972], 1:247–49).

[51]On Thomas Goodwin, see Toon, *Puritans, the Millennium and the Future of Israel*, 62–65.

[52]Irenaeus's premillennialism is well known. At the end of *Adversus Haereses*, 5, he presents an extended argument for the literal bodily resurrection and the millennial kingdom (on which see 5.32–34). Then he speaks of the new earth and new heaven, which he argues is substantially identical with the present heaven and earth. It is the "fashion" (1 Cor. 7:31) of the world, not its "substance," that passes away. The fashion has to do with sin (5.35–36, esp. 36.1). He does, however, argue that *some* human beings will be privileged to live in the new heaven while others are on the new earth.

[53]The views of these nineteenth-century premillennialists can be seen in the publications of the 1878 and 1886 international premillennial prophecy conferences (see Nathaniel West, ed., *Second Coming of Christ: Premillennial Essays of the Prophetic Conference Held in the Church of the Holy Trinity, New York City. With an Appendix of Critical Testimonie*. [Chicago: Fleming H. Revell, 1879]; *Prophetic Studies of the International Prophetic Conference (Chicago, November, 1886)* [Chicago: Fleming H. Revell, 1886]). See especially Chas. K. Imbrie, "The Regeneration," in *Second Coming of Christ*, 108–73. Imbrie speaks of those who understand the "regeneration" of Matt. 19:28 together with the "restitution of all things" in Acts 3:21 "to be a great and blessed change in reference to this earth and the race upon it. They understand it to comprehend the glorious appearing of the great God our Saviour to accomplish this

approach might be called *consistent or holistic premillennialism*. The work of George Ladd fits here as well.[54]

One can see that reductionist and holistic premillennialisms have two different views of the eternal state. Classical dispensationalism finds its historical location as an attempt to mediate these two approaches with a *dualist premillennialism*. This dualist approach did not prove stable in the long run. As a result, those who sought in the 1950s and 1960s to revise classical dispensationalism had to choose which view of the eternal state they were willing to affirm. Some, such as Ryrie, opted for a reductionist premillennialism, but added to it many of the dispensational distinctions that classical dispensationalism had affirmed. Others, such as Alva J. McClain and J. Dwight Pentecost, affirmed a new creation model of eternity. Their work paved the way for progressive dispensationalists to develop a consistent, holistic premillennialism.

George Ladd's category of historic premillennialism has had little value in understanding the history of premillennialism. It functioned primarily as a rallying point in the twentieth century for nondispensationalists. His great contribution, however, was the stimulation of a critical evangelical biblical scholarship focusing on biblical eschatology and apocalyptic. And that contribution has been helpful to dispensationalists and

---

Regeneration [in the millennial kingdom] ... [and] finally, at the close of the Millennial period ... the establishment on the earth of the redeemed forever." He continues, "This is the view of the Regeneration usually held by those who maintain the premillennial Advent of Christ," which he notes was the view of "the Church universally for the first three centuries.... It was received substantially by a number of the English Reformers and the godly and learned men who followed them in the sixteenth and seventeenth centuries ... and is held by a large number, of high reputation as biblical scholars, in the present day, notwithstanding it has at times met with opposition and even contempt" (pp. 115–16). Imbrie's new creation eschatology, embracing both millennial and eternal states, is typical of the other contributors in both this volume and the later collection of prophetic essays.

[54]"After the millennium when the Age to come has been inaugurated, John sees a new heaven and *a new earth*, unto which the holy city, the new Jerusalem, descends. Here is an important fact: the ultimate scene of the Kingdom of God is earthly. It is a transformed earth to be sure, but it is still an earthly destiny. Scripture everywhere teaches this. Paul says that 'the creation itself will be set free from bondage to decay and obtain the glorious liberty of the children of God' (Rom. 8:21). Corresponding to the new creation is the resurrection of the body ..." (George Eldon Ladd, *The Last Things* [Grand Rapids: Eerdmans, 1978], 112).

nondispensationalists alike.[55] Working in critical interaction, evangelical biblical scholarship has produced a common, broad-based understanding of the nature and revelatory progression of the eschatological kingdom of God, one that affirms an over-all new creation eschatology.[56] Premillennialists see the millennial kingdom of Christ as an integral feature of the progressive revelation of this kingdom.

Premillennialism and Apocalypticism

Many think of premillennialism from the standpoint of its association with apocalyptic readings of present or past church history. Not all premillennialists employ biblical apocalyptic in this manner. However, some have developed distinctive emphases, and we need to acknowledge them here. We have seen that from the time of the Reformation onward, Protestant interpreters of all three millennial views attempted to interpret their own times within the sometimes sequential and sometimes repetitive visions of Daniel and Revelation.

Historicist premillennialism refers to a distinctive type of apocalypticism that primarily existed between the seventeenth and late nineteenth centuries (before the dominance of dispensational premillennialism). They read church history as having fulfilled many of the visions of Daniel and Revelation, with remaining visions indicating the future course of church history.[57] Specifically, historicists were interested in certain numbers found in Daniel and Revelation, which, they believed, referred to years of church history. They followed a basic formula whereby days in biblical prophecy equaled years in the history

---

[55]Darrell Bock notes appreciation for Ladd and the similarity as well as difference between Ladd's views and those of progressive dispensationalism in "Why I Am a Dispensationalist With a Little 'd'," in a forthcoming issue of *Journal of the Evangelical Theological Society*. Bock helps to clear up the confusion of some who simply equate progressive dispensationalism with Ladd's historic premillennialism.

[56]For example, see Craig Blomberg's remarks in a review of G. R. Beasley-Murray's book, *Jesus and the Kingdom of God*, in which he notes "a growing consensus among evangelicals" regarding the inaugural and future aspects of the kingdom of God in the teaching of Jesus ("A Response to G. R. Beasley-Murray on the Kingdom," *Journal of the Evangelical Theological Society* 35 [1992]: 31–38).

[57]I am using the typology of historicist and futurist premillennialism given by Timothy Weber, *Living in the Shadow of the Second Coming*, 9–11.

of the church. Some on this basis even dared to predict the date of Christ's second coming.[58]

Dispensationalism precluded historicism by its separation of spiritual churchly and Jewish earthly eschatologies. Apocalyptic descriptions of the Tribulation, the Day of the Lord, and all associated number sequences were relegated to the Jewish earthly eschatology, which had nothing to do with the church, past, present, or future.

Dispensationalists rejected the year-day formula and took a strictly literal approach to the days and months numbered in Daniel and Revelation (such as 1260 days, 42 months). On this basis they proposed two clearly defined future periods of time—a seven-year Tribulation and a thousand-year millennial kingdom.[59]

Dispensationalism helped premillennialism abandon the instability that plagued all attempts to read church history in the numbered sequences of biblical apocalyptic. This helped in turn to shed the popular and somewhat sensationalist apocalypticism that seemed to characterize some well-known examples of premillennialism. And this in turn enabled premillennialists to

---

[58]The year-day theory appears from the sixteenth to the nineteenth century in apocalypticism of all types, postmillennial and amillennial as well as premillennial. The phenomenon is discussed by most of the works already cited regarding early modern millennialism. A helpful discussion can be found in Davidson, *The Logic of Millennial Thought*, 37–80. Much has been written on the Millerite use of this theory. For a summary, see Sandeen, *The Roots of Fundamentalism*, 42–58. For a comparison of the different approaches of William Miller and Hal Lindsey, see Stephen D. O'Leary, *Arguing the Apocalypse: A Theory of Millennial Rhetoric* (New York: Oxford, 1994).

[59]The seven-year Tribulation is primarily based on Daniel 9:24–27, which presents seventy sevens for Israel and Jerusalem to fulfill all prophecy (9:24). Sixty-nine sevens are recorded in vv. 25–26. Interpreters uniformly see these as a reference to history now past. Conservatives understand the sixty-nine sevens to terminate at the time of Christ because of the reference to the Messiah in v. 26. Dispensationalists postulate a gap between the sixty-ninth and the seventieth seven since all the "sevens" have to do with Israel. The last seven (v. 27) is understood to be the future Tribulation. This would seem to be confirmed by the fact that the abomination of desolation will be set up in the middle of that seven. Jesus refers to the abomination that was spoken by Daniel in Matthew 24:15. Paul also appears to reference the same thing in his comments about a future man of lawlessness (2 Thess. 2:3–8). Revelation also alludes to these same features in John's vision of a beast who rises out of the sea (Rev. 13:1–10) to exercise dominion for forty-two months (13:5), which is, of course, one-half of seven years (84 months), the length of time from the abomination to the end in Daniel 9:27.

study apocalyptic discourse without always having to ask the question of historical fulfillment.

In spite of all this, after the founding of the state of Israel in 1948, many dispensationalists developed their own form of popular apocalypticism by postulating that whereas Tribulation events could not transpire during church history, antecedents to those events could. Thus, interest developed in attempting to discern the elements of the apocalyptic scenario as they might be coming into formation. *Dispensational apocalypticism* became popular during the era of the Cold War and occasioned all kind of speculations about events during that period of history. One example of this, certainly the most well-known, are the writings of Hal Lindsey.[60]

Although dispensational apocalypticism has received much attention in the media and in studies of popular religion, where it continues to thrive, it has become peripheral to the point of absence in dispensational biblical scholarship. This is because of popular apocalypticism's loose relationship to the literary and historical study of Scripture and because of ongoing evangelical scholarly work on the interpretation of biblical apocalyptic. Furthermore, popular apocalypticism's penchant for relating future events in Scripture to headline news and even making predictions about how, when, and where future events will be fulfilled, including the date of Christ's return, has discredited it in the minds of many.

THE MILLENNIAL KINGDOM AND NEW CREATION ESCHATOLOGY

In the rest of this chapter, I will present a biblical argument for a holistic, consistent premillennialism. This can only be done in summary form because of the limitations of space in this publication. Certainly the reader should be aware that much has been written of an exegetical and expositional nature on Old and

---

[60]Hal Lindsey, *The Late Great Planet Earth* (Grand Rapids: Zondrvan, 1970); *There's a New World Coming: A "Prophetic Odyssey"* (Santa Ana, Calif.: Vision House, 1973); *The Terminal Generation* (Old Tappan, N.J.: Revell, 1976); *The 1980's: Countdown to Armageddon* (New York: Bantam, 1980). For an overview of popular apocalypticism, see P. Boyer, *When Time Shall Be No More: Prophecy Belief in Modern American Culture* (Cambridge, Mass.: Belknap Press, 1992).

New Testament eschatology that would bear on our subject. In these few pages we can only hope to outline key features of the argument.[61]

I will present these features in three parts: (1) the biblical theme of a coming eschatological kingdom; (2) the question of how compatible later revelation of a post-Advent millennial kingdom is with this common biblical theme; (3) John's vision in Revelation 20 within its context in the entire book, to demonstrate that in fact revelation has been given of a future millennial kingdom subsequent to the return of Christ and prior to the Final Judgment.

The Eschatological Kingdom in Old and New Testament Theology

A key feature in Old Testament eschatology concerns a future kingdom that God will set up on this earth and which will be everlasting in duration. We can see this in Daniel 2:34–35, 44; Isaiah 2:2–4; and Micah 4:1–8. This kingdom is not simply a higher order of spiritual reality that coexists with the present course of affairs, but it is a complete *replacement* of present conditions on earth with a new worldwide and multinational world order.[62] Promises found throughout the prophets regarding the future restoration of Israel are coterminous with this expectation of a worldwide kingdom. Personal and national blessings are extended to Gentiles as well.

---

[61]A more detailed exposition of the idea of biblical covenants and the eschatological kingdom of God can be found in Blaising and Bock, *Progressive Dispensationalism*, 128–283; and in various articles in Blaising and Bock, eds., *Dispensationalism, Israel and the Church*. One should also see the work in biblical theology by Ladd, noted above, esp. *The Presence of the Future* and *Crucial Questions About the Kingdom of God*. Campbell and Townsend, eds., *A Case for Premillennialism: A New Consensus*, has many excellent articles, although it is mixed between reductionist and holist approaches. For a biblical theology of the kingdom of God that affirms a new creation eschatology with many traditional dispensational features, note J. Dwight Pentecost, *Thy Kingdom Come* (Wheaton, Ill.: Victor, 1990). For an older premillennial work on the biblical theology of the kingdom that affirms a holist, consistent premillennialism, see Nathaniel West, *The Thousand Years in Both Testaments* (New York: Fleming H. Revell, 1880).

[62]It is important that one note this idea of *replacement* in the way the eschatological kingdom is set forth. See esp. Kenneth L. Barker, "Evidence From Daniel," in *A Case for Premillennialism*, 135–46.

Messianic prophecy also finds its fulfillment here. Daniel's future kingdom on earth, introduced in Daniel 2, is re-presented in 7:12–14, 27, under the rule of "one like a Son of Man." God's rule from Zion over all nations in Isaiah 2 is revealed in Isaiah 11 to be the rule of a future Davidite, "a shoot ... from the stump of Jesse" (11:1), who "will reign on David's throne and over his kingdom ... from that time on and forever" (9:7) and to whom "the nations will rally" (11:10). Jeremiah's prophecies of a coming Messiah (Jer. 23:3–7; 33:14–16) also coordinate with these expectations and together with Isaiah look back to Amos's earlier prediction that God would repair "David's fallen tent" so that the nations would bear the name of Yahweh (Amos 9:11–12).

The worldwide blessing for all peoples personally and nationally under the rule of the future Messiah from the house of David is continuous with the covenant structure of Scripture, in which God promised to bless Abraham's descendants and the land of their inheritance along with all peoples on earth through a descendant of David whose kingdom the Lord would establish forever (Gen. 12:1–3; 13:14–17; 15:18–21; 22:15–18; 2 Sam. 7:8–16; 1 Chron. 17:7–15; Ps. 89; 110; 132). The prophets' predictions of a future worldwide kingdom stand in direct relationship to these covenant promises. However, the prophets looked forward to an expansion of these blessings in the future establishment of a new covenant. This new covenant adds to the holistic scope of blessing through its emphasis on the forgiveness of and cleansing from sin along with the re-creation of human hearts indwelt by God's Spirit and inscribed with God's law (Isa. 59:21; Jer. 31:31–37; Ezek. 11:19–20; 36:22–37:14).

Spiritual blessings are predicted in these texts together with national and political blessings. They help to explain the holistic eschatological kingdom descriptions of righteousness, justice, peace, and joy, which Amos, Isaiah, Jeremiah, and Micah present to us. They also coordinate with Daniel's expectation of the coming end of sin, atonement for wickedness, and the institution of everlasting righteousness (Dan. 9:24) in conjunction with the kingdom that he saw as coming in the future.

The earthly context of blessing for the eschatological kingdom is further developed in Isaiah's prophecy about a new heaven and new earth (Isa. 65:17–25; 66:18–23). Similar phrases link the new earth prediction (65:25) to the prophecy of the future reign of Messiah (11:6–9). Promises of blessing on the land of Israel and of the future glory of Jerusalem coordinate with these promises of blessing on the earth. The particular and universal scope of earthly blessing recalls both the covenant with Abraham, in which the land was given, and the earlier covenant with Noah to bless the earth. Blessing on Israel and all nations, blessing on the land of Israel and on all the earth, come together in the holistic scope of the promised eschatological kingdom.[63]

The New Testament carries forward the Old Testament eschatological hope and adds to it the revelation that the Messiah of the eschatological kingdom is Jesus of Nazareth. Such is the announcement of the angel Gabriel at the beginning of the Gospel of Luke: "He will be great and will be called the Son of the Most High. The Lord God will give him the throne of his father David, and he will reign over the house of Jacob forever; his kingdom will never end" (Luke 1:32–33). The theme of Jesus' ministry is good news that the kingdom of God is near. No explanation for the meaning of this kingdom is given. An Old Testament contextual understanding of his message is assumed.

This good news was to be preached to Israel and to all nations. Jesus predicted the political reconstitution of Israel and referred to himself as the Son of Man, who would come on the clouds of glory. He predicted that he would go away and receive the authority of the kingdom and then return. His miracles demonstrated the physical and earthly aspects of kingdom peace and well-being. His exorcisms revealed the exclusion of demonic influence from that kingdom. His acts of forgiving sins, his promise of the Holy Spirit, and especially his yielding up of his own self as a ransom for sin revealed the kingdom's new covenant features (note esp. his remarks at the Last Supper, Luke 22:20). His longest discourse spoke of the coming of the Son of Man in glory to sit on his glorious throne and judge the nations for entrance into the "inheritance, the kingdom prepared for you since the creation of the world," which entrance is defined as "eternal life" (Matt. 25:31–46).

---

[63]The holistic scope of Old Testament eschatology is well presented by Donald E. Gowan, *Eschatology in the Old Testament* (Philadelphia: Fortress, 1986). Gowan's theme is that the coming transformation involves human hearts, human society, and the whole of nature (p. 2).

The theology of Luke-Acts teaches that when Jesus ascended into heaven, he was enthroned with kingdom authority.[64] Paul teaches that Jesus is presently seated at the right hand of God with all things in subjection under his feet (Eph. 1:19–23; Col. 1:13–18; cf. 1 Peter 3:22). New covenant blessings have been inaugurated through the cross and the outpouring of the Holy Spirit (1 Cor. 11:25; 2 Cor. 3:2–6). These blessings institute features of the promised eschatological kingdom. Jews and Gentiles who have been reconciled in Christ have received the Holy Spirit as a down payment on their future redemption and form a body of peoples united in peace by the Holy Spirit, demonstrating the new humanity of the eschatological kingdom (Eph. 1:13–14; 2:12–22). They have been transferred into the kingdom of God's Son (Col. 1:13) and have been made a kingdom and priests to serve the God and Father of Jesus Christ (Rev. 1:6). But these are only inaugural aspects. The fullness of the eschatological kingdom is yet to come.

Much of the New Testament's "heavenly" language, which spiritual vision and realized millennial views highlight, comes from texts that speak of the believers' present relation to the ascended Christ. These are inaugural aspects of the eschatological kingdom, which anticipate the future fullness of the kingdom, just as the pledge anticipates the future payment in full. Christians now are heirs of the kingdom (James 2:5; cf. 1 Cor. 6:9–10; Gal. 5:21; Eph. 5:5), for which they suffer (2 Thess. 1:5). Entrance into the kingdom is future (Acts 14:22; 2 Peter 1:11). The believers' inheritance is said to be "kept in heaven" because Christ is in heaven. The city of God is in heaven (Gal. 4:26; Phil. 3:20; Heb. 12:22), being prepared by Christ for us (John 14:2–3). That city and inheritance are coming with him when he returns (Heb. 2:5; 13:14). That coming will bring a renewal of the creation (Rom. 8:18–23), a new earth and new heaven, even as the Old Testament expected (2 Peter 3:13), along with blessing on Israel and on all nations (Acts 1:6; 3:21; Rom. 11:26–29).

We will see that the book of Revelation affirms this same new creation eschatology. Although believers are now a king-

---

[64]See esp. Darrell L. Bock, "The Reign of the Lord Christ," in *Dispensationalism, Israel and the Church*, 37–67; "Current Messianic Activity and O.T. Davidic Promise: Dispensationalism, Hermeneutics, and N.T. Fulfillment," *Trinity Journal* 15 n.s. (1994): 55–87.

dom of priests (Rev. 1:6), they will yet reign on the earth (5:10). The One who has already sat down on the Father's throne (2:21) will (in the future) rule the nations (19:15). He will reign forever and ever (11:15) over peoples from all nations (5:9–10) on a new earth without sin and death (21:1–5; 22:5).

But Revelation 20 also speaks of a millennial kingdom, which will transpire prior to the new world conditions in which the everlasting reign will be fulfilled. This millennial kingdom, as we will see, is best interpreted as a future phase or stage of that eschatological kingdom.

The Coming of the Eschatological Kingdom

How will the eschatological kingdom come? Some texts simply state that the Lord will establish, create, or raise it up in the last days (Isa. 2; Amos 9:15–16). The Lord will cause the stump of Jesse to sprout (Isa. 11:1); a son will be born (9:6) in Bethlehem (Mic. 5:2), and the government will be on his shoulders (Isa. 9:6). However, other texts specifically indicate that the eschatological kingdom will be established through a climactic act of judgment on world conditions. Daniel describes it coming like a falling rock pulverizing, obliterating, and then replacing existing world political structures (Dan. 2:34–35, 44). The Messiah to whom the kingdom will be given comes on the clouds of heaven in glory, just as judgment falls on the world order existing at that time (7:11–14). He and his saints exercise the dominion of the kingdom worldwide and forever in replacement of that previous order (7:14, 27).

Isaiah 24 foresees a day of the Lord, a common theme in the prophets concerning a divine visitation of judgment. Most often, the references to the Day of the Lord signify the Assyrian or Babylonian invasions that brought death, destruction, and exile (see Isa. 2:12–21; 13:6–13; 22:1–25; 34:1–17; Jer. 46:1–12; Ezek. 7:1–27; 13:5; 30:1–19; 38–39; Joel 1–3; Amos 5:18–20; 8:8–9; 9:5–6; Obad. 15–21; Nah. 1–3; Zeph. 1:7–8, 14–18; 2:1–3; 3:8; Zech. 14:1–21; Mal. 3–4). However, a typology was set up through these descriptions, reinforced through repetitive application, and projected into the future to describe the context in which the eschatological kingdom of God would come into existence. The coming Day of the Lord in Isaiah 24 contains the typical features, but it will come as a punishment of "the powers in the heavens

above and the kings on the earth below" (24:21). After this punishment, "the LORD Almighty will reign on Mount Zion and in
Jerusalem, and before its elders, gloriously" (24:23).

His kingdom reign is further described in Isaiah 25 as a
great banquet for all peoples. In Zechariah 14:5, "the LORD my
God will come, and all the holy ones with him." It will be "a day
of the LORD" (14:1), visiting judgment on all nations (cf. Joel 3).
"On that day, his feet will stand on the Mount of Olives. . . . It
will be a unique day. . . . The LORD will be king over the whole
earth. On that day there will be one LORD, and his name the only
name" (14:4, 7, 9). Zechariah 14:16–21 proceeds to describe the
subsequent reign of the Lord from Jerusalem over all nations.

The inaugurated form of the kingdom revealed in the New
Testament came into existence through the Cross (which is
described in the Gospels in "Day of the Lord" imagery), the resurrection of Jesus, and his ascension. But the future coming of the
kingdom is presented in the same way as in the Old Testament.

As Jesus proclaimed the nearness of the kingdom, he
warned his hearers to repent. He spoke repeatedly about this
coming judgment and about the future coming of the Son of Man
in glory and judgment. At one point, when his hearers thought
that perhaps he would walk right into Jerusalem and begin the
kingdom reign (Luke 19:11–28), he told them that he must go
away to receive the kingdom and then return. He warned them
about the judgment of his coming. In the Olivet Discourse, in
answer to a question about his coming, he presented a context
for his return structured with features from Daniel's description
of judgment and from the prophetic theme of the Day of the
Lord. The future kingdom of the Son of Man would be established on the earth through a catastrophic act of judgment, just
as the Old Testament had predicted (Matt. 24:1–25:46).

The rest of the New Testament clearly speaks of the future
coming of the kingdom consistent with the predictions of the
Old Testament and of Jesus. The future kingdom will come
when the Lord himself comes to establish it, and he will do that
in a time of judgment.[65]

---

[65]This point has been made repeatedly by premillennialists. For example, see
S. H. Kellogg, "Christ's Coming—Is It Pre-Millennial?" in *Second Coming of Christ:
Premillennial Essays*, 47–77. Also see J. Walvoord, "The Second Coming of Christ,"
in his *The Millennial Kingdom*, 263–75; James H. Bookes, *Maranatha* (New York: Fleming H. Revell, 1889).

The coming of Jesus Christ is the key event in the eschatology of the church. Paul writes in Titus 2:11–13 that the grace God has already given us instructs us to look "for the blessed hope—and the glorious appearing of our great God and Savior, Christ Jesus." Peter admonishes, "Set your hope fully on the grace to be given you when Jesus Christ is revealed" (1 Peter 1:13). The church at the present time is viewed as waiting "for his Son from heaven, whom he raised from the dead—Jesus, who rescues us from the coming wrath" (1 Thess. 1:10). That wrath will be brought by the Lord himself in a "day of the Lord" (1 Thess. 5:2), for, as Paul continues, "this will happen when the Lord Jesus is revealed from heaven in blazing fire with his powerful angels. He will punish those who do not know God and do not obey the gospel of our Lord Jesus. They will be punished with everlasting destruction and shut out from the presence of the Lord and from the majesty of his power on the day he comes to be glorified in his holy people and to be marveled at among all who have believed" (2 Thess. 1:7–10).

This future coming of Jesus, from the standpoint of the New Testament, will be the fulfillment of the eschatological Day of the Lord, even as he himself predicted in the Olivet Discourse. He, the Son of Man who will come on the clouds of glory and judgment, is the Lord who comes in the Day of the Lord. Consequently, it is now known as "the day of our Lord Jesus Christ" in which *Jesus* will be "revealed" from heaven (1 Cor. 1:7–8). All of these predictions of the revelation of Jesus point to a visible appearing (1 Peter 1:8, 13). They correlate with the angelic declaration at his ascension: "This same Jesus, who has been taken from you into heaven, will come back in the same way you have seen him go into heaven" (Acts 1:11).

Unique descriptions attributed to Jesus in the Olivet Discourse are incorporated along with traditional Old Testament typology into the epistolary correspondence about the coming Day of the Lord. The repetition of these sayings of Jesus (e.g., coming as a thief, in 1 Thess. 5:2; 2 Peter 3:10; Rev. 16:14–15) indicates a correlation of apostolic eschatology with that which the Lord himself presented. This in itself indicates that the apostles expected the future kingdom to come in and through the Day of the Lord. This certainly includes Jesus' teaching that the Day of the Lord would usher in the kingdom of the Son of Man on the earth.

This expectation is confirmed in the writings of Paul. In 1 Thessalonians 5:2 the apostle speaks of the Day of the Lord coming "like a thief." In 2 Thessalonians, he develops Daniel's theme of a future world ruler who will be destroyed in divine judgment at the time that the Son of Man comes, and he conflates the descriptions of the coming Lord with language from Isaiah's messianic rule (2 Thess. 2:3–4, 8). The church that in 1 Thessalonians 1:10 was said to be waiting "for his Son from heaven . . . who rescues us from the coming wrath," is now told to look forward to the fact that it will "share in the glory of our Lord Jesus Christ" (2 Thess. 2:14; cf. 1:7–10). That glory is none other than the kingdom that comes with his appearing (2 Tim. 4:1; relate to 2 Thess. 2:8), the glory that Jesus himself associated with his coming reign over all nations (Matt. 25:31–46; cf. 24:30).[66] It is the inheritance for which the church is now suffering (2 Thess. 1:5), which suffering will be relieved at the coming of Jesus (1:7–10).

A Millennial Phase of This Eschatological Kingdom?

My argument for premillennialism is that the millennial kingdom revealed to John, while new in its specific content, is compatible with this earlier revelation concerning the eschatological kingdom and the manner of its coming. Not only that, but now that we have the revelation of a future millennial kingdom, that revelation harmonizes with and clarifies earlier revelation that spoke of the coming eschatological kingdom in a more general manner. This of course is not the first example of such progressive revelation.

It was not entirely clear that Isaiah's predictions of a glorious Messiah (Isa. 11) and a Suffering Servant (Isa. 53) would be the same person, nor even how they *could* be so, until revelation was given of a progressive, sequential fulfillment of these prophecies in Jesus Christ. It was not clear prior to Jesus that the Old Testament prophecies regarding a future resurrection would be fulfilled in stages, with the Messiah being raised far in advance of the general resurrection. Yet, once that messianic resurrection is revealed, it clarifies not only the sequential nature

---

[66]The "appearing" of Christ in 2 Thess. 2:8 must be understood as the "coming" in 1:7 and 2:1.

in which the resurrection prophecies will be fulfilled but also the role of Messiah in the history of salvation. Certainly, no one would claim that the resurrection of the Messiah over two millennia in advance of a general resurrection is incompatible with Isaiah 25:7–8; 26:19; Daniel 12:2; or even Ezekiel 37:1–28, although nothing is said explicitly in these passages about stages of the Resurrection.

When we examine John's vision of a post-Advent Millennium in relation to earlier revelation about the coming of the eschatological kingdom, I believe we can see its compatibility with that earlier revelation in several ways. (1) John's revelation of the coming millennial kingdom is consistent with the New Testament's teaching about how the eschatological kingdom will come. The future kingdom will come when the Lord himself comes in the Day of the Lord. Accordingly, John envisions the millennial kingdom and the subsequent eternal reign as both following the coming of Jesus in the great Day of the Lord. Only as a consequence to this Great Tribulation and the coming of Jesus in glory is the eschatological kingdom instituted, first in a millennial form and then as everlasting. In this way, the premillennial expectation of a temporary phase of that future kingdom following the Lord's coming and preceding the Final Judgment is consistent and compatible with the extensive revelation given earlier about how a future kingdom of the Lord will come.

(2) Closely related to the above, the fact that a millennial kingdom will be established between Christ's coming and the Final Judgment preserves the hope of the church that, as we have seen, is consistently throughout the New Testament focused on the coming of Jesus Christ. The book of Revelation preserves and emphasizes this hope. Just as Peter wrote that we are to fix our hope completely on the grace to be given to us when Christ is revealed (1 Peter 1:13), so John in Revelation focuses his readers' attention on the coming of Christ (Rev. 1:7; 2:26; 3:3, 11; 19:11–16; 22:7, 12, 17, 20). The millennial kingdom is not a distraction from that hope, not some other program or blessing of God, but rather is part of that same grace, that inheritance that Scripture everywhere indicates is coming with the return of the Lord.

(3) When we inquire into the nature of the millennial kingdom in relation to what has been revealed about the eschatological

kingdom generally, not only the compatibility but also the harmonizing aspect of this progress in revelation becomes clear. The fact that the Millennium transpires prior to the Final Judgment has been enough for premillennialists to emphasize that this kingdom is nothing less than a political as well as spiritual order, which will be set up on this earth. It is this earthly nature that can now be seen as compatible with the new creation theology that everywhere informs biblical eschatology. But the closer we look at the earlier descriptions of the eschatological kingdom, the more evident it becomes that a temporary fulfillment prior to the Final Judgment and followed by an everlasting fulfillment exactly harmonizes those predictions even within a new creation eschatology.

Isaiah 65:17–25 describes the new world of the eschatological kingdom, a condition of joy and great blessing. But curiously death still remains a feature in that world order (65:20). Isaiah 25, however, in no uncertain terms predicts a reign of God in which death will be abolished. Accordingly, although the millennial kingdom that John envisioned will see some of the dead raised to reign with Christ, death itself will not be completely abolished until after the Millennium has passed (Rev. 20:12–21:4).

Some passages predict conditions for the eschatological kingdom in which sin is present while others exclude it altogether. Zechariah 14 plainly states that when the Lord comes in the Day of the Lord, when he descends to the earth and proceeds to reign from Jerusalem, he will require the nations to worship him and will punish those who refuse to do so (14:16–19). Micah 4:1–8, however, speaks of the nations streaming to Zion to learn the ways of the Lord. They beat their swords into plowshares and put an end to war. Daniel 9:24 likewise expects that when the kingdom comes, sin will come to an end. It is conceivable that the differences in these descriptions point to two different phases of the eschatological kingdom, one before and one following the Final Judgment on sin.

The theme of peace presented in Micah 4 and Isaiah 2 is also featured in the prediction of the messianic kingdom of Isaiah 9:6–7. In fact, that passage indicates that there will be no end of peace in that messianic reign. Yet Isaiah 11, which also presents the future messianic reign, speaks of the Messiah slaying the wicked with a word from his mouth (11:4). This could be a reference to the coming of the Messiah and the initiation of his reign. But the presence of the wicked could also refer to a temporal aspect of his reign that will later give way to the conditions described in chapter 9. The repetition of phrases between chapters 11 and 65 seems to relate both of those passages to the same eschatological conditions, and those conditions point to a situation prior to the final dealing with sin and death.

The structure of the oracle in Isaiah 24–25 indicates some kind of intermediate situation between the coming of God in the Day of the Lord and the everlasting reign in which sin and death are done away completely. After describing the destructive judgments of the Day of the Lord, Isaiah comments in 24:21–23:

> In that day the LORD will punish
>> the powers in the heavens above
>> and the kings of the earth below.
> They will be herded together
>> like prisoners in a dungeon;
> they will be shut up in prison
>> and be punished after many days.
> The moon will be abashed, the sun ashamed;
>> for the LORD Almighty will reign
> on Mount Zion and in Jerusalem,
>> before its elders, gloriously.

The many days of imprisonment between the coming of God in the Day of the Lord and the punishment after which the Lord reigns in glory greater than sun or moon bear a correspondence to the millennial period in Revelation 20, which also follows the coming of the Lord in the Day of the Lord (Rev. 6–19) and transpires between the imprisonment of the devil (20:1–3) and his future punishment (20:7–10).[67] After this intermediate order, new conditions are set up in which the new Zion is brighter than sun or moon (21:23). The descriptions of the new earth order in 21:3–4 also draw on the imagery and wording of Isaiah 25:6–9: the peoples of all nations as the inhabitants of the new order and God's wiping away all tears and eliminating death forever.

Paul's teaching about stages of resurrection in 1 Corinthians 15 is also compatible with the later revelation of a millennial

---

[67]A parallel can be found in 1 Enoch 10, where Azazel is bound and imprisoned for a period of time prior to the final, eternal judgment and new earth conditions.

kingdom bounded by two stages of resurrection. In verses 23–24, Paul lists three stages of resurrection: Christ, those who belong to Christ (raised) at his coming, and the end. The grammatical structure indicates that "the end" is the third stage of resurrection, differentiated not only from Christ's resurrection but also from a resurrection of those who believe in Christ. The end also correlates with the final subjugation of death, the last enemy, and the moment at which Christ presents the kingdom to the Father. Prior to this "he must reign until he has put all his enemies under his feet" (15:25). The grammar of the text allows the possibility of an interval of a reign of Christ between the resurrection of believers and the final resurrection.

The point I am making is not that Scripture prior to Revelation 20 explicitly teaches a millennial kingdom. Rather, it teaches a future eschatological kingdom, which the Lord will institute when he comes in the Day of the Lord. John's visions in Revelation confirm this expectation (Rev. 11:15; 21:1–5; 22:5). But what Scripture says about that eschatological kingdom is conducive to being sequenced in its fulfillment, just like the prophecies of Messiah.

Furthermore, prophecies concerning the resurrection of the dead are also amenable to a sequenced fulfillment. The resurrection of Jesus has already demonstrated that fact. A future sequencing of resurrection stages is predicted by Paul in 1 Corinthians 15—a sequence fully capable of being adapted to the millennial revelation that John received concerning the resurrection of saints at Christ's coming and a final resurrection to take place a millennium later. Isaiah 24–25 presents an intervening imprisonment between the coming of the Lord in the Day of the Lord and the final state of immortality. The key that puts all these features together is John's explicit revelation of a millennial kingdom between the return of Jesus and the Final Judgment.

PREMILLENNIALISM IN THE BOOK OF REVELATION

Normal literary grammatical interpretation requires that we understand John's visions recorded in Revelation 19–20 within the larger context of the entire book, which means we must have some understanding of how the book as a whole is structured.

That may seem a more daunting task than it really is. One may ask, isn't the book of Revelation subject to numerous interpretations? Yes, it is. But from a literary standpoint, some conclusions about the structure and development of the book are commonly recognized.[68]

For example, practically all interpreters recognize a prologue in Revelation 1:1–8 and an epilogue in 22:10–21. Furthermore, the letters addressed to the seven churches in 2:1–3:22 should obviously be grouped together. The vision of Jesus found just after the prologue introduces the seven letters (cf. 1:11–12, 20; 2:1) and may be grouped with them or distinguished separately in the structural outline.

The phrase "in the Spirit" is a commonly recognized structural indicator, appearing four times in the book: once just after the prologue (1:10–11), once just after the seven letters (4:1–2), and later to introduce the visions of Babylon (17:1–3) and the new Jerusalem (21:9–10). In each of these texts, John is addressed by someone from heaven and commanded to "write" (1:10–11) or "come," with the promise "I will show you" (4:1–2; 17:1–3; 21:9–10). The first such appearance is from the Lord Jesus Christ. He authorizes John to "write on a scroll what you see" (1:11) and further elaborates this as "write, therefore, what you have seen, what is now and what will take place later" (1:19). The second time John is again visited by the Lord Jesus, who now promises to show him "what must take place after this" (4:1). This promise repeats the wording of 1:19 (*ha . . . genesthai meta tauta*), reinforcing the structural significance of these remarks.

The last two heavenly appearances (17:1–3; 21:9–10) involve angels and are strikingly similar in construction: "One of the seven angels who had the seven bowls [21:9 adds, 'full of the seven last plagues'] came and said to me, 'Come, I will show

---

[68]A helpful approach is given by Christopher R. Smith, "The Structure of the Book of Revelation in Light of Apocalyptic Literary Conventions," *Novum Testamentum* 36 (1994): 373–93. Smith notes that "there is very broad agreement among Revelation's interpreters as to how its structure should be sought—through one of two sound principles of biblical interpretation: assessment of a book according to the conventions of its literary genre, or hermeneutical inquiry after indicated authorial intent." He then goes on to propose a "unified field" approach, which does not simply combine the contributions of others but will "use interactively the two methods one of which almost all interpreters apply" (p. 377). The following structural analysis will follow Smith's approach.

you...." The object to be shown in each case is a city—Babylon in chapter 17 and Jerusalem in chapter 21. The cities, while parallel, are set in contrast by their respective descriptions: 17:1— "Come, I will show you the punishment of the great prostitute who sits on many waters"; 21:9—"Come, I will show you the bride, the wife of the Lamb." In each case, John is carried away by the Spirit, but to different visionary locations—to "a desert" in chapter 17 and "to a mountain, great and high" in chapter 21. In each case, the section begun by these visions ends with the same feature—the rebuke of John's attempt to worship the angel (19:9–10; 22:8–9). From these observations, we can conclude that 17:1–19:10 and 21:9–22:9 also form major structural units in Revelation.

The remaining text not included in the above analysis extends from 4:1–16:21 and from 19:11–21:8. As we will see below, this portion of the text contains a vision of the heavenly court and its judgments and an apocalyptic narrative structured by the two advents of Christ. Two other structural markers will be noted below, one in 1:19 and the other in 10:11. In summary, we can observe the following divisions of this book (key structural markers are shown in italics):

Prologue   1:1–1:8
Visitation by Jesus while in the Spirit and command to write (1:9–10)

Letters to the Seven Churches   1:9–3:22
Command to write (1:19)
Visitation by Jesus while in the Spirit with a command to come and see (4:1)

The Heavenly Court and Its Judgment   4:1–11:19
Command to write again (10:11)

The Apocalyptic Narrative—
Between the Advents   [11:1–13]; 12:1–16:21
Visitation by an angel while in the Spirit with a command to come and see (17:1–3)

Babylon and Her Fall   17:1–19:10

The Apocalyptic Narrative—
The Second Advent and Beyond   19:11–21:8
Visitation by an angel while in the Spirit with a command to come and see (21:9–10)

The New Jerusalem Established Forever   21:9–22:9
Epilogue   22:10–22:21

Most commentators recognize the structural divisions we have noted even if they add various other divisions, subordinate some or elevate others in status. This confirms the point that an overall literary structure of Revelation can be discerned. We must now examine the visions in 4:1–16:21 and 19:11–21:8, the latter of which contains the millennial vision. Can the structure of these visions be identified?

This portion of Revelation contains a number of features that have often been observed. For example, there are the sevenfold series of seals, trumpets, thunders, and bowls. Some commentators have used the sevenfold sequence as an overall approach to the book.[69] There is also the phenomenon of intercalation, reiteration, or recapitulation. But drawing on features of apocalyptic genre along with structural indications in the text, an overall structure can be discerned in these visions that is consistent with historical, contextual, and literary concerns.

The Heavenly Court and Its Judgment

In chapters 4–5, John has a vision in which he ascends to heaven and sees the heavenly throne room, the One who sits on the throne, and the Lord Jesus Christ. Jesus takes a seven-sealed scroll, and as he opens each seal, a corresponding calamity comes on the world (6:1–8:1). The intensity increases when the last seal is broken, introducing another series of seven judgments—with seven trumpets announcing them (8:1–11:19; note 8:1–2, 7, 8, 10, 12; 9:1, 13; 10:7; 11:15). The intensity increases further as John gives a more elaborate description of the last three of these trumpet judgments and designates them as three woes (8:13; 9:12; 11:14). The end of the entire series announces the culmination of divine wrath and the judgment of the dead (11:8), together with the proclamation, "the kingdom of the world has become the kingdom of our Lord and of his Christ, and he will reign for ever and ever" (11:15).

There are two interludes to the unfolding of these serial judgments. (1) In 7:1–17, John sees "the servants of our God" (7:3), who are sealed from "all the tribes of Israel" (7:4–8), and "a

---

[69]For example, see W. Hendriksen, *More Than Conquerors: An Interpretation of the Book of Revelation* (Grand Rapids: Baker, 1939), 25–31; more recently, Adela Yarbro Collins, *The Apocalypse* (Wilmington, Del.: Michael Glazier, 1979).

great multitude ... from every nation, tribe, people and language ... who have come out of the great tribulation ... [and who] have washed their robes and made them white in the blood of the Lamb" (7:9, 14). This interlude is structurally connected with the worship of Christ in heaven in 5:9–10, the vision of the fifth seal (6:9–11), and the promise of the seventh trumpet (11:15–19).

(2) Revelation 10:1–11 announces further revelation, some of which remains a mystery and some of which John is commanded to disclose. The new revelation appears as a book brought down to John from heaven (10:2, 8–10), and he is commanded, "You must prophesy again about many peoples, nations, languages and kings" (10:11). Verse 7 indicates that this revelation relates to the seventh trumpet and the conclusion of all prophetic mysteries. Since the seventh trumpet is announced at the end of chapter 11, the prophecy of chapter 10 explains why the book of Revelation does not end at that point. Several visions will yet occur, beginning already in chapter 11 and running through chapter 22, which deal precisely with "peoples, nations, languages and kings."[70]

The Apocalyptic Narrative

Christopher Smith has observed how in many apocalypses, "a journey through heaven becomes an occasion for a revelation about the course of the future.... Usually such future-oriented sections in apocalyptic works have a 'historical' character because they begin with a lengthy review of history presented as prophecy (*vaticinia ex eventu*) in order to generate greater credence for the actual predictions made."[71] This phenomenon is coordinate with pseudepigraphy in extrabiblical apocalypses (such as Enoch, 4 Ezra, etc.). In their case, the author is portrayed as an ancient prophet, patriarch, or other important figure whose "prophecy" of what is now known as history conditions the reader to accept predictions made about what supposedly yet lies ahead.

The book of Revelation stands distinct from extrabiblical apocalypses in that John does not write pseudepigraphically but

---

[70]I am particularly indebted to J. Dwight Pentecost for this observation. See his *Things to Come*, 187–88; see also Collins, *The Apocalypse*, 3.

[71]Smith, "The Structure of the Book of Revelation," 390.

rather in his own name, as one commissioned by Jesus Christ. Consequently, he makes no pretense about predicting a history already known to his readers. However, the revelation given to him nevertheless parallels the genre of the extrabiblical apocalypses.[72] After his vision of the heavenly court and its judgments, John presents a group of visions in which key events constitute a plot line. As John records visions about "peoples, nations, languages and kings," we can discern the beginning, continuation, culmination, and conclusion of a narrative history.[73]

Smith observes that this plot concerns the Christian community from its beginning to its eschatological culmination. I believe the focus can be sharpened by stating that it concerns Jesus Christ and his saints—those who fear God and keep the testimony of Jesus.[74] While it is impossible to offer a detailed,

---

[72]Robert Thomas reviews the discussion of apocalyptic genre and notes the fact that Revelation does not share the feature of pseudonymity (*Revelation 1–7: An Exegetical Commentary* [Chicago: Moody, 1992], 23–29). He observes John's own indication that the work is prophecy (Rev. 1:3; 22:7, 10, 18, 19) and concludes that the genre should be classified as prophetic, not apocalyptic (or some combination genre in which apocalyptic is included) since "it does not allow for the preeminence of the book's prophetic character" (p. 28). But this is contradicted by his earlier statement, "Of the thirty-one characteristics that have been cited in attempts to define apocalyptic, all when properly understood could apply to prophecy as well, with the possible exception of pseudonymity ..." (p. 25). The similarities between Revelation and apocalyptic literature are well known. Genre features do not have to be followed slavishly and *in toto* in order to make a general classification. Often the particular distinctions from the common genre are what make a work stand out in its uniqueness. John's rejection of pseudonymity concurs with his own testimony as a prophet to the Christian community and distinguishes his "apocalypse" as true, in contrast to many others with which his readers might be familiar.

[73]This helps us to see how the oft-cited contrast between preterist and futurist approaches to the book is in fact a false dichotomy. John's narration includes events that are past as well as present to him and his community. But the narration of past and present events forms the basis for prophetic prediction regarding the future. Thus, both preterist and futurist interpretations have a point that needs to be brought together in a holistic understanding of the book (see Robert H. Mounce, *The Book of Revelation* [Grand Rapids: Eerdmans, 1977], 43–44).

[74]Dispensationalists traditionally have interpreted the Tribulation period described in Revelation as pertaining to Israel, not the church. Consequently, they argue the church is not in view after chapter 5 until chapters 21–22. The reference to "saints" in chs. 6–20 is understood to mean Jewish believers distinct from the church. This view coincides with the dispensationalist expectation that the pretribulational Rapture will remove the church prior to the beginning of the Tribulation

much more complete commentary on these chapters, the general features of this plot can be highlighted. The point is that through various visions there is a progression to this plot and that progression is important (though not in itself the determinative factor) to understanding John's view of the Millennium of 20:1–10. *The basic structure of this progression is the past and future history of Jesus Christ.*[75]

In Revelation 12, John records a vision of the birth of Christ and his ascension into heaven. His death and resurrection have already been stated in previous chapters; his future return is the focus of hope in Revelation (1:7; 2:16; 3:3, 11; 22:7, 12, 17, 20). The period between Jesus' ascension (ch. 12) and return (ch. 19) is the time of conflict for the saints.

The conflictual nature of a life for Christ in this world was a primary concern in the letters to the seven churches. Jesus informs these churches that conflict with the devil and unbelieving peoples can be expected for the church throughout its history (however long that may be) until the coming of Christ. John's visions in chapters 11–22, however, are not an overview of the ages and general course of church history. Rather, his visions here have to do with *the days of the seventh trumpet*, in which the mystery preached to the prophets will be concluded (10:7). After recording the ascension of Christ in 12:5, John's visions quickly focus on a time that is repeatedly referenced in three chapters in the same or similar ways: 1260 days (11:3; 12:6), 42 months (11:2; 13:5), time, times, half a time (12:14), all roughly equal to three and one-half years. It is with respect to *this particular period* between the advents, prior to the return of the previously ascended Christ, that John's narration of events is primarily concerned.

---

so that the program of the earthly people can begin again. Nondispensationalists reject the idea of a pretribulational Rapture and see these "saints" as the church. Progressive dispensationalists see these "saints" as part of the body of Christ, thus a part of the church as it is defined in the New Testament. However, they also affirm a pretribulational Rapture on the basis of 1 Thessalonians 4–5. Its purpose is not to distinguish between heavenly and earthly peoples and programs but as a sign of the future resurrection and transformation that will be given to all who come to faith in Christ.

[75]This accords with the fact that the book is a revelation of Christ and with the references at the beginning and end of the book to his past and future (1:8, 18 and 22:13).

Oppression in that time will come from the dragon, that is, the devil, just as was the case for John's readers in his own day. However, Satan's wrath will be great, a "woe to the earth and the sea . . . because he knows that his time is short" (12:12). The "woe" relates this vision intertextually to the "Woe! Woe! Woe to the inhabitants of the earth" in 8:13, which speaks of the final trumpet judgments. The short time harmonizes with the brief time period that is repeatedly invoked in these visions, which portray the devil playing a key role and speak of persecution for the saints.

The plot progresses as the devil gives authority to the beast (13:2) and speaks through the false prophet (13:11–12). Whereas the saints (some at least) receive some protection from the dragon in chapter 12, the beast, who is empowered by the dragon in chapter 13, is able to overcome them. This progression is already anticipated in chapter 11, where the two witnesses are overcome only by the beast when he appears on the scene. Chapter 14 presents warnings and anticipates the coming judgment on the beast and his followers. Chapters 15–16 present that judgment falling as a series of seven plagues. The vision of Babylon in chapters 17–18 looks at these themes in contrast to the coming city of God in chapters 21–22. The acquisition of power by the beast in chapter 13 is replayed in this vision of Babylon (17:11–18).

It is important to note that the coming of Christ in Revelation 19 marks a definite progression to the plot structure of these visions concerning peoples, nations, languages, and kings, which started with the two witnesses in Revelation 11, was positioned after the First Advent in chapter 12, and came to focus on the short period of three and one-half years. The coming of Jesus not only brings about the destruction of Babylon but also the crushing of the beast and false prophet and their expulsion into the lake of fire. Consequently, his coming brings to an end their period of authority, which has been highlighted so deliberately up to this time. All that remains after the punishment of the beast is the punishment of the devil (whose time of wrath on the nations was said to have been short, anticipating its coming termination), the judgment of the dead, and the eternal reign of the saints on the earth. It is precisely at this point that John tells us that these expectations will be fulfilled in a two-step process of one thousand years between the return of Christ and the final state.

Revelation 20:1–10 Within 19:11–21:8

We must now consider Revelation 19:11–21:8—visions that concern the coming of Christ and its consequent effects, namely, the unfolding judgment on the wicked and the fulfillment of blessing on the people of God. The Millennium is one of these consequences; it is not a vision of circumstances that exist prior to the Parousia.

Many of the more recent studies on the literary structure of Revelation acknowledge this. Bauckham writes, for example, "Between the two sections 17:1–19:10 and 21:9–22:9 comes a section [19:11–21:8] which must be understood as a single section describing the transition from one to the other."[76] Fiorenza notes that the capture of the devil in 20:1–3 and his final punishment in 20:7–11 is a two-part punishment that extends the victory of Christ won in chapter 19.[77] Michaels writes that structurally in the context of the visions themselves, the events of 19:11–21 lie in the past of the events of chapter 20. The Millennium itself, he notes, is a transitional reign between the coming of Christ and the new world.[78] "Its theological contributions to the Book of Revelation are its graphic pictures of the vindication of the martyrs and of Satan's final consignment to the lake of fire." It is "a kind of threshold to his visions of the new world and its new holy city" (chs. 21–22).[79]

Collins interprets the visions of 19:11–21:8 as an unnumbered series of seven visions and interprets them in a sequential manner, although she rejects any correspondence to actual future events. While she speaks about recapitulation in terms of themes already mentioned in Revelation, the actual plot line running through these visions is sequential.[80] Robert Wall sees 19:11–20:15 as a group of visions that describe "a single event, Christ's return to earth, and its various results, concluding with the establishment of the eschatological community in the garden of

---

[76]Richard Bauckham, *The Climax of Prophecy: Studies on the Book of Revelation* (Edinburgh: T. & T. Clark, 1993), 5.

[77]Elizabeth Schüssler Fiorenza, *Revelation: Vision of a Just World* (Minneapolis: Fortress, 1991), 103–9.

[78]J. Ramsey Michaels, *Interpreting the Book of Revelation* (Grand Rapids: Baker, 1992), 68.

[79]Ibid., 146.

[80]Collins, *The Apocalypse*, 133–34.

the city of God."[81] In contrast to traditional amillennial interpretation, both Wall and Collins relate the binding of Satan (20:1–3) to the Second Advent in 19:11–21 and contrast it with his casting down in Revelation 12 (a result of the First Advent).[82] Finally, we may note Jürgen Roloff, who argues:

> ... a clearly marked break exists between 19:10 and 11. The sections that now follow focus on the events that conclude the end-time event: the return of Jesus as judge of the world (19:11–21), the establishment of the messianic kingdom (20:1–10), the resurrection of the dead and the judgment of the world (20:11–15), as well as the new world and the consummation of the community of salvation.[83]

Many of these commentators, though not all, discount any predictive significance to these visions. That is not surprising given their view that biblical prophecy and apocalyptic is mythological. It is noteworthy, however, that when the issue of theological-historical significance is suspended and the question is strictly literary, there is general agreement that the events in the visions of 19:11–21:8 are correlative with or consequent to the Parousia of 19:11.

For evangelicals, the visions of 19:11–21:8 have referential significance. But that significance must be dependent on the literary-grammatical-contextual meaning of the visions themselves. Essential to this is the determination of the basic plot development of the visions. We can all agree that John gives little information about the Millennium of Revelation 20. But the question is: How do we understand contextually the little information he does give?

---

[81]Robert W. Wall, *Revelation* (Peabody, Mass.: Hendrickson, 1991), 227. Wall sees the Millennium as an aspect of the Second Advent (pp. 234–35). While he rejects the notion that it should be seen as a chronological period following the Second Advent, he also rejects the idea that it is a recapitulation of a period prior to that advent. Premillennialism, of course, argues that the millennial vision is indeed a period following the advent of ch. 19. However, the point to be noted here is that Wall sees the visions of 19:11–21:8 as developing or expanding the meaning of the Second Advent in Revelation. The series of visions are sequential in a literary sense as they expand this meaning. In that sense, his observations accord with the premillennial reading of the *literary* sequence of these visions.

[82]Ibid., 234; Collins, *The Apocalypse*, 141.

[83]Jürgen Roloff, *The Revelation of John: A Continental Commentary*, trans. John E. Alsup (Minneapolis: Fortress, 1993), 16.

There is no question that the Millennium is a one-thousand-year imprisonment of the devil and reign of the saints with Christ. Is it an imprisonment and reign *after* the return of Christ? When we see a basic consensus of people who study the literary structure of the book that John does in fact see an interregnum between the Parousia and the new world freely admitting this point (while dissociating any personal theological commitments from such an idea), then the question is: Why do some evangelicals committed to Scripture have such trouble seeing this? I suggest that the answer lies in traditional theological preunderstandings that are hostile to this interpretation, preunderstandings whose history we have sketched earlier in this chapter.

Six observations bear on the point that the thousand years of Satan's imprisonment and the saints' reign in Revelation 20 must be seen as consequent to the Parousia of Christ in chapter 19. In this we leave aside for the moment the exploration of the meaning of this Millennium. It is enough for now to establish the fact that whatever the Millennium means, whatever the imprisonment means, whatever the reigning is, it is something that John saw as occurring *subsequent* to a future coming of Christ and consequent thereon as something he himself establishes. It is *not* something John saw as a condition existing *prior to* the Parousia.

(1) The visions of 19:11–21:8 are positioned as a transition between the vision of Babylon and the view of the New Jerusalem. As such, they are best understood conceptually as a transition from one to another. In John's account, these two cities are not coexisting realities. Each city receives the allegiance, the support, and the participation of the nations, of the kings of the earth. The governments of the earth fornicate with Babylon; the saints are dead and dying under her dominion. This vision is oriented toward Babylon's end, her destruction by God, and the vindication of the saints. The vision of the New Jerusalem sees the nations walking by its light, the kings of earth bringing their glory into it. The saints thrive in the new city, serving the Lord. The emphasis of the two visions is on the establishment of the New Jerusalem.

In John's vision, the New Jerusalem succeeds and replaces Babylon. God removes Babylon for the purpose of revealing the new Jerusalem. The intervening visions tell us that the old order of earth and heaven give way to the new heaven and new earth, that the old things are passed away, that death, crying, and pain—characteristics of Babylon—have all passed as God makes all things new. The relation of the two cities in John's vision is sequential, not juxtapositional. As Michaels points out, the New Jerusalem does not reiterate (his word for recapitulate) Babylon "because the formal parallels between the two visions only serve to highlight the irreconcilable conflict between the two cities."[84] In the book of Revelation, the New Jerusalem is *not* an inaugurated kingdom. It is wholly future.[85]

With the two cities related to each other in terms of a replacement, the intervening visions explain the transition in which and by which the replacement takes place. Christ comes in 19:11 and judges the nations who fornicated with Babylon, who consolidated their loyalty with the beast, and who gathered to war against Christ. He casts the beast and false prophet into the lake of fire. He imprisons the devil. He raises the martyrs murdered by Babylon and the beast. He and his saints rule the nations with a rod of iron. Then, after the nations revolt upon the release of the devil, he casts the devil into the lake of fire to join the previously sentenced beast and false prophet. He raises the rest of the dead and judges them, damning the wicked to hell. All things are made new and he receives his bride, the New Jerusalem, in which his saints will dwell.

(2) The visions of 19:11–21:8 are structured in a unified sequence. *There is no structural indication of a major break within this sequence recapitulating pre-Parousia conditions.* The series is tied together by the frequent use of *kai eidon* ("and I saw"), a recognized structural marker. This phrase, although not determinative in itself of a chronological sequence, nevertheless can be used for such. The content of the visions helps to determine the chronology. The key point, however, is that *kai eidon* does *not* signify a major structural break at one point (such as 20:1), which would be contrary to its use throughout the entire group of visions.[86]

---

[84]Michaels, *Interpreting the Book of Revelation*, 66.

[85]This is in contrast to Paul, who speaks of our present citizenship of the heavenly Jerusalem (Gal. 4). Hebrews also speaks of the present reality of the heavenly Jerusalem (Heb. 12:22–24), but it also speaks of its future coming (13:14), consistent with its expectation of a coming kingdom (12:28), which correlates with "the world to come" (2:5).

[86]Commenting on 20:1, Robert Mounce writes, "It should be noted that the recurring 'and I saw' of 19:11, 17, 19; 20:1, 4, 12; and 21:1 appears to establish a

(3) Six out of the eight visions in 19:11–21:8 are commonly acknowledged as either contemporaneous with the Parousia or subsequent to it. These include 19:17–18, 19–21; 20:7–10, 11–15; 21:1, 2–8. The presumption is in favor of viewing the remaining two visions in a similar manner, a presumption that is reinforced by the preceding observations.

(4) The description of Satan's relation to the world in 20:1–3 is incompatible with the descriptions of that relationship envisioned by John as transpiring prior to the Parousia. Descriptions of the devil in relation to the nations in chapters 12–14 harmonize with descriptions of 20:1–3 only if the latter is understood as a subsequent, changed condition. The contrasts that set forth these changed conditions are well summarized by Johnson:

> That this whole action is not a recapitulation of earlier descriptions of Satan is evident from a number of points: (1) In 12:9 (q.v. for the same titles), Satan is "hurled" out of heaven "to the earth," where he goes forth

---

sequence of visions which carries through from the appearance of the Rider on the white horse (19:11) to the establishment of the new heaven and new earth (21:1ff). The interpretation that discovers recapitulation for the segment 20:1–6 must at least bear the burden of proof" (*The Book of Revelation*, 352). Recently, Fowler White has argued that the angelic descent in 20:1 is a structural indicator of a recapitulating sequence ("Reexamining the Evidence for Recapitulation in Rev. 20:1–10," *Westminster Theological Journal* 51 [1989]: 319–44). Although White says that this observation "does not *prove* recapitulation in chap. 20, . . . it does support that approach . . ." (p. 336). White believes that angelic descent in 7:2; 10:1; and 18:1 establishes a structural pattern in which the occurrence of angelic descent "initiate[s] a visional sequence which temporarily suspends historical progress . . . [within a larger structural sequence—such as the seals or trumpets series] and introduces a recapitulating interlude" (p. 338). In each case, White argues that the interlude takes the reader to a point prior to the beginning of the series in which the angelic descent interlude is located. On this basis, he argues that the angelic descent of 20:1 signals an interlude that recapitulates conditions prior to 19:11, that is, prior to the second coming of Christ. Since Rev. 20:1 introduces the Millennium, White concludes that the Millennium concerns conditions prior to the second coming of Christ. However, White's theory fails on literary-structural grounds. (1) In each of his examples (7:1; 10:1; 18:1) the structural indicator is distinct from the indicator used in the larger series (numbered sequence in the seals and trumpets visions; "and he [or the angel] said to me" in the Babylon vision). In 20:1, this is not the case; the structural indicator ("and I saw") is used for the series itself. As a result, the angel's coming down in 20:1 is a series item just as much as the opening of heaven in 19:11, as the angel standing in the sun in 19:16, as the assembling of the beast and the kings of the earth in 19:19, etc. (2) Each of White's examples involve a message from the angel, which also

with great fury to work his deception and persecute God's people (13:14; 18:23c). But in 20:1–3, the situation is completely different. Here Satan is cast *out of the earth* into a place where he is kept from "deceiving the nations." (2) The former period of Satan's restriction to earth is described as a "short time" (12:9, 12) while the time here (20:1–3) of his binding is a thousand years. (3) In the earlier references to Satan, he is very active on the earth (2:10, 13; 12:17; 16:13, cf. 1 Peter 5:8); here he is tightly sealed in "prison" (*phylaka*, v.7). The binding of Satan is concurrent with and inseparable from the thousand-year reign of resurrected martyrs.... If that reign is yet future, the binding is future. If the binding refers to an earthly situation—which it clearly does—the thousand-year reign most naturally refers to an earthly situation.[87]

We need to examine this fourth observation in more detail. The *isolation* implied by imprisonment in 20:1–3 is reinforced by comparison with John's vision in chapter 9. In Revelation 9, John

includes an explicit reference to the larger series (7:3; 10:7; 18:2). No such message appears in 20:1–10. There are other problems with White's presentation as well. (3) In 7:2, the angel *ascends*, disqualifying the entire passage from consideration in a *descending* angel typology. (4) White's discussion of chs. 10–11 ignores the structural significance of 10:11 for the two witnesses' vision in 11:3–13. As a result, he treats the two witnesses' vision as if it were part of the interlude in ch. 10, completely ignoring its structural connection to the visions of chs. 12–14. (5) Also, White ignores the reference to Babylon's destruction in 17:16 in his effort to locate the setting of 18:1 prior to ch. 17. But the attempt to locate ch. 18 prior to the bowls judgment in ch. 16 also runs counter to his typology because ch. 18 is not an interlude in the bowls series. In all of this, White's approach has the feel of an artificially constructed typology that ignores numerous textual details that argue against his reading of ch. 20. (6) Finally, one should note that for all of his focus in the descending angel of 20:1, White surprisingly makes no mention of Rev. 9:1–6, the only passage that truly offers a parallel description to that of 20:1–3. There, John saw "a star that had fallen ... to the earth." This star, a personal being (as is an angel), is given "the key to the shaft of the Abyss" (*hē kleis tou phreatos tēs abyssou*). The language is practically the same as in 20:1, where the angel who comes down has "the key to the Abyss" (*tēn klein tēs abysson*). A contrast is set up between 9:1–6 and 20:1–3 in the plot development of Revelation. The star, or angel, of 9:1 *releases* tormentors from the Abyss. The angel of 20:1 *imprisons* the devil in the Abyss. Then, in 20:7, the devil is *released* from the Abyss. Note that the vision of the star in 9:1 is *not a recapitulating vision* but rather part of a visionary sequence, just as is the angel of 20:1.

[87] Alan Johnson, "Revelation," in *The Expositor's Bible Commentary*, ed. Frank E. Gaebelein (Grand Rapids: Zondervan, 1981), 12:581–82.

sees a swarm of locusts coming up out of the pit. The harm caused by these pit locusts occurs only after they are released. The necessary implication is that their influence is not experienced by anyone as long as they are locked up in the pit. The graphic language about the key, opening the pit, subsequent instructions about harming, and coming on the earth (*eis tēn gēn*, v. 3), with the object being *tous anthrōpous hoitines ouk echousi tēn sphragida tou theou*, all converges to make the point that these "locusts" had *no* influence on earthly inhabitants prior to the time of their release. This does not mean that evil was nonexistent, but that these locusts themselves played no role prior to their release.

In 20:1–3, the language of key and pit is repeated, echoing the situation of chapter 9. But the notion of confinement is emphasized even more by words such as "chain," "bound" (*edēsen*), "locked" (*ekleisen*, implying the use of the "key," *kleis*), and "sealed . . . over him" (*esphragisen epanō autou*). The contrast between Satan's activity in chapters 12–13 and the inactivity in 20 could not be more greatly stressed.

The arguments of Augustine that being bound in 20:3 meant that "the angel . . . checked and repressed [Satan's] power to seduce and possess those destined to be set free [saved, given eternal life]," and that being bound means "being cast deeper [for he was already there] into the hearts of the nonelect," are without literary contextual support in the book of Revelation.[88] Mark 3:27 is too remote a context for interpreting John's words. Whatever contribution they may make can only be secondary to intercontextual interpretation in Revelation itself. But the comparison of contexts between Mark 3 and Revelation 20 leads clearly to the point that the two texts are speaking of different matters.[89] Johnson summarizes the point well when he writes:

> A careful examination of Mark 3:27 and Revelation 20:1–3 leads to the conclusion that the two passages are not teaching the same truth. There is a sense in which, according to the Gospel account, Satan is in the process of being

---

[88]Augustine, *City of God*, 20.7.

[89]Walvoord notes, "Opposed to the amillennial interpretation, however, is the uniform revelation of the New Testament which shows that Satan in the present age is a very active person." He then surveys the many texts that speak of Satan's activity at the present time (*The Revelation of Jesus Christ* [Chicago: Moody, 1966], 292–93).

bound by the activity of Christ and the kingdom of God; but this is clearly an event different from the total consigning of Satan to the Abyss as taught in Rev. 20:1–3.[90]

Another consideration in support of the transitional, nonrecapitulating nature of 20:1–3 is the explanation given by John that the binding of the devil is "to keep him from deceiving the nations anymore until the thousand years were ended." Richard Ostella has called attention to the significance of the word "anymore" or "no longer" (mē . . . eti) as signifying a *prior* action of deception that provoked the Parousia of 19:11–21.[91]

In 12:9, the devil's activity on earth following the ascension of Christ is seen in his characterization as the one "who leads the whole world astray" (ho planōn tēn oikoumenēn). The devil's activity progresses in chapter 13, where he gives power to the beast (13:4) and speaks through the false prophet (13:11) so that the latter "deceived the inhabitants of the earth" (plana tous katoikountas epi tēs gēs) through various signs and wonders (13:14). This deception reaches its climax in the gathering of the nations for the battle of Armageddon as is graphically described in 16:13–16: Three evil spirits are seen to come out of the mouths of the dragon, the beast, and the false prophet. The spirits perform miraculous signs and gather the kings of the whole world (tēs oikoumenēs holēs) for battle. This battle is the coming of Christ in 19:11–21, at which the beast and false prophet are seized, the latter described as the one who "deluded [eplanēsen] those who had received the mark of the beast."

Since Satan was the power behind this deception, the reader naturally expects judgment on him. Revelation 20:1–3 is the first part of that punishment, when the devil is seized and bound "to keep him from deceiving the nations anymore [hina mē planēsē eti ta ethnē] until the thousand years were ended." The deception then resumes (after the thousand years) in 20:7–10, where after Satan is released he will go out "to deceive the nations [planēsai ta ethnē] . . . to gather them for battle." It should be evident that 20:1–3 cannot describe pre-Parousia conditions since those conditions in the book of Revelation find the devil at work *deceiving the nations*. In Revelation 20, John says that the devil is

[90]Johnson, "Revelation," 582.

[91]Richard A. Ostella, "The Significance of Deception in Revelation 20:3," *Westminster Theological Journal* 37 (1975): 236–38.

bound so that he *deceives the nations no longer*. This indicates a termination to that deceptive activity described in the previous eight chapters, which has been building to a climax (from 16:13–16 to 19:11–21) and which has been emphasized through the repetition of the verb "deceive" (*planaō*, cf. 19:20; 20:3).[92]

(5) The next observation on the millennial vision of 20:1–10 as being subsequent to the Parousia is the fact that the rebellion after the Millennium (vv. 7–10) is described in terms that carefully distinguish it from the state of affairs that existed at the Parousia. The latter rebellion occurs on Satan's release from prison, whereas the earlier had occurred after his being cast down to the earth. The latter rebellion surrounds the saints and the beloved city (on earth), while the earlier rebellion gathered to resist the descent of Christ and the saints to the earth. The suppression of the earlier rebellion gave the bodies of the rebels to the carrion birds; the suppression of the latter consumes them by fire.

(6) The final observation on the post-Parousia, prefinal judgment nature of the Millennium envisioned by John comes

---

[92]White argues that a sequential interpretation of 19:11–20:3 is not logically coherent, that its "credibility … suffers considerably" because at the Parousia, Christ will destroy all the inhabitants of all the nations except the redeemed ("Reexamining the Evidence for Recapitulation in Rev. 20:1–10," 325). Thus, he concludes, there will be no nations left who were previously deceived and are now to be deceived no longer. But nowhere in 19:11–21 does it say that Christ at the Parousia will destroy all the inhabitants of all the nations. Rev. 16:13–16 and 19:11–21 describe a military battle. The gathering of the nations for this battle is not a gathering of all their inhabitants but of their armies. This point is made explicit in 19:19: "I saw the beast and the kings of the earth and their armies gathered together to make war against the rider on the horse [Christ] and his army." When 19:21 says, "the rest of them were killed with the sword that came out of the mouth [of Christ]," it refers to the destruction of these *armies, not all the inhabitants* or even all the wicked inhabitants of the nations, as White apparently thinks (see Harold W. Hoehner, "Evidence From Revelation 20," in Campbell and Townsend, eds., *A Case for Premillennialism*, 252). While he quotes 19:15, White overlooks the phrase "he will rule them with an iron scepter." This *future*, or *subsequent rule* is a stated purpose in his coming, and the "them" refers to the nations. If he completely destroyed them all, he could hardly fulfill his intent to rule them. Furthermore, the "iron scepter" recalls Ps. 2:9 as well as the rod of Isa. 11:4. The description conveys the image of potentially rebellious subjects. The pattern of Parousia followed by a rule over restless subjects, even involving discipline of those subjects, has already been set in Zech. 14. The use of the rod of iron description in Rev. 19 fits well with the subsequent millennial rule as described in 20:1–10, after which the potential of rebellion finds actual expression and is suppressed. But the language is ill suited to describe the conditions of the new earth.

from the description that John gives of the millennial reign of the saints in 20:4–6. It is to this description that we now turn.

The Crux Interpretum: Revelation 20:4–6

In Revelation 20:4, John first sees "thrones on which were seated those who had been given authority to judge." The identity of the occupants of these thrones is not crucial to resolving the millennial question, but it is plausible to see them as those who next come into focus in the following lines of the vision.[93] John sees "the souls of those who had been beheaded because of their testimony for Jesus and because of the word of God." They are joined by a greater company (see NASB), or less preferably, are themselves further described as those who "had not worshiped the beast or his image and had not received his mark on their foreheads or on their hands."

These descriptions take us back to 6:9, where underneath the altar of God in heaven, John saw "the souls of those who had been slain because of the word of God and the testimony they had maintained." Those souls are told to wait for justice and vindication "until the number of their fellow servants and brothers who were to be killed as they had been was completed" (6:11). Revelation 12 tells of the conflict between the devil and "those who obey God's commandments and hold to the testimony of Jesus" (12:17). They are able to overcome the devil "by the blood of the Lamb and by the word of their testimony" (12:11). But at least some will die because he adds, "they did not love their lives so much as to shrink from death" (12:11).

Chapter 13 envisions the devil giving power to the beast (13:2). So empowered, the beast is then able to "make war against the saints and to conquer them" (13:7). All are required to worship the beast, and those who refuse are killed (13:15). Everyone who survives is required "to receive a mark on his right hand or on his forehead" (13:16). The death of the saints is again seen in 17:6, where Babylon the Great, the harlot of the nations, is "drunk with the blood of the saints, the blood of those who bore testimony to Jesus" (see also 18:24).

The phrases of 20:4 identify those who have been martyred as none other than believers in Christ—the same as those who

---

[93]For a survey of views on the identity of these who reign with Christ, see John P. Newport, *The Lion and the Lamb* (Nashville: Broadman, 1986).

suffered physical death as described in John's preceding vision. While he specifies "beheaded" as the manner in which these martyrs had died, his reference to others (*kai hoitines*) and the use of phrases such as "testimony," "because of the word of God," and refusal to worship the beast tie this whole company to the martyrs in the preceding visions. Revelation 6:9, 11 introduced the expectation that some justice would be executed by God on their behalf, and they wait for that justice even as they are joined in waiting by subsequent martyrs. But the letters to the seven churches also gave readers the expectation that those who die for their faith in Christ will receive "the crown of life" (2:10), given to them by none other than Christ himself, "who died and came to life again" (2:8). Furthermore, they expect that to the one who overcomes will be given authority to rule the nations (2:26–27) and will be granted "the right to sit with me [Christ] on my throne" (3:21), all of which is reinforced in the later promise that "they will reign on the earth" (5:10).

With these expectations in mind, we read in 20:4 that these martyrs "came to life and reigned with Christ [recall 3:21] a thousand years." That is, what John sees is the just vindication of believers who were slain for their faith, the fulfillment to them of promises made by Christ himself. They will be raised from physical death and will reign on the earth with the resurrected Jesus. The only new element added is a temporal duration of one thousand years.

John interprets his own words in verses 5b–6. This coming to life is the "first resurrection." "The second death has no power over them" recalls the promise of 2:11, that they will receive "the crown of life" from Jesus, who himself had come to life. John further specifies that these resurrected martyrs "will be priests of God and of Christ" and repeats the fact that they "will reign with him for a thousand years." This description not only picks up the language of 1:6 but also the promise of 5:10, which specifies a future "reign on the earth." In his elaboration, John clarifies that he has resurrection from physical death in view, followed by a reign of the resurrected with Christ on the earth, and he repeats that this reign will last a thousand years.

Working from the standpoint of a contextual, grammatical, and literary interpretation of 20:4–6, certain interpretations of these verses are implausible at best and otherwise without foundation. Augustine's often-repeated suggestion that "came to life" means spiritual birth, regeneration to spiritual life, is simply not possible.[94] In Revelation, the only other uses of *zaō* in the aorist are for bodily resurrection, one genuine (2:8, of Christ who died and came to life) and one apparent (13:14, of the beast, who appeared to receive a fatal wound yet lived).

Consistently through John's visions, martyrs are those who lose their physical lives for Christ's sake. They have a promise from the One who died and yet came to life in resurrection (*ezēsen* in 2:8) that they will receive the crown of life (2:10) and that they will reign on the earth (5:10). These promises are fulfilled when at the end of the book they come to life (*ezēsan*) and reign with Christ (20:4). References to Paul's use of words for rising or being made alive with Christ and being seated with him (Rom. 6:4; Eph. 2:5–6; 5:14; Col. 3:1) are not relevant to Revelation 20:4 because John is not talking about a coming to life from spiritual death. The martyrs in Revelation are not spiritually dead prior to their coming to life. They are dead "because of their testimony for Jesus." They already had spiritual life, as evidenced by this faith that led to their martyrdom.

Nor can one establish the interpretation that the martyrs were simply alive spiritually in spite of being dead physically—an interpretation that eliminates the ingressive sense of *ezēsan* (i.e., *came to* life, *began to* live [as would be the case in a resurrection]). Such a view argues that John is stating a simple contrast: They were dead (physically) yet were alive (spiritually).[95] But this has no support contextually. The ingressive sense is the proper sense in the other uses of the word (2:8; 13:14), and they mean bodily resurrection. Even outside Revelation, *ezēsan* or *ezēsen* is never used to describe the life of a disembodied soul. On the contrary, it is used with an ingressive sense to denote resurrection (cf. LXX of Ezek. 37:10). It is even used interchangeably with *anazaō*, which means definitely "to live again" (see Luke 15:24, 32).

John's meaning is established by his use of the word "resurrection" (*anastasis*) to clarify "came to life" (*ezēsan*). The word *anastasis* is never used in the Bible for the continuing existence

---

[94]Augustine, *City of God*, 20.

[95]This interpretation was argued by James A. Hughes, "Revelation 20:4–6 and the Question of the Millennium," *Westminster Theological Journal* 35 (1973): 290–92. It was correctly refuted by Jack S. Deere, "Premillennialism in Revelation 20:4–6," *Bibliotheca Sacra* 135 (1978): 66–67.

of the physically dead. Other than an instance in which it has no reference to death (Luke 2:34, although an oblique reference to resurrection cannot be ruled out), it *always* refers to *the elimination of the condition of physical death through bodily resurrection.*

Besides grammatical and lexical incoherence, the argument that John is asserting the contrasting fact of life in heaven for dead martyrs destroys the plot of judgment and blessing for martyrs running through the visions and coming to climax at this point in the book. The martyrs have been promised bodily resurrection (2:10) and a future reign with Christ (2:26–27; 3:21) on the earth (5:10). Their deaths by martyrdom, the spilling of their blood on the earth, has been a repeated theme up to this point. In their state of death they are never described as reigning or as seated on thrones, but as resting, waiting, and positioned under the altar until justice is done for them (6:9–10; 14:13). But in 20:4, their condition is changed. At the time that judgment comes on their enemies, they come to life and reign. This is the beginning of the fulfillment of the promise and reward for which they have been waiting throughout the book.[96]

Interpretations of these martyrs' coming to life spiritually (as if from spiritual death) or simply living spiritually while physically dead are not valid within the parameters of contextual, grammatical, and literary interpretation of the book of Revelation. Nor are they valid as a historical-grammatical interpretation within the broader contexts of the Old and New Testaments. These interpretations can only be accounted for as the importation of some external context of meaning that is hostile to the notion of a post-Parousia, prefinal judgment reign of the resurrected on the earth.

Revelation 20:5a is also important in understanding John's vision of the Millennium because it explains how the Christian expectation of a universal resurrection will take place. John writes

---

[96]In light of this it seems incredible that Meredith Kline could devote two articles attempting to defend a traditional amillennial view of "the first resurrection" by means of an argument on the word "first," completely ignoring the operative term "resurrection" ("The First Resurrection," *Westminster Theological Journal* 37 [1975]: 366–75; "The First Resurrection: A Reaffirmation," *Westminster Theological Journal* 39 [1976]: 117–19). The latter is a response to J. Ramsey Michaels, "The First Resurrection: A Response," *Westminster Theological Journal* 39 (1976): 100–109 (see Hoehner, "Evidence From Revelation 20," 255). Unsurpassed on this topic is A. J. Gordon's essay written almost 130 years ago, "The First Resurrection," in *Second Coming of Christ: Premillennial Essays*, 78–107.

that "the rest of the dead did not come to life until the thousand years were ended." The typical postmillennial and amillennial interpretations of "came to life" are once again seen to be deficient from a grammatical, contextual, and literary standpoint.

Premillennialists have always argued that "came to life" must mean the same thing in 20:5 as it does in 20:4.[97] Typical amillennial and postmillennial interpretations usually try to acknowledge this point but face a problem with the universal extent of the phrase "rest of the dead" and the implication that they too will come to life when the thousand years are ended. Obviously, if "came to life" means to have or begin to have *spiritual life*, then "the rest of the dead" (whether physically or spiritually) will all receive *spiritual life* at the end of the Millennium, whatever the Millennium is taken to mean. Since "the rest" appears to be comprehensive (few debate this comprehensiveness), then universalism would be the result! But that interpretation immediately conflicts with 20:11–14 (note also 14:9–11, which describes the future of those who do worship the beast and receive the mark in contrast to the martyrs of 20:4—those dead whose deaths are recorded in 14:17–20 and 19:15–21, along with others who have died in the judgments leading up to that point [6:8; 9:18], as well as all the dead in Hades [20:12–13], all of whom are included in the contextual meaning of "the rest of the dead").

Augustine attempted to avoid this problem by discounting the sense of "until the thousand years were ended," arguing that it means something like "during or up to the point of the thousand years," thus implying no expected changes *after* that millennial period (whatever it refers to) has been terminated.[98] Once again, this interpretative sense is imported into the text contrary to grammatical, contextual meaning. While *achri* ("until") may of itself indicate a simple limit, its use as a conjunction with *teleō* ("to complete, fulfill, end") in the book of Revelation consistently indicates a reversal of conditions[99] (see this combination in 15:8;

---

[97]Alford's consternation is typical of many premillennialists: "If, in a passage where *two resurrections* are mentioned . . . the first resurrection may be understood to mean *spiritual* rising with Christ, while the second means *literal* rising from the grave;—then there is an end of all significance in language, and Scripture is wiped out as a definite testimony to anything" ("Apocalypse of John," *The Greek Testament* [Chicago: Moody, 1958], 4:732).

[98]Augustine, *City of God*, 20.9.

[99]Cf. Deere, "Premillennialism in Revelation 20:4–6," 68–69.

17:17; 20:3 [which is the same as 20:5]). In these passages it contributes to the theme of the future fulfillment of God's judgment and promised blessing by signifying the temporary nature of present conditions.

In the immediate context of 20:3, the revelation that the devil will be kept from deceiving the nations "until the thousand years were ended" clearly intends a change of conditions, since 20:7–8 tells us that when the thousand years were over, "Satan will be released ... to deceive the nations." In 20:5a, the expected reversal is further confirmed in 20:13, when (after the thousand years, 20:7) death and Hades (the intermediate state of the dead) give up the dead. This is the final resurrection, which constitutes the reversal of state for the rest of the dead in 20:5.

To summarize at this point, "came to life" in 20:5 must have the same meaning as 20:4. It cannot mean "came to spiritual life" or "lived spiritually" for two reasons: (1) It cannot mean this in 20:4, as has been shown, and (2) by virtue of the syntax of *achri teleō*, either sense would entail a major contradiction with the teaching of Revelation (as with biblical theology generally) on the destiny of the unbelieving dead. The only way to avoid these problems while maintaining these meanings is to remove 20:4–5 from its literary and grammatical context in the book of Revelation and set it within some external field of meaning.

Establishing the fact that John really envisions the physical resurrection of martyrs to reign with Christ on earth is the crucial point. For once this is seen, the objection to the sequence of 19:11–21:8 becomes irrelevant. No such bodily resurrection of martyrs for Christ has occurred nor is any expected by anyone (including amillennial or postmillennial) until Christ returns. Furthermore, arguments about the literal meaning of the "thousand years" also become irrelevant. The issue is not how *exact* are the thousand years, for we know that Scripture often uses round numbers in reference to time as well as in other quantitative measurements. Nor is the issue the fact that the Bible uses numbers symbolically, such as the seven heads of the beast. Even as a symbol, a number has some meaning, figuratively referring to some kind of sequence, quantity, or duration.

In Revelation 11–22, John uses numbers to mark the time of his visionary narrative. One set of numbers consistently refers to the "short time" of the devil's wrath and deception prior to the Parousia. One figure—significantly larger—refers to the period of the saints' vindication and the devil's imprisonment after the Parousia and before the Final Judgment and the revelation of the new earth and the new Jerusalem. The point is that John sees a passage of time, which he calls "a thousand years," transpiring between two physical resurrections, a period of history in which the first resurrected ones reign on earth with Christ and during which Satan's relation to the earth and its inhabitants is changed.

CONCLUSION

We have seen that Jesus Christ gave to John the specific revelation that after his coming, believers who had given their lives for him would be raised from the dead and reign with him on the earth for a thousand years before the Final Judgment and the everlasting conditions of the new heaven and earth. We have seen that this revelation is consistent with the new creation eschatology that characterizes Old and New Testaments and that it fits with the progressive revelation of the eschatological kingdom of God. On this basis, I would submit that premillennialism is biblically sound, and as such, it should be affirmed as true.

Why do some evangelicals deny it? Assuming the acknowledgment of biblical authority, the answer lies in hermeneutics. In spite of the fact that most evangelicals expressly affirm literary, grammatical, and historical hermeneutics, we do have preunderstandings, traditional and even confessional precommitments, that affect the way we read and understand Scripture. Some of these traditional views have roots in hermeneutical practices no longer recognized as valid or sound. To the extent that this may be true, whether for premillennialists, amillennialists, or postmillennialists, the biblical authority we commonly confess requires all of us to submit our views for testing, reconfirmation, or reformulation if need be. This has been my intent in this chapter. I believe the same desire is shared by the other contributors to this book. May God grant each of us, contributors and readers alike, to grow in grace as well as in the knowledge of his Son until we reach that unity in faith and maturity in Christ, of which the same Scripture speaks (Eph. 4:13).

A POSTMILLENNIAL RESPONSE TO CRAIG A. BLAISING

Kenneth L. Gentry Jr.

COMMENDATION AND APPRECIATION

I must open with a commendation to Dr. Blaising for his important contribution to this book. His chapter is a model of argumentative clarity, theological erudition, and evangelical exegesis. I also appreciate his pioneering work in the ongoing restructuring of dispensationalism, of which his chapter is a fine specimen. As dispensationalist Feinberg noted a decade ago, dispensationalism is moving in a more covenantal direction, allowing greater continuity between the Testaments.[1] As a covenantal Christian I applaud this reorientation. In fact, as a result I find many points of agreement with Blaising's chapter: He recognizes Christ's present kingly reign, the Christian's present participation in that reign, new covenantal blessings for the church, and more. Of course, I wish he did not interpret these as partial fulfillments expecting a catastrophic final fulfillment in a distinct future dispensation.

Now allow me briefly to engage a few of the salient differences between us.[2]

---

[1]John S. Feinberg, ed., *Continuity and Discontinuity: Perspectives on the Relationship Between the Old and New Testaments* (Westchester, Ill.: Crossway, 1988), xii, 64, 310.

[2]Normal space constraints for rejoinders forbid thorough, point-for-point analysis.

HISTORY AND PARADIGM

Blaising provides an interesting summation of a theological paradigm shift in the church's developing understanding of the Christian's eternal destiny. I endorse the basics of Blaising's preferred new creation model for eternity, wherein we learn that the "scope of eternal life is essentially continuous with that of present earthly life except for the absence of sin and death." In fact, I argued for a new creation model in my *He Shall Have Dominion*.[3] Of course, Blaising puts a progressive dispensational spin on the data, with which I cannot concur. I will offer a three-fold response.

Presentational Bias

First, Blaising's overview is such that the uninformed reader will deem postmillennialism an alarming prospect. I am confident Blaising did not intentionally poison the well, but he introduces postmillennialism to his readers as a cause (or at least a corollary) of anarchical militarism represented by "debacles such as the Anabaptist rebellions of the sixteenth century and the English Fifth Monarchy movement of the seventeenth." Such ultimately generates Western colonial oppression, the American Civil War, and "various military conflicts." This is not an endearing construct. Blaising has postmillennialists struggling over whether Christ's rule in human affairs should be effected by "military forces" or by the forces of "revival," with the revivalists winning out only much later in the eighteenth century under the influence of Whitby and Edwards.[4]

The historical situations are more complicated than his brief, selective analysis suggests. The Reformation generated

---

[3]See, for example, chapter 13: "Consummation," in *He Shall Have Dominion: A Postmillennial Eschatology* (Tyler, Tex.: Institute for Christian Economics, 1992, rev. 1997). Matthew Henry, an earlier postmillennialist (1662–1714), writes of 2 Peter 3: "This dissolution is in order to their being restored to their primitive beauty and excellency.... In these new heavens and earth, freed from the vanity the former were subject to, and the sin they were polluted with, only righteousness shall dwell; this is to be the habitation of such righteous persons as do righteousness, and are free from the power and pollution of sin" (*Matthew Henry's Commentary on the Whole Bible*, vol. 6 [Old Tappan, N.J.: Revell, n.d.], 1057).

[4]I highly recommend as a corrective the reading of Iain Murray's *The Puritan Hope: Revival and the Interpretation of Prophecy* (Edinburgh: Banner of Truth, 1971).

enormous cultural upheaval, shaking the very foundations of social order—even by simply declaring the priesthood of believers and salvation by grace through faith! Undoubtedly, some restless extremists in these dismal times picked up on certain postmillennial themes, misapplied them, and took the law into their own hands to correct political and ecclesiastical tyranny. Oftentimes though, the seeds of anarchy were sown by the alarmist preaching of those premillennialists expecting the immediate apocalyptic return of Christ.

For instance, premillennialist Kromminga notes of the social context of the Fifth Monarchy debacle: "Back of this emergence of political chiliasm lay doubtless the hopes and longings for the return of Christ which the long time of suffering and repression under [Queen] Elizabeth and the early Stuarts had intensified in the hearts of the dissenters."[5] This dangerous mixture of current social unrest and imminent apocalyptic-premillennial hope served as a passion-inflaming intoxicant for the Anabaptist radicals and the Munster upheaval. Kromminga notes that "when the expected return of Christ does not eventuate at the calculated moment, the social-political aims, if realized, must therefore immediately be reinterpreted in a postmillennial sense."[6] Indeed, the masses were stirred with apocalyptic hope by such premillennial preachers as Melchior Hofmann (though he himself was not a militant).

Surely Blaising would wince if I introduced premillennialism by quoting Hengstenberg: "It is not quite accidental, that sects have constantly had a predilection for Chiliasm, while the church has been disinclined to adopt it."[7] The cultic predilection for premillennialism (Mormonism, Jehovah's Witnesses, Seventh-Day Adventism, Worldwide Church of God) should not color our study of all premillennialism.[8]

---

[5]D. H. Kromminga, *The Millennium in the Church* (Grand Rapids: Eerdmans, 1945), 180.

[6]Ibid., 187.

[7]E. W. Hengstenberg, *The Revelation of St. John*, vol. 2 in *The Works of Hengstenberg* (Cherry Hill, N.J.: Mack, rep. n.d.), 287.

[8]Unfortunately, all eschatological views have their embarrassing advocates or annoying "look-alikes." Besides cultic expressions, date-setting apocalypticism is a perennial problem among dispensational populists, as Blaising is well aware. As for postmillennialism, one of the early known "postmillennial-like" advocates is Origen, who in many respects was heretical. Amillennialism, of course, has its liberal

Furthermore, although Blaising associates the arising of the spiritual model of eternity with the birth of amillennialism and postmillennialism, both of these nonpremillennial eschatologies now strongly affirm a new creation model—just as does Blaising as one aspect of the novelty of his new brand of dispensationalism. I have already mentioned my 1992 postmillennial study in this regard; our other contributor, Robert Strimple, affirms such in his contribution. Indeed, amillennialist Hoekema provides a thorough presentation of the new creation model in his 1979 book, *The Bible and the Future*.[9] In fact, the new covenant model appears in the writings of anti-premillennialist John Calvin in the 1500s.[10]

Historical Anomalies

Second, Blaising explains the early decline of premillennialism: "The ancient Christian premillennialism weakened to the point of disappearance when the spiritual vision model of eternity became dominant in the church." A part of the problem revolves around hermeneutic recapitulation in Revelation. Blaising argues that Augustine's spiritual model was defended "by rejecting the narrative-historical sequence in John's vision" and by allowing "these visions [to] recapitulate the same events." For early representatives of the new creation model he points to rabbinic Judaism and the Christian Irenaeus.

---

advocates. As I mentioned in my main chapter above, by definition there can be no liberal postmillennialist: What liberal believes Christ will return visibly and gloriously after ("post") the "Millennium" to end history and judge all men?

[9]Anthony A. Hoekema, *The Bible and the Future* (Grand Rapids: Eerdmans, 1979). Even earlier still, Louis Berkhof noted that "Reformed theologians prefer" the view of a "renewal of the present creation" as our eternal destiny (*Systematic Theology* [Grand Rapids: Eerdmans, 1941], 736–37).

[10]John Calvin, *The Epistles of Paul to the Romans and to the Thessalonians*, trans. by R. MacKenzie (Grand Rapids: Eerdmans, 1960), 174: "God will restore the present fallen world to perfect condition at the same time as the human race." See also his comment on 2 Peter 3:10 in *The Epistle of Paul the Apostle to the Hebrews and the First and Second Epistles of St. Peter*, trans. by W. B. Johnston (Grand Rapids: Eerdmans, 1963), 365: "Heaven and earth will be cleansed by fire so that they may be fit for the kingdom of Christ." Indeed, "I shall say just one thing about the elements of the world, that they will be consumed only in order to receive a new quality while their substance remains the same, as can easily be concluded from Romans 8:21 and other passages."

Unfortunately, his analysis is torn by dialectical tension. In his footnote regarding Irenaeus we discover an interesting admission: Irenaeus "does, however, argue that *some* human beings will be privileged to dwell in the new heaven while others are on the new earth." In fact, Irenaeus argues (in a neo-Platonic fashion) that the more spiritual Christians inhabit heaven whereas the less spiritual dwell on the new earth: "Those who are deemed worthy of an abode in heaven shall go there, others shall enjoy the delights of paradise, and others shall possess the splendour of the city" (the New Jerusalem in the new creation).[11] Thus, Blaising's earliest premillennialist example already had neo-Platonic tendencies regarding eternal destinies, tendencies that Blaising suggests undermine premillennialism.

As Blaising explains the paradigm shift he deems destructive of premillennialism (spiritual model and recapitulation), he makes some observations that undercut his own case. (1) He notes that premillennialists have employed the spiritual model and recapitulation.[12] He shows how medieval premillennialist Mede employed recapitulation and viewed the final state "in the traditional spiritual manner." He also admits that classic dispensationalism and much of revised dispensationalism long

---

[11]Irenaeus, *Adversus Haereses*, 5.36.1. He continues: "There is this distinction between the habitation of those who produce an hundred-fold, and that of those who produce sixty-fold, and that of those who produce thirty-fold: for the first will be taken up into the heavens, the second will dwell in paradise, the last will inhabit the city" (ibid., 5.36.2). Thus, Christians on the lowest level are relegated to the new earth. In fact, even the Millennium for Irenaeus is so that we might be "gradually accustomed to partake of the divine nature" (5.32.1). As Kromminga notes: "This idea of the service of the millennial kingdom in the gradual perfection of the saints is not a passing thought with Irenaeus but an important element. He dwells on it repeatedly" (*The Millennium and the Church*, 94).

[12]Though not mentioned by Blaising, Victorinus of Pettau, a premillennialist, was the earliest commentator on Revelation. Victorinus is problematic for Blaising's analysis for two reasons: (a) Victorinus employs recapitulation. As David E. Aune notes, "Victorinus of Pettau proposed that the seven bowl plagues (15:1–16:21) do not chronologically follow the seven trumpet plagues (8:6–11:15) as part of a continuous series but are actually parallel accounts of the same events, which they recapitulate in another form" (*Revelation*, Word Biblical Commentary [Dallas: Word, 1997], 1:xci). (b) Victorinus employs spiritualization principles. As Henry A. Wace observes of Victorinus: "In consequence, perhaps, of his Millennarian tendencies, or of his relations to Origen, his works were classed as 'apocrypha' in the *Decretum de Libris Recipendis*" (*A Dictionary of Christian Biography*, ed. Henry A. Wace and William C. Piercy [Peabody, Mass.: Hendrikson, rep. 1994 (1911)], 1010).

held to the spiritual model: From the time of dispensationalism's own historical origin in the 1830s it set forth "two separate coexisting eternal realms of salvation, one heavenly and one earthly."

(2) Blaising admits that spiritual model advocates may be sequentialists. He recognizes—contrary to his own concerns—that "even those who preferred a sequential rather than a recapitulatory reading of John's visions tended to accept Augustine's interpretation of these features."

(3) Blaising himself allows recapitulation. He argues that Augustine's spiritual model was defended "by rejecting the narrative-historical sequence in John's vision" and by allowing "these visions [to] recapitulate the same events." But then Blaising recognizes recapitulatory features in Revelation: "The acquisition of power by the beast in Revelation 13 is replayed in this vision of Babylon (17:11–18)."

In fact, on Blaising's analysis Revelation 11 reaches a conclusion seemingly requiring the immediate appearance of the Millennium: "The end of the entire series announces the culmination of divine wrath and the judgment of the dead (11:8), together with the proclamation, 'the kingdom of the world has become the kingdom of our Lord and of his Christ, and he will reign for ever and ever' (11:15)." This sounds like Millennium-establishing judgments. But the Millennium appears much later—and "out of sequence," as it were.[13]

In light of these observations, how can the arising of the spiritual model and recapitulation explain the demise of premillennialism in the medieval church? His paradigm explanation is *non causa pro causa*.

Interpretive Failure

Blaising supports his argument for the new creation model from several passages of Scripture: "Following the language of Isaiah 25, 65, and 66, of Revelation 21, and of Romans 8, the new

---

[13]On literalistic assumptions, who can avoid recapitulation? Rev. 6:12–14, for instance, appears to be a climactic, world-ending event: "I watched as he opened the sixth seal. There was a great earthquake. The sun turned black like sackcloth made of goat hair, the whole moon turned blood red, and the stars in the sky fell to earth, as late figs drop from a fig tree when shaken by a strong wind. The sky receded like a scroll, rolling up, and every mountain and island was removed from its place." Somehow, however, pre-Second Advent history continues for another thirteen chapters.

creation model expects the earth and the cosmic order to be renewed and made everlasting through the same creating power that grants immortal and resurrection life to the saints." Yet even Blaising later recognizes that in one of his foundational passages for the "renewed" and "everlasting" new creation order (Isa. 65), "curiously death still remains a feature in that world order (Isa. 65:20)." This curiosity is explained by a proper understanding of Revelation 21:1–22:5 (another of Blaising's passages) in its original context. Immediately after the new creation/Jerusalem appears in Revelation 21–22, we read: "'These words are trustworthy and true. The Lord, the God of the spirits of the prophets, sent his angel to show to his servants the things that *must soon take place'*.... Then he told me, 'Do not seal up the words of the prophecy of this book, because *the time is near*'" (Rev. 22:6, 10, emphasis added).

Below I will provide more detail, but for now please note that preteristic postmillennialism sees in these passages the coming of the new heavens/earth/Jerusalem in the *permanent establishing* of Christianity in God's judgment on Israel when he destroyed the old Jewish order in A.D. 70.[14] Consequently, the new order began *legally and spiritually* under Christ and his apostles (e.g., 2 Cor. 5:17; Gal. 6:15; cf. Luke 4:16–21; Eph. 2:10, 12–16; 4:24); it was confirmed *publicly and dramatically* in A.D. 70 by removing the typological, old covenant order (which "will soon disappear," Heb. 8:13) so that the final new covenant order could be firmly established (12:22–28).[15] The "great tribulation" (Matt.

---

[14]See Kenneth L. Gentry Jr., *A Tale of Two Cities: A Brief Introductory Commentary on Revelation* (Atlanta: American Vision, 1998) and my chapter in C. Marvin Pate, ed., *Four Views on the Book of Revelation* (Grand Rapids: Zondervan, 1998), ch. 1. See also my taped lectures: "The Divorce of Israel: Introduction and Survey of Revelation," "Preterism and Futurism," and "Postmillennialism: New Testament Evidence" (Texarkana, Ark.: Covenant Media Foundation).

[15]Cf. Matt. 8:10–12; Mark 9:1; Luke 13:32–35; 19:41–44; 21:20–24; 23:27–31; Acts 2:16–21; Gal. 4:24–31. For a fascinating and insightful discussion of the Lucan passages see Peter W. L. Walker, *Jesus and the Holy City: New Testament Perspectives on Jerusalem* (Grand Rapids: Eerdmans, 1996), 69–79. R. T. France, citing Strecker, notes that "the fall of Jerusalem" is the "visible expression of the rejection which has already been effected" (*Matthew: Evangelist and Teacher* [Grand Rapids: Zondervan, 1989], 200). France's works on Matthew are extremely helpful for understanding the significance of the A.D. 70 catastrophe. See also his *The Gospel According to Matthew* (Grand Rapids: Eerdmans, 1987). As Richard B. Gaffin well observes in "Theonomy

24:21; Rev. 7:14) against the first-century temple (Matt. 23:38–24:3, 15; Rev. 11:1–2) in Judea (Matt. 24:16; Rev. 11:8) was to occur in "this generation" (24:34; cf. Rev. 1:1, 2).[16]

As I argue in my chapter above, the postmillennial eschatological schema involves *gradualistic* development of the kingdom of God in history. This is opposed to the premillennial catastrophism, which imposes a bureaucratic, political, temple-based kingdom on a recalcitrant world at the battle of Armageddon. The seed principles of the new order are legally established in Christ's redemptive work (A.D. 30) and publicly demonstrated in Christ's judgment of Israel (A.D. 70). The outworking of the kingdom/new covenant/new creation/millennial principle begins progressing in an upward and linear fashion by incremental development through history. Ultimately this upward progress will be superseded by final perfection at the Second Advent, which will establish the consummate, eternal new

---

and Eschatology," William S. Barker and W. Robert Godfrey, eds., *Theonomy: A Reformed Critique* (Grand Rapids: Zondervan, 1990), 205:

> The fall of Jerusalem, by the way, is to be closely associated with the above-mentioned events [death, resurrection, ascension] preceding it; with them it is one in a unified complex of events. As such, like those other events, it does point to and anticipate the second coming. . . . The destruction of Jerusalem and the temple begins already on Good Friday, when God himself radically desecrates "the holy city" [Mt 27:53] in its inner sanctum. Already then the city is desolated at its vital center as the temple curtain is torn "in two from top to bottom" [v. 51; cf. Mk 15:38; Lk 23:45]. What happens in A.D. 70, despite the untold suffering and violence, is but the inevitable aftermath, nothing more than a secondary after shock.

[16]This is why John's vision of the new Jerusalem's establishment following old Jerusalem's destruction has God's people inside while Satan's people still exist outside—though not in the lake of fire (Rev. 22:14–15). See Kenneth L. Gentry Jr., *Perilous Times: A Study in Eschatological Evil* (Bethesda, Md.: Christian Universities Press, 1998); Thomas D. Ice and Kenneth L. Gentry Jr., *The Great Tribulation: Past or Future?* (Grand Rapids: Kregel, 1998); J. Marcellus Kik, *The Eschatology of Victory* (Nutley, N.J.: Presbyterian and Reformed, 1971); Roderick Campbell, *Israel and the New Covenant* (Tyler, Tex.: Geneva Divinity School, 1954 [rep. n.d.]); France, *The Gospel According to Matthew*, ad loc.; John Lightfoot, *Commentary on the New Testament from the Talmud and Hebraica: Matthew–1 Corinthians*, vol. 1 (Peabody, Mass.: Hendrickson, rep. 1989 [1674], ad loc.); Gary DeMar, *Last Days Madness: Obsession of the Modern Church* (Atlanta: American Vision, 1994); David Chilton, *The Great Tribulation* (Fort Worth: Dominion, 1987).

creation order (see chart on next page). Thus, Blaising rightly desires "a holistic future hope in which the Millennium forms one part." Unfortunately, he looks for the wrong type of Millennium (Zionistic politicism), produced by the wrong method (catastrophic imposition).

THEOLOGY AND EXEGESIS

Blaising opens his chapter with an important statement on his "two most central convictions," the first and foremost of which is the "conviction ... that Jesus is coming back." As a postmillennialist I wholeheartedly concur. But then he adds a "second central conviction," which "has to do with the *millennial* part of *premillennial*. This is the belief that after Jesus comes, he will establish and rule over a kingdom on this earth for a millennium, that is, for a thousand years." Here problems arise even within his own system.

Premillennialism's Dependence on Revelation

By his own repeated admission, Blaising's entire eschatological system ultimately hinges on his (semi-literalistic) understanding of Revelation—especially chapter 20. This lone revelation of the thousand-year reign of Christ appears in one chapter in the most hotly debated and variously interpreted book of the Bible, a book so difficult that John himself could not understand portions of it (7:13–14; 17:6–7). As has been facetiously lamented: Wherever you find five commentators on Revelation, you will find six different views.

Note how forcefully and frequently Blaising's admission appears (emphases are mine):

- "The *basic structure* of premillennial belief *is taken from John's vision* of the return of Jesus and a millennium subsequent to that return in the book of Revelation."
- The millennial kingdom is *"explicitly* found *only* in Revelation 20."
- "For premillennialism, the *crucial hermeneutical question* had to do with those features in Revelation 19–20 that set the Millennium apart from all preceding visions."

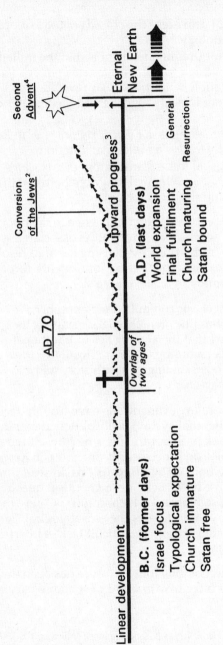

POSTMILLENNIAL CHART

Linear development

Second Advent[4]

Eternal
New Earth

Conversion of the Jews[2]

upward progress[3]

General Resurrection

AD 70

Overlap of two ages[1]

B.C. (former days)
Israel focus
Typological expectation
Church immature
Satan free

A.D. (last days)
World expansion
Final fulfillment
Church maturing
Satan bound

NOTES:
[1] Demise of old covenant Israel rise of new covenant church. Temple system removed A.D. 70.
[2] Massive conversions to Christ among the Jews. Accelerated advance of Christianity in world.
[3] Growing influence of Christianity bringing about worldwide righteousness, peace, and prosperity.
[4] Satan released, instigating a brief rebellion against Christianity just prior to the Second Advent

- Revelation 19–20 provides "the *crucial sequence* of premillennial eschatology."
- "My argument for premillennialism is that the millennial kingdom revealed to John, *while new in its specific content*, is compatible with this earlier revelation concerning the eschatological kingdom and the manner of its coming."
- "The point I am making is *not that Scripture prior to Revelation 20 explicitly teaches* a millennial kingdom."
- "*The key* that puts all these features together is *John's explicit revelation* of a millennial kingdom between the return of Jesus and the Final Judgment."

In my chapter above, I only reluctantly engage the book of Revelation because of the enormous difficulties associated with its interpretation. Such admissions by Blaising seem to resolve one of his own perplexities and deflect one of his forceful charges against nonpremillennialists. He asks:

> Why do some evangelicals committed to Scripture have such trouble seeing this [the premillennial structure of the kingdom]? I suggest that the answer lies in traditional theological preunderstandings that are hostile to this interpretation, preunderstandings whose history we have sketched earlier in this chapter.

(1) The reason why many evangelicals have trouble seeing it is because the premillennial system is absolutely dependent on the most difficult book of Scripture. Blaising himself repeatedly admits premillennialism is necessarily anchored in Revelation (esp. ch. 20). Only here do we find its "basic structure," which helps us to resolve its "crucial hermeneutical question" and discern its "crucial sequence," which in turn is "new in its specific content," thereby providing us the eschatological "key."

Most scholars note the extremely difficult task of interpreting Revelation. For example:

- Terry: "No portion of the Holy Scripture has been the subject of so much controversy and of so many varying interpretations."[17]

---

[17]Milton S. Terry, *Biblical Hermeneutics* (Grand Rapids: Zondervan, n.d.), 466.

- Reuss: "Ideas of the Apocalypse are so widely different that a summary notice of the exegetical literature, mingling all together, would be inexpedient."[18]
- Warfield: Revelation is "the most difficult book of the Bible: it has always been the most variously understood, the most arbitrarily interpreted, the most exegetically tortured."[19]
- Vincent: "This document has given rise to voluminous controversy."[20]
- Swete: "To comment on this great prophecy is a harder task than to comment on a Gospel, and he who undertakes it exposes himself to the charge of presumption. I have been led to venture upon on what I know to be dangerous ground."[21]
- Beckwith: "No other book, whether in sacred or profane literature, has received in whole or in part so many different interpretations. Doubtless no other book has so perplexed biblical students throughout the Christian centuries down to our own times."[22]
- Robertson: "Perhaps no single book in the New Testament presents so many and so formidable problems as the Apocalypse of John."[23]
- Beasley-Murray: "Revelation is probably the most disputed and difficult book in the New Testament."[24]
- Ladd: "Revelation is the most difficult of all New Testament books to interpret."[25]

---

[18]Eduard Wilhelm Reuss, *History of the Sacred Scriptures of the New Testament* (Edinburgh: T. & T. Clark, 1884), 155.

[19]B. B. Warfield, "The Book of Revelation," in *A Religious Encyclopedia* (New York: Funk and Wagnalls, 1883), 2:80.

[20]Marvin R. Vincent, *Word Studies in the New Testament*, vol. 2, *The Writings of John* (Grand Rapids: Eerdmans, rep. 1985 [1887]), 16.

[21]Henry B. Swete, *Commentary on Revelation* (Grand Rapids: Kregel, rep. 1977 [1906]), xii.

[22]John T. Beckwith, *The Apocalypse of John: Studies in Introduction* (Grand Rapids: Baker, 1919 [1967]), 1.

[23]A. T. Robertson, *Word Pictures in the New Testament* (Nashville: Broadman, 1933), 6:269.

[24]G. R. Beasley-Murray, *The Book of Revelation*, New Century Bible (London: Marshall, Morgan, and Scott, 1974), 5.

[25]George Eldon Ladd, *A Commentary on the Revelation of John* (Grand Rapids: Eerdmans, 1972), 10.

- Walvoord: "Attempts at its exposition are almost without number, yet there continues the widest divergence of interpretation."[26]
- Morris: "Some of the problems of this book are enormously difficult and I certainly have not the capacity to solve them." Indeed, it is "by common consent one of the most difficult of all the books of the Bible."[27]
- Johnson: For "the modern reader ... [Revelation] is the most obscure and controversial book in the Bible."[28]
- Pate: "The Apocalypse is arguably the most controversial book in the Bible. . . . A hermeneutical thicket awaits the interpreter of Revelation."[29]

Premillennialism's dependence on Revelation should send up a red flag. I do not say this as one hesitant to deal with Revelation, for I wrote my doctoral dissertation on it,[30] authored two books on it,[31] have been involved in another Zondervan Counterpoints book debating it,[32] and am currently preparing a commentary on it.[33] But because of the obvious matters of difficulty associated with Revelation's imagery and premillennialism's total dependence on it, I believe Blaising seriously overstates the matter when he writes:

> Amillennial and postmillennial rejections of premillennialism traditionally have had more to do with a preunderstanding of what is "proper," "fitting," or "plausible" in relation to their traditional expectations about eternal life than with any specific biblical teaching contradicting the premillennial coming of Christ.

---

[26]John F. Walvoord, *The Revelation of Jesus Christ* (Chicago: Moody, 1966), 7.

[27]Leon Morris, *The Revelation of St. John*, Tyndale New Testament Commentaries (Grand Rapids: Eerdmans, 1969), 13, 15.

[28]Alan F. Johnson, *Revelation*, The Bible Study Commentary (Grand Rapids: Zondervan, 1983), 9.

[29]C. Marvin Pate, in Pate, ed., *Four Views on the Book of Revelation*, 172, 173.

[30]Kenneth L. Gentry Jr., "Dating the Book of Revelation: An Exegetical and Historical Argument for a Pre-A.D. 70 Composition" (Th.D. diss., Whitefield Theological Seminary, 1988).

[31]Kenneth L. Gentry Jr., *Before Jerusalem Fell*, 2d ed. (Bethesda, Md.: Christian Universities Press, 1996); *The Beast of Revelation*, 2d ed. (Tyler, Tex.: Institute for Christian Economics, 1989).

[32]I contributed the chapter on a preterist understanding of Revelation in Pate, ed., *Four Views on the Book of Revelation*.

[33]Tentatively entitled *A Tale of Two Cities*.

(2) Most interesting, the first half of Blaising's entire presentation outlines *his own historico-theological preunderstanding of eschatology*, in which he adopts the new creation motif over against the spiritual motif. Then in most of the other half he exegetes Revelation 20 (and its context) to fill out that preunderstanding. Thus, Blaising's foundational arguments for premillennialism are: (a) his own theological preunderstanding (which he warns against in others); and (b) his theological dependence on Revelation (which exposes the risky nature of his enterprise).

(3) In light of all this, what are we to make of Blaising's claim that premillennialism re-emerged in church history after the Reformation because of "the recovery of the literal sense of Revelation 20"? Who can seriously argue for a "literal sense" in a book such as Revelation? After all, (a) John informs us that Revelation is given to *signify* his prophetic insights for an angel "sent and *signified*[34] it" (Rev. 1:1, KJV). These symbolic signs, remember, sometimes even confuse John (7:13–14; 17:6–7).

(b) John illustrates the manner of symbolic interpretation in a number of cases, thereby undercutting literalistic approaches. He specifically informs us that sometimes lampstands represent churches (1:20), eyes represent the Spirit (5:6), incense represents prayers (5:8), a serpent represents Satan (12:9), heads represent mountains (17:9), horns represent kings (17:12), waters represent people (17:15), and so forth.

(c) John confounds us by presenting us with creatures full of eyes and with six wings (4:6), a seven-eyed lamb (5:6), people talking to mountains (6:16), people washing robes in blood (7:14), locusts with human faces (9:7), lion-headed horses (9:17), fire-breathing prophets (11:5), a woman clothed with the sun while standing on the moon (12:1), a seven-headed dragon that pulls stars down from heaven (12:3–4), a serpent vomiting out a river (12:15), a seven-headed beast (13:1), frogs coming out of the mouth of a dragon (16:13), a blood-drinking harlot (17:6), Jesus returning from heaven on a horse and with a sword in his mouth (19:11, 15), a 1,500-mile-high city floating down out of the sky (21:16), one tree bearing twelve different fruits (22:2)—and more.

---

[34]A. T. Robertson notes that the Greek word used here is "from *sēma*, sign or token, for which see John 12:33; Acts 11:28." He continues: "*Sēmaino* (only here in the Apocalypse) suits admirably the symbolic character of the book" (*Word Pictures in the New Testament*, 6:284).

And what becomes of Blaising's claimed literalism in dealing with John's own specifically defined time-frame indicators? John dogmatically and frequently claims the prophetic events will occur "soon" (1:1; 22:6); indeed, they are "about to come" (3:10, NASB[35]) after waiting just "a little longer" (6:11) because "the time is near" (1:3; 22:10). Yet Blaising's system delays the events for untold centuries—so far.

And what of the literal interpretation of Revelation 20 itself? A literal reading of Revelation 20:1–6 requires a physical chain to bind Satan (20:1–2[36]) and demands a thousand-year period ruled over *only* by martyred saints and/or those committed believers who live *during the time of the beast* (20:4a-b). Blaising seems oblivious to this problem: "The phrases of 20:4 identify those who have been martyred as none other than believers in Christ—the same as those who suffered physical death as described in John's preceding vision." "Consistently through John's visions, martyrs are those who lose their physical lives for Christ's sake." What becomes of the millions of unmartyred saints of the church age, per his dispensationalism? Besides, John promises that the martyrs *in his own day* (1:9; 2:9–10, 12) will have to await vindication only "a little longer" (cf. 6:9–11). But today almost two thousand years have passed. Moreover, Blaising and Bock themselves question the literal length of the one-thousand-year time frame.[37]

Early in his presentation, Blaising claims that Revelation 19–20 provides "the basic structure of premillennial belief." But all sorts of problems arise at this point. (1) Where is the premillennial, pretribulational Rapture of the church in this "basic structure"? Nothing in Revelation—and especially in Blaising's preferred section, chapters 19–20—suggests a rapture. At best it is a suppressed premise early in Revelation.

(2) As a pretribulational premillennialist, Blaising informs us that "premillennialists believe that when Jesus comes, he will

---

[35]Alfred A. Marshall, *Interlinear Greek-English New Testament* (Grand Rapids: Zondervan, 1959), ad loc.

[36]Cf. same word (*deō*) in Acts 12:6; 2 Tim. 2:9.

[37]Surprisingly, though Blaising's "second central conviction" regards a "kingdom on earth . . . for a thousand years," he later confesses: "Arguments about the literal meaning of the thousand years also become irrelevant. The issue is not how *exact* are the thousand years, for we know that Scripture often uses round numbers in reference to time as well as in other quantitative measurements."

raise the dead in two stages." In multiplying eschatological comings, resurrections, and judgments, premillennialism suffers from what Jay Adams calls eschatological "diplopia."[38] This leads to enormous systemic problems. For example, Blaising emphatically argues for a physical resurrection from death as the necessary meaning of 20:4–5, but this leaves out those raptured at Christ's return and who, therefore, never die. Furthermore, according to Blaising's sequencing of Revelation 19–20, his pretribulational Rapture scheme has the "first resurrection" out of sequence: It is supposed to occur seven years *prior* to the beginning of the Millennium, even though 20:4 ties the resurrection to its beginning.

Furthermore, what becomes of those saints converted in and dying during the Tribulation (e.g., 7:14) *after* the first resurrection at the pretribulational Rapture? When are they resurrected? They have already "missed" the first resurrection in the pretribulational scheme. And what of those Tribulation converts who live through the post-Rapture Tribulation to enter the Millennium in unresurrected bodies? When they eventually die in the Millennium, where is their resurrection? Unfortunately, these classes of believers are lost in the shuffle, for in the premillennial system the resurrection of God's people (the first resurrection) has already occurred; only the resurrection of the lost remains.

(3) Why should we believe that the New Testament everywhere teaches a general, singular resurrection on the last day, only to discover later in the most difficult book of the Bible that there are actually two specific, distantly separated resurrections for different classes of people? This is all the more remarkable in that even John himself records our Lord's express teaching on the singular, general resurrection: "Do not be amazed at this, for a time is coming when *all who are in their graves* will hear his voice and come out—those who have done good will rise to live, and those who have done evil will rise to be condemned" (John 5:28–29, emphasis added). Indeed, this is the teaching of all Scripture elsewhere, as Blaising admits[39] (e.g., Dan. 12:2; Acts

---

[38]Jay E. Adams, *The Time Is at Hand* (Philadelphia: Presbyterian and Reformed, 1966), 10.

[39]Blaising writes: "It was not clear prior to Jesus that the Old Testament prophecies regarding a future resurrection would be fulfilled in stages."

24:15; Rev. 20:13–15). In fact, the Lord informs us that this resurrection will be on the *last* day—not 1,007 years prior to the last day (John 6:39, 40, 44, 54; 11:24; 1 Cor. 15:23–24, 52). Blaising claims that "as a matter of progressive revelation" the Millennium in Revelation "adds to and helps harmonize the broader biblical teaching." It would appear, however, that it wholly reinterprets everything else, not merely "adds" to it.[40]

Premillennialism's Misunderstanding of Revelation

Not only is premillennialism dependent on Revelation— but on a *misunderstanding* of it. Blaising complains that the non-premillennialist employs a "double hermeneutic movement" to get around the Revelation 19–20 chronological sequencing, which he (Blaising) sees as presenting: (1) Christ's second coming, followed by (2) the binding of Satan, issuing forth in (3) the resurrection of martyrs at (4) the onset of the millennial reign of Christ. He complains that the twofold hermeneutic maneuver involves an unwarranted recapitulation and a surprising reinterpretation of the facts.[41]

Even though Blaising and I both allow recapitulation in certain places in Revelation, it is *not* necessary to recapitulate in chapter 20. In fact, I believe this chapter *does* follow from chapter 19. But this sequencing does not lead to premillennialism. I interpret John's sequencing in light of Revelation's dogmatic assertions of the nearness of the events, coupled with his decla-

---

[40]Blaising sees in 1 Cor. 15 a possible allusion to the Millennium: "The end also correlates with the final subjugation of death, the last enemy, and the moment in which Christ presents the kingdom to the Father. Prior to this 'he must reign until he has put all his enemies under his feet' (15:25). The grammar of the text allows the possibility of an interval between the resurrection of believers and the final resurrection, which would be a reign of Christ." But fellow premillennialist commentator Robert Mounce admits: "The attempt to attribute to Paul a belief in the millennium on the basis of 1 Cor. 15:20–28 is unconvincing" (*The Book of Revelation*, New International Commentary on the New Testament [Grand Rapids: Eerdmans, 1977], 357, n. 15).

[41]A part of Blaising's suggestive proof that Rev. 20 is sequential and not a new vision recapitulating a previous vision is counterproductive. Blaising notes that Rev. 20:1 begins with *kai eidon*, which "although not determinative in itself of a chronological sequence, nevertheless can be used for such." If he presses *kai eidon* as a structural marker for sequence, then its presence in 20:4 would indicate that the millennial reign of the saints begins only after the thousand-year binding of Satan!

ration of the theme of the book (1:7). Let me briefly explain this preterist approach.[42]

Remember, John wrote to a first-century audience of literal churches (1:4, 11; chs. 2–3). Both John and these churches were already in "tribulation" as he sought to comfort and instruct them (1:9; 2:9). Christ urged the seven churches to repent, reform, and persevere (2:5, 16, 21–22; 3:3, 19) because of the impending judgments that would soon erupt in full scale (2:5, 16; 3:11; 22:12, 20). In the case of the Philadelphia church, for instance, Christ promised to shield them from those judgments: "Because you have kept the word of My perseverance, I also will keep you from the hour of testing, that *hour* which is about to come upon the whole world, to test those who dwell upon the earth" (3:10, NASB). At the outset of Revelation he informed those persecuted saints that the prophesied events "must soon take place" (1:1; 22:6) because "the time is near" (1:3; 22:10). That was two thousand years ago!

Then John states his theme just four verses after these temporal delimiters: "Look, he is coming with the clouds, and every eye will see him, even those who pierced him; and all the peoples of the earth will mourn because of him. So shall it be! Amen" (1:7). This theme summarily mirrors Christ's "coming" in Revelation 19, just as the preceding verse (1:6) reflects the kingdom reign in 20:6.[43]

I am convinced that Revelation's main point is to prophesy *the coming destruction of Jerusalem and the temple in A.D. 70.*[44] In so

---

[42]The word "preterist" is based on a Latin word *praeteritus*, meaning "gone by," i.e., past. For more detail on the preterist interpretation, see my chapter in Pate, ed., *Four Views on the Book of Revelation*, or in my forthcoming commentary on Revelation, *A Tale of Two Cities*. See also Steve Gregg, *Revelation: Four Views: A Parallel Commentary* (Nashville: Nelson, 1996).

[43]Compare 1:6, "[Christ] has made us to be a kingdom and priests to serve his God and Father—to him be glory and power for ever and ever! Amen" with 20:6, "Blessed and holy are those who have part in the first resurrection. The second death has no power over them, but they will be priests of God and of Christ and will reign with him for a thousand years."

[44]I hold John wrote this book prior to the destruction of the temple in A.D. 70 (c. A.D. 65). Those readers who are surprised that Revelation's dramatic judgment language can refer to historical judgments prior to the Second Advent should read Homer Heater Jr., "Do the Prophets Teach That Babylonia Will Be Rebuilt in the Eschaton?" *Journal of the Evangelical Theological Society* 41:1 (March, 1998): 23–44. He offers a fine explanation of stereotypical judgment language.

doing, John is expanding on Christ's teaching in Matthew 23–24, in which the Lord abandoned the first-century temple (Matt. 23:38; 24:1), promised its destruction (24:2), and then urgently warned his followers to flee Judea (24:16) at that temple's "desolation" (24:15; cf. Luke 21:20), which is "the great tribulation" (24:21); "all these things" (i.e., 24:4–33) were to occur in "this generation" (24:34). Revelation 1:7 is similar to Matthew 24:30: "At that time the sign of the Son of Man will appear in the sky, and all the nations of the earth will mourn. They will see the Son of Man coming on the clouds of the sky, with power and great glory"; in the space of five verses, John declares Christ's "coming" is "near" (Rev. 1:3, 7).

Indeed, the theme of imminent judgment is prominent in the whole New Testament. Dramatic divine judgments are "soon," "near," "at hand," "at the door," "present," and so forth. They inform us that "the hour has come," "the time is short," "the wrath of God is coming," "the day is approaching" in "just a little while." Thus, these events will occur in "this generation," before "some of you standing here taste of death."[45]

Revelation 1:7 *must* prophesy A.D. 70 as Christ's judgment on Jerusalem for various reasons. (1) The time frame demands it (1:1, 3; 3:11; 6:11; 22:6, 10; cf. Matt. 24:34). How else could John have expressed nearness in time if not by these terms? *All* English translations use terms expressing temporal nearness. While Blaising well notes that "John ... focuses his readers' attention on the coming of Christ (Rev. 1:7; 2:26; 3:3, 11; 19:11–16; 22:7, 12, 17, 20)," he overlooks the time frame of that "coming."

(2) The relevance to the original recipients of Revelation expects it (1:4, 9, 11; chs. 2–3). Though Revelation is an apocalyptically framed prophecy, it also partakes of the character of an occasional letter. That is, John is concerned with the historic occasion of his audience. To delay the events for thousands of years (so far) cruelly mocks the present suffering of his followers.

(3) The parallels of Revelation with the Olivet Discourse suggest it.[46] Both prophecies involve the "temple" (Matt. 24:2,

---

[45]Matt. 23:36–24:3; 22:34; 26:64; Mark 9:1; John 4:20–24; Acts 2:16–20; Rom. 13:11, 12; 16:20; 1 Cor. 7:26, 29–31; Col. 3:6; 1 Thess. 2:16; Heb. 2:5; 10:25, 37; 12:18–29; James 5:8–9; 1 Peter 4:5, 7; 1 John 2:17–18.

[46]"Revelation can be seen as an updating of [Jesus'] apocalypse, given on the Mount of Olives" (J. P. M. Sweet, *Revelation* [Philadelphia: Westminster, 1979], 2). This is also the view of the Puritan Talmudic scholar, John Lightfoot, who applies both apocalypses to A.D. 70 and the destruction of the temple (*Commentary on the New Testament from the Talmud and Hebraica*, 2:319, 422).

15; Rev. 11:1–2) during the "great tribulation" (Matt. 24:21; Rev. 7:14). I agree with Blaising that the Olivet Discourse relates a "catastrophic act of judgment." This, in fact, occurred in A.D. 70. Darrell Bock, Blaising's associate and friend, notes of A.D. 70: "Jerusalem's fall is part of God's total eschatological plan."[47] Indeed, A.D. 70 and Christ's second coming are "a pair of related events" because "for Jesus the destruction of Jerusalem is like the end-time," in that "the fall of Jerusalem in A.D. 70 is part of God's plan and judgment. This fall pictures the end."[48]

(4) The "coming with the clouds" language allows it. Apocalyptic expressions commonly portray historical divine judgments on nations (e.g., Isa. 19:1).[49] In fact, premillennial commentator Henry Alford observes of such "coming" language in Matthew 21:40:

> We may observe that our Lord makes "when the Lord cometh" coincide with the destruction of Jerusalem, which is incontestably the overthrow of the wicked husbandmen. This passage therefore forms an important key to our Lord's prophecies, and a decisive justification for those who like myself, firmly hold that the coming of the Lord is, in many places, to be identified, primarily, with that overthrow.[50]

Here in Revelation 1:7 the divine judgment befalls Israel in A.D. 70 for crucifying her Messiah. The (still future) Second Advent will be a physical, visible coming (Acts 1:11), but that event was not "shortly to come to pass" in the first century.

(5) This coming judgment is morally relevant. It is directed against "those who pierced him." That is, it is against the first-century Jews, who demand his crucifixion. The Lord and the apostles lay the covenantal blame on the first-century Jews (Acts 3:14–15; 4:8–10).[51]

---

[47]Darrell L. Bock, *Luke 9:51–24:53* (Grand Rapids: Baker, 1994), 1657.

[48]Ibid., 1650, 1656.

[49]See confirmation of this statement in Dallas Theological Seminary's *Bible Knowledge Commentary: Old Testament* (Wheaton, Ill.: Victor, 1985) at the following similar passages: Ps. 18:7–15; 104:3; Isa. 13:1, 9–13; 19:1; Joel 2:1–2; Mic. 1:3–4.

[50]Henry Alford, *The Greek New Testament*, 4 vols. (Chicago: Moody, rep. 1958 [1849–1861]), 1:216.

[51]See also Matt. 20:18; 21:33–43; Luke 9:22; Acts 4:10a; cf. John 19:5–15; Acts 2:22–23, 36; 5:30; 10:39; 1 Thess. 2:14–16. This fact is so evident that liberals claim that later Christians reworked Christ's history in the gospel record as an anti-Semitic

(6) This coming is historically relevant. It brings mourning on "all the tribes of the earth." We may literally render this phrase "the tribes of *the land*" (Gk.: *tēs gēs*), that is, the well-known Promised Land.[52] That is why Jesus urged his followers to flee Judea (Matt. 24:16) in light of his coming against "the tribes of the land" (lit. trans. of 24:30).

(7) This judgment in A.D. 70 is prophetically expected; it is "the great day of their wrath," which John expressly mentions in Revelation 6:17. Interestingly, the Pentecostal outpouring of the Spirit resulted in miraculous tongues, which were harbingers of the approach of this day (Acts 2:5, 12, 16–20) on the inhabitants of Jerusalem (cf. Acts 2:14, 22, 36, 40).[53] Blaising is partially correct: "The future kingdom will come when the Lord himself comes in the Day of the Lord"; but he wrongly projects "the Day of the Lord" into *our* future.

Gathering all of this data together, Blaising correctly calls for a sequential flow between Revelation 19 and 20. The historical nature of the flow, however, is altogether different from what he presents. Revelation 19 serves as a dramatic exhibition of John's seminal theme in 1:7, in which Jesus providentially "comes" in judgment on Israel in A.D. 70.[54] After that judgment,

---

polemic. See, for example, John Dominic Crossan, *Who Killed Jesus? The Roots of Anti-Semitism in the Gospel Story of the Death of Jesus* (New York: HarperCollins, 1996). For a study of the ancient history of this problem see M. Dibelius, *An die Thessalonicher,* in *Handbuch zum Neuen Testament,* 3d ed. (Tübingen: J. C. B. Mohr, 1937); Ernst Käsemann, "Paul and Israel," *New Testament Questions of Today* (1969). For helpful evangelical analyses of the judgment of Israel as a major theme in the Gospels see N. T. Wright, *Jesus and the Victory of God* (Minneapolis: Fortress, 1996); France, *Matthew: Evangelist and Teacher*; Walker, *Jesus and the Holy City.*

[52]Matt. 8:11–12; 21:43–45; 22:1–7. See Alan James Beagley, *The "Sitz im Leben" of the Apocalypse with Particular Reference to the Role of the Church's Enemies* (New York: Walter de Gruyter, 1987). See also Gentry, *Before Jerusalem Fell,* ch. 8.

[53]Cf. Heb. 10:25 with 8:13. Tongues are a sign of judgment on the first-century Jews (1 Cor. 14:21–22; cf. Deut. 28:49; Isa. 28:11ff.; 33:19; Jer. 5:15; Ezek. 3:5). See Kenneth L. Gentry Jr., *The Charismatic Gift of Prophecy: A Reformed Response to Wayne Grudem,* 2d ed. (Memphis: Footstool, 1989); O. Palmer Robertson, *The Final Word: A Biblical Response to the Case for Tongues and Prophecy Today* (Edinburgh: Banner of Truth, 1993). The Pentecostal events and their interpretation may be the reason why believers in Jerusalem sold their property (Acts 2:45; 4:32): It was soon to be of zero value.

[54]Cf. Matt. 8:11–12; 21:43–45; 22:1–7. For a fuller exegesis of this approach to the Olivet Discourse, see Ice and Gentry, *The Great Tribulation: Past or Future?*

the reign of Christ (the Millennium) is *publicly exhibited* and his people *dramatically vindicated*: Those saints who died for his testimony are enthroned in heaven (cf. 6:9–11; 14:13), and those on earth are emboldened against their oppressors, knowing that even they are seated with Christ "in heavenly realms" (Eph. 2:6; cf. Rev. 1:6)—which is the point of Revelation 20:4.

Hort, a preterist commentator, observes:

> Under the pressure of the sufferings and terrors of that crisis men's faith in the reality of His presence might well fail. It might seem as though His resurrection and ascension were an idle tale, since He shewed himself no more to His sorely tempted servants. Then this revelation of Him is given that it may be shewn to them. Having been hidden from sight, He is seen with the veil rent away: having been supposed to be absent, He is found to be present.[55]

Christ's reign *legally* began at his exaltation (Matt. 28:18; Acts 2:29–36; Eph. 1:19–21; Phil. 2:8–11); it was *publicly exhibited* in A.D. 70 (cf. Mark 9:1; Matt. 24:29–30, 34; 1 Thess. 2:14–16). Thus the Jewish Sanhedrin, who condemned Christ, would experience his judgment (Matt. 26:64; cf. 23:32–37).[56]

Elsewhere Blaising points to Babylon as a "transition" to the New Jerusalem by noting that "the New Jerusalem succeeds and replaces Babylon." Once again I agree—but not in the way Blaising prefers. Historically, the new Jerusalem (i.e., Christianity; cf. Gal. 3:28–29; 4:24–27; 6:15; Heb. 12:22) dramatically replaces the old, earthly Jerusalem, which has become the enemy of God, a virtual Babylon.[57] The Babylon of Revelation is a derogatory name for the Christ-rejecting Jerusalem of the first century.[58]

---

[55] F. J. A. Hort, *The Apocalypse of St. John: I—III* (London: Macmillan, 1908), 4.

[56] This two-phased scenario—legal-principial, then dramatic-historical—follows the pattern of the giving of the Spirit: He is given privately to the disciples in John 20:22, then publicly to the church in Acts 2.

[57] Note especially Paul's contrasting of the earthly Jerusalem and heavenly Jerusalem in Gal. 4:25–31. The writer of Hebrews provides the same sequential contrast in Heb. 12:18–22.

[58] Rev. 11:8; cf. Matt. 23:37; Luke 23:38–41. For an excellent study of Jerusalem's first-century sin and judgment as revealed in the New Testament see Peter W. L. Walker, *Jesus and the Holy City*. For proof of the Babylon=Jerusalem interpretation see Gentry, "The Preterist View," in Pate, ed., *Four Views on the Book of Revelation*,

If Blaising approached Revelation preteristically—giving full credence to the time indicators (1:1, 3), original audience relevance (1:4, 11), and the parallels to the Olivet Discourse—he would still have his sequencing. With only slight word changes I can affirm his claim that "only as a consequence to this Great Tribulation and the coming of Jesus in glory is the eschatological kingdom instituted." But my sequencing develops in the first-century initiation of the new covenant era in historical judgment.

Premillennialism's Focus in Revelation

I have spent much space on Revelation in general, hoping to show that premillennialism misreads it altogether. My previous comments should provide the reader pause before accepting Blaising's view of chapter 20. But there is more. Now I must briefly mention additional problems I have with his exposition of the focal passage, 20:1–6.[59]

Although Blaising provides a fine sample of exegetical methodology, his approach is more appropriate for John's Gospel than for his Revelation. Special rules are often called for as a result of the dramatic, overdrawn, visionary character of Revelation—just as many commentators note the need even for

---

73–79. See also Iain Provon, "Foul Spirits, Fornication and Finance: Revelation 18 From an Old Testament Perspective," *Journal for the Study of the New Testament* 64 (December 1996): 96; Cornelis Vanderwaal, *Search the Scriptures: Hebrews—Revelation*, vol. 10 (St. Catherines, Ont.: Paideia, 1979), 79–111; Milton S. Terry, *Biblical Apocalyptics: A Study of the Most Notable Revelations of God and of Christ* (Grand Rapids: Zondervan, rep. 1988 [1898]), 426–39; J. Massyngberde Ford, *Revelation*, The Anchor Bible (Garden City, N.Y.: Doubleday, 1975), 54–55, 93, 259–307.

[59]Please note that because of space limitations, my chapter outlining the case for postmillennialism glossed over the details of the A.D. 70 backdrop of Revelation 20, focusing rather on the spiritual nature of the "first resurrection" as opposed to the premillennial argument for a physical one. In the present response to Blaising, I will flesh out more of the contextual setting and theological details to show how John framed the issue in terms of his first-century audience, which contained martyrs and beast-resistors. Of course, the glorious redemptive truths applicable to the first-century faithful under the oppression of the beast are true also for the ongoing church of the faithful, as well; the same blood of the Lamb covers us as it did them. The difference between this presentation and my earlier one is the difference between a more detailed analysis and a summary overview. It is like the difference between saying, "There is a cat on the mat" and then saying, "There is a black cat on the red mat."

a special *grammar* for Revelation.[60] H. B. Swete, the prince of Revelation commentators, notes that John's grammatical irregularities often relate to his "desire of giving movement and vivid reality to his vision."[61]

Often John dramatically projects visionary scenes that vividly portray more mundane spiritual realities. For instance, I rather doubt that the martyrs in 6:9 were literally at the foot of a physical altar in heaven, crying out for vengeance. This colorful imagery portrays the necessity of their vindication as a divine response to their cruel martyrdom. As such it reminds us of the Old Testament's image of "innocent blood" crying out from the ground.[62] The martyrs' deaths not only demand vindication but explain and justify the judgments to follow.[63] This is dramatic imagery—as is chapter 20—which, like parabolic discourse and poetic song, may not be pressed according to the standard rules of grammar.

Furthermore, does not Blaising argue that Revelation *adds* to our understanding of prior biblical revelation? Note his following observations (all emphases mine):

- "As a matter of progressive revelation, the Millennium *adds to* and helps to harmonize the broader biblical teaching."
- "Premillennialists see the *millennial kingdom* of Christ as an integral feature of the *progressive revelation* of this kingdom."
- "*It was not clear prior to Jesus* that the Old Testament prophecies regarding *a future resurrection would be*

---

[60]The most recent special grammar appears in David Aune, *Revelation*, secs. 7 and 8. See also R. H. Charles, *The Revelation of St. John*, International Critical Commentary (Edinburgh: T. & T. Clark, 1920), 1:cxvii-clix. According to H. B. Swete, in the last century Revelation grammars were written by various scholars: Vögel, Winer, Ewald, Lücke, Hitzig, Bousset, S. Davidson, A. Lee, Archbishop Benson (see Swete's *Commentary on Revelation* [Grand Rapids: Kregel, rep. 1977 (1906)], cxxiii).

[61]Swete, *Revelation*, cxxv. A. T. Robertson agrees that certain peculiarities in Revelation are "due to the vividness of conception in the book" (*A New Short Grammar of the Greek Testament* [Grand Rapids: Baker, 1958], 402). In his book on Greek idioms, C. F. D. Moule warns: "No attempt has been made to treat the idioms of the Apocalypse systematically. That is a study in itself" (*An Idiom-Book of New Testament Greek* [Cambridge: Cambridge Univ. Press, 1960], vii).

[62]Gen. 4:10; 19:13; Ps. 115:17; Heb. 12:24; cf. Gen. 18:20; 19:13; Deut. 19:10, 13; 21:9; 2 Kings 24:4; Jer. 7:6; 19:4; 26:15; Joel 3:19.

[63]See Rev. 16:6; 17:6; 18:24; 19:2; 20:4–5.

fulfilled in stages, with the Messiah being raised far in advance of the general resurrection. Yet, once that messianic resurrection is revealed, *it clarifies* not only the sequential nature in which the Resurrection prophecies will be fulfilled but also the role of Messiah in the history of salvation."

- Revelation brings before us material that is *"new in its specific content."*
- "The point I am making is *not that Scripture prior to Revelation 20 explicitly teaches* a millennial kingdom. . . . But what Scripture says about the eschatological kingdom is *conducive to* being sequenced in its fulfillment. . . ."

Why, then, may not this "[coming] to life" (20:4) be a surprising recasting of a prior revealed truth? That is, in light of John's expansion on previous revelation in remarkable ways, why may he not dramatically portray the vindication of sorely tested martyrs as if such were a coming to life? Though a cruel enemy may slay the Lamb's faithful followers, they will be vindicated and their lives be gloriously affirmed by God's divine wrath in A.D. 70. They "live again" despite their deaths.[64] As Swete warns: "To infer from this statement, as many expositors have done, that the *ezēsan* of v. 4 must be understood of bodily resuscitation, is to interpret apocalyptic imagery by methods of exegesis which are proper to ordinary narrative."[65] In fact, in Revelation 20 other spiritual transactions are given physical dimensions, such as Satan's binding with a chain. Why may not

---

[64]Because of space limitations in my chapter in Pate's *Four Views on the Book of Revelation*, I was unable even there to flesh out the full significance of the martyr theme in Revelation 20. But briefly, John expressly focuses on these martyrs who, despite losing their earthly lives, are in reality saved through the blood of the Lamb (which brings a newness of life on the order of a spiritual resurrection, John 5:24; 1 John 3:14). Their vindication (and the church's) occurs in the destruction of their first enemy, Israel, in A.D. 70. John focuses on the A.D. 70 phenomenon as the clear and public "proof" of the reality of salvation, just as the Lord informs his judges during his trial that he (and his message) will be vindicated upon them: "'Yes, it is as you say,' Jesus replied. 'But I say to all of you: In the future you will see the Son of Man sitting at the right hand of the Mighty One and coming on the clouds of heaven'" (Matt. 26:64). Thus, he encourages his followers to know that "some who are standing here will not taste death before they see the kingdom of God come with power"—at A.D. 70 (Mark 9:1)—although others will taste of death.

[65]Swete, *Revelation*, 263.

John present the martyrs' salvation-vindication at A.D. 70 as a "coming to life"?

Blaising complains that disallowing a physical resurrection here in Revelation 20:4 necessarily "eliminates the ingressive sense" of the aorist *ezēsan*. That may well be. But the functions of verbal *Aktionsart* are somewhat subjective determinations anyway. For instance, renowned Greek scholar Robertson suggests that this *ezēsan* may be a *constative* aorist, suggesting an "increased spiritual life"[66]—more in keeping with my view. In fact, he notes this constative use of the aorist "clearly" appears in the attached statement that they "reigned" (*ebasileusan*) in the same verse.

Furthermore, Blaising notes that the word *anastasis* ("resurrection") always indicates physical resurrection, *except in Luke 2:34*. Interestingly, Bock's dispensational commentary on Luke 2:34 notes that *anastasis* there probably indicates that "those who accept him in faith are headed for vindication."[67] I believe this is true in Revelation 20 also.

This heightened "positioning" of the martyrs seems to reflect John's earlier statement: "The nations were angry; and your wrath has come. The time has come for judging the dead, and for rewarding your servants the prophets and your saints and those who reverence your name, both small and great—and for destroying those who destroy the earth" (11:18). This passage

---

[66]Robertson, *Word Pictures*, 6:459. Interestingly, the prodigal son parable employs *anezēsen* in a metaphorical, nonliteral way of the son's return to the father and reestablishment in the home. The son, as it were, receives a fuller life, having left feeding pigs and having returned to the love and wealth of his father. The prodigal son parable ultimately portrays the salvation of the outcasts of Israel over against the lostness of the Pharisees (cf. Luke 15:1–3).

[67]Bock, *Luke 1:1–9:50*, 247. He cites Joachim Jeremias, who sees this *anastasis* as the believers' faith vindicated. Jeremias, "λίθος," in Gerhard Kittel, *Theological Dictionary of the New Testament*, trans. and ed. by Geoffrey W. Bromiley (Grand Rapids: Eerdmans, 1967), 4:277. Bock also allows that Paul's phrase in Rom. 11:15—"life from the dead"—refers to the future, when "Israelites will believe again en masse," despite its sounding like a physical resurrection (Bock, *Luke*, 2:1240, n. 22). J. Dwight Pentecost seems torn over the proper interpretation of Romans 11:15. In his *Things to Come: A Study in Biblical Eschatology* (Grand Rapids: Zondervan, 1958) he allows that its language "is used figuratively, to express spiritual life out of the deadness of sin" (397), whereas earlier he lists Romans 11:15 as one of the verses on the physical resurrection (175).

fits the overall theme of the book: judgment on Israel for cruci-fying her Messiah (1:7; cf. 2:9; 3:9; 11:1–2).[68]

The time has come for the vindication of the martyrs on those who destroy the Promised Land; the temple and Jerusalem will be destroyed (Matt. 24:2, 15, 34; Rev. 1:1, 3; 11:1–2). This is how those "faithful, even to the point of death," receive the "*crown* of life" (Rev. 2:10, emphasis added) in the dramatic imagery of Revelation: God will publicly vindicate them in the collapse of their first enemy, Israel. These martyrs "have not lost everything. They have gained royalty and triumph."[69] This is dramatically demonstrated in history in A.D. 70. Remember, 20:4 is what *John* "saw"; that is, he sees in A.D. 70 the vindication of the saints. Then he reports it to the beleaguered confessors still living—as an encouragement to their perseverance and faith-fulness. Though the martyrs may have died physically, they will not have to die the "second death," which will be the fate of their enemies (in addition to their physical destruction in A.D. 70).

Blaising complains: "Interpretations of these martyrs' com-ing to life spiritually (as if from spiritual death) or simply living spiritually while physically dead are not valid within the param-eters of contextual, grammatical, and literary interpretation of the book of Revelation." But the martyrs' coming to life here does not merely express the point of salvation, but rather vindi-cated innocence rooted in their salvation by the blood of the Lamb[70]—hence John's dramatic imagery.

CONCLUSION

Many theological problems remain with the premillennial scenario because of the wholesale restructuring of biblical the-ology and redemptive history generated from the most difficult book in the Bible. Note the following examples:

---

[68]Morris notes that the "given authority to judge" may really mean judgment was given in behalf of, which is the theme of the book (Rev. 6:10–11) (*The Revelation of St. John*, 237).

[69]Ibid., 237.

[70]See Rev. 1:5; 5:9; 7:14; 12:11. Though the judgments of Revelation ultimately avenge the blood of Christ, they also avenge the blood of his saints who align them-selves with and follow him (17:6; cf. 6:10; 12:11; 16:6; 19:2). To afflict the corporate body of Christ is to afflict Christ (cf. Matt. 25:40).

(1) the convenient and surprising imposition of enormous time gaps in prophecy, such as in Daniel 2 (where after successive kingdoms a gap exists between the ancient Roman Empire and the future Antichrist) and in Daniel 9 (where the gap stretches from Christ's ministry to the future Great Tribulation—despite Daniel's providing a careful, unified measure of "seventy weeks")[71]

(2) the future appearance of the fullness of Christ's kingdom in an age (dispensation) separate and distinct from the present era, despite this present era's being the "last days" (Acts 2:16–17, 24[72]), the fullness of times (Gal. 4:4).[73] If these are the "last days," how can *more* days follow in a whole new era? Yet Blaising sees the millennial era as a "complete *replacement* of present conditions on earth with a new worldwide and multinational world order"

(3) the thousand-year period in which glorified, resurrected saints intermingle on earth with mortal, fallen sinners, who will eventually attack the undying immortals (20:7–9)

(4) the second humiliation of Christ, when he returns to rule on the earth (his footstool, Isa. 66:1; Matt. 5:35; Acts 7:49), only to have his kingdom rebel against his personal administration and surround him in Jerusalem at the end (Rev. 20:7–9)

(5) the retrogression back to a typological temple-sacrificial approach to worship.

---

[71]For a detailed exegesis see my *Perilous Times: A Study in Eschatological Evil* (Bethesda, Md.: Christian Universities Press, 1998).

[72]Cf. also 1 Cor. 10:11; 2 Tim. 3:1; Heb. 1:1–2; 9:26; 1 Peter 1:20; 1 John 2:18.

[73]Cf. Mark 1:15; Luke 4:18–19; 2 Cor. 6:2.

AN AMILLENNIAL RESPONSE TO CRAIG A. BLAISING

Robert B. Strimple

Given the nature of this book and the necessarily brief space available for responses, each respondent must focus now on those points where his view of "the Millennium and beyond" differs from that of his colleague. Unfortunately, this may give the reader the impression that those points at which evangelical Christians disagree with regard to their biblical hope are more significant than those on which they confidently and joyfully agree. That would be a most inaccurate impression indeed, and we look forward to our editor's correcting it in his concluding remarks.

Professor Blaising's chapter reveals encouraging interpretative advances over earlier forms of dispensationalism—in particular, (1) his recognition of the fundamental creation/fall/new creation structure of biblical thought; (2) his appreciation of the "already" aspects of the risen and exalted Christ's fulfillment of Old Testament eschatological hope; (3) his emphasis on the significance of the *literary structure* of Revelation for the correct interpretation of that book; and (4) his recognition of the role played by the interpreter's theological "preunderstandings" in his interpretation of Scripture, and thus of the importance of striving to ensure that those preunderstandings are themselves truly biblical (what earlier Christians referred to as "the analogy of faith," comparing Scripture with Scripture). It is my sincere conviction that continued reflection on biblical revelation in accordance with those fundamental insights will lead the interpreter eventually to abandon the distinctively premillennial elements in eschatology.[1]

Blaising devotes the first lengthy section of his stimulating essay to the presentation of essentially one argument, an argument from the history of theology. His thesis is that

> amillennial and postmillennial rejections of premillennialism traditionally have had more to do with a preunderstanding of what is "proper," "fitting," or "plausible" in relation to their traditional expectations about eternal life than with any specific biblical teaching contradicting the premillennial coming of Christ.

That controlling preunderstanding, Blaising insists, has been the "spiritual vision" model of the eternal state, which was tied to the early church's allegorical/mystical method of interpretation, which then spiritualized the literal, earthly aspect of the biblical hope. It was the Reformers, according to Blaising, who "emphasized the authority of the Bible's literal sense in theological expression" and thus introduced the possibility of a "new creation" model of eschatology and the reemergence of premillennialism.

In presenting the case for amillennialism, I chose not to survey the history of theology, but rather to concentrate on the biblical revelation, simply because it is by the study of the Scriptures that our doctrine must be finally determined. But it must be noted that Professor Blaising's historical argument is unsupportable from any direction. (1) What evidence does he offer, for example, to support the alleged link between early amillennial thought and Greek philosophical dualism? In 1992 Charles E. Hill published a careful and comprehensive study of premillennialism

---

[1]Contemporary defenders of classical dispensationalism have decried what they see as the progressives' drift toward amillennialism and covenant theology. "As for the present effort toward rapprochement between covenant theologians and modified dispensationalists, it seems that most of the 'give' is from dispensationalists and not from covenant people." "It is not inconceivable ... that the Millennium and the eternal state could become so blurred or merged that the Millennium disappears and amillennialism takes over" (Charles C. Ryrie, "Update on Dispensationalism," in *Issues in Dispensationalism*, ed. Wesley R. Willis and John R. Master [Chicago: Moody, 1994], 24 and 25).The progressive position does not reflect amillennialism nor covenant theology. What its presence has done is open up a healthy dialogue across traditional lines, which has also improved the tone of the debate.

(chiliasm[2]) in the early church, in which he concluded that orthodox nonchiliasm

> which looked for a return of Christ to be followed, with-
> out an interregnum, by a last judgment and an eternal state
> was no less "realistic," no less "historical" and no more
> "allegorical," "mystical" or "Greek" than was chiliasm.

Of special significance is the fact that early orthodox amillennialism "does not appear to have held any prejudice whatsoever
against the belief in a future resurrection of the body," a belief
considered the height of foolishness by Greek philosophy.[3]

Hill's extensively documented thesis is that the real doctrinal link was between (a) the early chiliasts' affirmation of a
future millennial reign of Christ on the present earth and (b) *their
rejection of the doctrine that believers go immediately after death into
the presence of God in heaven*, insisting instead that the souls of the
righteous are detained in Hades, the subterranean abode of the
dead, until the resurrection. The logical connection between
these two doctrines is drawn most explicitly by Irenaeus in
Adversus Haereses (5.31–32), where he argued that

> if souls are ushered into heaven, into the very presence
> of God and Christ, immediately after death and not
> detained in refreshing sub-earthly vaults, a future, earthly
> kingdom would seem at best an anticlimactic appendage
> to salvation history, at worst a serious and uncon-
> scionable retrogression.

Hill traces the link between these two doctrines in Papias, Justin,
Tertullian, Commodianus, Victorinus of Pettau, and Lactantius;
and he finds "the well-spring of this association in a particular
strand of Jewish apocalyptic piety, best exemplified by 2 *Baruch*
and 4 *Ezra*."[4]

(2) While Blaising offers little evidence for the thesis that
amillennial interpretation of the Bible before the Reformation
was governed by philosophical prejudice against the biblical
emphasis on a new creation, no evidence is offered to support

---

[2]*Chiliasm* and *millennialism* are synonymous terms, the former from the Greek
word for "a thousand" and the latter from the Latin word.

[3]Charles E. Hill, *Regnum Caelorum: Patterns of Future Hope in Early Christianity*
(Oxford: Clarendon Press, 1992), 182, 183.

[4]Ibid., 17; cf. 178.

the idea that such a bias is present in *modern* amillennialism. When we read modern amillennialists themselves, do we find them expressing a purely "spiritual" (i.e., nonphysical) eschatological hope? Not at all. A few representative affirmations will quickly make this point. They could, of course, be multiplied.

We are indebted to the Dutch Reformed Translation Society for the recent publication in English of Herman Bavinck's classic amillennial study of *The Last Things: Hope for This World and the Next*. In his introductory summary of chapter 7, "The Renewal of Creation," editor John Bolt writes: "Biblical hope, rooted in incarnation and resurrection is creational, this-worldly, visible, physical, bodily hope." And this is indeed the accent we find in Bavinck:

> God's honor consists precisely in the fact that he redeems and renews the same humanity, the same world, the same heaven, and the same earth that have been corrupted and polluted by sin.

> All that is true, honorable, just, pure, pleasing, and commendable in the whole of creation in heaven and on earth, is gathered up in the future city of God—renewed, re-created, boosted to its highest glory.

> Scripture consistently maintains the intimate connectedness of the spiritual and the natural.

> As the new heaven and earth are formed out of the elements of this world, and the believing community is a re-creation of the human race that fell in Adam, so the life of the redeemed in the hereafter is to be conceived as analogous with the life of believers here on earth.... It is a genuinely natural life but unfolded by grace to its highest splendor and its most bountiful beauty.[5]

One of the most influential American amillennialists was the great Princeton biblical theologian Geerhardus Vos. In an essay on "The Eternal State," Vos argues against any "hyper-spiritualizing of the content of the future life," and he concludes that "the only reasonable interpretation of the Genesis-account (*e mente Pauli*) is this, that provision was made and probation was instituted for a still higher state, both ethico-religiously *and physically*

---

[5]Herman Bavinck, *The Last Things*, ed. John Bolt, trans. John Vriend (Grand Rapids: Baker, 1996), 155, 157, 160, 161, 162.

complexioned, than was at that time in the possession of man."[6] With regard to the location of the saints eternally, Vos took the position that while "the scene of the consummate state is the new heaven and the new earth ... the central abode of the redeemed will be in heaven, although the renewed earth will remain accessible to them and a part of the inheritance (Matt. 5:5; John 14:2–3; Rom. 8:18–22; and the closing visions of the Apocalypse)."[7]

A later amillennialist, Anthony Hoekema, presented an even more earth-oriented vision:

> The Bible assures us that God will create a new earth on which we shall live to God's praise in glorified, resurrected bodies.
>
> The total work of Christ is nothing less than to redeem this entire creation from the effects of sin. That purpose will not be accomplished until God has ushered in the new earth, until Paradise Lost has become Paradise Regained.[8]

There is, of course, no reason to see such an emphasis as somehow an inconsistency or aberration in amillennial thought. Blaising assumes that the promise of a new creation carries with it the concept of an earthly millennial reign of Christ. But why— unless the Millennium will take place on the new earth? In his recent inaugural lecture as professor of New Testament at Gordon-Conwell Theological Seminary, Greg K. Beale presented the outlines of an attempt "to understand eschatology exhaustively as 'new creation' ... and to contend that the perspective of the 'already and not yet,' latter-day new creation is the heuristic lens for understanding all of the major doctrines of the New Testament."[9] The new creation concept cannot be given more preeminence in Scripture than that—and Professor Beale is an amillennialist![10]

---

[6]Geerhardus Vos, *The Pauline Eschatology* (Grand Rapids: Eerdmans, 1953), 304, 309.

[7]Geerhardus Vos, *Redemptive History and Biblical Interpretation*, ed. Richard B. Gaffin Jr. (Phillipsburg, N.J.: Presbyterian and Reformed, 1980), 55.

[8]Anthony A. Hoekema, *The Bible and the Future* (Grand Rapids: Eerdmans, 1979), 274, 275.

[9]Greg K. Beale, "The Eschatological Conception of New Testament Theology," in *The Reader Must Understand* (Leicester, Eng.: Inter-Varsity, 1997), 11.

[10]See Beale's soon-to-be-published commentary on Revelation in The New International Greek New Testament Commentary series (Grand Rapids: Eerdmans).

(3) Professor Blaising also fails to make clear either (a) that a "spiritual vision" understanding of the eternal state is incompatible with belief in an earthly millennial reign of Christ, or (b) that it was the "new creation" model that triggered the post-Reformation revival of premillennial thought. As a matter of fact, Blaising himself tells us that the earliest modern premillennialists (Alsted, Mede, Goodwin) still viewed the final state "in the traditional manner" and that the earliest dispensationalist premillennialists (Darby, Scofield, and especially Chafer) "promoted a highly mystical form of Christian spirituality that drew heavily on the traditional spiritual vision model of heaven as the final destiny for Christian believers." Blaising seeks to blunt the force of the problem this poses for his thesis by categorizing such premillennialisms as "reductionist" or "dualist" rather than "consistent," but the fact remains that historically the link between the new creation model and premillennialism has not been as clear and strong as his thesis implies.

(4) Likewise, the contention that it was the Reformers' emphasis on the literal meaning of Scripture that opened the way for the reemergence of premillennialism is without foundation. Neither the Lutherans nor the Calvinists were premillennialists. In addressing "the error of the chiliasts (millenarians)" in section 3.25.5 of the *Institutes*, Calvin expresses his opinion that "their fiction is too childish either to need or to be worth a refutation. And the Apocalypse, from which they undoubtedly drew a pretext for their error, does not support them."[11] Interestingly (in the light of Charles E. Hill's thesis referred to above) it was within the so-called "radical" Reformation that new forms of chiliasm were developed *along with a doctrine of the soul's sleep (or death) between death and resurrection*. Calvin's first theological treatise was a refutation of this "soul-sleep" teaching, and in his argument Calvin expresses briefly the interpretation of the "first resurrection" announced in Revelation 20:6 that I presented in my chapter on amillennialism. Calvin begins with a look at Revelation 6:10–11:

> Again, if the souls of the dead cried aloud, they were not sleeping.... Accordingly, in the same book John has

---

[11]John Calvin, *Institutes of the Christian Religion*, vol. 21 in The Library of Christian Classics, ed. John T. McNeill, trans. Ford Lewis Battles (Philadelphia: Westminster, 1960), 995.

described a twofold Resurrection as well as a twofold death; namely, one of the soul before judgment, and another when the body will be raised up, and when the soul also will be raised up to glory. "Blessed," says he, "are those who have part in the first Resurrection; on them the second death takes no effect" (Rev. xx.6). Well, then, may you be afraid who refuse to acknowledge that first Resurrection, which, however, is the only entrance to glory.[12]

Blaising's error at this point stems from his misunderstanding of the Reformers' desire to discover the literal meaning of Scripture. The Reformers did not mean by the term *literal* what classical dispensationalists later meant when they insisted that the biblical text must be interpreted "literally wherever possible," where the literal is opposed to the figurative, poetical, symbolical, or typological. A reading of the Reformers reveals that they were certainly not "literalists" in their reading of the Old Testament prophets as premillennialists have defined that term. For them the literal sense of the Scripture is simply the *true* sense, the intended sense, whatever that sense is (historical or figurative); and only a careful study of the words in their sentences in their contexts (their ultimate context being the whole of the biblical revelation) can determine that.[13]

Richard Muller and John Thompson have well summarized the Reformers' approach to biblical interpretation:

The meaning of a text is governed by the scope and goal of the biblical book in the context of the scope and goal of the canonical revelation of God. . . . Reformation-era exegetes . . . assumed that the exegete needed to come to terms with the historical and theological unity of the whole of Scripture as an integral part of the attempt to understand a particular book or passage. The point is

---

[12]John Calvin, *Tracts and Treatises in Defense of the Reformed Faith*, vol. 3, trans. Henry Beveridge (Grand Rapids: Eerdmans, 1958), 446.

[13]Jacques Lefevre defined the literal sense as "the sense intended by the prophet and by the Holy Spirit speaking in him" (*Introductory Letter to Fivefold Psalter*, cited in Philip Edgcumbe Hughes, *Lefevre: Pioneer of Ecclesiastical Renewal in France* [Grand Rapids: Eerdmans, 1984], 55). Hughes comments that for Lefevre, "this literal-spiritual sense may be historical, allegorical, tropological, or anagogical—or, more simply, historical or figurative—in accordance with the meaning proper to the text" (63).

perhaps best illustrated by the constant use of Scripture to explain Scripture—an interpretative technique that well supported the *sola Scriptura* of the Reformation. . . . Thus (for example) the text of the Old Testament is illuminated by its fulfillment in the New Testament; the Psalter is illuminated by the use of the Psalter in the Gospels, the Acts, and the Epistles; the story of creation in Genesis 1 is illuminated by the first chapter of the Gospel of John; and so on.[14]

It is amillennialism, not premillennialism, that has followed in the footsteps of the Reformers in allowing the New Testament revelation of the risen, exalted, Spirit-outpouring Christ to illuminate the Old Testament revelation.

When Professor Blaising begins his "biblical argument for a holistic, consistent premillennialism," he first considers the Bible apart from Revelation 20 and then concentrates on 20:1–10 within the context of the book of Revelation as a whole. Not only does he devote many more pages to chapter 20 than to any other, but he is also candid and clear throughout his essay (even clearer perhaps than premillennialists before him) about the fact that *all* his evidential eggs rest in that one basket. He alerts us to this at the outset of his essay: "As we will see, the basic structure of premillennial belief is taken from John's vision of the return of Jesus and a Millennium subsequent to that return in the book of Revelation."

This is indeed an amazing statement—that "the basic structure," the foundation and overarching design of the entire eschatological edifice, is to be drawn from one passage, and that a passage in an apocalypse, somewhat enigmatic and highly symbolical, and thus subject to more variety of interpretation in the history of the church than any other New Testament book. Professor Blaising's essay gives the distinct impression of one who has started with a commitment to a certain interpretation of Revelation 20 and then searched for both a rationale for this Millennium and a way of fitting it into the eschatology presented in the rest of the Bible.

He does insist, of course, that though "a thousand-year kingdom transpiring between the coming of Christ and the Final

---

[14]*Biblical Interpretation in the Era of the Reformation*, ed. Richard A. Muller and John L. Thompson (Grand Rapids: Eerdmans, 1996), 340.

Judgment is explicitly found only in Revelation 20 . . . the Millennium is compatible with . . . the broadly based biblical theme of a coming eschatological kingdom of God." But is it? Nowhere does Professor Blaising deal with the evidence marshaled in the second part of my essay, evidence that not only does the New Testament (aside from Rev. 20) not teach a future millennial kingdom, but it also *rules out* an earthly millennial kingdom following Christ's return because it teaches clearly, and in several passages, that all the dramatic events forming the grand eschatological finale of redemptive history are clustered together at the second coming of Christ: the resurrection of believers, the resurrection of the unjust, judgment for all, the End, the new heaven and new earth, and the inauguration of the final kingdom of God, the eternal state of the redeemed.

For example, in making the point that "the coming of Jesus Christ is the key event in the eschatology of the church," Blaising points out that "the wrath to come" from which Jesus will deliver us (1 Thess. 1:10) "will be brought by the Lord himself" at his coming, and he quotes 2 Thessalonians 1:7–10. He speaks also of the glorious "inheritance for which the church is now suffering (2 Thess. 1:5), which suffering will be relieved at the coming of Jesus (1:7–10)." But he does not address the question of how Jesus' bringing eschatological wrath for the wicked and eternal rest for the righteous *at his Parousia* is to be harmonized with the notion that a thousand-year kingdom will intervene before either that punishment or that blessing is received.

In arguing that "messianic prophecy also finds its fulfillment" in "a future kingdom that God will set up on this earth," he appeals to Amos's prediction that God would repair David's fallen tent so that the nations would bear the name of Yahweh (Amos 9:11–12), but he makes no reference to Acts 15:15–18. I suspect Blaising agrees that James properly saw the fulfillment of Amos's prophecy in the resurrection and exaltation of Christ and the consequent conversion of the Gentiles through the preaching of the apostles, but how then does that prophecy make Blaising's point that the premillennial vision is compatible with Old Testament prophecy?

Professor Blaising emphasizes the significance of the interpreter's preunderstanding as he comes to the biblical text. But he presents no persuasive argument to show that the Christian's interpretation of the Old Testament prophets should be governed by the demands of literalism and a premillennial understanding of Revelation 20:1–10.

Frankly, I was surprised and disappointed to find Professor Blaising emphasizing throughout this chapter "the literal sense," "the literal interpretation," "the literal reading," as though sticking with the literal (as opposed to a possibly figurative) interpretation of any prophetic passage is the key to interpreting it correctly. In an earlier article surveying the development of dispensational hermeneutics[15] in recent years, Blaising had emphasized that "literal hermeneutics does not mean literalistic" and that "consistently literal exegesis is inadequate to describe the essential distinctive of dispensationalism";[16] and I had looked forward to his developing further what *is* the key to interpreting Old Testament prophecy.

To cite just one example of falsely "literal" interpretation, Blaising (like the postmillennialist Kenneth Gentry) argues that although "Isaiah 65:17–25 describes the new world of the eschatological kingdom, a condition of joy and great blessing," the passage cannot be describing the eternal state because "curiously death still remains a feature in that world order (65:20)"; therefore, the passage must be describing the Millennium. He then contrasts Isaiah 65 with chapter 25, which "in no uncertain terms predicts a reign of God in which death will be abolished" and which therefore speaks of the new heaven and new earth of Revelation 21, the eternal state, because Revelation 21:4 picks up "the imagery and wording of Isaiah 25:6–9" about "God's wiping away all tears and eliminating death forever."

But note well that the interpreter does not need to go to Isaiah 25 to find that imagery and wording about the removal of tears (thinking that it is somehow in contrast to what appears in ch. 65). We find the same thing in Isaiah 65:19: "I will rejoice over Jerusalem and take delight in my people; the sound of weeping and of crying will be heard in it no more." That fact should have alerted Blaising (and Gentry) to the fact that Peter (in 2 Peter 3:13) and John (in Rev. 21:1) give us the authoritative apostolic interpretation of Isaiah's vision of the new heavens and the new

---

[15]"Hermeneutics" means the science of biblical interpretation.

[16]Craig A. Blaising, "Developing Dispensationalism Part 2," *Bibliotheca Sacra* 145 (1988): 269, 272.

earth (Isa. 65:17 and 66:22) as the *eternal* dwelling place of God's people, who are the New Jerusalem. Yes, were it literally true that a man who died at a hundred would be considered a mere youth (65:20), then tears would be shed at his passing. But surely that does not mean that we are to view verse 19 as describing the eternal state and verse 20 the Millennium.

Moreover, surely it does not require too great a "poetic soul" to see that in the Old Testament the coming messianic kingdom

> is sketched by the prophets in hues and colors, under figures and forms, which have all been derived from the historical circumstances in which they lived. Palestine will be reconquered, Jerusalem rebuilt, the temple with its sacrificial worship restored. Edom, Moab, Ammon, Assyria, and Babylon will be subdued. All citizens will be given a long life and a relaxed setting under vine and fig tree. The [projected] image of the future is Old Testament-like through and through.... But into those sensuous earthly forms prophecy puts everlasting content. In that shell is an imperishable core which, sometimes even in the Old Testament itself, breaks through.... In Jesus' day ... these forms and images were taken literally. The shell was mistaken for the core, the image of it for the thing itself, and the form for the essence.... Accordingly, chiliasm is not of Christian but of Jewish and Persian origin.... It would appear that its strength lies in the Old Testament, but actually this is not the case. The Old Testament is decidedly not chiliastic. In its depiction of the messianic kingdom it describes the completed kingdom of God that is without end and lasts forever (Dan. 2:44), preceded by judgment, resurrection, and world renewal.... The benefits of salvation promised and foreshadowed under the Old Testament have become manifest in Christ as eternal and authentic reality.[17]

Again, Blaising can appeal to the Old Testament prophetic hope of a renewed Israel as evidence for premillennialism only

---

[17]Bavinck, *The Last Things*, 90, 91, 97. Contrary to Blaising's argument that "the structure of the oracle in Isaiah 24–25 indicates some kind of intermediate situation between the coming of God in the Day of the Lord and the everlasting reign in which sin and death are done away completely," see Meredith G. Kline, "Death, Leviathan, and the Martyrs: Isaiah 24:1—27:1," in *A Tribute to Gleason Archer*, ed. Walter C. Kaiser Jr. and Ronald F. Youngblood (Chicago: Moody, 1986), 229–49.

because he insists that such prophecy must be read "literally" and in light of the Revelation 20:1–10 (even though those ten verses are devoid of any reference to a renewed Israel, a return to the Promised Land, or a rebuilt temple or throne of David— *anything* that might link John's vision to these Old Testament prophecies concerning Israel). As I emphasized in the first part of my defense of amillennialism, the proper *Christian* preunderstanding in reading Old Testament prophetic passages is the authoritative apostolic, post-Pentecost, New Testament interpretative pattern, which consistently sees these prophecies as fulfilled in Christ and his messianic kingdom, both in its present, partially realized phase and in its future, fully realized phase.

According to Blaising, Jesus and all the apostles interpreted the Old Testament without benefit of the explicit revelation that a thousand-year kingdom on this earth would intervene between the resurrection of believers at the second coming of Christ and the resurrection of unbelievers, the Final Judgment, and the eternal state, because that revelation was given for the first time to John in the vision of Revelation 20. Can we say that the nonpremillennial reading of the Old Testament by Jesus and his apostles is not a sufficient guide to *our* reading of the Old Testament? Yes, answers Blaising, because this is simply another example of the progressive nature of biblical revelation, which all Christians must accept. Note, however, that all the examples "of such progressive revelation" he gives are Old Testament prophecies that have now been clarified by the New Testament revelation. Blaising can offer no comparable example within the New Testament canon itself of such a fundamental, structural, theological alteration as this.[18]

Again (as I emphasized in my defense of amillennialism) it is not simply that the New Testament before Revelation 20 is silent with regard to an earthly kingdom that intervenes between Christ's Parousia and the Final Judgment and the cosmic renewal. Jesus and the New Testament writers do speak to this matter and *rule out* such a conception, and Scripture does not contradict Scripture. Geerhardus Vos speaks of the "attractiveness" to many of premillennialism's "progressive revelation" argument, but then he observes:

---

[18]I am indebted to my former student C. Lee Irons for this insight.

As a matter of fact, however, all warrant for thus resolving the future coming of Christ into two successive events is lacking in the New Testament. . . . The one expected coming of Christ is throughout associated with the absolute consummation of this world and not with the ushering in of a merely provisional order of affairs (cf. Matt. 25:31ff.; Mark 13:27; 14:62; Luke 9:26; John 5:29; 6:40; Acts 2:20, 21; I Cor. 1:8; 3:13; 5:5; Phil. 3:21; II Thess. 1:7–9; II Tim. 1:18; 4:8; Heb. 9:27, 28; I Pet. 5:4; II Pet. 3:10–13).[19]

Is the evidence for the premillennial interpretation of Revelation 20:1–10 strong enough to stand against the forceful tide of the entire scriptural revelation? One consistent strand running through the uniform eschatological outlook of the New Testament is the contrast between "this age" and "the age to come." We find this contrast in the teaching of our Lord (Matt. 12:32; Mark 10:30; Luke 20:34–35) and especially in Paul, for whom the contrast between the two ages is the contrast "between the evil and transitory and the perfect and abiding."[20] As John Murray notes:

It is quite consonant with this perspective that the present age has a distinctly depreciatory complexion—it is an evil age and Satan is the God of this age (Gal. 1:4; II Cor. 4:4). Because it is evil the rulers of this age did not know the Lord of Glory (I Cor. 2:6–8). This depreciation of the present age arises to a considerable extent from the contrast with the age to come. The age to come is the age of consummation, of consummated righteousness and bliss and therefore bears a distinctly favourable complexion. So much is this the case that it can be equated with the reward of the righteous and therefore represented as unqualifiedly good (Luke 20:35). . . . It is the age associated with and introduced by the appearing of the glory of the great God and our Saviour Jesus Christ.[21]

Where does the Millennium fit into this fundamental structure of New Testament eschatology? Will it be the final phase of "this age" or the initial phase of "the age to come"? Will it take place

---

[19]Vos, *Redemptive History and Biblical Interpretation*, 415–16.

[20]Ibid., 28.

[21]John Murray, "Structural Strands in New Testament Eschatology," in *Kerux: A Journal of Biblical-Theological Preaching* 6:3 (1991): 21-22.

on this present, sin-cursed earth or on the renewed earth of the consummation?

There are problems, of course, with either answer to that last question. Some premillennialists have been so impressed with the clear teaching of Paul and Peter (Rom. 8:17–23; 2 Peter 3) that this material universe will experience its renewal when God's people experience theirs (i.e., at the coming of Christ and the resurrection of believers[22]) that they have followed the lead of Theodore Zahn[23] in suggesting that the cosmic renewal will indeed take place at Christ's Parousia, with the Millennium following on the new earth (thus Rev. 21–22 describes the Millennium).

It is for good reason, however, that this suggestion has been adopted by very few. This "revised" premillennialism must assume the coexistence during the Millennium of the glorious freedom from sin of the children of God with the continuing presence of sin and indeed a worldwide rebellion against God and God's people at Satan's instigation at the end of Christ's thousand-year reign (Rev. 20:7–10)—bringing as a consequence, we must assume, a reversion to cosmic curse again (since sin's wage is death and destruction not only for humankind but also for the realm it rules). But that is impossible. The creation's deliverance spoken of in Romans 8 must be as permanent and irrevocable as the glorious final freedom of the children of God. The victory Paul describes in Romans 8 is final, total, absolute, everlasting victory for both believers and the creation at the second coming of Christ.

Blaising also views the Millennium as a hybrid of the two ages, but in a way different from Zahn. In his conception, although the Millennium will be "a temporary phase of that future kingdom," it will take place on this present earth, still under the curse. The incompatibility of such a conception with the biblical teaching should be apparent. In the New Testament the return of Christ, the resurrection of believers, the Final Judgment, the cosmic renewal, and the eternal state are all concurrent. When this biblical convergence is torn apart and a millennial kingdom on this earth inserted, we are faced with a

---

[22]See my treatment of those two passages in the chapter presenting amillennialism.

[23]Theodore Zahn, *Die Offenbarung des Johannes* (Leipzig: Deichert, 1924–1926), 2:611–25.

situation in which believers will be resurrected to live in glorified bodies on this sin-ravaged earth alongside the unbelieving and unresurrected. It is one thing to say that bodily resurrection prepares the believer for life on earth. It is quite another to say that bodily resurrection prepares for "life on this earth *as we know it*" (emphasis added). According to the apostle's teaching in 1 Corinthians 15, it is in order to inherit that final, eternal kingdom of God that believers are raised by Christ's Spirit, glorified and immortal.

Having acknowledged that the teaching that there is to be a millennial reign of Christ on this earth between his second coming and the Final Judgment "is explicitly found only in Revelation 20," what is the nature of the evidence Blaising presents that this teaching is found in that passage? (1) He appeals to the literary structure of the book of Revelation. As noted above, I believe that recognition of the importance of the overall literary structure for the exegesis of each individual passage opens the door for fruitful studies of Revelation on the part of premillennialists and amillennialists working together; and I hope we will soon see such studies undertaken. But exactly how the literary structure *requires* the chronologically sequential understanding of 19:11–20:10, and rules out any recapitulation, Blaising does not make clear.

That 20:1–10 "is not a vision of circumstances that exist prior to the Parousia" must be established, not merely asserted. General appeals to "the literary-grammatical-contextual meaning of the visions" count for nothing. And the appeal to "a basic consensus" among more recent studies does not constitute evidence, since the compelling reasons for the consensus are not presented. Most of the citations give no argument at all, and Collins's contention that "the actual plot line running through these visions is sequential" simply reflects the error of assuming that the visionary-literary sequence must express the historical-chronological sequence.

(2) Blaising presents "six observations [that] bear on the point that the thousand years ... must be seen as consequent to the Parousia of Christ in chapter 19." (Note that he does not claim for these six observations that they prove the point; they simply "bear on" it.) Let us look at them briefly. (a) "The visions of 19:11–21:8 are positioned as a transition between the vision

of Babylon and the view of the New Jerusalem ... these two cities are not coexisting realities." True enough, but amillennialists do not see these two realities as coexisting. Babylon relates to this present evil age and the New Jerusalem to the consummation age to come, and the transition between them is the great final battle of Gog/Antichrist and the Parousia of Christ.

While Blaising agrees that "God removes Babylon for the purpose of revealing the New Jerusalem," he sees that purpose postponed for a thousand years rather than being realized immediately. In this millennial transition period, do the characteristics of Babylon (pain, crying, death) persist? In that case the Millennium will be in some sense still an expression of Babylon. Or are those Babylonian characteristics eliminated at the beginning of the Millennium with the bodily resurrection of the saints and the destruction of the last enemy, death (1 Cor. 15:26, 54)? If that is the case, what will be "new" about the New Jerusalem? Does not Blaising's important point that "the New Jerusalem succeeds and replaces Babylon" argue strongly that the fall of Babylon occurs in the battle of 20:7–10, which entails the destruction of the devil and the effects of his evil working in the earth, leading immediately therefore to the descent of the New Jerusalem, in which the effects of the curse cannot be found?[24]

(b) *"There is no structural indication of a major break within this sequence recapitulating pre-Parousia conditions."* What structural indication is present in 12:1 (which Blaising agrees begins a recapitulating break in the chronological sequence) that is *not* present in 20:1? Blaising acknowledges that *kai eidon* ("and I saw") does not always indicate chronological sequence. If it did, its appearance in verse 4 would mean that verses 4–6 refer to *another* thousand-year period following the one spoken of in verses 1–3. But we know that is not so, because the reference in verse 7 to *"the* thousand years" clearly refers us back (recapitulation) to the thousand years of Satan's being bound (vv. 1–3). Likewise, when we read in verse 8 that Satan is loosed to gather the nations for *"the* battle" (v. 8, "the" is in the Gk.), this is again a clear textual indicator of recapitulation; that is, the battle described is the same battle described in chapters 16 and 19 (see below and the arguments for this interpretation presented in my chapter).

---

[24]See Dennis E. Johnson, *Revelation: Windows on the War of the Ages* (Phillipsburg, N.J.: Presbyterian and Reformed, forthcoming).

(c) The statistical argument that since "six out of the eight visions in 19:11–21:8 are commonly acknowledged as either contemporaneous with the Parousia or subsequent to it," there is therefore a "presumption ... in favor of viewing the remaining two visions in a similar manner" carries no evidential weight.

(d) Alan Johnson begs the question when he argues that "if the binding [of Satan] refers to an earthly situation—which it clearly does—the thousand-year reign most naturally refers to an earthly situation." In my chapter I point out some of the indicators that verses 4–6 of Revelation 20 are, as a matter of fact, a heavenly scene. To the points made there it might be added that Daniel 7:9, the prophetic vision alluded to in Revelation 20:4, locates the thrones in heaven (see also below).

Blaising insists that the description of the binding of the serpent in verses 1–3 is too "graphic" and "total" to be a reference to any victory that Christ has already won over Satan. Specifically, "Mark 3:27 is too remote a context for interpreting John's words." But in what sense is the Markan reference (along with the parallel texts in Matthew and Luke) "too remote"?[25] *Spatially*—the one appearing near the beginning of our New Testament canon and the other at the end? *Temporally*—the two books being written some years apart? The many allusions to the Old Testament prophets throughout the book of Revelation and their significance for the interpretation of Revelation argue against drawing conclusions based on spatial or temporal remoteness.

Is the concern, then, that the Markan reference is too remote *lexically*, or *theologically*? In terms of vocabulary (*lexically*), the verb the NIV translates "ties up" in Mark 3:27 and "bound" in Revelation 20:2 is the *same* Greek verb, *deō* (aorist active subjunctive in Mark and aorist active indicative in Revelation).

Finally, the interpretation that sees the Markan reference as instructive for the reading of the Revelation reference yields an understanding of Revelation 20:1–3 and 7–10 that is in perfect accord *theologically* with the uniform structure of New Testament eschatology, which sets before us two climactic points (not three) at which Christ's victory over Satan is secured: the first in his first coming (in his miraculous ministry, atoning death, and triumphant resurrection) and the second at his consummating second coming, when all will be set right and the *shalom* of God is

---

[25]I am indebted to my student Lane Tipton for helpful suggestions at this point.

established for all eternity. Satan continues to persecute Christ's church at the present time, true (12:13–17); but he is restrained from deceiving the nations in such a way as to gather them together for an all-out assault against God's saints until the thousand years are over and that great final battle is fought (cf. vv. 3 and 7).

Blaising insists that non-premillennialists do not agree with the premillennial interpretation of Revelation 20:1–7 because of "traditional theological preunderstandings that are hostile to this interpretation," but (as noted early in this response) he offers no evidence to establish this claim. The exegetical arguments of amillennialists must be answered, not waved aside as not being the real reasons for their interpretation of Revelation 20. At the heart of the amillennialists' exegetical concern are the many clear evidences that 16:14–16; 19:19–21; and 20:7–10 are not describing three different battles that will take place at three different times, but rather are all descriptions of *one and the same battle*, with new information about that battle revealed each time. Because the exegetical evidence is extensive and cannot be presented in the space available here, the reader is urged to read two studies in particular: R. Fowler White, "Reexamining the Evidence for Recapitulation in Rev. 20:1–10," and Meredith G. Kline, "*Har Magedon* [Armageddon]: The End of the Millennium."[26]

In note 92 Blaising responds to White's argument "that a sequential interpretation of 19:11–20:3 is not logically coherent . . . because at the Parousia Christ will destroy all the inhabitants of all the nations except the redeemed" by arguing that 19:21 refers not to the destruction of all the inhabitants of all the nations but only to "their armies" since only the armies have been gathered together for this battle. But this overlooks the immediately preceding sentence (v. 18), which summons the birds of prey to "eat the flesh of kings, generals, and mighty men, of horses and their riders, *and the flesh of all people. . .*" (emphasis added). That final category is then further spelled out in a chiasm,[27] the point of which is to make clear that the "all

---

[26]R. Fowler White, "Reexamining the Evidence for Recapitulation in Rev. 20:1–10," *Westminster Theological Journal* 51 (1989):319–44; Meredith G. Kline, "*Har Magedon* [Armageddon]: The End of the Millennium," *Journal of the Evangelical Theological Society* 39 (June 1996): 207–22.

[27]In rhetoric, chiasm is the inversion of the second of two parallel phrases, clauses, etc.; for example, "she went to Paris, to London went he."

people" in view is indeed all-inclusive: "free and slave, small and great."

When Blaising appeals to 19:15 as if a distinction is there being made between the armies (who will be struck down by the sharp sword proceeding out of Christ's mouth) and all the people (over whom Christ will rule), he fails to recognize (as the postmillennialist likewise does) that the phrase from Psalm 2:9 (he "will rule them with an iron scepter") does not imply a long period of coercive dominion over restless subjects but rather a decisive blow of definitive judgment. The first time that phrase is quoted by John (Rev. 2:27) the immediately following (and explicating) phrase in Psalm 2 is also quoted: He "will dash them to pieces like pottery." Thus White's point is well taken: With the destruction (in the great battle at the end of ch. 19) of all those who oppose the Lord, who are left to be ruled over, or to be deceived no longer, during the Millennium?

Every commentator on Revelation, it seems to me, must recognize recapitulation at some points in this book. This phenomenon was recognized in the earliest known commentary, that of Tyconius, and it is recognized by all the recent scholars cited by Blaising as representative of a new "consensus." The question, therefore, is not *whether* such a pattern can be found but *where*. Blaising himself sees 20:4–6 as recapitulating the time period covered in verses 1–3, before the author goes on in verses 7–10 to tell what will happen at the end of that period. Earlier Blaising recognized recapitulation at 12:1ff. Indeed, he sees the battle of 16:13–16 recapitulated in 19:11–21, for he writes regarding the battle of Armageddon described in 16:13–16: "This battle is the coming of Christ in 19:11–21." It is not clear, therefore, why another recapitulation must be ruled out in 20:7–10.

To the contrary, there is every reason to see that another description of the one final battle is exactly what we have in chapter 20. John reveals three major evil figures: the dragon, the beast, and the false prophet. In keeping with the chiastic pattern we have already noted, the dragon's appearance is described first (ch. 12) and his destruction is described last (ch. 20). Especially impressive is Meredith Kline's detailed argument that the repeated allusions in these battle scenes to the Gog-Magog conflict of Ezekiel 38–39 show conclusively that "the Har Magedon crisis of Rev. 16:14–16 (and the series of parallel passages in Revelation) is to be identified with the millennium-ending Gog-Magog event of 20:7–10." Thus, "Har Magedon is not a prelude to the Millennium, but a postlude. Har Magedon marks the end of the Millennium. And that conclusion spells the end of pre-millennialism."

(e) It is such exegetical (not philosophical) concerns that influence the amillennial interpreter as he approaches what the premillennialist sees as the *crux interpretum*, Revelation 20:4–6. As argued in my chapter, this vision of the saints living and reigning with Christ is a heavenly scene, not an earthly one. Such a drawing back of the veil separating heaven from earth, so that the church militant may be encouraged by a glimpse of the church triumphant, is not unique at this point in the book. Interestingly, Blaising himself describes chapter 7 as an "inter-lude . . . structurally connected with the worship of Christ in heaven in 5:9–10, the vision of the fifth seal (6:9–11 [the vision of the souls under the altar]), and the promise of the seventh trumpet (11:15–19 ['loud voices in heaven'])." Like 14:13, John's message in 20:4–6 brings comfort and reassurance to saints still undergoing trials on this earth with respect to the blissful condition of the departed saints.[28]

At this point I must confess what is rarely confessed in such an exercise, that I have actually been convinced by my brother's argument at one point. In my chapter I stated that the "until" in verse 5 is eschatologically terminating. Blaising acknowledges that this Greek word "may of itself indicate a simple limit," but he notes that "its use as a conjunction with *teleō* ('to complete, fulfill, end') in the book of Revelation consistently indicates a reversal of conditions." I believe his point is well taken; therefore, there is a reference in verse 5 to "the rest of the dead" coming to life in the sense of a bodily resurrection at the end of the thousand years. This, however, only underscores the various and sometimes paradoxical nature of John's references to death and to life as experienced by believers on the one hand and by unbelievers on the other.

Blaising notes that "premillennialists have always argued that 'came to life' must mean the same thing in 20:5 as it does in

---

[28]Blaising himself writes that the descriptions of 20:4–6 "take us back to 6:9, where underneath the altar of God *in heaven*, John saw..." [emphasis added], but he does not reflect on what that might tell us about the setting of 20:4–6.

20:4." But does he apply the same principle to John's references to "death"? The reference to "the rest of the dead" in verse 5 refers to psycho-physical death, but the reference to "the second death" in verse 6 does not. John by the Spirit would have us see that those who trust in Christ will experience one death (unless the Lord returns before then) but two resurrections. That one death (psycho-physical) of the believer John reveals to be in truth a resurrection into the very presence of the Savior in heaven, to be followed by a second resurrection (bodily) at Christ's second coming, so that the whole person (body and soul) may enjoy eternal life in the new creation order. But in stark contrast to that glorious hope, John sees the unbelieving as having before them one resurrection—and that a resurrection to condemnation, so that it hardly warrants the name—but two deaths, the one psycho-physical on this earth and the second eternal following the judgment.

SUMMARY ESSAY

Darrell L. Bock

SUMMARY ESSAY

Darrell L. Bock

Mention the Millennium and many people will share with you a joke that circulates in church settings. It goes something like this. A person was once asked on an ordination exam, "What view of the Millennium do you hold? Are you postmillennial, amillennial, or premillennial? Explain why." The reply came back quickly. "I'm none of those." The examination committee, thinking they had covered all the options, then asked the candidate, "Well then, what view do you hold?" The candidate answered, "I'm a panmillennialist, because I believe it will all pan out in the end." As much as this joke makes me laugh and although some use it as an explanation to avoid discussing eschatology, the attitude it represents is not that which underlies the presentation of these essays.

This book is written because each contributor is convinced that thinking theologically about the culmination of God's plan represents an important area of doctrine that should not be dismissed as irrelevant. It is worthwhile to engage one another on this topic and think through the nature of our differences about it. Wrapped up in these discussions are views that show the inherent unity of Scripture, since ultimately salvation and Christology express themselves in a history that has an overriding purpose and design. Just as the last chapter is important to understanding any story in a book, so appreciating eschatology is important to apprehending what God is about in his partnership with humanity. These essays reveal significant differences in the various views, yet they all affirm the ultimate victory of

God—a victory that has fundamental significance for all Christians in expressing the hope that is part of the gospel.

But how can such good and godly people disagree so much on something so important and fundamental as the nature of the end of God's plan? The answer is found in the complexity of the topic and the extent of integration required to answer the question of the Millennium and beyond. The key to assessing a problem of interpretation often depends on getting the elements of the problem clearly set out. It is a complexity worth appreciating as one seeks to determine what Scripture says.

My task, then, is to draw this discussion together and enumerate the various issues that are being discussed, briefly noting where the sides fall. The debate surrounding the Millennium is like other areas where theological difference surfaces. They are as much about the integration of texts as they are about how to read individual passages. To take a parallel example, the women's debate centers not just on individual texts, but on how various kinds of texts relate to each other. That is, the Scripture has texts that affirm the rights of women in an unqualified way, along with texts that describe them as engaged in various practices, but it also has passages that affirm restriction of practice. The crucial question becomes which passages control the discussion: the passages where no limits seem to be expressed or those that do. Different sides take different positions based on whether they regard the nonrestrictive texts to be more fundamental to determining the view or the restrictive texts.

Many of the arguments surrounding texts such as these debate their meaning based on the perception of a passage's scope (e.g., is a passage culturally limited and thus not universally applicable, or is it grounded in a distinction made at the creation and thus universally prescriptive?). Thus the debate and differences are *both* textual *and* integrational, often at the same time. This is often why the topic seems to cycle through a tortuous kind of circularity when people debate it, seemingly getting nowhere. My goal is not to discuss the women's issue, but to illustrate how it is typical of contentious areas where significant disagreement abounds in the church. Many debates involving large areas of biblical synthesis are really as much hermeneutical as they are textual.

That same integrative premise applies to this discussion of eschatology. There are both issues of interpretation related to individual passages, and there are integrative questions about the relationship of various passages that come into play. Attempts to work around this (or avoid real engagement of the foundational issues) can be seen in the various interpretive maxims that one hears when futuristic eschatology is the topic. The claims "that one must interpret literally" or that "apocalyptic is symbolic and needs to be interpreted accordingly" are competing slogans that often hide complex interpretive issues, which in turn is a more complex matter than a "one-size-fits-all occasions" hermeneutical rule. Competing claims that these texts are clear or obscure (made about the same passages!) show just how much these foundational questions impact the reader's perception of what is required. One of the benefits of the essays we have studied is that each side has to make the case for both the synthetic claims and the particular interpretations being defended.

I propose to trace the discussion of the essays by examining the disagreements in three basic categories: integrative hermeneutical categories, textual hermeneutical issues, and basic structural implications. It might strike the reader odd that no clear category of "exegetical" is found in the list, but this is because in many cases *how* the text's language is being read is determined by more fundamental hermeneutical judgments made before one gets to the specifics of the passage in question. A glance at the preliminary remarks of each essay and response when discussing certain key texts like Revelation 20 shows how important these preunderstandings are to the reading of the texts. It may be fair to say that in no area of theology is this reality more apparent than in eschatological discussion. I would also note that the specifics of particular arguments for particular passages are well set forth by the representatives of each view, so there is little reason to repeat those arguments here.

One of the side discussions that emerges from the essays and responses is a debate over what history teaches. I will not engage this discussion at all. All of our responders agree that the most important issue is what Scripture teaches. Whether the early church was influenced by dualism or not and whether the basic eschatological model of that church reflects a new creation model or a move to a more static "spiritual vision" model is a question for another place. In addition, the best way to read Irenaeus's *Adversus Haereses* 5.31–32, 2 Baruch, or 4 Ezra cannot be developed here in light of our focus on Scripture. Was the early church too influenced initially by "Jewish materialistic" readings of the end or were they simply following the lead of the language of the Hebrew Scriptures?

This question spills over into considerations about the New Testament's use of the Old Testament, a question we will discuss. Nevertheless, what should not be missed in the midst of the debate over history is that all the responses affirm a biblical emphasis on the presence of "new creation" motifs as important for eschatological hope, though each view understands what is meant by "new creation" differently from the others. Defining what the movement toward this realization of the renewal of creation is and what it will eventually look like represents one of the central aspects of considering what Scripture teaches about the Millennium and beyond.

What do each of the categories treating the elements of disagreement represent? By "hermeneutical integration" I am referring to issues that are raised by the ways sets of texts are understood to relate to each other: Here I have seven issues to note:

(1) issues of preunderstanding involving simplicity, God's sovereignty, apocalyptic genre, the role of temporal language about the immediacy of the end-time events, and the nature of eternity

(2) the relationship of Old Testament to New Testament texts (explanatory and determinative commentary or complementary?)

(3) typology (its function: "shadow" or pattern?; its potential for repetition of motif, especially in judgment texts and issues related to the destruction of Jerusalem in A.D. 70; its possible role in linking more closely together events as one that may well be separated in time)

(4) the role of Israel in texts with its "this earth" and "among the nations" language

(5) the role of the book of Revelation (gives fresh information or develops what is already established?; mostly sequential or recapitulatory?)

(6) the issue of dualism (relationship of heavenly and earthly texts)

(7) the fact and nature of the Millennium (precluded by biblical teaching or allowed for it in Scripture?; also the possibility of an "intermediate kingdom" before the end).

These are all integrative and basic hermeneutical stances. The case made for the exegesis of a passage's details often stands on predecisions made about what these texts can denote interpretively, given the topic or genre.

By the category "textual hermeneutical" issues I am alluding to more literary kinds of interpretive issues. Here I have two separate concerns:

(1) What is the nature of the book of Revelation as apocalyptic literature? How does it communicate its truth through its symbolism? How does that symbolism work? Does the fact that Revelation is apocalyptic make it inherently a more obscure work?

(2) What is the role of numbers in apocalyptic? Certainly for the question of a time period like that which might be implied by Revelation's use of "a thousand years," this is an important issue.

Once all of these questions are considered, one can then turn to the fundamental implication that remains. By "implication" I am alluding to the basic worldview that results from each system. What implications do the different views have on our theological-ethical understanding of eschatology and the mission and expectation of the church?

The survey leaves us with a basic question and three fundamental options. Does Scripture indicate a *Zwischenreich* (i.e., the existence of an intermediate kingdom—a broader question than the millennial question, which more narrowly specifies time frame)? Is the end (1) a gradual improvement where we will see the church usher in the victory with Christ (so postmillennialism); (2) does it involve an apocalyptic act of Christ moving us directly into eternity (so amillennialism); or (3) is it the coming of victory on this earth through Christ in the completion of promises yet to be realized in the midst of catastrophic judgment and earthly rule (so premillennialism)? Only consideration of the various factors raised in the earlier questions can help us clear the way to get a sense of why Christians do not agree on the choice between these basic structural options. Only through an appreciation of the complexity of the discussion can one begin to get a sense of how each of these subissues can be addressed so that one can consider how the debate might be scripturally resolved.

POINTS OF AGREEMENT

Before I turn to disagreements, I will briefly trace some fundamental lines of agreement and commitments among the authors, which should not be forgotten as we proceed.

(1) All are committed to the Scripture as the ultimate authority in this discussion. In one way, this may be stating what is obvious from the essays, especially given the attention each essay has given to specific texts. But this is an important point. The alternative syntheses argued for here each represent an attempt to respect what Scripture teaches. Each view attempts to synthesize Scripture into a sensible whole, contending for that unified understanding. Each essay is written with a conviction that ultimately we must examine our views by the standards and concepts that Scripture sets. Since none of us possesses omniscience, the kind of interactive discussion represented in this book is helpful because it has the potential to reveal where a view defended might possess blind spots, as well as which issues each view sees as most significant. Often disagreements emerge because one view sees one contentious point as more central than another point considered more central by another view.

(2) There has been a sense of fellowship, even in the midst of the disagreement. The absolute affirmation of the lordship of Christ, though differently conceived in the details, breathes through every page of this discussion. There is an inherent recognition that in the larger scheme of issues debated in the world about religious belief, this is an internal discussion among brothers and sisters in Christ. Internal discussions are important, as any family knows. Such debates also can be contentious at points and require directness in engagement, but it is just as important to appreciate the family members as members of the same body.

Christians have a tendency to major on their differences with one another and exaggerate them to an extent that the effectiveness of their witness before a needy world is undermined. Lost are the points of inherent unity they possess with other believers who are committed to pursuing truth, even where their perceptions on it differ. Also often lost is a recognition that what is affirmed means that they are much closer together as brothers and sisters in Christ than what is being affirmed by those outside the faith.

(3) Each view represented here foresees the eventual victory of Christ to the glory of God. Though the routes taken to get there differ—and these differences have important implications in terms of the priorities of ministry and church practice—we should not lose sight of the fact that each view foresees a day when God will visibly, eternally, and indubitably display his authority with an exalted Christ at his side. This is one of the fundamental points that unite all Christians who embrace the message and hope of Scripture.

HERMENEUTICAL INTEGRATION ISSUES

Issues of Preunderstanding

Preunderstanding is difficult to write about, because it deals with often subconscious theological ideas we take as given, whether we have examined them carefully or not. For example, for the person who accepts that God is personal, it is often difficult to set about proving that he is, as one must often do in Eastern culture, where the divine is not thought of instinctively in those terms. Certain preunderstandings make other options often seem odd and inherently wrong. The feeling is that one is trying to prove what would seem obvious, like trying to demonstrate that air is there.

Preunderstandings mean that certain approaches to questions often draw us in favorably almost by default, not because we have examined the issues carefully, but because we are already predisposed to accept a certain orientation over another. It is important, of course, to appreciate that preunderstanding is not bad. It is actually unavoidable—we all have them, whether we are aware of it or not—and some preunderstandings are good and biblically sound. These preunderstandings deserve to be presented and defended. They are best defended in a context where they may be challenged to see if they really are preunderstandings worth maintaining.

However, preunderstandings are also tricky, because we tend to embrace them tenaciously. Sometimes we cling to them so tightly that we cannot see things any differently and inherently reject other options. Such preunderstandings, if wrongly held, can predispose us to accept something as likely that may not be the case and that may be unbiblical. Thus, reflecting about our preunderstanding is often a helpful exercise.

On preunderstanding and simplicity. In the area of eschatology, preunderstanding can show up subtly in various ways. For example, we might be predisposed to argue or even feel that the articulation of God's plan that is the simplest in structure is best. The claim of a simple structure has an appeal because it is clear and lacks the complication of other options. Such a straightforward reading has a seemingly inherent plausibility. It is here that amillennialism and postmillennialism like to make a point. There is something simple about having eternity follow right on the heels of Christ's return. No one will get lost in the detail of the amillennial or postmillennial approach as a matter of structure. Certainly the point is one that makes amillennialism or postmillennialism attractive. But it is important to point out that this kind of argument represents a kind of appeal to logic and preunderstanding as opposed to being automatically reflected in the text. A claim that the simplest approach is inherently superior is a claim at the level of preunderstanding, not a textual argument. By itself, the claim has no merit, unless the text can sustain the claim.

On preunderstanding and God's sovereignty. One of the points of agreement noted above was that all the views argue for God's sovereignly leading us to victory in the future. However, the essay for postmillennialism makes a developed argument for this point. Grounding the plan of God in creational purpose, sovereign power, and provision for blessing among God's people, and appealing to the positive thrust of texts like Matthew 13 and 28:18–20, the author argues that inherent in this idea is the notion that sovereignty means victory in history and that this view possesses a "historical optimism" for the present-day church era the other options lack.

Ironically, premillennialism makes the same argument but does so in the context of seeing an era yet to come when Christ brings the victory in the next stage of this history. Their emphasis on the plan being encased within Old Testament prophecy about Israel is a claim of sovereign design as well.

Amillennialism sees the sovereign victory in the manifestation of Christ's authority immediately upon his return, reversing the conditions of sin in a fallen world for all time. Ironically again, amillennialists and premillennialists agree that our current history is headed for a decisive confrontation between God and the world, in contrast to the postmillennialists' appeal to a gradual reversal and advance in the face of enduring confrontation between God and the world. The difference is that amillennialists see the resolution in this era, while premillennialists see it in one more phase to come.

The question to consider here is whether the category of sovereignty equals optimism about this phase of history. Is this equation a given or does it reflect another type of logical argument based on a preunderstanding about the current success of God's work in the church? The variety of options presented shows how contested this point is.

On preunderstanding and apocalyptic genre. This question is important enough to receive its own category in the discussion of textual hermeneutical issues. The point of placing an initial discussion here is that expectations of what apocalyptic is impact how we read Revelation. I remember a conversation I had with a scholar writing a commentary on Revelation. I asked him how long a section he would write on the genre of apocalyptic in the introductory section of his commentary. He replied that he was not writing on it at all, because such a literary discussion was a distraction from the content of the text and because Revelation was "prophetic" genre, not apocalyptic. Here was a commentator so trapped in his preunderstanding that he was unable to conceive of the possibility that Revelation could be read differently than he conceived of it. He also could not appreciate that the categories of prophecy and apocalyptic are not mutually exclusive as genre classifications but that apocalyptic is a special form of presenting prophetic declaration. What is minimized as a result is a careful discussion of the relationship between symbol and meaning in the material of Revelation. I am pleased that here is one issue none of our contributors ignores.

The essays in this work show how essential a preunderstanding of this question is. It makes a significant difference in interpreting the bulk of the book of Revelation whether it is a symbolic rendering of contemporary, first-century history (as postmillennialists argue), or a symbolic, cyclical portrayal of the history of the church from the first century to the future (as many amillennialists suggest), or a symbolic presentation of a future period (as some premillennialists suggest). One can also claim that it is a representation of literal referents in language where the prophet was doing his best to describe what he really saw, as if a videotape of future events was before him. Other premillennialists have argued for this understanding in their defense of a "literal" reading.

It is to the credit of our contributors that none of them ignored this question, but tackled it fully, each making the case for his reading. It is a sign of the difficulty of this area that often it is hard for us to seriously consider the other options, once our preunderstanding is firmed up on this question. The one exhortation I can give to the reader here is to listen carefully to the arguments at this point. They are often a major key to the view adopted.

I add a further observation here. In the last century, much attention has been given to the study of apocalyptic as a genre within New Testament studies. It often surprises the average Christian to be told that numerous examples of this genre existed in Judaism. Apocalyptic was a prevalent form of literary-religious expression in this period. These works helped to create an expectation of what such types of works were seeking to communicate and how they did it. I am not suggesting these works are canonical, only that the style they used was familiar and thus created expectations in its audience about what type of work apocalyptic is.

I am not sure that all that could be done in reflecting on the nature of this genre has been applied to this debate. Since historically many of the lines of reading the book of Revelation and the preunderstanding that emerged about it predated the discovery and analysis of these Jewish apocalyptic works, we might all do well to consider how the existence and prevalence of this genre in the ancient world helped to set the expectations of this kind of literature. Here is a potential fruitful area for future study, taking a much different path from my commentator friend noted above.

On preunderstanding and time terminology. This area has in mind the postmillennial emphasis that the end comes soon—that is, that it must come in the generation of Jesus because of texts that express this kind of a time frame for the events of the end. This leads to an emphasis on the role of A.D. 70 and the destruction of the temple as the coming of Jesus. On the other hand, there are texts like 2 Peter 3:8–9 where the sense of delay of the end is strong. In addition, many of these time texts belong in contexts where it is possible that typology (Olivet Discourse) or the discussion of patterns of activity across time are in play (the symbolism of judgment in Revelation). Thus, this subcategory illustrates how overlapping these discussions become. Those who prioritize these temporal references may well conclude that the end must have come in those years. Others, citing the literary elements of the contexts in which these remarks appear, may not be so convinced of this conclusion.

On preunderstanding and the nature of eternity. The importance of this question was noted in the essay on premillennialism. Assumptions about how static eternity is and how quickly we move into it influences how texts about consummation in the Old Testament are read. If the argument is accepted that the New Testament consummation texts in some way "update" the more earthly language of the Old Testament consummation texts, then reading these Old Testament texts in light of the beatific eternal state becomes an easy move, and some expressions of amillennialism or postmillennialism follow. If that argument is rejected as unbiblical, then the balance tilts in favor of some form of premillennialism.

Here we begin to see how preunderstanding and the relationship of the Old and New Testaments become intertwined in the argument. Beyond this, the preunderstanding that consummation in eternity is the only category for consummation also impacts this discussion. If, on the other hand, consummation itself comes in stages, then other options open up for the reading of the consummation and "new creation" texts.

Summarizing preunderstanding. A consideration of preunderstanding issues shows just how complex discussion of the Millennium and beyond actually is. Much like a juggler who has to keep track of many balls in the air at once, so the student of the eschatological debate is constantly having to track the discussion at many levels simultaneously. The point is not made to discourage the student, but simply to describe the nature and complexity of the problem clearly. What has been tragic about Christian discussion of this topic in the past is that in contending for our convictions about eschatology, we have been slow to admit to the complexity of the discussion, suggesting in the process that someone who holds a different view is either incompetent or disingenuous.

Many of the differences we see in the debate emerge because an individual has made certain judgments about what the text is saying or even what is possible from the text. Many times these judgments reflect an inherent prioritization of concerns that rest on issues of preunderstanding. It is important to know what options exist before making a judgment, rather than ruling them out ahead of time. It is also helpful to recognize how concerns are prioritized when the various options are examined. I trust these essays help us to see the nature of the choices about which the interpreter must make good judgments.

The Relationship of Old Testament to New Testament Texts

The way in which the Testaments are tied together is also an important consideration for each of the views. Amillennial and postmillennial interpretation contend that texts about Israel are now about the church. Each of these essays clearly laid out the argument for how this can be seen to take place. In effect, the New Testament serves as an explanatory and determinative commentator on Old Testament promises.

A major element in this reading is noting how Old Testament texts get applied to the church in the New Testament in fulfillment contexts. Postmillennialists and amillennialists argue that in a real sense Israel has been incorporated into the church in the New Testament; in light of fuller revelation, this fact must impact the way the Old Testament is now read. Moreover, what was said of Israel is now said of the church as a result of this incorporation. This is perhaps the strongest argument for these schools, for it is an internal scriptural argument. The case has not been taken seriously enough by premillennialists until the middle of this century.

Premillennialists take one of two approaches here. Some treat all "Israelitish" texts as referring to Israel and argue that New Testament texts that apply Old Testament texts to the church are arguing either by analogy based on future fulfillment in Israel or by indirect application with ultimate fulfillment coming in God's future work in Israel. This position has been popular among some forms of dispensationalism, notably traditional dispensationalism and revised dispensationalism, which became popular in the middle part of this century. Other premillennialists acknowledge that the New Testament does acknowledge degrees of direct, initial Old Testament fulfillment in the church today, but because this fulfillment is "already/not yet," the present fulfillment complements or supplies only a piece of what is ultimately alluded to in the Old Testament. The premillennial essay in the present book treats this issue when it speaks of the hope of an intermediate kingdom involving Israel in the midst of the nations. The contention is that these basic structures never get removed by subsequent revelation.

Historical premillennialists are the least clear on how all of this works, as most will speak of a conversion of Jews in the future, but they do not discuss how or whether the nation of Israel fits into the plan. Progressive dispensationalists speak of a strictly complementary relationship between the Testaments, where the New Testament adds to what the Old Testament promises affirm but does not merely elaborate on/replace/redefine/more precisely define what appeared to be promises to Israel. (The slashes in the previous sentence indicate the various ways this relationship is described by those nondispensationalists who affirm this relationship.)

Thus, both historical premillennialists and progressive dispensationalists take the "incorporation" language in New Testament texts as acknowledging the soteriological equality that is established in Christ for Jew and Gentile alike. They also acknowledge that these texts have a connection to promises of the Old Testament, but they argue that this affirmation does not need to eliminate how *ethnic* Israel has promises to her fulfilled. In an interesting development in the last few decades, more amillennialists are acknowledging as well such a possibility for *ethnic* Israel before the end (rather than seeing Rom. 11 as referring to the church as "elect Israel").

This is one area where the scope of our topic has prevented a full treatment of this question. For a staunch defense for Israel's being fully incorporated into the church within the New Testament, see the amillennial essay. That essay also argues that though ethnic Israel is referred to in Romans 11, this does not entail a prediction of a future national conversion. For the opposite contention, that Israel still refers in this text to Israel and that conversion is anticipated for the bulk of Israel, one can check commentaries on Romans by Cranfield or Moo, the study on Romans 9–11 by S. Lewis Johnson in *A Case for Premillennialism*, or the work by J. Lanier Burns on Romans 11 in *Dispensationalism, Israel and the Church*. Recent developments among the views show that affirming the presence of incorporation language in the New Testament does not need to answer the question of a future for ethnic Israel. Fulfillment can take place in the church without removing the hope of fulfillment for Jews or Israel.

This issue, however, still has one more level of discussion attached to it: If Romans 11 affirms a response by the Jewish nation viewed as a whole, then does that suggest a future for Israel as a national structure (most premillennialists, except for some historical premillenarians, who are not clear on this question)? Here one can discuss a potential distinction between a future for *ethnic* Jews as a whole and the need for a hope for Israel *as a nation*. Or does Romans 11 merely affirm that many ethnic Jews will come to faith in the future (as taught by those amillennialists and postmillennialists who do not understand Israel as referring exclusively to the church)? How one answers this question about the implications of Romans 11 is dependent less on this text than how one reads the hope of Scripture as a whole. One's answer to that question emerges from an assessment of many of the related questions we are examining.

Progressives go one step further than historical premillennialists in arguing that the millennial kingdom anticipates an administrative structure where national Israel again assumes a central place as the home of the reigning Messiah, in the midst of the nations who also respond to the Christ. Progressives do not argue this point in such a way as to deny the fundamental equality of Jew and Gentile in the benefits of salvation. So progressives speak openly, as other dispensationalists do, of a future for *national* Israel among the nations in the Millennium. It is this detail that makes a premillennial view dispensational.

Once again this entire area represents an integrative question. There are numerous key texts here, but perhaps the most visible are the speeches of Acts 2, 3, 13, and 15, along with the many texts like Galatians 3, 1 Peter 2, or Romans 9, where metaphors or covenants related to Israel in the Old Testament are discussed in relationship to the current era. One's general approach to how the Old Testament works when cited in the New Testament determines how the details of New Testament fulfillment, or even of Old Testament promise, are read. All sides are making a textual appeal here. The question is which synthesis is the more persuasive and comprehensive in treating the material.

Typology

Bound up in the discussion of the relationship between the Old and New Testaments is the question of typology. Typology is a crucial component of the discussion of these texts because it contains three distinct issues that require assessment. I believe the essays in this volume reveal the scope of options nicely, as well as providing ways to assess them.

(1) Important in the discussion is whether the typology coming out of the Old Testament points to a pattern that the New Testament completes in total fulfillment, so that the Old Testament imagery is eclipsed, or whether the New Testament use reflects a pattern of activity that is realized in a fresh way in the new era without necessarily excluding the old imagery for the future, or whether it is a mixture of both, depending on what is discussed. Obviously, of course, if there is no belief in an earthly intermediate kingdom, then the question of the reappearance of some or all of these things becomes moot. But for those who accept an earthly Millennium, the question of its form is a live option.

How do the earthly models of the Old Testament faith (law, sacrifices, temple, a nation of God's people) relate to the realities proclaimed in the New Testament? Postmillennial and amillennial interpreters appeal to the model of worship in passages like Hebrews 8–10 and argue that the typology or patterns of Old Testament worship are "shadows" of realities that now have come; they are never to be resumed. The roots of such claims are found in remarks such as Jesus made in John 2:18–22 or Stephen in Acts 7. Just as sacrifices have been done away with forever in Christ, so also all the patterns of Israel's worship have been permanently removed, since the shadow is removed in the fulfilling reality that is in Christ.

In other words, the principle applied to sacrifices and other elements of the temple worship in Hebrews is turned into a general interpretive principle for all of eschatological hope. On this basis, the hope of a nation of Israel or worship in a reestablished temple are ruled out. Ezekiel 40–48 then becomes an elaborate metaphor for genuine worship in the church or in heaven, not about a future earthly temple.

Premillennialists, by contrast, raise the question whether the principle argued for from Hebrews 8–10 should be elevated to a principle that applies across the board to eschatological categories. The typology that it represents involves only a specific pattern of realization, but the question as to the principle's extent must be determined by the specific declaration of passages and the treatment of other texts that, it is argued, give no hint of this shift of imagery into a new sphere. To premillennialists, it is better to take texts on a case-by-case basis, assessing how typology works in one text or instance at a time.

Some premillennialists are willing to consider whether some imagery is recast through a typological reading. Others, emphasizing "literalness," tend to see these images in Old Testament-like terms, looking for a return to worship around a rebuilt temple. All, however, do recognize that the cross has forever altered how sacrifices should be seen, so that discussion of a retrogression to Old Testament reality does not fairly describe what is present.

(2) The next issue is how typology can perhaps permit present and future events to be addressed simultaneously in the "pattern" that the typology represents. The effect of this category could be that events in the world today form a pattern for how the end also will look and how history will move towards its culminating phases. Specific discussion of this issue has not been prominent in this book.

The essence of typology is that it creates a "representative" description of a reality that may reappear in a fresh form at a later date. Such representation then gives the possibility that what is portrayed in one time period as taking place may "reappear" in the same general form in another time period, so that the two events can share an identification. The Olivet Discourse, for example, has these elements in it, according to premillennialists and amillennialists. The Old Testament treatment of the

Day of the Lord is a primary example of this type of typology acknowledged by all. It can refer to events in Joel's time while also picturing how the Final Judgment will come.

Could it be that the image of the beast is first-century Rome at one level or at least includes it in some way, since it was the evil world empire opposing the saints at the time of John's writing, and yet it is also genealogically and typologically related to the world power of the end, which Jesus will ultimately judge one day in the future? Could not images like Babylon and the beast represent similar kinds of connections, so that the struggle of history current in John's time is a type of cipher and precursor for the ultimate future struggle? If there are parts of Revelation that work this way, there may be ways in which the book is able at points to address the present, while at the same time pointing to the future.

(3) Another effect of typology is that two events can be discussed at once as one event, even though distinct in time, because one event "mirrors" the other in sharing the same pattern (thus the destruction of the temple in A.D. 70 can "mirror" the events of the end in such a way that both events can be seen as a part of the picture of the end). Cyclical readings of Revelation like those in the amillennial view may fall into this category, but they are not the only way in which typology may influence such a reading of Revelation. If this option is actually taking place in one form or another, then the old debate between choosing between Revelation as a book about the future from Revelation 4 on or about the present may be moot.

Is it possible that the end, which lies in the future, is pictured through the mirror of present events—a dual perspective that typology is capable of conveying? If so, then the end is like the present in the struggle that exists between the forces of evil and those who are the people of God, though in the end—with Christ's return—there will be unprecedented suffering and, ultimately, vindication for those who believe. The treatment by Marvin Pate in another Zondervan Counterpoints book (on interpreting Revelation) tries to argue this way. At the least, such options must be considered and need to be assessed.

The significance of the relationship of time and typology was noted in the discussion on preunderstanding. Events of the end start to unwind with signs that lead to the destruction of

Jerusalem in A.D. 70. Postmillennialists argue for more than a start to the path to the end. They argue that these predictions make that destruction the presence of the end and the establishment of the return, leading into a symbolic Millennium that ends in triumph. These texts also suggest to postmillennialists that Revelation should be read in preterist terms, since that also makes the book more relevant to the setting of its readers.

But amillennialists and those premillennialists who read the bulk of Revelation in a futurist way argue that the presence of typology helps one make better sense of the sequence of the end. Other premillennialists simply argue that the bulk of the book is futurist from the start. They define the issue of the shortness of time merely as imminence and as short on the scale of being the next event in God's plan that includes eternity.

Given the way such typology can work in the Old Testament and the fact that Revelation draws so heavily on Old Testament imagery, considering how typology might impact these discussions cannot be ruled out a priori. The result may be that some of the choices that the old debate raised over these issues by casting them as either/or options may, in fact, be both/and answers, with each side having some things right and other points wrong by the exclusive emphases that they brought to the reading. Here is another area where I believe future work on the question must concentrate. I am not certain whether we have all the answers here yet.

The Role of Israel

All that has been said about the Old Testament and the New Testament sets up the discussion of the role of Israel in texts with its "this earth" and "among the nations" language. The fundamental question here is whether Israel has been reconstituted in the church. If the church is reconstituted Israel, then what does that mean for the category of national and ethnic Israel as a part of God's promise, especially as it is expressed in texts of the Old Testament?

It is here that the question has become more complicated in recent years. One used to be able to say that if one saw the church as reconstituted Israel, then one would not hold to a future return to faith for Jews within Israel as a nation. If Israel is now the church and believers are the "true inward Jews" of today, then one need not expect a massive turn to faith in Christ by ethnic Jews that entailed as well a future role for national Israel—a view often tied to amillennialism or postmillennialism. But in recent years, some who held to these options have begun to consider the possibility of a massive Jewish conversion in the end times, as Romans 11 may indicate, which may imply a future for national Israel as well. The difference with premillennialists is that this possibility is not seen as requiring an earthly Millennium; rather, it places elect, ethnic, national Israel in the church, which has now become the true Israel.

Premillennialists have tended to argue that whether one views the millennial kingdom as representing a continuation of the church (historical premillennialism) or as the nation of Israel reestablished under a returned and reigning Christ (dispensationalism), one could anticipate a rule of Christ among the nations from Jerusalem. Such views meant that earthly Israelitish texts or texts about the kingdom residing among the nations were read in terms of this history and in terms of realization ultimately in the context of the intermediate kingdom and its aftermath.

The importance of this question is one of the reasons why Romans 11 receives so much attention in this debate. If there is a future for ethnic Jews, it raises the likelihood—though it need not guarantee it—that national Israel in the midst of the nations has a future as well. This is especially the case if Old Testament structural categories in Old Testament promise texts have a futuristic dimension to them. Since Romans 11 is considering the faithfulness of God in light of his past promises, the question can be raised about points of continuity implied in this argument as it reaches back into Old Testament expectation. Again, the point I wish to make is the importance of realizing all the interpretive options.

The Role of the Book of Revelation

The hermeneutical function of the book of Revelation is important and complex. Both the amillennial and postmillennial essays have argued that Revelation is obscure and that one should form the structures of one's eschatology from the thrust of Scripture before we get to this book. In this approach, Revelation merely develops symbolically what Scripture has already established about the future. This point applies whether one reads this book as a metaphor of the ongoing struggle of the church with evil in this era or if it looks futuristically to the end of our era before Christ ushers in eternity.

Premillennialists are aware of how difficult a genre Revelation is, but argue that it gives us the most carefully set forth disclosure about the end. As such, and as an important part of the canon, its fresh information explains and helps to establish the structures that are a part of the end. In short, Revelation is the key book for futuristic eschatology because it is devoted to that topic. Thus, it should be given careful attention when this topic is raised. Rather than highlighting its obscurity, it is a central text for this topic that demands our careful attention.

Here is one of the points where the various views could not be further apart. On the one hand, it is ironic that those views that emphasize so much the prominence of later revelation in the New Testament as definitive for many areas argue for a more limited role of this final New Testament book. On the other hand, those who argue for so much futurity in this work have to explain clearly the first-century relevance of a book that is so dedicated to what is clearly now a long-term future perspective.

The Issue of Dualism

The importance of the relationship of heavenly and earthly texts was noted above both in the discussion of typology and in the discussions on historical issues. It was also highlighted in the premillennial essay and in the responses to it. The superiority of "heavenly" forms to the material nature of the earth has a rich history in Western philosophy. What is debated is how much this influence has left its trace in the eschatology of the early centuries of the church. It is an important question to consider if this philosophical doctrine is reflected in Scripture or has colored the way biblical texts are read. It has presumably led to the development of a Christian instinct that "up there" is better.

Such a reading is not unique to any particular view of the Millennium, for some expressions of dispensational premillennialism have asserted the greatness of the church as God's heavenly people and of heaven itself on the basis of this dualism. On this point, the earliest classical dispensationalism was identical to the earlier amillennialist emphasis on a redemption involving a purely heavenly experience.

But the essays raise an interesting question. If God remakes the heavens and the earth and restores them to a pure, thoroughly redeemed state, then why should heaven be seen as better than the earth? If God brings a new heaven and a new earth, then does not the renewed character of that remade creation sanctify all of it fully? The newness of the ultimate redemption is something of which all the views could afford to reflect more. It may become a source for moving all of the options to a greater unity as they contemplate what is beyond the Millennium, however it is conceived. Interestingly, each view as expressed in this book has affirmed this dimension of eschatological hope, even though each one sees the point slightly differently.

The Millennium as an Intermediate Earthly Kingdom

Does Scripture allow for the Millennium as an intermediate earthly kingdom? In many ways, this is the basic ultimate question. The remaining sections of this summary chapter continually come back to this question in one form or another. All the essays deal with this question as a major burden, with key texts like 1 Corinthians 15 and Revelation 20 receiving careful attention from each of our contributors. I have tried to show that getting to this question presupposes several other questions before an answer can even begin to be developed. In a real sense, the judgment made here is the sum of judgments already made about other points.

HERMENEUTICAL TEXTUAL ISSUES

This category of consideration turns in particular to literary issues impacting the reading of the question. Much of what was said above about typology or the relationship between the Old and New Testaments could fit here as well. Yet I have reserved this category for two features of discussion about the book of Revelation: the book as apocalyptic and the role of numbers in apocalyptic literature.

The Book of Revelation as Apocalyptic

As noted above, the nature of apocalyptic literature is an important consideration about how the book of Revelation should be read. John's work addressed itself to an audience familiar with this style of presentation. Certain ancient conventions existed throughout this literature for how to address the hope of resolution by God in the end. Jewish apocalyptic works like 1 Enoch or 4 Ezra show what these expectations were, as well as the way the imagery was applied to present the message of the book. It is a fundamental characteristic of apocalyptic that it describes both symbolically and in a way that presents real history and hope.

Apocalyptic shows how the apocalyptic author foresaw God's resolving the current plight of his people. Apocalyptic has rightly been described as "crisis" literature. God's people are persecuted in the world by the world, so how will God execute his decisive judgment and deliver them? It is also decidedly "hope" literature, because what is portrayed is the final victory of God. Thus, by the end of the work, one can be confident that ultimately this work is futuristic. In this, of course, as a general category, all of our contributors agree. In this general judgment they are merely reflecting that this is what apocalyptic literature does.

However, one should note that the postmillennial and amillennial readings of Revelation place a bulk of its subject matter in the current age, while premillennialists tend to emphasize a futurist reading. Thus, the views that emphasize direct, first-century applicability are attractive to those who think Revelation must speak fairly consistently to the first-century situation. These readings also more simply relate how the current era of the church relates to victory in the end.[1] Thus, although all see the ultimate futurity of Revelation, it is more disputed exactly how the story turns toward the future. How Jewish apocalyptic literature works is important, since it indicates what an author of an apocalyptic work might be indicating to a reader of apocalyptic.

A work like 1 Enoch goes through a review of history extending back as far as Genesis 6 to make its case for how ultimate judgment comes (1 Enoch 6–10). These kinds of historical

---

[1]How the claim to simplicity relates to this subject was addressed above, under the heading "Issues of Preunderstanding."

reviews embedded within the sequence of an apocalyptic account mean that sometimes the writer engages in a type of historical review or overview even as the story proceeds in its sequence. Thus, one can hold to a sequence of events moving forward within an apocalyptic work and still have places where the imagery moves to review or summarize events whose roots may look back from the sequence portrayed. The characteristics of this genre should lead us to anticipate some mixture of present, past, and future in the movement of the events. At the least, one must consider what the options might be here. At the same time, however, the presence of reflective elements in the midst of a futuristic portrayal does not mean that a cyclical reading is established for the entire work. One must move through the text itself carefully piece by piece.

It is here that readers of any apocalyptic work must pay careful attention to the Old Testament imagery presented in the work. These allusions become the key for how to read the movement of the work and its timing. However, the genre does teach us to expect a movement ultimately toward the end of history and its resolution. Apocalyptic is designed to move forward to the story of the victorious end.

It is also here where the debate becomes complex, as several of the categories noted above coalesce. For example, should Jewish imagery of the 144,000 in Revelation 7 be read as the "tribes of Israel" picturing the reappearance of national Israel into a central role in the future (as many premillennialists have argued)? Or is this imagery merely a symbolic way of depicting God's people in the church today as bearers of the message of the gospel (as historical premillennialists, amillennialists, and postmillennialists argue)? Obviously, the answer to such a question depends not just on how one reads Revelation but also on how one puts together the relationship of Old Testament imagery in the New Testament, a category already treated above. Watch how these arguments are made in the essays, for they are crucial to the debate.

In noting the forward-moving characteristic of apocalyptic, one other point about the genre needs attention. Jewish apocalyptic tradition does have a category for an intermediate rule, though its duration is never the same across the various works and its details differ from that of Revelation. First Enoch 91:12–17, for example, refers to a period involving an "eighth" and then a "ninth" week in which righteousness is established and judgment is given before the "tenth" week, which extends into "many weeks without number forever." Here we see the inherent calendrical quality that often shows up in Jewish apocalyptic literature indicating a forward sequence of events.

Another text, 4 Ezra 7:28–29, speaks of an intermediate messianic kingdom of four hundred years for a messiah who dies at the end before the Final Judgment and eternity come. The detail is important because it reflects the calendrical dimension of apocalyptic as it depicts the movement toward the end. A major question is whether John reflects a similar pattern or is distinct from it at a literary level. How this question is answered impacts one's reading of Revelation 20.

One final point needs attention under this heading. How one conceives of the imagery's making its point within the genre is important. Two options exist: (1) The author makes his point with symbolic imagery that represents some described reality, or (2) the author sees in his vision some reality that he describes pictorially the best he can. The difference is important. Most interpreters of all camps have operated with the first view in some form, but some premillennial dispensationalists have argued the second is what is taking place. For example, when Revelation 9:3–11 raises the images of scorpions, some a generation ago argued that what John really saw was something like B-29s because these planes were well protected and "stung from the tail." A current view might update the reference to stealth bombers. The point of the example should be clear: The assumption of the reading is that John wrote down exactly what he saw in the best ancient language he could.

There are implications of that form of reading, however, that show it to be problematic. (a) It means that no reader in John's time, or for many centuries thereafter, had a chance of really understanding the prophet's message. (b) It assumes that the era of fulfillment for the text is our own, which is not certain either. (c) It ignores the very character of the genre, which is the theme of this section of the essay. The imagery of scorpions (or other images like it in Revelation, such as locusts) has a history as judgment imagery from the Old Testament. This previous biblical use of the imagery, along with the nature of symbolism itself, may provide the guidelines for how the image should be understood within the book. Along this line, the scorpion represents an agent who brings a painful and destructive type of venom to the judgment being described at this point of the text. The backdrop for the locusts is the Day of the Lord judgment from Joel. The imagery's connection with the underworld in Revelation describes the activity of cosmic forces of evil.

Such details reflect the apocalyptic characteristic of the spiritual forces of evil that operate "behind the scenes" in the struggle over humanity in history. The unusual physical description of the scorpion with faces like people, hair like a woman, teeth like a lion, scales like iron, and wings like the chariots of many horses reflect the aesthetic tendency of apocalyptic. Here the apocalypticist describes the enemy as a fearsome, almost unnatural being, adding the emotive note of foreboding to the judgment described. The goal of the genre is to get an almost visceral, emotive reaction and revulsion to the terror being described.

The point of looking at such an image in detail is to highlight how the imagery of Revelation works as symbolism within the limits set by the genre. A real judgment is portrayed, which is where the genre's realism shows, but it is presented often in symbolic, aesthetic, even emotive terms. The clues for understanding the imagery are not to be found in our time but in the interpretive categories that the imagery and its genre set for itself. The text, in its most futuristic reading, may address our time or it may not; we cannot be certain of this. Most often the roots for understanding the imagery comes from the Old Testament or other apocalyptic texts. As a result, such connections should be sought and noted, for they are the keys to appreciating the prophet's message. The possibility of typology, as noted above, also should be considered. It is this combination of factors that does make Revelation a difficult book. Nonetheless God did not reveal it to us to leave it a mystery. As part of the canon, it deserves careful reflection.

The Role of Numbers in Revelation

What needs to be noted here has already been suggested in the discussion of numbers and calendar in the previous section. All the authors agree that there is a prevalent use of symbolic numbers in Revelation, of which the most predominant are seven (as the number of completeness), four, three, twelve, and the multiples of these.

For the issue of the Millennium, the question is whether the number "one thousand" should be seen in a similar way. This number is not the only one to consider. There are other "calendrical" numbers, such as those texts that describe periods of about three and a half years by counting the numbers of days (e.g., 1,260 days in 20:6). Is 20:4–6 referring to one thousand literal years (premillennialists)? Or is it a symbol for a long period, namely, a period much longer than the other period of weeks and days noted elsewhere within the book (amillennialists and postmillennialists)? Placing this discussion within the calendrical progress typical of apocalyptic might suggest an answer where these numbers should be seen differently (i.e., more literally) than other numbers within the book, but the question also obscures another point that could be made by those reading the book in futuristic terms.

Is it not possible to see the thousand years as symbolic of, yet still referring to, an intermediate period that would be an earthly, "millennial," intermediate kingdom? In other words, the issue of the potential symbolism of the number does not really answer the question whether the deliverance portrayed in Revelation 20:4–6 precludes an intermediate kingdom. If one has resurrection bracketing the beginning and end of what is described here, then it is possible to have an intermediate stage regardless of how long it lasts.

I make this point not to argue whether the number is or is not symbolic, though I think my own view is evident in what I have said. Rather, I wish to point out that the answer to that "one thousand years" question may be ultimately irrelevant to the more fundamental question of whether Scripture portrays the existence of an intermediate kingdom. It is the existence of an intermediate kingdom in Scripture that is the most fundamental question to answer. What has traditionally been a linked question between the existence of such a kingdom and its duration may not necessarily be linked.

I make the point as well to show that the fundamental question revolving around futuristic eschatology is not how long the intermediate kingdom is (i.e., whether it is a thousand years or not), but whether it is present in Scripture, including in the New Testament. Whether an intermediate kingdom exists at all is the most basic question for this topic.

The issue of the Millennium in Scripture is not primarily a debate over its duration, but whether it is presented within Scripture as an intermediate period of kingdom rule on the earth distinct from the current era. How one answers this question goes a long way to determining which option of the Millennium and beyond one embraces. A belief in an intermediate kingdom leads to premillennialism. A belief that the church represents that victorious era (postmillennialism) or that only the victorious consummation into eternity is left (amillennialism) leads into the other two options.

Thus, I urge readers attempting to resolve the issue of the Millennium and beyond to pay careful attention to how each essay makes the case for its view when it comes to the arguments for or against an intermediate kingdom. Obviously, how one sees Revelation integrating into the whole of Scripture is an important component in the case that each author makes. As we have seen, it is in the myriad of factors that determine how one reads Revelation that many of the most crucial questions for determining one's view reside.

STRUCTURAL IMPLICATIONS AND CONCLUSION

One can see how many factors figure into the decision about how ultimate fulfillment is treated in Scripture. I would like to treat the structural implications of the various views, so one can see what is practically at stake in the options in terms of worldview and church mission.

The Impact of One's Eschatological View on One's Practice

Here I have in mind one question: What implications do the different views bring for our theological-ethical understanding of eschatology and our role in mission? My goal here is to be descriptive and less suggestive than I have been in the earlier sections. I make no real assessment of the differences in the views. It was not the assignment of any of the essays to deal with this question. I raise it simply to indicate how practically the differences in view can impact mission and outreach.

Postmillennialism claims to be the most optimistic of the views. It certainly possesses the most ambitious agenda growing out of its view. The church's call and, more important, even her destiny involve the declaration and establishment of the Lord's sovereignty over all the social-political-religious structures on earth. In seeing the church as steadily moving toward victory, the church becomes a locus not only of service but also of the exercise of divine power. Victory will emerge through her. There is no sphere outside the touch of the authority of the church's mission.

The call and vision of such a victory drive a full-blown cultural mandate, where the church goes about the purpose of achieving her call in all areas of life. Thus, a full engagement in politics, often in the context of confrontation with a fallen and sinful world, is the result. Theonomic postmillennialism expresses this goal most comprehensively with its desire to present the Old Testament law as part of this structure of realization, while other expressions of postmillennialism are more restrained and hermeneutically nuanced on this question. The difference results in differences of the scope of application of many texts, especially Old Testament legal texts, by postmillennialists.

Amillennialism shares the commitment to God's sovereignty, but incorporates a view of the depravity of humankind in the world that results in a less triumphant view of the church's fate than postmillennialists possess. The church struggles with a fallen world to testify to the grace of God in every sphere of life. The goal is not a belief that the church will ultimately succeed. Rather, she is called to be a faithful witness. The church should raise the challenge of the call to faithfulness and God's sovereignty to every person in the world and in every sphere of life, but victory is something that will come in the Lord's sovereign timing. It is not something that the church itself will bring. The image of church as light in the world is a dominating image in this view.

Premillennialism tends to split into two types of expression on such questions, yet in one other point they tend to agree. Premillennialists see a special place for Israel at the end in their approach because they believe that God is not done with Israel yet. Other views may have such a view of Israel—at least for ethnic Israel—but a future role for national Israel is not present as it is in premillennialism.

What, then, are the two expressions of premillennialism? Some, believing the world is driving to ever-increasing depravity until the end, concentrate on the "spiritual" dimensions of the church's call, since the social-political redemption comes with Christ in the era to come. Attention is given to the health of the church and to issues of her discipleship and evangelistic mission. Engagement in and with the larger world tends to be limited to expressions of personal humanitarian outreach with an explicit evangelistic goal—medical missions, individual relief efforts in catastrophic settings, outreach to some groups of the needy, evangelistic-oriented gospel missions to the homeless, and so forth. These show how God loves individuals. The other views are also engaged in such activities, but this expression of premillennialism tends to keep its focus and energy exclusively to these areas. Issues that touch more corporate structures, such as the plight of the poor as a social structural matter, are left to others. Evangelism and service are the keys here.

Other premillennialists share an outlook similar to amillennialists. They do not see the church as bringing about the victory, but as called to reflect the wholeness of salvation in their interaction with the larger culture. Thus, even though the world is ultimately headed toward a catastrophic judgment, the call of the church is still to function as light in the world and to show how the presence of a redeeming perspective impacts relationships at every social-political-religious level. One of the most powerful ways to show this reality is for the church to reflect fully such values in the way she functions internally and in how she serves, engages, and critiques the world.

The one place where these premillennialists are likely to differ with their amillennial colleagues are in certain readings of the Old Testament. Both want to apply the moral standards of inter-human relations raised by the prophets, but these premillennialists tend to believe and respond with an approach that accepts a degree of separation of church and state. Many amillennial denominations have tended to function within the context of a state church. Premillennialists, on the other hand, have tended to view such a close relationship between nation and church with skepticism, viewing it as often having compromised the prophetic role of the church in a fallen world.

What is fascinating about this brief overview is something we have seen in different configurations in the other subsections. One's view does not always mean that one lines up with others in his or her camp within a particular subcategory. The way in which the variations fall within a view means that at some points of application a person in one camp may look like someone in a subcamp of another view.

The Fundamental Eschatological Question— Is There an Intermediate Earthly Kingdom?

Our survey has drawn to a conclusion. I have tried to show the various elements that go into deciding whether or not the end of history consists simply of a move to eternity or to an intermediate earthly kingdom followed by eternity. I have not tried to make a case for any view, though you deserve to know that I am a premillennialist, so any bias in my presentation surely leans in that direction. The basic question is whether history is moving to culmination in two steps or one. I hope I have shown that many elements go into making a decision on the question. I have tried to show how our contributors have done us a service in outlining the issues. The joy of reflection and deliberation remains as you seek to become a better student of eschatology.

CONCLUSION

In the midst of all this complexity, some students will surely despair about the possibility of determining what Scripture says. But debate, complexity, and nuance, which Scripture contains in many areas, are not adequate reasons to avoid the responsibility of coming to an attempted understanding of what it teaches. Developing one's own view of God's Word is a part of good discipleship and stewardship before the Lord. If we take Scripture seriously, we want to know what it says, so we can believe what it teaches and respond to its call, embracing what it instructs us to do. Maturity means understanding why one holds to a conviction and why others may differ with that view. This work attempts to help us all achieve such a level of maturity even as we all seek vigorously to come to a knowledge of the truth.

As the reader seeks resolution, he or she should keep one basic appeal in mind, an appeal the contributors, I am sure, would share. Search the Scriptures. Read them in their histori-cal-grammatical-theological-literary context. Try to move toward the solution that most fully integrates all of these factors the best. Realize that you are making judgments in these matters and that each view has strengths and weaknesses. Recognize that the integration of the various features involved in the discussion is complex. This means that each view has some issues that it addresses clearly and other points of detail where it has to work to defend its structure. This is often the case when one engages in theological synthesis. Also realize that good people do dis-agree on these matters. Perhaps this book has helped you to appreciate why different positions exist and has laid the building blocks to help you to appreciate all the elements that go into determining a scriptural resolution to the question of the Mil-lennium and beyond.

We know in part now, and we make our case recognizing that we are trying our best to understand Scripture within the limitations we now possess. One day we will know fully—and more importantly—be fully known (1 Cor. 13:12). All of us look forward to that wonderful eternity in the beyond when we can rejoice together in a unity about which now we can only dream.

SELECT BIBLIOGRAPHIES

POSTMILLENNIALISM

Books

Alexander, J. A. *Commentary on the Prophecies of Isaiah.* Grand Rapids: Zondervan, rep. 1977 (1878).

Bahnsen, Greg L. *Theonomy in Christian Ethics.* 2d ed. Phillipsburg, N.J.: Presbyterian and Reformed, 1984.

Boettner, Loraine. *The Millennium.* 2d ed. Phillipsburg, N.J.: Presbyterian and Reformed, 1984.

Brown, David. *Christ's Second Coming: Will It Be Premillennial?* Edmonton, Alta.: Still Waters Revival, rep. 1990 (1882).

Chilton, David. *Paradise Restored: An Eschatology of Dominion.* Fort Worth: Dominion, 1985.

Davis, John Jefferson. *Christ's Victorious Kingdom.* Moscow, Ida.: Canon, 1995.

DeMar, Gary, *Last Days Madness: Obsession of the Modern Church.* 3d ed. Atlanta: American Vision, 1997.

Gentry, Kenneth L. Jr. *The Greatness of the Great Commission: The Christian Enterprise in a Fallen World.* 2d ed. Tyler, Tex.: Institute for Christian Economics, 1993.

_____. *The Beast of Revelation.* 2d ed. Tyler, Tex.: Institute for Christian Economics, 1995.

_____. *Before Jerusalem Fell: Dating the Book of Revelation.* 2d ed. Bethesda, Md.: Christian Universities Publications, 1996.

_____. *God's Law in the Modern World: The Continuing Relevance of Old Testament Law.* 2d ed. Tyler, Tex.: Institute for Christian Economics, 1997.

_____. *He Shall Have Dominion: A Postmillennial Eschatology.* 2d. ed. Tyler, Tex.: Institute for Christian Economics, 1997.

_____. *Perilous Times: A Study in Eschatological Evil*. Bethesda, Md.: Christian Universities Press, 1998.

Gentry, Kenneth L. Jr., Gary DeMar, and Ralph Barker. *Demystifying Revelation* (video cassette interview of Gentry). Atlanta: American Vision, 1997.

Henry, Matthew. *Commentary on the Whole Bible*. Old Tappan, N.J.: Revell, n.d.

Ice, Thomas D., and Kenneth L. Gentry Jr. *The Great Tribulation: Past or Future?* Grand Rapids: Kregel, 1998.

Kik, J. Marcellus. *The Eschatology of Victory*. Phillipsburg, N.J.: Presbyterian and Reformed, 1971.

Murray, Iain. *The Puritan Hope: Revival and the Interpretation of Prophecy*. Edinburgh: Banner of Truth, 1971.

Murray, John. *The Epistle to the Romans*. New International Commentary on the New Testament. 2 vols. Grand Rapids: Eerdmans, 1965.

North, Gary. *The Dominion Covenant: Genesis*. Tyler, Tex.: Institute for Christian Economics, 1982.

_____. *Millennialism and Social Theory*. Tyler, Tex.: Institute for Christian Economics, 1990.

Pate, C. Marvin, ed. *Four Views on the Book of Revelation*. Grand Rapids: Zondervan, 1998.

Rushdoony, Rousas J. *God's Plan for Victory: The Meaning of Postmillennialism*. Vallecito, Calif.: Ross House, 1977.

Sandlin, Andrew. *A Postmillennial Primer*. Vallecito, Calif.: Chalcedon, 1997.

Symington, William. *Messiah the Prince*. Edmonton: Alta.: Still Waters Revival, rep. 1990 (1884).

Terry, Milton S. *Biblical Apocalyptics: A Study of the Most Notable Revelations of God and of Christ*. Grand Rapids: Baker, rep. 1988 (1898).

Warfield, Benjamin B. *Biblical and Theological Studies*. Phillipsburg, N.J.: Presbyterian and Reformed, 1952.

Audio and Audio-Visual Resources

Christian Education Materials, 1749 Kingston Rd., Placentia, CA 92870

Christian Reconstruction Audio, P.O. Box 328, Conestee, SC 29636

Covenant Media Foundation, 4425 Jefferson Ave., Suite 108, Texarkana, AR 71854

Foundations for Biblical Studies, 234 N. Titmus Dr., Mastic, NY 11950

Southern California Center for Christian Studies, P.O. Box 328, Placentia, CA 92871

Postmillennial Periodicals

Christianity & Society, P.O. Box 20514, Seattle, WA 98102 or P.O. Box 2, Taunton, Somerset TAI 2WZ England

Contra Mundum, P.O. Box 32652, Fridley, MN 55432–0652

The Counsel of Chalcedon, P.O. Box 888022, Dunwoody, GA 30356–0022

Credena/Agenda, P.O. Box 8741, Moscow, ID 83843–1241

Dispensationalism in Transition newsletter (e-mail: SEND TO: list-request@metanet.net; TEXT BOX: subscribe transition-list)

The Journal of Christian Reconstruction, P.O. Box 158, Vallecito, CA 95251

AMILLENNIALISM

Adams, Jay. *The Time Is at Hand*. Nutley, N.J.: Presbyterian and Reformed, 1966.

Bavinck, Herman. *The Last Things*. Ed. John Bolt. Trans. John Vriend. Grand Rapids: Baker, 1996.

Beale, Greg K. *Revelation*. The New International Greek New Testament Commentary. Grand Rapids: Eerdmans, forthcoming.

Berkhof, Louis. *The Second Coming of Christ*. Grand Rapids: Eerdmans, 1953.

Berkouwer, G. C. *The Return of Christ*. Grand Rapids: Eerdmans, 1972.

Clouse, Robert G., ed. *The Meaning of the Millennium: Four Views*. Downers Grove, Ill.: InterVarsity, 1977.

Clowney, Edmund P. "The Final Temple." In *Studying the New Testament Today*, ed. John H. Skilton. Philadelphia: Presbyterian and Reformed, 1974.

Cox, William E. *These Last Days*. Philadelphia: Presbyterian and Reformed, 1964.

_____. *Amillennialism Today*. Philadelphia: Presbyterian and Reformed, 1972.

De Young, James. *Jerusalem in the New Testament*. Kampen: Kok, 1960.

Fairbairn, Patrick. *The Interpretation of Prophecy*. London: Banner of Truth Trust, rep. 1964 (1856).

_____. *The Prophetic Prospects of the Jews*. Grand Rapids: Eerdmans, 1930.

_____. *The Typology of Scripture*. Grand Rapids: Zondervan, 1975.

Grier, W. J. *The Momentous Event*. Belfast: Evangelical Book Shop, 1945.

Hamilton, Floyd. *The Basis of Millennial Faith*. Grand Rapids: Eerdmans, 1952.

Hendriksen, W. *More Than Conquerors: An Interpretation of the Book of Revelation*. Grand Rapids: Baker, 1939.

_____. *Israel in Prophecy*. Grand Rapids: Baker, 1968.

Hill, Charles E. *Regnum Caelorum: Patterns of Future Hope in Early Christianity*. Oxford: Clarendon, 1992.

Hodges, Jesse Wilson. *Christ's Kingdom and Coming*. Grand Rapids: Eerdmans, 1957.

Hoekema, Anthony. *The Bible and the Future*. Grand Rapids: Eerdmans, 1979.

Holwerda, David E. *Jesus and Israel: One Covenant or Two?* Grand Rapids: Eerdmans, 1995.

Hughes, Archibald. *A New Heaven and a New Earth*. Philadelphia: Presbyterian and Reformed, 1958.

Hughes, Philip E. *Interpreting Prophecy*. Grand Rapids: Eerdmans, 1980.

Kline, Meredith G. "The First Resurrection," *Westminster Theological Journal* 37 (Spring 1975): 366–75.

_____. "The First Resurrection: A Reaffirmation," *Westminster Theological Journal* 39 (Fall 1976): 117–19.

_____. "Har Magedon [Armageddon]: The End of the Millennium," *Journal of the Evangelical Theological Society* 39 (June 1996): 207–22.

Konig, Adrio. *The Eclipse of Christ in Eschatology*. Grand Rapids: Eerdmans, 1989.

Milne, Bruce. *What the Bible Says About the End of the World*. Lottbridge Drove, Eng.: Kingsway, 1979.

Murray, George L. *Millennial Studies*. Grand Rapids: Baker, 1948.

Peters, George N. H. *The Theocratic Kingdom*. Grand Rapids: Kregel, 1952.

Pieters, Albertus. *The Seed of Abraham*. Grand Rapids: Eerdmans, 1950.

Ridderbos, Herman. *The Coming of the Kingdom*. Philadelphia: Presbyterian and Reformed, 1962.

Robertson, O. Palmer, "Is There a Distinctive Future for Ethnic Israel in Romans 11?" In *Perspectives on Evangelical Theology*, ed. Kenneth S. Kantzer and Stanley N. Gundry. Grand Rapids: Baker, 1979.

Robinson, William Childs. *Christ—The Hope of Glory*. Grand Rapids: Eerdmans, 1947.

Travis, Stephen. *The Jesus Hope*. Downers Grove, Ill.: InterVarsity, 1976.

Vos, Geerhardus, *The Pauline Eschatology*. Grand Rapids: Eerdmans, 1953.

_____. *Redemptive History and Biblical Interpretation*. Ed. Richard B. Gaffin Jr. Phillipsburg, N.J.: Presbyterian and Reformed, 1980.

Wyngaarden, Martin J. *The Future of the Kingdom in Prophecy and Fulfillment*. Grand Rapids: Zondervan, 1934.

PREMILLENNIALISM

Many works have been published on premillennialism. The following is only a sample. The reader is also directed to commentaries on the book of Revelation, such as those of Johnson, Mounce, Walvoord, Ladd, Newport, and Thomas cited in the footnotes of the article on premillennialism.

Blackstone, W. E. *Jesus Is Coming*. Chicago: Fleming H. Revell, 1989.

Blaising, Craig A., and Darrell L. Bock. *Progressive Dispensationalism*. Wheaton, Ill.: Victor, 1993.

Campbell, Donald K., and Jeffrey L. Townsend, eds. *A Case for Premillennialism: A New Consensus*. Chicago: Moody, 1992.

Clouse, Robert G., ed. *The Meaning of the Millennium: Four Views*. Downers Grove, Ill.: InterVarsity, 1977.

Feinberg, Charles L. *Millennialism: The Two Major Views*. 3d ed. Chicago: Moody, 1980.

Hoyt, Herman A. *The End Times*. Chicago: Moody, 1969.

Ladd, George E. *Crucial Questions About the Kingdom of God*. Grand Rapids: Eerdmans, 1952.

_____. *The Presence of the Future: The Eschatology of Biblical Realism*. Grand Rapids: Eerdmans, 1974.

McClain, Alva J. *The Greatness of the Kingdom*. Winona Lake, Ind.: BMH Books, 1959.

Pentecost, J. Dwight. *Things to Come: A Study in Biblical Eschatology*. Grand Rapids: Zondervan, 1958.

_____. *Thy Kingdom Come*. Wheaton, Ill.: Victor, 1990.

Saucy, Robert L. *The Case for Progressive Dispensationalism*. Grand Rapids: Zondervan, 1993.

Walvoord, John. *The Millennial Kingdom*. Grand Rapids: Zondervan, 1959.

_____. *Major Bible Prophecies*. Grand Rapids: Zondervan, 1991.

West, Nathaniel. *Second Coming of Christ: Premillennial Essays*. Chicago: Fleming H. Revell, 1879.

_____. *The Thousand Years in Both Testaments*. New York: Fleming H. Revell, 1880.

GENERAL INDEX

Abraham, the father of many nations, 146
Abrahamic covenant, 29–30
achri, 225
Adam and Eve, 26
Adams, Jay E., 22
Alford, Henry, 247
Alsted, Johann, 179
Ambrose, 168
amillennialism, 83–129; and Canaan, 90–91; and Jerusalem, 91–93; and the judgment, 102–3; and the kingdom of David, 94–97; and Old Testament prophecy, 84; postmillennial response to, 130–42; premillennial response to, 143–53; and renewal of the earth, 91; and its response to postmillennialism, 58–71; and its response to premillennialism, 256–76; and second coming, 100–112; and the temple, 97–99; the term, 83; and the true Israel, 87
Anabaptist rebellions, 178
anagogy, 168
analogy of faith, 256, 263
anastasis, 223, 253
anazaō, 223
Ancient of Days, 47
angels, bound, 124
Anointed One, 33
Antichrist, 21, 65, 180, 255
Apocalypse, visions of the, 260
apocalyptic genre, 287–88
apocalyptic literature, nature of, 300–301
apocalyptic narrative, 208–9
apocalypticism, premillennialism and, 190–92
apokalypsis, 103, 106, 110
Apostle's Creed, 14
Armageddon, battle of, 219, 235, 274

Athanasius, 16, 68
Augustine, 16, 72, 167, 178–79, 218
Augustinian view, of the Millennium, 172
authority, Christ is "bestowed," 45

Babylon, 211, 214–15, 249, 271
battle, the, 124–25
Bauckham, Richard, 212
Bavinck, Herman, 259
Beale, Greg K., 260
Beasley-Murray, G. R., 239
beast, the, 65, 221, 274
Beckwith, John T., 239
Berkhof, Louis, 83
Berkouwer, G. C., 62, 110, 134, 147, 151
Beza, Theodore, 17
Bible, authority of, 257. *See also* Scripture
Blevins, James L., 50
Bloesch, Donald G., 15–17
Bock, Darrell, 247
Boettner, Loraine, 51, 75
book of life, 126
bound, Satan's being, 122
Brightman, Thomas, 16–17
Brooks, Thomas, 18
Bucer, Martin, 17

Calvin, John, 17, 41, 68, 114, 231, 261–62
Canaan, 90
Chafer, Lewis Sperry, 182
chiliasm, 258
Christ, is "bestowed" authority, 45; rule of, 53; second coming of, 65–67; the true Israel, 87
Christian Reconstructionism, 19, 58–60
church fathers, 15–16
church, in amillennialism, 306; as the city of God, 173; continues to live in this age, 63–64; as the focal

SCRIPTURE INDEX

CONSIDER ALL POINTS OF VIEW WITH COUNTERPOINTS!

Four Views on the Book of Revelation

Is the book of Revelation a prophecy fulfilled when the temple fell in A.D. 70, a metaphor for the battle between good and evil raging until Christ's return, a chronological record of events between Christ's ascension and the new heavens and new earth, or an already/not yet prophetic dichotomy of fulfillment and waiting?

Four Views on the Book of Revelation will expand your understanding of the Bible's most mystifying book, and it may even change your mind.

Moody professor C. Marvin Pate mediates the lively dialogue and adds his own view to those of Kenneth L. Gentry Jr., Sam Hamstra Jr., and Robert L. Thomas.

ISBN: 0-310-21080-1

Three Views on the Rapture

Eschatology doesn't end when you decide how to approach the book of Revelation. If you believe in a premillennial rapture, you want to know whether it happens before, during, or after the Great Tribulation.

Richard Reiter introduces *Three Views on the Rapture* (formerly titled *The Rapture*) with an essay tracing the history of this debate in American evangelicalism. Gleason L. Archer Jr., Paul D. Feinberg, and Douglas J. Moo represent and defend each view.

ISBN: 0-310-21043-8

COUNTERPOINTS COVER KEY DOCTRINAL ISSUES!

Five Views on Law and Gospel

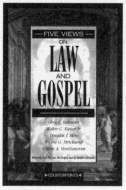

Examine the relevance of the Old Testament law to Christian life with five scholars representing the most common evangelical Christian views.

Douglas J. Moo presents a modified Lutheran answer, Wayne G. Strickland defends the Dispensational view, while Walter C. Kaiser Jr. argues that the "weightier issues" of the Mosaic Law still apply to Christians. Willem VanGemeren and Greg Bahnsen present Theonomic and Non-theonomic Reformed points of view.

ISBN: 0-310-21217-5

Five Views on Sanctification

Five Views on Sanctification will deepen your understanding of the moral perfection of Christ as it presents differing ideas about how that perfection affects the Christian life.

Can we live up to the Wesleyan ideal of "entire sanctification" held by Melvin E. Dieter, or are Reformed scholars like Anthony J. Hoekema correct that complete holiness in this life is impossible? What role do Pentecostals like Stanley M. Horton say transforming gifts of the Holy Spirit play? What is the Keswick tradition of J. Robertson McQuilkin, and what wisdom on this issue has John F. Walvoord found in the writings of St. Augustine?

ISBN: 0-310-21269-3

We want to hear from you. Please send your comments about this book to us in care of the address below. Thank you.

ZondervanPublishingHouse
Grand Rapids, Michigan
http://www.zondervan.com

A Division of HarperCollins*Publishers*

Stanley N. Gundry (S.T.D., Lutheran School of Theology at Chicago) is Vice President and Editor-in-Chief of the Book Group at Zondervan Publishing House. He graduated summa cum laude from both the Los Angeles Baptist College and Talbot Theological Seminary before receiving his Masters of Sacred Theology from Union College, University of British Columbia. With more than 35 years of teaching, pastoring, and publishing experience, he is the author or coauthor of numerous books and a contributor to numerous periodicals.